全国船舶工业职业教育教学指导委员会推荐教材

U0868455

气体保护焊方法及应用

主　编　孙淑侠　韩　喆
参　编　莫芝林　王　飞　杨　金
　　　　杨　帅　官　旭　邱　鹏
　　　　王　静　周飞霓
主　审　赵宗合　潘文欢　代能武

哈爾濱工程大學出版社
Harbin Engineering University Press

内容简介

本教材为中英双语教材，通过理论和实践的结合，融合了岗课赛证的技术技能需求，介绍了气体保护焊方法的基本理论和实际生产中典型项目节点的工艺操作流程。本教材包括气体保护焊安全与防护、熔化极气体保护焊及应用和手工钨极氩弧焊及应用三个模块共计十五个项目，学习者可以通过学习和训练，理解气体保护焊基本原理、设备组成、焊接工艺等基本知识，掌握气体保护焊工艺编制、设备运维、参数调节以及板板和管板的多位置焊接基本技巧、规范及操作方法，获得气体保护焊所需要的基本知识和技能训练，具备气体保护焊方法的实际操作技能、典型结构焊接工艺编制和焊接质量控制能力，胜任对应焊接技术岗位工作。

教材可用于中、高职和应用型本科院校焊接技能学习、职业资格证书考核培训和焊接技能竞赛训练，也可用于焊接行业工程技术人员工作参考和其他相关从业人员岗前培训。

图书在版编目(CIP)数据

气体保护焊方法及应用 : 汉英对照 / 孙淑侠, 韩喆主编. -- 哈尔滨 : 哈尔滨工程大学出版社, 2025. 1.

ISBN 978-7-5661-4393-8

Ⅰ. TG444

中国国家版本馆 CIP 数据核字第 2024PZ0710 号

气体保护焊方法及应用

QITI BAOHUHAN FANGFA JI YINGYONG

选题策划 史大伟
责任编辑 丁月华
封面设计 李海波

出版发行 哈尔滨工程大学出版社
社　　址 哈尔滨市南岗区南通大街 145 号
邮政编码 150001
发行电话 0451-82519328
传　　真 0451-82519699
经　　销 新华书店
印　　刷 哈尔滨市海德利商务印刷有限公司
开　　本 787 mm×1 092 mm　1/16
印　　张 19.75
字　　数 600 千字
版　　次 2025 年 1 月第 1 版
印　　次 2025 年 1 月第 1 次印刷
书　　号 ISBN 978-7-5661-4393-8
定　　价 69.80 元

http://www.hrbeupress.com
E-mail:heupress@hrbeu.edu.cn

前　　言

随着现代制造业的飞速发展，作为支撑技术之一的焊接技术不断创新和突破。气体保护焊凭借其高效、优质、便捷、经济、低污染、易于实现自动化和智能化的特性，仍然是众多领域必不可少的焊接方法。不论是船舶、桥梁、建筑等大型钢结构建造中的二氧化碳气体保护焊，还是航天、储罐、深海等特殊钢结构建造以及新能源、新材料、新工艺研制中的惰性气体保护焊，亦或自动化、智能化焊接生产线的研制和应用，都依赖于手工操作技术的支撑。

然而，兼具一定理论知识和高水平操作技术、能够解决高端装备制造业生产实际问题、深度参与智能化焊接设备和工艺研制、有效进行智能化焊接生产线操作的高端焊接人才尚有较大欠缺。为了顺应时代需求，培养更多满足现代制造业结构复合化、操作高端化、工作研究化等新需求的焊接技术技能人才，我们精心编写了这本包含一定理论知识和初、中、高等级操作技能的《气体保护焊方法与应用》教材。

同时，考虑到要使教材具备完整体系性和广泛适用性，适应制造业全球发展的需求，响应国家职教出海的号召，遂将教材进行了双语编写，以方便中外合作教学和培训，助力境外同仁教育和学习。

教材框架遵照职业成长规律，基于当前产业端人才需求状态，强化焊接技术技能人才的理实一体化培养过程。内容构建结合产业端实际工作项目和任务，融合气体保护焊方法及工艺的理论与实操内容，融入焊接竞赛规程和技能证书标准，秉承“项目引领、任务驱动、行动导向”理念，让学习者在一系列职业活动中掌握技能知识、形成岗位能力。

教材内容包括气体保护焊安全与防护、熔化极气体保护焊及应用和手工钨极氩弧焊及应用三个模块共计十五个项目。模块一以培养设备安全操作和人身安全防护为目标，让学习者先建立良好的职业素养和安全意识，包含理论、操作和案例，强化综合职业能力；模块二、模块三以培养专业能力为目标，包含理论知识和实操技术，提升核心职业能力。各个项目包含学习目标、学习任务和任务考核等内容。

教材可作为中、高职教育，应用型本科相关专业的教学用书和焊接行业工程技术人员的参考用书，也可作为气体保护焊方法职业技能等级证书的培训用书，适用于同类职业技能资格证书培训、教学、自学和考核评价。对应课程一般为《气体保护焊方法与操作》等相关课程，由于教材为项目化活页式的灵活形式，也可按模块对应专业的《焊接安全生产》《熔化极气体保护焊》《手工钨极氩弧焊》等相关焊接课程。

本教材具有以下特色：

1. 突出职业能力导向。对接先进装备制造生产模式和岗位需求，以模块引导、项目驱动、任务实施的方式进行编写，每个模块由若干个理实结合、由易到难、螺旋上升的项目和任务构成，符合学习者知识认知和技能操作规律，使学生在完成任务过程中，逐步积累知识、掌握技能。

2. 强化育才先育人功能。针对焊接操作职业的特殊性，以安全防护和安全操作模块开篇，让学习者熟悉职业特性，强化安全意识，坚定职业信念，提升职业素养，带着良好的职业素养进行专业知识和操作的学习，更有助于成人、成才。

3. 深化岗课赛证融合度。教材实操项目全部是装备制造中大型钢结构典型焊接节点，做到既满足教学需求，又满足岗位需求；融合职业技能等级证书和技能竞赛内容及考核标准；邀请专业技术岗位人员和技能大师加入教材编写团队，及时吸收一线岗位新技术、新工艺和新方法，实现"岗、课、赛、证"有机融通，提升核心职业能力。

4. 丰富学习资源形式。教材配套微课视频、三维动画、课件(PPT)、任务考核及答案、教师工作页、学生实验实训页等助教助学富媒体资源，教材中各个项目均设置了配套数字化资源的二维码，可随扫随学。

本教材充分融合产业端岗位需求，编写和审核都有经验丰富的企业一线技术技能人员参与。

教材由武汉船舶职业技术学院孙淑侠、韩喆主编，中国一冶集团有限公司赵宗合、中国船级社武汉规范研究所潘文欢、武昌船舶重工集团有限公司代能武主审，具体参编人员及分工如下：

中国一冶集团有限公司莫芝林负责模块三项目三、四的中文编写；武昌船舶重工集团有限公司王飞负责模块三项目五、六的中文编写；武汉船舶职业技术学院：杨金、周飞霓负责模块三项目三、四、五、六的英文编写，杨帅、官旭负责模块三项目一、二的中英文编写，邱鹏、王静负责模块二项目五、六、七的中英文编写，韩喆负责模块一的中、英文编写，孙淑侠负责前言、模块二项目一、二、三、四的中英文编写以及全书统稿。

本教材编写过程中参阅了大量国内外相关教材和文献，并获得了多位焊接行业专家和一线技术人员的大力支持和帮助，在此一并感谢。

囿于编者水平有限，教材中难免存在疏漏和不足，恳请同行专家和读者批评指正。

Preface

With the rapid development of modern manufacturing industry, welding technology, as a supporting technology, continues to innovate and break through. Gas shielded welding method is still an essential welding method in many industries due to its high efficiency, high quality, convenience, economy, low pollution, and ease of automation and intelligence. Whether it is the carbon dioxide gas shielded welding method in the construction of large steel structures such as ships, bridges, and buildings, or the inert gas shielded welding method in the construction of special steel structures such as aerospace, storage tanks, and deep sea, as well as the development and application of new energy, new materials, and new processes, and the development and application of automated and intelligent welding production lines, all rely on the support of manual operation technology.

However, there is still a significant lack of high-end welding talents who possess certain theoretical knowledge and high-level operational skills, can solve practical production problems in the high-end equipment manufacturing industry, deeply participate in the development of intelligent welding equipment and processes, and effectively operate intelligent welding production lines. In order to meet the needs of the times and cultivate more welding technology and skilled talents who can meet the new demands of modern manufacturing such as structural complexity, high-end operation, and research-based work, we have carefully compiled this textbook "Gas Shielded Welding Method and Application", which includes certain theoretical knowledge and initial, intermediate, and high-level operational skills.

At the same time, considering that the textbooks have a complete system and wide applicability, adapt to the global development needs of the manufacturing industry, and respond to the national call for vocational education to go global, the textbooks have been bilingual, facilitating Sino foreign cooperative teaching and training, and assisting overseas colleagues in education and learning.

The textbook framework follows the laws of professional growth and is based on the current demand for talent in the industry, strengthening the integrated training process of welding technology and skilled personnel in theory and practice. The content construction is based on actual work projects and tasks in the industry, integrating the theoretical and practical content of gas shielded welding methods and processes, incorporating welding competition regulations and skill certificate standards, adhering to the concept of "project led, task driven, action oriented", allowing learners to master skill knowledge and form job abilities in a series of professional activities.

The textbook includes three modules: gas shielded welding safety and protection, melting electrode gas shielded welding and its application, and manual tungsten inert gas welding and its application, totaling fifteen projects. Module one aims to cultivate equipment safety operation and personal safety protection, enabling learners to establish good professional literacy and safety awareness, including theory, operation, and case studies, and strengthen comprehensive professional abilities; Modules two and three aim to cultivate professional abilities, including theoretical knowledge and practical skills, to enhance core vocational skills; Each project includes learning objectives, learning tasks, and task assessments.

Textbooks can be used as teaching materials for secondary and higher vocational education, applied undergraduate related majors, and reference materials for engineering and technical personnel in the welding industry. They can also be used as training materials for gas shielded welding method vocational skill level certificates, and are suitable for training, teaching, self-learning, and assessment of similar vocational skill qualification certificates. The corresponding courses are generally related courses such as "Gas Shielded Welding Method and Operation". Due to the flexible project-based form of the textbook, it can also correspond to professional welding courses such as "Welding Safety Production", "Gas Metal Arc Welding", "Tungsten Inert Gas Welding", etc. by module.

Characteristics of textbooks:

1. Highlighting vocational ability orientation. Integrate advanced equipment manufacturing production modes and job requirements, and write them in a module guided, project driven, and task implementation manner. Each module consists of several projects and tasks that combine theory and practice, go from easy to difficult, and spiral upwards, in line with learners' knowledge cognition and skill operation rules, enabling students to gradually accumulate knowledge and master skills in the process of completing tasks.

2. Strengthening the function of educating talents first. In response to the particularity of the welding operation profession, the safety protection and safety operation module is introduced to familiarize learners with the professional characteristics, strengthen safety awareness, strengthen professional beliefs, enhance professional qualities, and carry out professional knowledge and operation learning with good professional qualities, which is more conducive to adulthood and success.

3. Deepen the integration of job, course, competition and certification. All practical projects in the textbook are typical welding nodes of large steel structures in equipment manufacturing, achieving both learning and practice, teaching and production, and meeting job requirements; Integrate vocational skill level certificates and skill competition content and assessment standards; Invite professional technical personnel and skill masters to join the textbook writing team, timely absorb new technologies, processes, and methods from frontline positions, achieve organic integration of "job, course, competition, and certification", and enhance core professional abilities.

4. Rich forms of learning resources. The teaching materials are accompanied by micro lesson videos, 3D animations, PowerPoint presentations, task assessments and answers, teacher work pages, student experimental training pages, and other rich media resources for teaching assistance. Each item in the teaching materials is equipped with QR codes for supporting digital resources, which can be scanned and learned at any time.

This textbook fully integrates the job requirements of the industry, and experienced front-line technical and skilled personnel from enterprises participate in both the writing and review.

The textbook ' s editors in chief is Shuxia Sun and Zhe Han from Wuhan Institute Of Shipbuilding Technology. And the main reviewers is Zonghe Zhao from China First Metallurgical Group Co. , Ltd and Wenhuan Pan from Wuhan Rules & Research Institute of China Classification Society and Nengwu Dai Wuchang Shipbuilding Industry Group Co. , Ltd. The specific participating personnel and division of labor are as follows:

Zhilin Mo from China First Metallurgical Group Co. , Ltd is responsible for the Chinese language writing of projects 3, 4 in module 3; Fei Wang from Wuchang Shipbuilding Industry Group Co. , Ltd is responsible for the Chinese writing of projects 3, 4 in module 3; Wuhan Institute Of Shipbuilding Technology: Jin Yang and Feini Zhou are responsible for the English writing of projects 3, 4, 5, and 6 in module 3, Shuai Yang and Xu Guan are responsible for the Chinese and English writing of projects 1 and 2 in module 3, Peng Qiu and Jing Wang are responsible for the Chinese and English writing of projects 5, 6, and 7 in module 2, Zhe Han is responsible for the Chinese and English writing of module 1, and Shuxia Sun is responsible for the Chinese and English writing of the preface, projects 1, 2, 3, and 4 in module 2, as well as the overall manuscript of the book.

During the process of writing this textbook, a large number of relevant textbooks and literature from both domestic and foreign sources were consulted, and we have received strong support and assistance from many welding industry experts and frontline technicians. We would like to express our gratitude for this.

Due to the limited level of the editor, there are inevitably omissions and deficiencies in the textbook. We sincerely request peer experts and readers to criticize and correct us.

目　　录

Contents

模块一

气体保护焊安全与防护

项目一　安全用电用气

【学习目标】

1. 掌握用电安全基础知识；
2. 掌握焊接触电事故的预防措施；
3. 掌握用气安全基础知识；
4. 掌握防止气瓶爆炸的措施；
5. 掌握常用防火防爆措施。

任务1：掌握用电安全基础知识

1. 安全电压与危险电压

安全电压是指有效值小于 36 V 的电压，危险电压通常指有效值大于 36 V 的电压。气体保护焊弧焊电源的输入端电压一般为 50 Hz 的 220 V 或 380 V 电压，输出端的空载电压一般也在 60 V 以上，均属于危险电压，因此焊工在操作过程中要遵守操作规程，防止触电。

2. 电击对人体的危害

接触带电部件将有电流流过人体，导致电击。电击的伤害程度取决于以下几个因素。

(1) 电流大小

不大于 1 mA 的电流仅使触电者有微弱的刺痛感；1~5 mA 的电流会使人很难受但不痛；6~30 mA 的电流会引起疼痛，使人失去对肌肉的控制，不能够行走，还可能会引起烧伤；50~150 mA 的电流会引起严重疼痛，导致严重的肌肉收缩、深度烧伤、击倒并可能会导致死亡；1 000~4 300 mA 的电流会引起心室纤维性颤动（心电图节奏被打乱，心脏跳动剧烈，且由于心室收缩无法同步，不能送出血液），可能会导致死亡；电流为 10 000 mA 时，会导致心脏停搏、严重烧伤，死亡可能性很大。

尽管电击对人体的作用是以电流大小来衡量的，但由于通过人体的电流是不可能事先计算出来的，因此安全条件不是按照安全电流，而是按照安全电压来确定的。不同环境条件下，人体电阻是不相同的，安全电压也各不相同。一般情况下，36 V 以下的电压不会导致伤亡，因此规定低于 36 V 的电压为安全电压。

(2)电击持续时间

电击持续时间越长，电击伤害程度就越严重。这是因为随着通电时间的延长，人体电阻因出汗或其他原因而下降，导致电流增大，触电危险性增加。此外，人的心脏每收缩扩张一次，中间约有 0.1 s 的间歇时间，人体在这 0.1 s 的间歇时间内对电流最为敏感。如果电流在这一瞬间通过心脏，即使电流只有几十毫安，也会引起心脏震颤。电流不在该瞬间通过心脏时，即使电流达 10 A，也不会引起心脏停搏。由此可知，如果电流持续时间超过 1 s，则必将与心脏最敏感的间歇时间重合，带来很大危险。

(3)电流种类(直流或交流)、交流电流的频率

对于人体来说，最危险的频率为 25~300 Hz，2 000 Hz 以上的高频对人体的影响很小，这是因为高频有集肤效应。直流电压的危害也小于工频交流电压。

(4)电流在人体中的流通路径

电流从手到脚流通的危险性最大，因为沿这条路径流通的电流有较多的机会通过心脏、肺部和脊髓等重要器官；其次是从手到手的流通路径；而从脚到脚的电流路径危险性最小。

(5)人体电阻

当外加电压一定时，人体电阻越大，危险性越小。人体电阻主要由体内电阻和皮肤电阻组成。体内电阻基本上不受外界条件的影响，其数值不低于 500 Ω。皮肤电阻受很多外界因素的影响，例如皮肤上的汗液、损伤、黏附的粉尘等都会降低皮肤电阻，增大危险性。

3. 电击事故的常见原因

因具体情况的不同，发生电击的原因很多，但大致可分为两类：一类是直接电击，即直接接触正常运行时带电的部件所发生的电击；另一类为间接电击，即触及意外带电体所发生的电击。意外带电体是指正常情况下不带电，由于绝缘损坏或电气元部件故障而带电的物体，如漏电的焊机外壳、绝缘外皮破损的电缆等。

(1)直接电击事故

进行以下操作时易发生这类事故：

①焊接开始前更换电极或整理焊枪上的焊丝时，不小心接触到焊枪上的导电部位。

②在接线、调节焊接电流或移动焊接设备时，手或身体碰到接线柱、极板等带电体。

③在登高焊接时触及低压线路或靠近高压网络。

(2)间接电击事故

焊接发生间接电击事故的原因主要是触及漏电的焊机外壳或绝缘破损的电缆。焊机外壳漏电的主要原因有线圈潮湿、焊机长期超负荷运行、短路发热、安装地点和方法不符合安全要求、因振动或碰击而使线圈或引线的绝缘受到机械性损伤、金属物(如铁丝、铁屑、铜线或小铁管头)进入焊机外壳内。

4. 触电类型

触电可分为以下几种情况。

(1)低压单相触电

低压单相触电指人体某一部位触及连接单相电压的带电体。大部分触电事故都是单相触电事故。

(2)低压两相触电

低压两相触电即人体两处同时触及两相带电体。此时,人体所受到的电压可高达380 V,危险性很大。

(3)跨步电压触电

电气设备发生接地故障时,接地电流通过接地导体流向大地,人在接地点周围,两脚之间的电位差称为跨步电压。过大的跨步电压也会引起触电事故。高压设备的接地故障处或有大电流流过的接地装置附近,都可能出现较高的跨步电压。

任务2:掌握焊接触电事故的预防措施

为了保证焊接设备的安全使用,设备在出厂前就采取了许多安全措施,如隔离防护措施、绝缘措施等。为了确保用电安全,在设备安装及焊接操作过程中除了应遵守随机附带的使用说明外,还应注意以下几点。

1. 焊机外壳的保护接地

如果焊机不接地,变压器初级绕组由于某种原因与外壳短路后,将带有很高的电压,人触及外壳后就会导致电击。因此,所有焊机外壳均必须接地。所谓接地就是用导线将焊机外壳与大地连接,提供一条连接地面的低电阻路径。这样,在焊机外壳漏电时,将有很大的对地短路电流产生,从而使保险丝烧断或断路器跳闸,将整个电路切断并同时向用户发出报警信号,如图 1-1-1 所示。

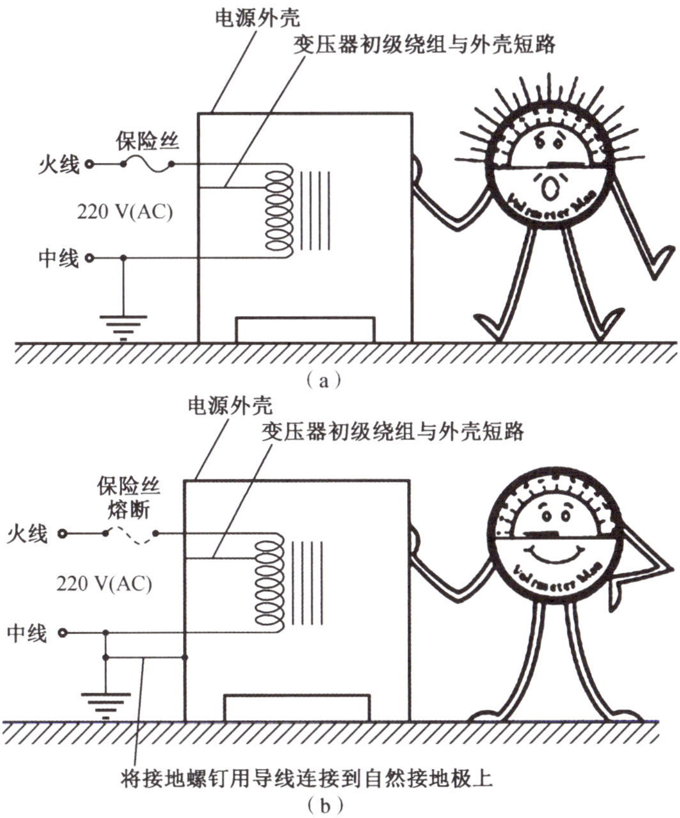

图 1-1-1　电源外壳的接地

焊机的外壳上大部分设有专用的接地螺钉(有些采用三相四线制供电的焊机没有该螺钉,四根电缆线中有一根线接到电网的地线上),应利用导线将该螺钉连接到接地极上,而且接地电阻应小于4 Ω。可采用专用接地极或自然接地极。

一般可利用插入地下深度超过1 m的铜棒或无缝钢管作为专用接地极(或称人工接地极)。自然接地极是指原有的可靠接地的装置,例如已可靠接地的建筑物金属结构件(建筑规程通常要求金属结构件接地)、地下水管等。经常移动的焊机一般采用自然接地极。注意,不得使用氧气管道或易燃易爆气体管道作为接地极,也不要利用避雷针作为接地极,这是因为避雷针经长久的风吹日晒后,接地电阻会变大。

对于接地线,有如下几个要求:

①要有足够的截面积,不得小于相线截面积的1/3~1/2。

②接地线必须是整根的,中间不得有任何接头。焊机与接地线的连接必须牢固可靠。对于经常移动的焊接设备,应利用螺栓拧紧,最好使用弹簧垫圈、防松螺帽以防变松;对于固定安装的焊机,接地线最好采用焊接方式进行连接。

③多台焊机共用一个接地极时,只能采用并联连接,不得串联到接地极上。

④接地线上不得设置熔断器或开关,以保证接地的永久性和可靠性。

⑤连接接地线时,应先接到接地极上,再接到焊机外壳上;拆除时顺序正好相反。

2. 保护接零

所谓保护接零,就是通过连接零线进行保护,即利用一根导线将焊机的金属外壳与电源线的零线连接起来,如图1-1-2所示。这是三相四线制供电电源的正确连接方法,四根线中有一根用来将焊机的金属外壳与电源线的零线连接起来。当某一相与焊机外壳短路时,焊机外壳将该相与零线短路,产生很大的单相短路电流,使该相保险丝熔断,该相电源被切断,外壳带电现象立刻终止。

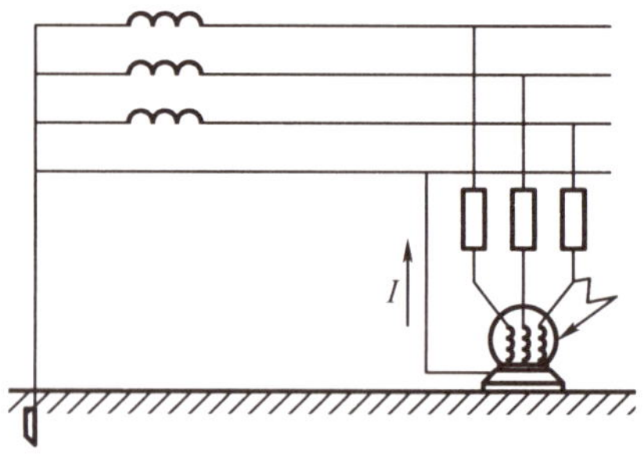

图1-1-2　保护接零

一些用户通过将外壳连接到大地上来代替零线的连接,这是不正确的。这是因为当某一相的绝缘被破坏而导致漏电时,外壳可能产生相当于相电压一半的电压,不能保证安全。

在焊机二次绕组一端接地或接零时,焊件不得接地,也不得接零。焊机二次绕组和焊件同时接地或接零时,如果电焊机二次回路接触不良,接地线或接零线上可能会产生很大电流,将地线或零线熔断,失去接地或接零保护功能。这不但危及焊工的人身安全,而且易引起火灾。因此,在焊接已牢固接地的工件时,必须将焊机的二次绕组的接地线或接零线暂时拆除,焊接后再恢复。图1-1-3比较了几种正确接地或接零方法。

对于接零线,有如下几个要求:

①接零线要有足够的截面积,其许用电流应大于焊机的主电源熔断器额定电流的2.5倍,或者大于对应自动开关跳闸电流的1.2倍。

②接零线必须是整根的,中间不得有接头。焊机外壳与接零线的连接应利用螺栓拧紧,最好使用弹簧垫圈、防松螺帽等以防长时间使用时变松;对于固定安装的焊机,可采用焊接方式连接。

③多台焊机不得以串联方式连接到零线上，只能采用并联方式。

④接零线上不得设置熔断器或开关。

⑤连接时，先将接零线接到零线上，再接到焊机外壳上；拆除时顺序正好相反。

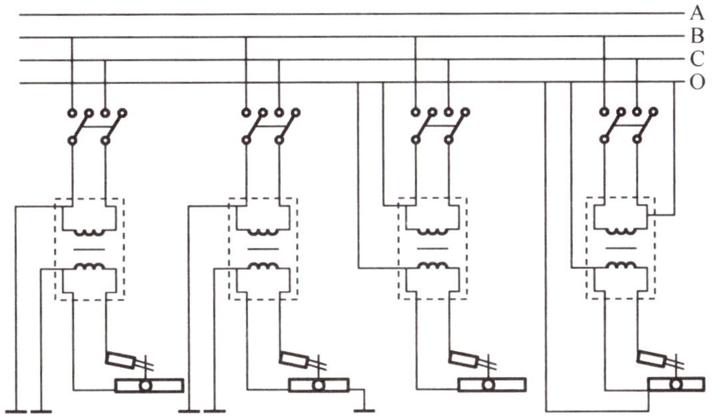

图 1-1-3　接地或接零正误方法比较

3. 采用接地故障断路器

在潮湿环境(如多雨的施工现场)中工作时，仅仅采用接地或接零是不能保证焊工安全的，这种情况下最好采用接地故障断路器。

接地故障断路器对由电网流入焊机的电流进行测量，并将其与流出焊机的电流进行比较。如果这两个电流有明显的差别，接地故障断路器将在几毫秒的时间内断开焊机与电网间的连接。流入焊机的电流与流出弧焊电源的电流之间的不平衡一般是因对地短路造成的。接地故障断路器以很快的速度断开电源，因此流向地面的短路电流不会造成人身伤害。应采用接地故障断路器、设备接地和合适的保险丝来提供最好的保护。即使焊机不接地，接地故障断路器仍然能进行保护，如图 1-1-4 所示。

4. 气体保护焊焊工需要记住的电气安全要点

①确保所有设备均可靠地接地或接零，在电源的输入侧最好使用接地故障断路器进行保护，并定期检查它们的可靠性。

②焊机持续工作时间应符合其铭牌的规定值，不得长时间超时运行。

③焊工操作时必须按劳动保护规定穿戴防护工作服、绝缘鞋和焊工手套。

④不要在雷雨天施焊，特别是焊接高度大的钢结构时，若雷电击中焊接电缆焊工将有生命危险。

⑤确保电源和电缆保持良好的工作状态。

⑥在焊接过程中、维护弧焊电源时或操作开关时不要站在湿地上或水泥地上。

⑦救助不幸被电击的人时一定要小心，以免自己成为另一个受害者。如果不知道如何做，那就等待急救服务。

⑧了解应急用断路器及熔断器的位置。

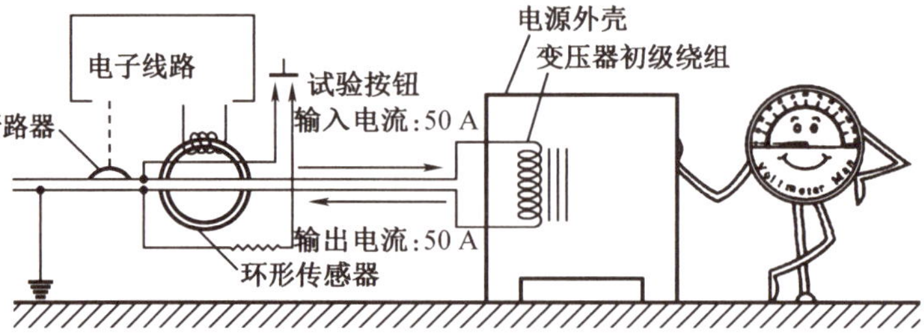

(a) 当流入焊机的电流与流出焊机的电流相等时，接地故障诊断器闭合

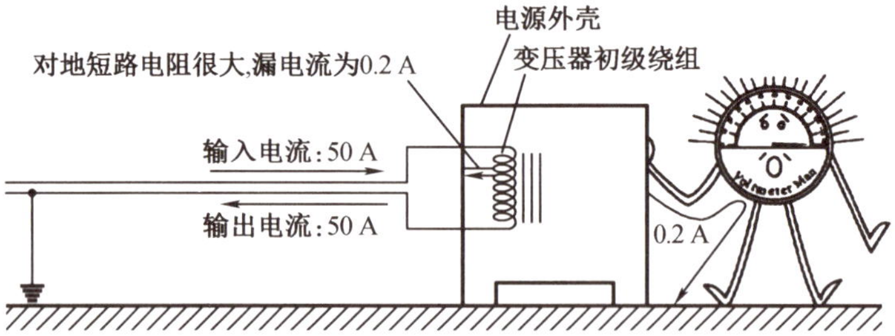

(b) 当没有安装接地故障诊断器时，小电流的对地短路故障不会熔断保险丝，但有危险

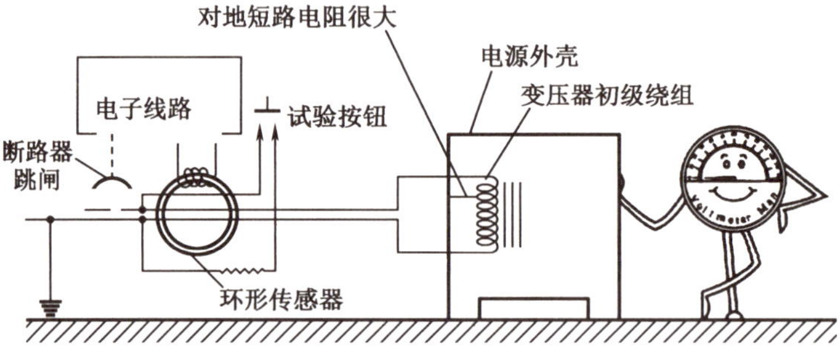

(c) 故障断路器检测到很小的短路故障电流后立即跳闸，保护焊工安全

图 1-1-4　接地故障断路器保护原理

⑨维修设备前应关断焊接设备的外部电源。光线不足时,照明灯的电压应为不高于 36 V 的安全电压。

⑩在狭小空间或容器内进行焊接时,必须两人轮换操作,并互相照应,一人留在外面监护,以便发生意外时及时切断电源进行抢救。

5. 触电抢救措施

万一有焊工触电,应遵守如下规定:

①最好先迅速地将电源切断。如果因某种原因(例如离开关较远)来不及切断电源,则应利用干燥的手套、木棒等绝缘物拉开触电者或挑开电线。切勿赤手或用导电物体去接触触电者,以防自己触电。单手操作比双手操作要安全些。

②切断电源后,如果触电焊工仍呈昏迷状态,应立即使其平卧,并进行心肺复苏或拨打 120 电话求助。

任务3：掌握用气安全基础知识

1. 常用气瓶及标识

气体保护焊常用的保护气体（如氩气（Ar）、氦气（He）、氧气（O_2）及二氧化碳（CO_2））是分别盛放在气瓶中的，焊接时，通过软管以一定的流量和压力将单一气体或混合气体导入焊接区。每种气瓶都有醒目的标识，如表 1-1-1 所示。不同的气瓶不能混用。

表 1-1-1　各种气瓶的标识方法

气体		Ar	He	O_2	CO_2	H_2
标识	气瓶外表面颜色	灰色	银灰色	天蓝色	铝白色	淡绿色
	字样	绿色“氩气”	绿色“氦气”	黑色“氧气”	黄色“二氧化碳”	红色“氢气”

2. 气瓶引起爆炸的原因

焊接用气瓶有氧气瓶、乙炔气瓶、氢气瓶、氩气瓶、二氧化碳气瓶和液化石油气瓶等，属Ⅱ、Ⅲ类受压容器，使用不当时可能引起爆炸，危险极大。引起气瓶爆炸的主要原因如下：

①气瓶的材质、结构或制造工艺不符合要求。

②由于保管和使用不当，受阳光直接暴晒、明火以及其他热源的辐射加热作用，使气瓶中气体受热膨胀而引起爆炸。

③搬运装卸时，气瓶从高处坠落、倾倒或滚动等，发生剧烈碰撞。

④放气速度太快，气体迅速流经阀门时产生静电火花。

⑤氧气瓶口上沾有油脂或氧气瓶内混入其他可燃气体。

⑥乙炔瓶内多孔物质下沉，产生净空间，使乙炔气处于高压状态。

⑦乙炔瓶内丙酮量过少。

⑧液化石油气充灌过满，受热时瓶内压力过高。

任务4：掌握防止气瓶爆炸的措施

1. 防震

在运输、储存和使用过程中应避免气瓶受剧烈振动和碰撞冲击。尤其是冬天，瓶体金属更容易发生脆裂而导致爆炸。气瓶应戴有安全帽，防止摔断瓶阀，造成事故，瓶身应有橡胶圈。搬运气瓶时，必须使用专门的抬架或小车，不得直接用肩膀扛运或直接搬运，车辆运输时，应用波浪形瓶架等将气瓶妥善固定，最好垫上橡皮或其他软物，以减少振动。应轻装轻卸，严禁从高处滑下或在地面上滚动。氧气瓶储存和使用时，应尽可能垂直立放，并设有支架固定，以防倾倒，发生碰撞。乙炔气瓶使用时必须立放，不能横躺卧放，以防丙酮流出，引起燃烧爆炸。

2. 防热

在运输和使用气瓶时，都要预防气瓶直接受热。夏天用车辆运输或室外使用气瓶时，瓶身应加以覆盖，避免阳光暴晒。气瓶存放和使用时，应当远离高温、明火、熔融金属飞溅和易燃易爆物质等，距离应当在10m以上。

3. 严格检查

使用气瓶时要检查气瓶试压日期是否过期，装上减压器后检查是否漏气，表针是否灵活。

4. 精心操作

①开启阀门时不要面对阀门接口，应站在气瓶接口的一侧或垂直方向的位置上，以免气流或减压气射出伤人。

②未装减压器之前，应先缓慢地打开气瓶阀门，吹除污物，以免灰尘和水分进入减压器。

③开启阀门的动作要缓慢，以免气流过速产生静电火花或减压器里的气体经压缩而发生燃烧爆炸事故。

④冬季瓶阀或减压器可能有结冻现象，只能用热水或蒸汽解冻，严禁使用火焰烘烤或用铁器猛击瓶阀，更不能猛拧减压器的调节螺丝，以防气体大量冲出，造成事故。

⑤氧气瓶阀和减压器不得染上油脂。

⑥氧气瓶和乙炔气瓶及其他可燃气瓶相互接触时，一旦发生漏气着火，容易引起燃烧爆炸，因此不得同车运输和在一起存放。

⑦禁止用起重设备直接吊运钢瓶及用氧气瓶代替压缩空气进行喷漆等。

⑧使用液化石油气瓶时，液体不能充得过满，必须按规定留出气化空间。因液化石油气对普通橡胶导管和衬垫有腐蚀作用，应采用耐油性强的橡胶导管和衬垫。

⑨储存和使用石油气的场所，其通风孔除设在高处外，低处亦应设有通风孔，以利空气对流。

⑩用石油气瓶焊割点火时，应先点燃引火物，后打开瓶阀，不要颠倒次序。气瓶内气体不能全部用完，应保留一定的气量，瓶内保证正压，以防空气进入气瓶。

5. 加强气瓶的安全技术检验

气瓶在使用过程中，必须按国家《气瓶安全监察规程》的要求，对充装无腐蚀性气体的气瓶，每三年检验一次；充装有腐蚀性气体的气瓶，每两年检验一次。在使用过程中，如发现有严重腐蚀、损伤和怀疑有问题时，可提前进行检验。气瓶的检验项目一般包括内外表面检验和水压试验。

任务5：掌握常用防火防爆措施

1. 防火防爆措施

焊接过程中，飞溅的颗粒如果落到可燃物品上，易导致火灾，因此应采取如下措施防止火灾：

①焊前应先检查焊接现场周围是否有易燃、易爆物品（如油漆、煤油、木屑等）。如有，则应将这些物品搬离，或利用绝热材料进行可靠的覆盖。

②在对储存容器、管道等进行修复焊时，应检查该容器内是否存放过易燃、易爆物。如果是，则必须先将容器内残留的介质清理干净，并用碱水清洗内壁，再用压缩空气吹干，确认安全可靠后方可进行焊接。

③在对压力容器、筒体、管道进行焊接时，必须先将压力释放后才能开始工作，防止发生爆炸。

2. 灭火措施

作业现场应配有灭火器。万一发生火灾，应首先切断电源，最好将气瓶移走，然后采取灭火措施。常用的灭火器材有四氯化碳灭火器、二氧化碳灭火器和干粉灭火器。

任务考核

1. 能引起人体轻度痉挛的交流电为( )mA。

A. 5　　B. 10　　C. 35　　D. 50

2. 电流通过人体时，最危险的途径是( )。

A. 从手到手　　B. 从肩到手　　C. 从脚到脚　　D. 从手到脚

3. 流经人体的电流越大，则电击造成的伤亡程度( )。

A. 越小　　B. 越大　　C. 无影响　　D. 无规律变化

4. 对人体来说最危险的电流频率是( )。

A. 50　　B. 200　　C. 500　　D. 1 000

5. 当皮肤潮湿多汗或在水下电焊时，人体电阻为( )。

A. 200~300　　B. 400　　C. 650　　D. 1 000

6. 因电流的机械效应而发生电伤时，电流( )人体。

A. 通过　　B. 不通过　　C. 只通过表皮　　D. 少量通过

7. 在潮湿而且触电危险性大的环境下进行电焊时，安全电压应( )V。

A. 2.5　　B. 12　　C. 36　　D. 45

8. 模压底绝缘鞋的电阻为 10 000 Ω，两只脚平行并联的电阻为( )Ω。

A. 5 000　　B. 10 000　　C. 20 000　　D. 40 000

9. 属于意外带电体的是( )。

A. 接线柱　　B. 焊钳口　　C. 焊条　　D. 绝缘破损的电缆

10. 安全规程规定，确需延长焊机电源线时，应离地面 2.5 m，该规定属于( )保护措施。

A. 绝缘　　B. 屏护　　C. 间隔　　D. 个人防护

Module Ⅰ

Gas Shielded Welding Safety and Protection

Project Ⅰ Safe Use of Electricity and Gas

【Learning Objectives】

1. Master the basic knowledge of electrical safety;
2. Master the preventive measures for welding electric shock accidents;
3. Master the basic knowledge of gas safety;
4. Master the measures to prevent gas cylinder explosion;
5. Master common fire and explosion prevention measures.

Task 1:Master the Basic Knowledge about Electrical Safety

1. Safe voltage and hazardous voltage

Safe voltage refers to a voltage with an effective value less than 36 V, while dangerous voltage usually refers to a voltage with an effective value greater than 36 V. The input terminal voltage of a shielded arc welding power supply is generally 50 Hz, 220 V or 380 V, and the no-load voltage at the output terminal is generally above 60 V, both of which are considered dangerous voltages. Therefore, welding machines must follow operating procedures to prevent electric shock.

2. Hazards of electric shock on the human body

Contact with live parts will result in current flowing through the human body, leading to electric shock. The extent of injury caused by electric shock depends on the following factors.

(1) Current magnitude

The current of not more than 1 mA will only cause a slight tingling sensation for the electric shock victim; a current of 1-5 mA will be discomforting but not painful; a current of 6-30 mA will cause pain, result in loss of muscle control, inability to walk, and may even cause burns; a current of 50-150 mA will cause severe pain, leading to severe muscle contractions, deep burns, knockdown, and possibly death. The current of 1,000 – 4,300 mA will cause ventricular fibrillation (the disruption of the electrocardiogram's rhythm, causing violent heartbeats and the inability to pump blood due to ventricular desynchronization), which may result in death; when the current is 10,000 mA, the heart will stop beating, with severe burns and a high likelihood of death.

Although the effect of electric shock on the human body is measured by the magnitude of current, since the current passing through the human body cannot be calculated in advance, safety conditions are determined based on safe voltage rather than safe current. The resistance of the human body varies under different environmental conditions, and the safety voltage also differs. Generally, voltage below 36 V will not cause casualties, hence it is defined as a safe voltage.

(2) Duration of electric shock

The longer the duration of electric shock, the more severe the degree of electric shock injury. This is because as the power-on time extends, the body resistance decreases due to sweating or other reasons, resulting in an increase in current and an increased risk of electric shock. In addition, there is an interval of about 0.1 s for each contraction and expansion of the human heart, during which the human body is most sensitive to current. If an electric current passes through the heart at this moment, even if it is only a few tens of milliamperes, it can cause heart tremors. When the current does not pass through the heart at that moment, even if the current reaches 10 A, it will not cause cardiac paralysis. It can be seen that if the current lasts for more than 1 s, it will certainly coincide with the most sensitive interval of the heart, causing great danger.

(3) Type of current (DC or AC), frequency of alternating current

For the human body, the most dangerous frequency is between 25 and 300 Hz. Frequencies above 2,000 Hz have minimal impact on the human body due to the skin effect. The harm caused by DC voltage is also less than that of power frequency AC voltage.

(4) Flow path of electric current in the human body

The most hazardous path is from hand to foot, as the current flowing along this route has a greater chance of passing through vital organs such as the heart, lungs, and spinal cord. Next is the path from hand to hand, while the path from foot to foot is the least dangerous.

(5) Body resistance

When the applied voltage remains constant, a higher resistance in the human body results in a lower risk. Human body resistance is primarily composed of internal resistance and skin resistance. The internal resistance is not significantly affected by external conditions and has a minimum value of 500 Ω. Skin resistance, on the other hand, is influenced by various external factors such as sweat, skin damage, and the presence of adhered dust. These factors reduce skin resistance and increase the risk.

3. Common causes of electric shock accidents

There are many causes of electric shocks due to different specific circumstances, but they can be roughly divided into two categories: One is direct electric shock, which occurs when live parts are directly contacted during normal operation; the other is indirect electric shock, which occurs when accidental charged bodies are touched. Accidental charged bodies refer to objects that are normally uncharged but become charged due to insulation damage or electrical component failure, such as welding machine shells with electric leakage and cables with damaged insulation sheaths.

(1) Direct electric shock accident

These types of accidents are likely to occur when the following operations are conducted:

①Accidentally touching the conductive part of the welding gun when replacing the electrode or arranging the welding wire on the welding gun before welding.

②Touching charged bodies such as binding posts and electrode plates with hands or body when wiring, adjusting welding current, or moving welding equipment.

③Touching low-voltage lines or getting close to high-voltage networks during welding at heights.

(2) Accidental indirect electric shock

Indirect electric shock accidents during welding are mainly caused by touching the live welding machine shell or damaged insulation on the cables. The main reasons for electrical leakage from the welding machine shell include: Moisture in the coil, prolonged overload operation, short-circuit heating, improper installation location and method that do not meet safety requirements, mechanical damage to the insulation of the coil or lead due to vibration or impact, and the entry of metal objects such as iron wires, iron filings, copper wires, or small iron pipe heads into the welding machine shell.

4. Type of electric shock

Electric shock can be categorized into the following situations.

(1) Low-voltage single-phase electric shock

A certain body part of a person comes into contact with a charged object connected to single-phase voltage. Most electrical accidents involve single-phase electric shocks.

(2) Low-voltage two-phase electric shock

Two parts of the human body simultaneously come into contact with two-phase charged objects. During this time, the voltage experienced by the human body can reach as high as 380 V, posing a significant danger.

(3) Step voltage electric shock

When an electrical equipment experiences a grounding fault, the grounding current flows through the grounding conductor to the earth. When people are near the grounding point, the potential difference between their two feet is referred to as step voltage. Excessive step voltage can also lead to electric shock accidents. High step voltage may occur at the location of a grounding fault in high-voltage equipment or near a grounding device with a high current flow.

Task 2:Master the Preventive Measures for Electric Shock Accidents during Welding

To ensure the safety of welding equipment usage, various safety measures have been implemented before the equipment leaves the factory, including isolation protection and insulation measures. To ensure electrical safety, apart from following the provided instructions during equipment installation and welding operations, attention should be given to the following points.

1. Protective grounding of welding machine shell

If the welding machine is not grounded, the primary winding of the transformer will generate a high voltage when short-circuited with the housing for some reason, causing electric shock when people touch the housing. Therefore, all welding machine shells must be grounded. Grounding, in simple terms, is connecting the welding machine shell to the ground using a wire, providing a low-resistance path to the ground. This ensures that when the welding machine shell experiences electrical leakage, a significant short-circuit current to the ground is generated. This current will burn out the fuse or trip the circuit interrupter, effectively cutting off the entire circuit and simultaneously sending an alarm signal to the user, as shown in Fig. 1-1-1.

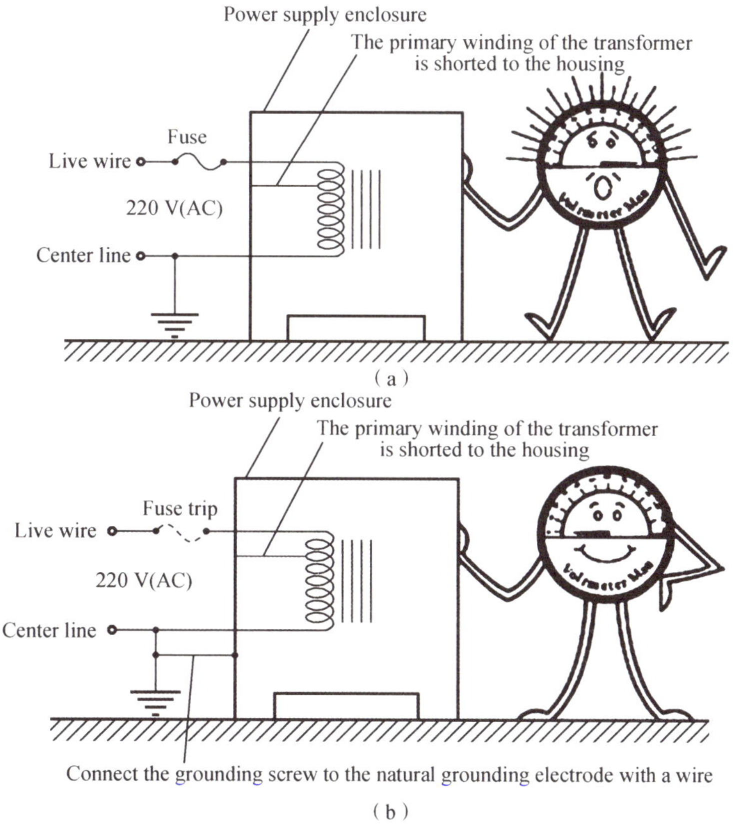

Fig. 1-1-1 Grounding of Power Supply Enclosure

Most welding machine shells are equipped with dedicated grounding screws (some welding machines with three-phase four-wire power supply do not have such screws, and one of the four cables is connected to the grounding wire of the power grid). These screws should be connected to the grounding electrode using wires, and the grounding resistance should be less than 4 Ω. Special grounding electrodes or natural grounding electrodes can be used.

Generally, copper rods or seamless steel pipes inserted into the ground with a depth of more than 1 m can be used as specialized grounding electrodes (or artificial grounding electrodes). Natural grounding electrodes refer to existing reliable grounding devices, such as metal structural members of buildings that have been reliably grounded (metal structural members are usually required to be grounded in building regulations), underground water pipes, etc. Natural grounding electrodes are generally used for welding machines that are frequently moved. Note: Do not use oxygen pipelines or flammable and explosive gas pipelines as grounding electrodes, and do not use lightning rods as grounding electrodes. The grounding resistance will increase after the lightning rod is exposed to wind and sun for a long time.

There are several requirements for grounding wires:

①There should be sufficient cross-sectional area, not less than 1/3-1/2 of the phase line's cross-sectional area.

②The grounding wire must be a single piece without any joints in the middle. The connection between the welding machine and the grounding wire must be strong and reliable. For welding equipment that is moved frequently, it should be tightened with bolts, it is advisable to use spring washers and locknuts to prevent loosening; for fixed welding machines, the grounding wires are best connected by welding.

③ When multiple welding machines share one grounding electrode, they can only be connected in parallel and must not be connected in series to the grounding electrode.

④No fuse or switch should be installed on the grounding wire to ensure the permanence and reliability of grounding.

⑤When connecting the grounding wire, first connect it to the grounding electrode and then to the welding machine shell. The removal order is reversed.

2. Protective connect to neutral

The so-calledprotective connect to neutral is to provide protection by connecting to the neutral wire. It involves connecting the metal shell of the welding machine to the neutral wire of the power cord using a wire, as shown in Fig. 1-1-2. This is the correct method of connecting a three-phase four-wire power supply. One of the four wires is used to connect the metal shell of the welding machine to the neutral wire of the power cord. When a certain phase is short-circuited with the welding machine shell, the welding machine shell will create a large single-phase short-circuit current by short-circuiting this phase

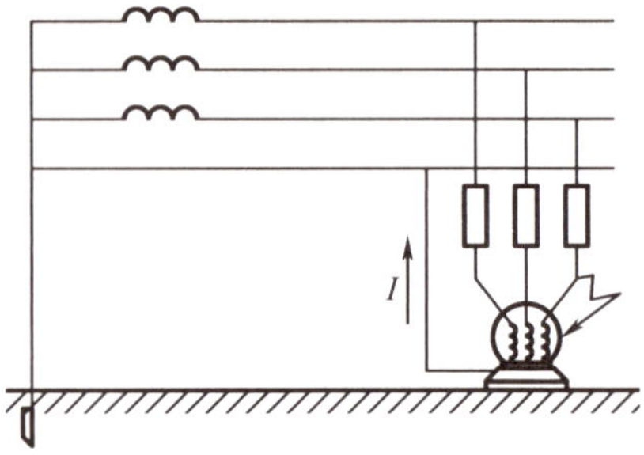

Fig. 1-1-2 Protective Connect to Neutral

with the neutral wire. As a result, the fuse of this phase blows, cutting off the power supply of this phase, and immediately terminating the electrified phenomenon of the shell.

Some users incorrectly replace the neutral wire connection with connecting the shell to earth. This is because when the insulation of a certain phase is damaged and causes leakage, the shell may generate a voltage equivalent to half of the phase voltage, which cannot guarantee safety.

When one end of the secondary winding of the welding machine is grounded or connected to neutral, the weldment should not be grounded or connected to neutral. If both the secondary winding of the welding machine and the weldment are simultaneously grounded or connected to neutral, a large current may be generated on the grounding wire or wire connecting to neutral due to poor contact in the secondary circuit of the welding machine, resulting in the fusion of the grounding wire or neutral wire and the loss of the grounding or neutral protection function. This not only jeopardizes the personal safety of welding machines but also easily leads to fires. Therefore, when welding workpieces firmly grounded, the grounding wire or wire connecting to neutral of the secondary winding of the welding machine must be temporarily disconnected and restored after welding. Fig. 1-1-3 compares several correct grounding or neutral wire connection methods.

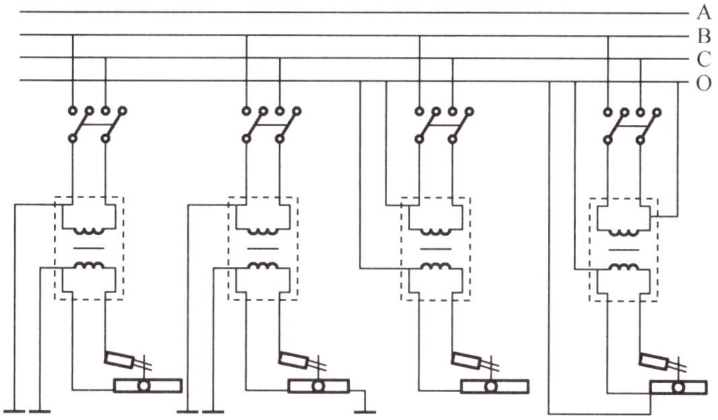

Fig. 1-1-3 Comparison of Grounding or Neutral Wire Connection Methods

There are the following requirements for thewire connecting to neutral:

①Thewire connecting to neutral shall have a sufficient cross - sectional area, and its allowable current should be greater than 2. 5 times the rated current of the main power fuse of the welding machine or greater than 1. 2 times the tripping current of the corresponding recloser.

②Thewire connecting to neutral must be continuous without any joints. The connection between the welding machine shell and the wire connecting to neutral should be tightened with bolts. It is preferable to use spring washers, lock nuts, etc. to prevent them from loosening after long-term use. For fixed welding machines, they can be connected by welding.

③Multiple welding machines should not be connected to the neutral wire in series, but only in parallel.

④No fuses or switches are allowed to be installed on thewire connecting to neutral.

⑤During connection, first connect thewire connecting to neutral to the neutral wire and then to the welding machine shell. The removal order is reversed.

3. Utilize grounding fault circuit interrupter (GFCI)

When working in a humid environment (such as a rainy construction site), the safety of welding machines cannot be ensured solely through grounding or neutral wire connection. It is recommended to use a GFCI in such cases.

The GFCI measures the current flowing from the electrical grid into the welding machine and compares it with the current flowing out of the welding machine. If there is a significant difference between these two currents, the GFCI will disconnect the welding machine from the grid within a few milliseconds. The imbalance between the current flowing into the welding machine and the current flowing out of the arc welding powersupply is generally caused by a short circuit to ground. The GFCI quickly disconnects the power supply, so the short-circuit current flowing to the ground will not cause personal injury. To ensure the best protection, it is important to use the GFCI, equipment grounding, and appropriate fuses. The GFCI provides protection even when the welding machine is not grounded, as depicted in Fig. 1-1-4.

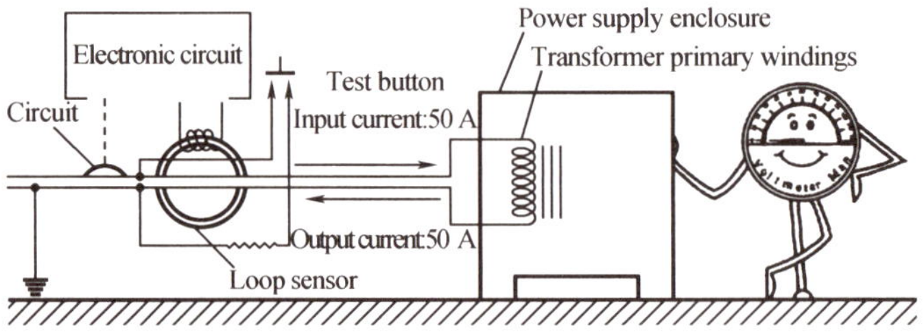

(a) When the current entering and exiting the welding machine are equal, the GFCI closes

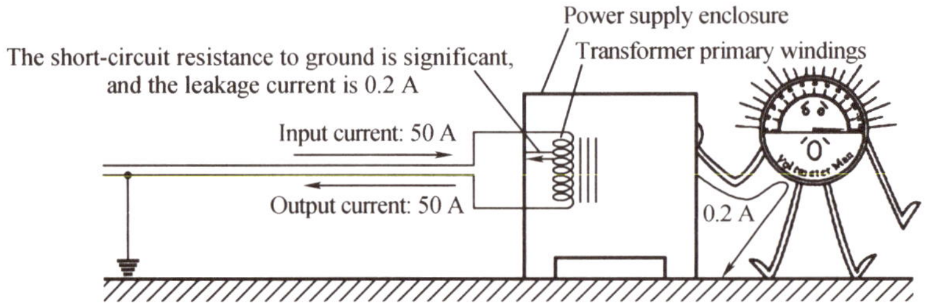

(b) When a GFCI is not installed, a low-current short-to-ground fault will not cause the fuse to blow, but it is still hazardous

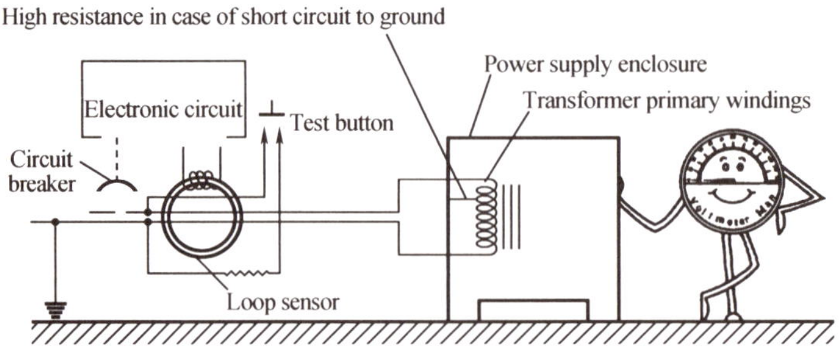

(c) Protect the welding machine by immediately tripping the failed circuit breaker upon detection of a small short-circuit fault current

Fig. 1-1-4 GFCI Protection Principle

4. Electrical safety points that gas shielded welding welding machines need to remember

①Ensure that all equipment is properly grounded or connected to the neutral. It is recommended to use a GFCI for protection on the power supply input side, and regularly check their reliability.

②The welding machine's continuous operating time must comply with the specified value on its nameplate and should not exceed the allowed overtime for an extended period.

③Welding machines must wear protective work clothing, insulated footwear, and welding gloves according to labor protection regulations during operation.

④Avoid welding during thunderstorms, especially when working on steel structures with significant heights, as lightning striking the welding cables can be life-threatening.

⑤Ensure that the power supply and cables are in good working condition.

⑥Do not stand on wet or cement floors while welding, performing maintenance on the arc welding power supply, or operating switches.

⑦Exercise caution when rescuing someone who has been electrocuted to avoid becoming another victim. If unsure of what to do, wait for emergency services.

⑧Familiarize yourself with the location of emergency circuit interrupters and fuses.

⑨Before maintenance, switch off the external power supply of the welding equipment. In case of insufficient lighting, the voltage of the illumination lamp should not exceed the safe voltage of 36 V.

⑩When welding in confined spaces or containers, two individuals must take turns operating and supervising each other. One person should remain outside to monitor and cut off the power supply promptly in case of an accident.

5. Rescue measures for electric shock

In the event of an electric shock to welding machines, the following regulations shall be adhered to:

①It is best to quickly cut off the power supply. If it is not possible to cut off the power supply in time for some reason (for example, if it is far away from the switch), use dry gloves, wooden sticks, and other insulating materials to move the electric shock victim or remove the wire. Do not touch the victim or conductive objects with bare hands to avoid getting an electric shock yourself. It is safer to operate with one hand instead of two hands.

② After cutting off the power supply, if the electric shock welding machine is still unconscious, they should immediately lie down and perform artificial respiration or call 120 for help.

Task 3:Master the Basic Knowledge about Gas Safety

1. Commonly used gas cylinders and signage

The protective gases (such as argon(Ar), helium(He), oxygen(O_2), and CO_2) used for gas shielded welding are stored separately in gas cylinders. During welding, single gas or a mixture of gas is introduced into the welding area through hoses at a specific flow rate and pressure. Each type of gas cylinder has a distinctive mark, as shown in Table 1-1-1. Different cylinders cannot be mixed.

Table 1-1-1 Identification Methods of Various Gas Cylinders

Gas		Ar	He	O_2	CO_2	H_2
Identification	Color of gas cylinder outer surface	Gray	Silver gray	Sky blue	Aluminum white	Pale green
	Words	Green "Argon"	Green "Helium"	Black "Oxygen"	Yellow "CO_2"	Red "Hydrogen"

2. Causes of gas cylinder explosions

Gas cylinders used for welding purposes include oxygen cylinders, acetylene cylinders, hydrogen cylinders, argon cylinders, CO_2 cylinders, and liquefied petroleum gas cylinders. These cylinders belong to Class Ⅱ and Ⅲ pressure vessels. Improper use may lead to explosions, which can be extremely dangerous. The primary causes of cylinder explosions are as follows:

①The material, structure, or manufacturing process of the gas cylinder does not meet the requirements.

②Due to improper storage and use, direct exposure to sunlight, open flames, and radiation heating from other heat sources, the gas in the cylinder is heated and expands, causing an explosion.

③During handling, loading, and unloading, the gas cylinder falls from a high place, tips over, or rolls, resulting in violent collisions.

④The gas is released too quickly, generating static sparks when it flows rapidly through the valve.

⑤The oxygen cylinder mouth is contaminated with grease, or other combustible gases are mixed in the oxygen cylinder.

⑥The porous substance in the acetylene cylinder sinks, creating a clear space, causing the acetylene gas to be under high pressure.

⑦The acetylene cylinder contains insufficient amounts of acetone.

⑧The LPG cylinder is overfilled, resulting in excessively high pressure when heated.

Task 4:Master the Measures to Prevent Gas Cylinder Explosions

1. Anti-vibration

During transportation, storage, and use, gas cylinders should be protected from severe vibration and impact. Especially in winter, the metal of the cylinder is more prone to embrittlement and explosion. Gas cylinders should be equipped with safety caps to prevent accidents caused by broken cylinder valves, and the cylinder body should have rubber gaskets. When handling gas cylinders, a specialized lifting frame or trolley must be used. It is not allowed to carry them directly on the shoulder or handle them directly. During vehicle transportation, gas cylinders should be properly secured with wave-shaped cylinder racks, etc. It is recommended to pad rubber or other soft objects to reduce vibration. They should be handled with care and it is strictly prohibited to slide down from a height or roll on the ground. When storing and using oxygen cylinders, they should be placed vertically as much as possible and secured with brackets to prevent tipping and collisions. Acetylene cylinders must be stored upright rather than horizontally to prevent acetone from flowing out and causing combustion and explosion.

2. Heat insulation

When transporting and using gas cylinders, ensure they are not directly exposed to heat. When transporting gas cylinders by vehicles or using them outdoors in summer, the cylinder body should be covered to prevent exposure to sunlight. The gas cylinder warehouse and the use of gas cylinders should be kept away from high temperatures, open flames, molten metal splashes, and flammable and explosive substances, with a distance of over 10 m.

3. Thorough examination

Check the expiration date of the pressure test for the gas cylinder when using it. After installing the pressure reducer, inspect for any air leakage and ensure the gauge needle is flexible.

4. Meticulous operation

①When opening the valve, do not face the valve interface. Stand on one side of the gas cylinder interface or in a vertical direction to avoid injury from airflow or decompressed gas ejection.

②Before installing the pressure reducer, slowly open the cylinder valve and blow off dirt to prevent dust and moisture from entering the pressure reducer.

③Open the valve slowly to avoid electrostatic sparks caused by excessive airflow or combustion and explosion accidents caused by compressed gas in the pressure reducer.

④In winter, the cylinder valve or pressure reducer may freeze. Only hot water or steam can be used to unfreeze it. It is strictly prohibited to use flame to heat or hit the cylinder valve with iron tools. It is also not allowed to forcefully turn the adjusting screw of the pressure reducer to prevent a large amount of gas from rushing out and causing accidents.

⑤Oxygen cylinder valves and pressure reducers should not be greased.

⑥When oxygen cylinders, acetylene cylinders, and other combustible gas cylinders come into contact with each other, the leakage and ignition can easily cause combustion and explosion. Therefore, they should not be transported or stored together.

⑦It is prohibited to directly lift steel cylinders with lifting equipment and to spray paint using oxygen cylinders instead of compressed air.

⑧When using liquefied petroleum gas cylinders, the liquid must not be overfilled, and a gasification space must be reserved as required by regulations. Since LPG has a corrosive effect on ordinary rubber conduits and gaskets, rubber conduits and gaskets with strong oil resistance should be used.

⑨Ventilation holes should be placed at both high and low positions in locations where LPG is stored and used to facilitate air convection.

⑩When welding, cutting, and igniting with petroleum gas cylinders, the ignition source should be lit first, followed by opening the cylinder valve. The order should not be reversed. The gas in the cylinder should not be completely used up, and a certain amount of gas should be reserved. Positive pressure should be maintained in the cylinder to prevent air from entering.

5. Enhance the safety technical inspection of gas cylinders

During the use of gas cylinders, they must be inspected every three years according to the requirements of the national *Safety Supervision Regulations for Gas Cylinders*. Gas cylinders filled with non-corrosive gases shall be inspected every two years. If serious corrosion or damage is found during use and there are doubts about it, an inspection can be carried out in advance. Generally, the inspection items for cylinders include internal and external surface inspection and hydrostatic testing.

Task 5:Master Common Fire and Explosion Prevention Measures

1. Fire and explosion prevention measures

During the welding process, if splashing particles fly onto combustible materials, it can easily result in a fire. Therefore, the following measures must be taken to prevent fires:

①Before welding, check for flammable and explosive materials (such as paint, kerosene, wood chips, etc.) in the vicinity of the welding site. If any are present, these items should be removed or adequately covered with thermal insulation materials.

②When carrying out repair welding on storage containers, pipes, etc., check if flammable and explosive materials have been stored in the containers. If so, the remaining contents in the container must be drained first, and the inner wall should be cleaned with alkaline water, followed by drying with compressed air. Welding can only proceed after confirming it to be safe and reliable.

③Prior to welding on pressure vessels, cylinders, and pipes, the pressure must be released before commencing work to prevent explosions.

2. Fire extinguishing measures

Fire extinguishers should be provided at the work site. In the event of a fire, the power supply should be cut off first. It is preferable to remove the gas cylinder before taking fire extinguishing measures. Commonly used fire extinguishers include carbon tetrachloride, CO_2, and dry powder extinguishers.

Task Assessment

1. The alternating current that can cause mild spasms in the human body is ( ) mA.

A. 5 B. 10 C. 35 D. 50

2. When current passes through the human body, the most dangerous pathway is ( ).

A. from hand to hand B. from shoulder to hand

C. from foot to foot D. from hand to foot

3. The greater the intensity of current flowing through the human body, the higher the degree of casualties caused by electric shock will be ( ).

A. smaller B. larger C. no impact D. irregular changes

4. The most dangerous current frequency for the human body is ( ).

A. 50 B. 200 C. 500 D. 1,000

5. When the skin is wet and sweaty or underwater welding is carried out, the electrical resistance of the human body is ( ).

A. 200-300 B. 400 C. 650 D. 1,000

6. When an electric injury occurs due to the mechanical effect of current, the current ( ) the human body.

A. pass through

B. did not pass through

C. only passes through the surface layer

D. pass a small amount

7. When welding is carried out in a damp environment with a high risk of electric shock, the safe voltage should be ( ) V.

A. 2.5 B. 12 C. 36 D. 45

8. The resistance of molded insulating shoes is 10,000 Ω, and the parallel resistance of both feet is ( ) Ω.

A. 5,000 B. 10,000 C. 20,000 D. 40,000

9. The object with accidental charge is ( ).

A. terminal post B. welding clamp

C. welding electrode D. insulation damaged cable

10. The safety regulations state that when it is absolutely necessary to extend the power cord of the welding machine, it must be 2.5 m above the ground. This provision falls under ( ) protective measures.

A. insulation B. shielding

C. spacing D. personal protective equipment

项目二 个人危害及防护

【学习目标】

1. 掌握弧光辐射的危害及防护措施;
2. 掌握高频磁场辐射的危害及防护措施;
3. 掌握放射性辐射的危害及防护措施;
4. 掌握焊接烟尘的危害及防护措施。

任务1:掌握弧光辐射的危害及防护措施

1. 弧光辐射的危害

弧光包括红外线、可见光、紫外线三种射线。紫外线对焊工的危害最大,尤其对眼睛和皮肤。眼睛受到长时间的弧光紫外线辐射后,会严重影响视力,引起电光性眼炎。电光性眼炎的主要症状为疼痛、有砂粒感、多泪、怕风吹等。皮肤经常受到紫外线照射,会导致发红、触痛、变黑、脱皮等,严重的还会诱发皮肤癌。另外,紫外线对纤维织物还有破坏和褪色作用。气体保护焊电弧温度高,其电弧光辐射比焊条电弧焊强得多,例如,氩弧焊的紫外线辐射强度是焊条电弧焊的13倍,因此更应加强防护。

2. 防护措施

应采取下列弧光辐射防护措施:

①引弧前应戴好专用头盔或面罩,保护好面部(特别是眼睛),还要注意周围是否有其他人员,以免强烈弧光灼伤别人的眼睛。

②焊前应穿戴好高领帆布工作服和专用手套(最好是白色的),防止弧光灼伤皮肤。

③多人使用多台焊机同时进行焊接作业时,弧光辐射源较多,应使用防护屏相互遮挡,避免受其他焊机弧光的伤害。防护屏可用玻璃纤维布及薄钢板等制作,并涂上灰色或黑色的无光漆。

任务2:掌握高频磁场辐射的危害及防护措施

1. 高频磁场辐射的危害

钨极氩弧焊采用高频振荡引弧,因此引弧时焊工易受到高频磁场的辐射。人体长时间受高频磁场辐射时,各种器官的温度会升高,出现头晕、乏力、多梦、脱发和记忆力下降等症状。

2. 防护措施

通常采用如下防护措施:

①提高高频振荡引弧的可靠性,减少引弧次数及时间;可靠引弧时,引弧时间只有0.2 s左右,影响较小,但是如果频繁引弧则影响较大。

②工件可靠地接地。工件接地能够显著降低高频辐射强度。

③降低工作环境的温度和湿度。环境温度和湿度越高，人体对高频辐射的敏感性越大，因此加强通风，降低工作环境温度和湿度是减少高频辐射的重要手段。

④屏蔽高频振荡器。将高频振荡器用金属外壳屏蔽起来，可降低高频磁场辐射强度；最好将焊枪内的电缆、连接焊枪至焊机的电缆也利用铜质软编织层屏蔽起来。

任务3：掌握放射性辐射的危害及防护措施

1. 放射性辐射的危害

钨极氩弧焊经常采用钍钨极。这种钨极中含有少量的 ThO_2，具有轻微的放射性。对焊工的危害主要是体外照射和体内照射。体外照射就是钨极发射出的放射性射线所产生的照射。在正常焊接中，由于钍钨极本身放射性并不大，焊接持续时间不长，因此体外照射是不需要进行屏蔽的。所谓体内辐射即钍及其衰变产物以气溶胶的形式进入人体，这种气溶胶具有很高的生物活性，很难被排出，长期作用于体内，从而形成体内照射，引起放射性疾病。主要表现为免疫力降低、体重减轻、衰弱无力、造血系统受到破坏。

2. 防护措施

采取如下措施进行放射性辐射防护：

①尽量不采用钍钨极，而选用铈钨极。铈钨极放射性比钍钨极低两个数量级。

②焊接时务必戴上头盔，防止蒸发出的钨极进入体内。

③根据电流选择合适直径的钨极，防止钨极的过量烧损。

④钍钨极应利用铅或铁质箱子盛放，存放在独立的地下储藏室中；储藏室应配置排气系统，随时将被放射性物质污染的空气排出。

⑤打磨钨极时务必穿上专用工作服，并戴上口罩和手套；砂轮必须安装在通风良好的地方。

⑥对打磨场地或焊接场地及时进行湿式清理；对收集的放射性粉尘应进行深埋处理。

⑦接触钍钨棒后应利用流动的水和肥皂洗手，工作服和手套应经常清洗，最好使用一次性口罩。

任务4：掌握焊接烟尘的危害及防护措施

1. 焊接烟尘的危害

焊接过程会放出烟尘，这些烟尘主要由金属、氧化物和氟化物等微粒以及臭氧、氧化氮和一氧化碳等有害气体组成。气体保护焊焊接烟尘各种组分的危害性见表 1-2-1。具体成分和数量主要取决于采用的焊接方法、焊接参数等。实际上焊接烟尘是影响最大的有害因素。因此，应采取有效措施来进行防护，特别是在通风情况欠佳的环境下，如在密闭容器、船舱或管道里进行焊接时。

2. 通风防护措施

通风是焊接烟尘最常用、最有效的防护方法，而且通风还是降低焊接热污染的主要措施。在室内、各种容器及管道内进行焊接作业时，均应采取通风措施，以保证操作人员的身体健康。根据通风动力源的不同，通风可分为自然通风和机械通风两种。

表 1-2-1　气体保护焊焊接烟尘各组分的危害性

烟尘成分		来源	危害	症状
粉尘	铝、氧化铝	铝的焊接及切割	铝尘肺	气短、胸闷、咳嗽、咳痰、无力、神经衰弱等
	铬、氧化铬	钢,特别是不锈钢的焊接及切割	慢性非特异性肺病、支气管炎、癌症	气短、胸闷、咳嗽、咳痰、无力、气喘、神经衰弱等
	铁、氧化铁	钢的焊接、切割	铁尘肺	气短、胸闷、咳嗽、咳痰、无力、神经衰弱等
	锰、氧化锰	钢的焊接,特别是 CO_2 气体保护焊	锰中毒、肺炎	头疼、乏力、失眠、神经功能紊乱等
	氧化硅	钢的焊接,特别是 CO_2 气体保护焊	尘肺	气短、胸闷、咳嗽、咳痰、无力、神经衰弱等
有毒气体	臭氧	主要是钨极氩弧焊和熔化极氩弧焊	支气管炎	咳嗽、胸闷、乏力、食欲不振、头晕、全身疼痛
	氮氧化合物	各种气体保护焊	慢性中毒、慢性支气管炎	头疼、失眠、食欲不振、呼吸困难、虚脱、全身软弱无力等
	一氧化碳	各种气体保护焊	一氧化碳中毒	头疼、全身乏力、脉搏加快、呕吐、头昏等

(1)自然通风

自然通风依靠焊接工作场所与外界的温差及自然风力将焊接烟尘排出,这种方式的特点是通风量小,不够稳定,受外界条件影响大。由于焊接车间内的温度高于外界,在温度差的作用下,室内空气和室外空气之间自然会发生交换,形成自然通风。在车间设计过程中,通过适当调整车间结构可改善自然通风条件;通过合理安排车间内的设备布局也可改善自然通风。自然通风只能作为辅助通风措施。

(2)机械通风

机械通风是利用风机产生的压力来进行换气的,具有通风量大,通风稳定的特点。根据通风范围,机械通风可分为全面机械通风和局部机械通风两种。而根据风机类型,机械通风可分为机械送风与机械排风两种方式。机械排风的效果较好,是目前焊接通风采用的主要方式。

①全面机械通风

全面机械通风利用通风系统对整个车间进行通风换气,根据通风方向可分为上抽排烟、下抽排烟和侧抽排烟等三种。表 1-2-2 对这三种全面机械通风方式进行了比较。

表 1-2-2　三种全面机械通风方式的比较

通风方式	简图	特点	效果
上抽排烟	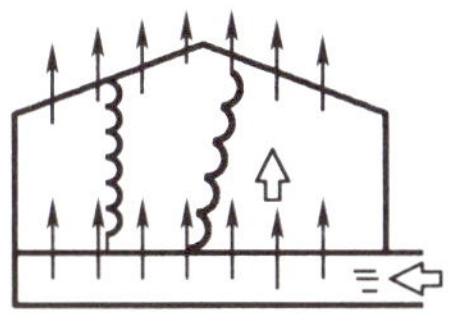	室外空气从地表送入，室内污染空气从房顶排出，烟流与新鲜空气的流动方向相同，消耗能量小	焊接工作位置仍有一定污染，排烟效果一般，适用于新建车间
下抽排烟	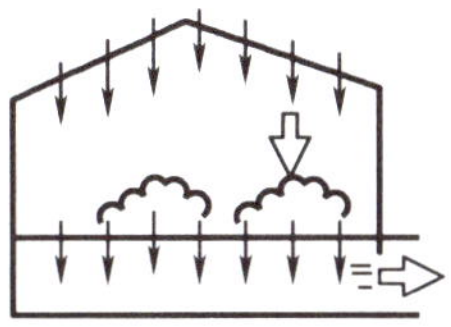	室外空气从房顶送入，室内污染空气从地表排出，烟流与新鲜空气的流动方向相反，消耗能量大	排烟效果好，适用于新建车间
侧抽排烟	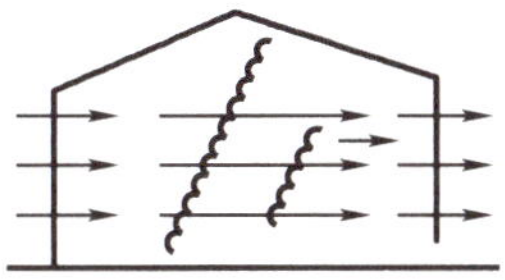	室外空气从一侧送入，从另一侧送出，上风口的效果好于下风口	排烟效果差，适用于老厂房改造

全面通风时，应保持每个焊工有一定的通风量，但很难保证各个焊工均有良好的通风量，因此全面机械通风一般也仅仅作为辅助通风措施。

②局部机械通风

采用局部机械通风时，焊接烟尘和有害气体刚一产生，就被近距离安装的排风罩口迅速吸走，因此所需风量小，且不污染环境，不影响焊工，通风效果好，是目前焊接所采用的主要通风措施。

局部机械通风主要通过抽风机来进行，设备由排气罩、风管、净化装置和风机四部分组成。局部机械通风设备可分为固定式局部排烟除尘机和移动式排烟除尘机两类。

a. 固定式局部排烟除尘机

在焊工工作区安装固定的通风排气管路，进行局部的排烟除尘处理。适用于焊接工作区和焊接工作台固定的情况。固定式排烟除尘机分上抽、下抽和侧抽三种形式，如图 1-2-1 所示，其中下抽式效果最好，而且其安装位置不影响焊工的操作。

b. 移动式排烟除尘机

这类通风装置具有结构简单、轻便的特点，可随工作地点和操作位置移动而移动，主要用在密闭容器或管道内施焊时。使用时，只需将吸风头放置在电弧附近，开动风机，就可有效地将有毒气体和粉尘吸走。移动式排烟除尘机通常带有净化器，如图 1-2-2 所示。

焊接大而长的工件时，常采用多吸头排烟除尘机，此除尘机属于固定式局部排烟除尘机。每个排气支管可根据焊件的大小和高低进行适当的调整，排气口的数量也可根据焊件长短进行调整，如图 1-2-3 所示。

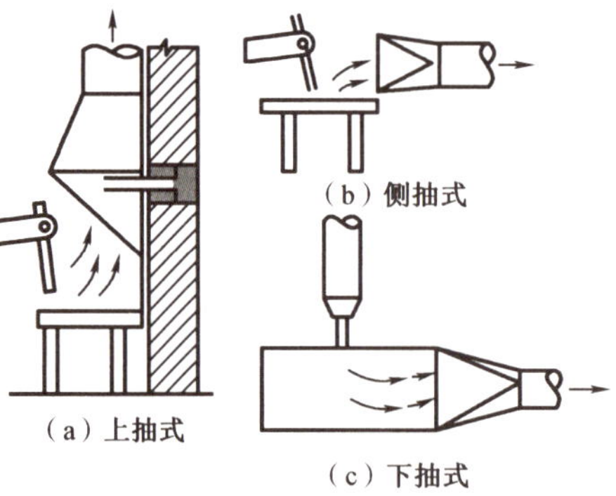

图 1-2-1　固定式局部排烟除尘机

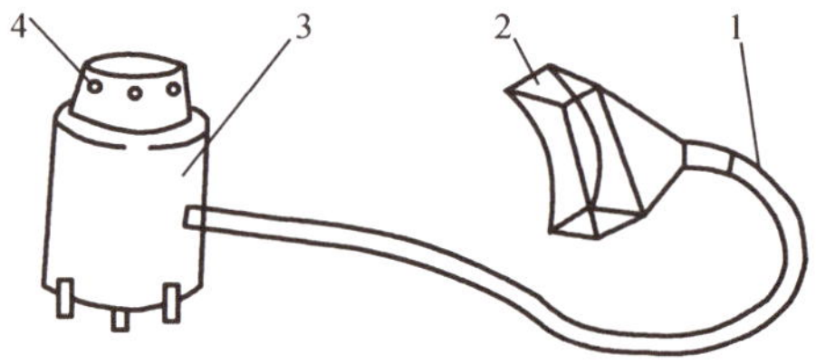

1—软管；2—吸风头；3—净化器；4—出气孔。

图 1-2-2　移动式排烟除尘机

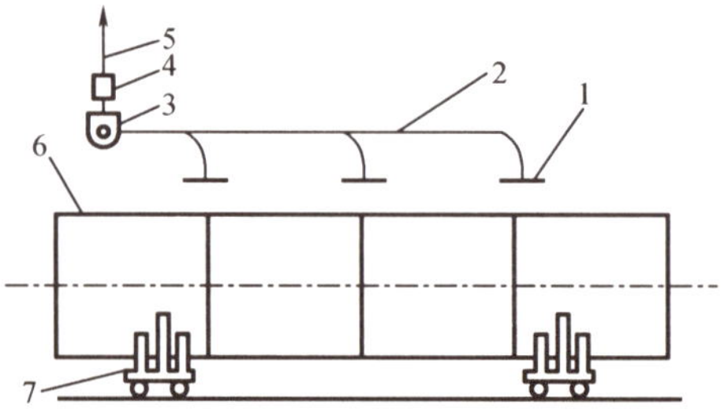

1—排烟罩；2—排烟管；3—风机；4—净化器；5—排出口；6—容器；7—转动轮。

图 1-2-3　多吸头排烟除尘机

3. 焊工个人防护

在某些通风不易解决的特殊作业场合，例如封闭容器内进行焊接作业时，个人防护措施是最行之有效的手段。在这种恶劣的工作环境下工作时，加强个人的防护措施至关重要。一般个人防护措施除穿戴好工作服、鞋、帽、手套、眼镜、口罩、面罩等防护用品外，必要时可采用送风盔式面罩（图 1-2-4）及防护口罩（图 1-2-5）。

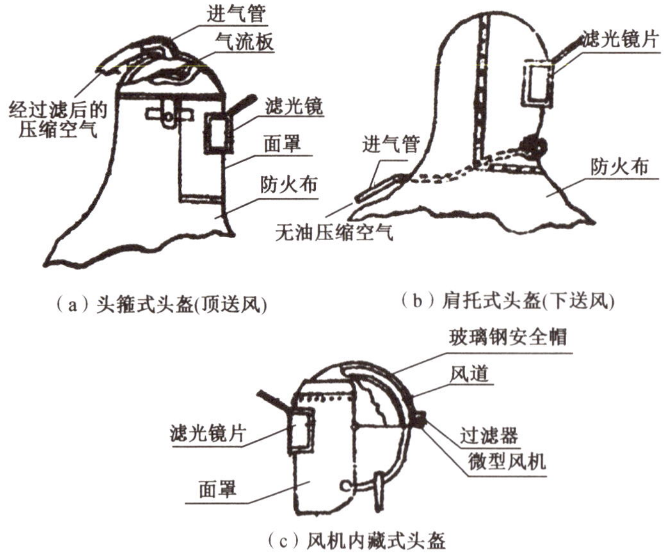

图 1-2-4　送风盔式面罩

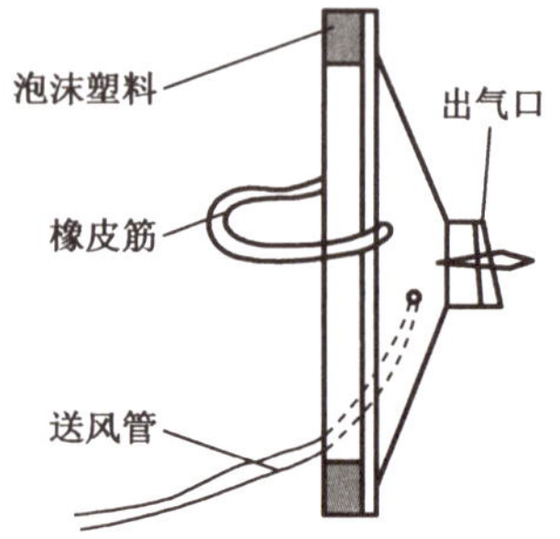

图 1-2-5　防护口罩

任务考核

1. 焊接弧光辐射能引起电光性眼炎的光线是(　　)。

A. 红外线　　B. 紫外线　　C. 可见光　　D. 紫光

2. 焊接弧光辐射的可见光会造成(　　)。

A. 白内障　　B. 皮炎　　C. “电焊晃眼”　　D. 电光性眼炎

3. 电焊烟尘的成分中占比最大的是(　　)元素。

A. 铁　　B. 硅　　C. 锰　　D. 钙

4. 金属烟尘中容易造成“金属热”职业病的烟尘粒径是(　　)μm。

A. 0.01~0.02　　B. 0.05~0.5　　C. 0.6~0.9　　D. 1.1~1.3

5. 空气中的氧在焊接电弧的(　　)激发下,大量地被破坏而形成臭氧。

A. 红外线　　B. 强烈的可见光　　C. 长波紫外线　　D. 短波紫外线

6. 氮氧化物是由于焊接电弧的(　　)作用,使空气的氧、氮分子离解,重新结合而形成的。

A. 高温　　B. 可见光　　C. 紫外线　　D. 紫光

7. 各种明弧焊中产生一氧化碳浓度最高的焊接工艺是(　　)。

A. 焊条电弧焊　　B. 氩弧焊　　C. 二氧化碳焊　　D. 电渣焊

8. 我国卫生标准规定,臭氧最高允许浓度为(　　)mg/m^3。

A. 0.01　　B. 0.05　　C. 0.2　　D. 0.3

9. 容易同橡胶、棉织物发生化学作用的有毒气体是(　　)。

A. 氮氧化物　　B. 一氧化碳　　C. 氟化氢　　D. 臭氧

10. 焊接弧光辐射中(　　)对纤维的破坏能力很强。

A. 紫外线　　B. 可见光　　C. 红外线　　D. 紫光

Project Ⅱ　Personal Hazards and Protection

【Learning Objectives】

1. Master the hazards and protective measures of arc radiation;
2. Master the hazards and protective measures of high-frequency magnetic field radiation;
3. Master the hazards of radioactive radiation and protective measures;
4. Master the hazards of welding fumes and protective measures.

Task 1:Master the Hazards of Arc Radiation and Protective Measures

1. Hazards of arc radiation

Arc light includes infrared, visible, and ultraviolet rays. Ultraviolet rays are the most harmful to welders, especially the eyes and skin. Prolonged exposure to arc ultraviolet radiation can seriously affect vision and cause electric ophthalmia. The main symptoms of electric ophthalmia are pain, gritty sensation, excessive tearing, and sensitivity to wind. The skin, when frequently exposed to ultraviolet light, can become red, tender, darkened, and peel, and in severe cases, it can even lead to skin cancer. Additionally, ultraviolet rays also cause damage and fading to fiber fabrics. The arc temperature of gas shielded welding is high, and its arc light radiation is much stronger than that of electrode arc welding. For instance, the ultraviolet radiation intensity of argon arc welding is 13 times greater than that of electrode arc welding. Therefore, stronger protective measures should be implemented.

2. Protective measures

The following measures should be taken to protect against arc radiation:

①Before striking an arc, put on a specialized helmet or mask to protect the face (especially the eyes). Also, be mindful of others nearby to avoid injuring their eyes with intense arc light.

② Prior to welding, wear high-collared canvas work clothes and specialized gloves (preferably white) to prevent the arc light from burning the skin.

③ When multiple people use multiple welding machins simultaneously for welding operations, there are multiple sources of arc radiation. Protective screens should be used to shield each other and prevent damage from the arc light of other welding machins. The protective screen can be made of materials such as glass fiber cloth and thin steel plate, and it should be coated with gray or black matte paint.

Task 2:Master the Hazards of High-frequency Magnetic Field Radiation and Protective Measures

1. Hazards of high-frequency magnetic field radiation

Argon tungsten arc welding utilizes high-frequency oscillation to strike the arc, making welders susceptible to radiation from high-frequency magnetic fields. Prolonged exposure to high-frequency magnetic field radiation can lead to increased temperatures in various organs, resulting in symptoms such as dizziness, fatigue, vivid dreams, hair loss, and decreased memory.

2. Protective measures

The usual preventive measures are typically adopted:

①Enhance the reliability of high-frequency oscillation arc striking and reduce the frequency and duration of arc striking. During reliable arc striking, the duration of arc striking is only about 0.2 s, which has minimal impact. However, frequent arc striking will have a significant impact.

②The workpiece is effectively grounded. Grounding the workpiece can significantly reduce the intensity of high-frequency radiation.

③Decrease the temperature and humidity of the working environment. The higher the ambient temperature and humidity, the greater the human body's sensitivity to high-frequency radiation. Therefore, enhancing ventilation and reducing the temperature and humidity of the working environment are crucial measures to reduce high-frequency radiation.

④Shield the high-frequency oscillator. Shielding the high-frequency oscillator with a metal casing can reduce the intensity of high-frequency magnetic field radiation. It is recommended to shield both the cable inside the welding gun and the cable connecting the welding gun to the welding machine using a copper soft braided layer.

Task 3:Master the Hazards of Radioactive Radiation and Protective Measures

1. Hazards of radioactive radiation

Thoriated tungsten electrodes are commonly used forargon tungsten arc welding. These tungsten electrodes contain a small amount of ThO_2 and are slightly radioactive. The hazards to welders mainly include external exposure and internal exposure. External exposure refers to the irradiation caused by radioactive rays emitted from the tungsten electrode. In normal welding, since the radioactivity of thoriated tungsten electrodes itself is not large and the welding duration is not long, external irradiation does not require shielding. Internal radiation refers to thorium and its decay products entering the human body in the form of aerosol, which is highly biologically active and difficult to excrete. It acts on the body for a long time, causing internal irradiation and leading to radioactive diseases. It is mainly characterized by decreased immunity, weight loss, weakness, and damage to the hematopoietic system.

2. Protective measures

The following measures are taken for protection against radioactive radiation:

①Try not to use thoriated tungsten electrode, but choose ceriated tungsten electrode. The radioactivity of ceriated tungsten electrode is two orders of magnitude lower than that of thoriated tungsten electrode.

②Remember to wear a helmet when welding to prevent vaporized tungsten electrode from entering the body.

③Select the tungsten electrode with the appropriate diameter based on the current to avoid excessive burning loss.

④Thoriated tungsten electrodes should be stored in lead or iron containers and kept in a separate underground storage room equipped with an exhaust system to release air polluted by radioactive substances at any time.

⑤Always wear special work clothing, masks, and gloves when grinding tungsten electrodes; the grinding wheel should be installed in a well-ventilated area.

⑥The grinding or welding site needs to be cleaned with wet methods promptly; collect and deeply bury any radioactive dust.

⑦After handling thoriated tungsten rods, wash hands thoroughly with running water and soap. Frequently clean work clothing and gloves, and preferably use disposable masks.

Task 4:Master the Hazards of Welding Fumes and Protective Measures

1. Hazards associated with welding fumes

The welding process will release fumes, mainly composed of particles such as metals, oxides, and fluorides, as well as harmful gases like ozone, nitrogen oxides, and carbon monoxide. Refer to Table 1-2-1 for the hazards of various components of welding fumes from gas shielded welding. The specific composition and quantity mainly depend on the welding method used, welding parameters, etc. In fact, welding fumes are the most harmful factor in the affected area. Therefore, effective measures should be taken for protection, especially in poorly ventilated environments such as welding in closed containers, cabins, or pipelines.

2. Ventilation protective measures

Ventilation is the most commonly used and effective protection method for welding fumes, and it is also the main measure to reduce welding heat pollution. When welding is carried out indoors and in various containers and pipes, ventilation measures should be taken to ensure the health of operators. Ventilation is divided into natural ventilation and mechanical ventilation according to different sources of ventilation power.

(1) Natural ventilation

Natural ventilation exhausts welding fumes by relying on the temperature difference between the welding workplace and the outside world, as well as natural wind power. This method is characterized by a small volume of ventilation, instability, and a significant influence from external conditions. As the temperature in the welding workshop is higher than outside, there will be natural exchange between indoor and outdoor air to form natural ventilation under the influence of temperature difference. During the workshop design process, natural ventilation conditions can be improved by properly enhancing the workshop structure. Additionally, the arrangement of equipment layout in the workshop can also enhance natural ventilation. However, natural ventilation can only be used as an auxiliary ventilation measure.

(2) Mechanical ventilation

Mechanical ventilation utilizes the pressure generated by fans to facilitate air exchange, with the characteristics of high ventilation capacity and stable airflow. It can be classified into comprehensive mechanical ventilation and local mechanical ventilation based on the scope of ventilation. Based on the type of fan, mechanical ventilation can be categorized into mechanical air supply and mechanical exhaust. Mechanical exhaust ventilation has proven to be highly effective and is the primary method utilized for welding ventilation presently.

Table 1-2-1 Hazards of Each Component of Welding Fume from Gas Shielded Arc Welding

Composition of smoke particles		Source	Hazards	Symptoms
Dust	Aluminum, aluminum oxide	Aluminum Welding and Cutting	Aluminum dust lung	Shortness of breath, chest tightness, cough, sputum production, weakness, symptoms of neurasthenia, etc.
	Chromium, chromic oxide	Welding and cutting of steel, especially stainless steel	Chronic non - specific lung disease, bronchitis, cancer	Shortness of breath, chest tightness, cough, sputum production, weakness, asthma, symptoms of neurasthenia, etc.
	Iron, iron oxide	Steel welding and cutting	Iron dust lung	Shortness of breath, chest tightness, cough, sputum production, weakness, symptoms of neurasthenia, etc.
	Manganese, manganese oxide	Welding of steels, especially CO_2 welding	Manganese toxicity, pneumonia	Headache, fatigue, insomnia, and neurological dysfunction, etc.
	Silicon dioxide	Welding of steels, especially CO_2 welding	Pneumoconiosis	Shortness of breath, chest tightness, cough, sputum production, weakness, symptoms of neurasthenia, etc.
Toxic gases	Ozone	Mainly include argon tungsten arc welding and GMAW	Bronchitis	Coughing, chest tightness, fatigue, decreased appetite, dizziness, and body aches
	Nitrogen oxides	Various gas shielded welding	Chronic poisoning, chronic bronchitis	Headache, insomnia, loss of appetite, difficulty breathing, collapse, overall weakness, etc.
	Carbon monoxide	Various gas shielded welding	Carbon monoxide poisoning	Headache, overall weakness, increased pulse, vomiting, dizziness, etc.

①Full mechanical ventilation

The comprehensive mechanical ventilation utilizes a ventilation system to provide ventilation for the entire workshop. Based on the direction of ventilation, it can be divided into upper smoke extraction, lower smoke extraction, and side smoke extraction. Table 1-2-2 compares these three modes of comprehensive mechanical ventilation.

Table 1-2-2 Comparison of Three Comprehensive Mechanical Ventilation Modes

Ventilation mode	Rough draft	Features	Effect
Upward exhaust	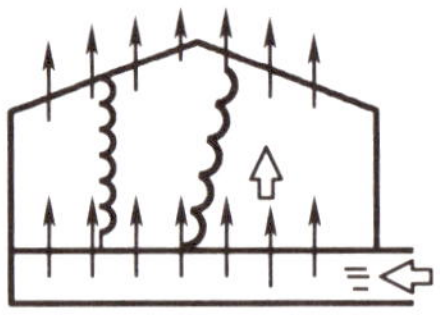	Outdoor air is supplied from the ground, and indoor polluted air is discharged from the roof. The smoke flow direction is the same as that of fresh air, resulting in low energy consumption	There is still some pollution at the welding work position, and the smoke exhaust effect is general. It is suitable for new workshops
Downdraft smoke exhaust		Outdoor air is supplied from the roof, and indoor polluted air is discharged from the ground. The flow direction of smoke is opposite to that of fresh air, which consumes a lot of energy	Good smoke extraction effect, suitable for newly built workshops
Side-drawn smoke extraction	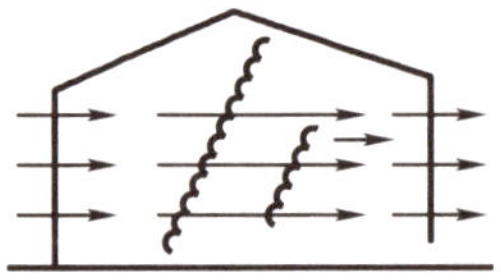	Outdoor air is supplied from one side and sent out from the other side. The upper air outlet is more effective than the lower air outlet	Poor smoke exhaust effect, suitable for renovating old factory buildings

During comprehensive ventilation, a specific amount of airflow should be maintained for each welder, but it is difficult to ensure that all welders have adequate ventilation. Therefore, comprehensive mechanical ventilation is generally used only as an additional ventilation measure.

②Local mechanical ventilation

When using local mechanical ventilation, welding fumes and harmful gases are immediately sucked away by the exhaust hood installed nearby as soon as they are generated. This ensures a small required air volume, no environmental pollution, and does not impact welders, resulting in effective ventilation. It is currently the primary ventilation measure used in welding.

Mechanical local ventilation is primarily achieved through the use of exhaust fans. It is comprised of four components: An exhaust hood, air duct, purification device, and fan. This system can be categorized into two types: Fixed local smoke exhaust dust machines and mobile smoke exhaust dust machines.

a. Fixed local smoke exhaust dust remover

Fixed ventilation and exhaust pipelines should be installed in the welder's working area for local smoke and dust removal. This applies to situations where the welding work area and the welding table are stationary. The fixed smoke exhaust and dust remover are categorized into three types: Up-drafting, down-drafting, and side-drafting, as shown in Fig. 1-2-1. Among them, the down-drafting type has the best effectiveness, and its installation position does not affect the welder's operation.

b. Mobile smoke and dust extractor

This type of ventilation device is characterized by its simple and lightweight structure, allowing it to easily move along with the working place and operation position. It is mainly used for welding inside closed containers or pipelines. During usage, the toxic gas and dust can be effectively suctioned away by placing the suction head near the electric arc and starting the fan.

The mobile smoke exhaust dust remover is typically equipped with a purifier, as illustrated in Fig. 1-2-2.

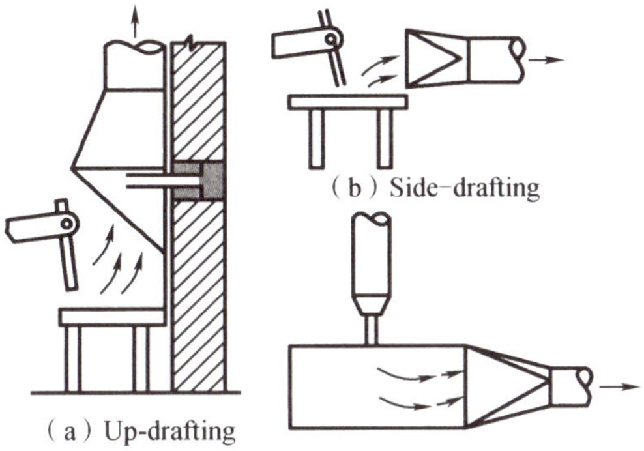

Fig. 1-2-1 Fixed Local Smoke and Dust Exhaust Machine

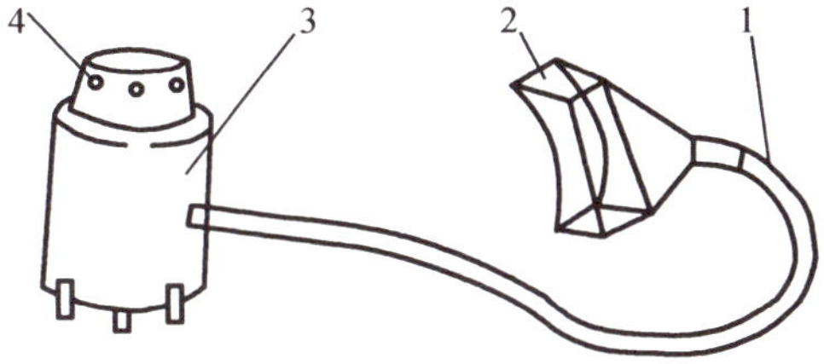

1—Hose; 2—Suction nozzle; 3—Purifier; 4—Air vent.

Fig. 1-2-2 Mobile Smoke Exhaust and Dust Collector

For welding large and long workpieces, the multi-suction head smoke exhaust dust remover is often used. This type of dust remover belongs to a fixed local smoke exhaust dust remover. Each exhaust branch can be properly adjusted according to the size and height of the weldment, and the number of exhaust ports can also be adjusted according to the length of the weldment, as shown in Fig. 1-2-3.

3. Welder's personal protective equipment

Personal protective measures are the most effective means in certain special operation situations where ventilation is difficult to solve, such as welding operations inside closed containers. It is crucial to enhance personal protective measures when working in such harsh environments. Besides wearing protective equipment like work clothes, shoes, caps, gloves, glasses, masks, and face shields, general personal protective measures can also include the use of air supply helmet-type masks (Fig. 1-2-4) and protective respirators (Fig. 1-2-5).

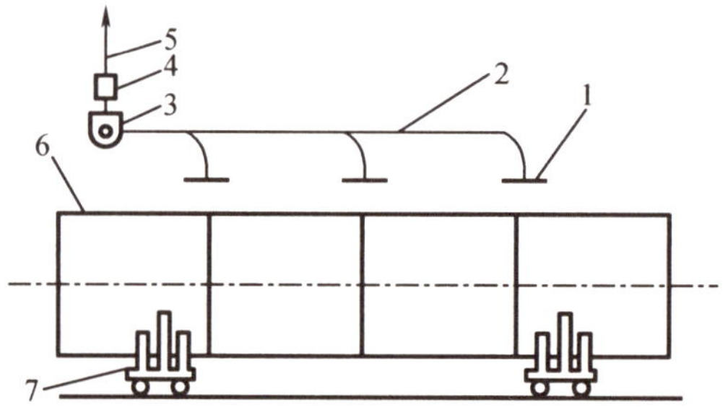

1—Exhaust hood; 2—Smoke exhaust pipe; 3—Fan; 4—Purifier; 5—Discharge port; 6—Container; 7—Rotating wheel.

Fig. 1-2-3 Multi-suction Head Smoke and Dust Exhaust Machine

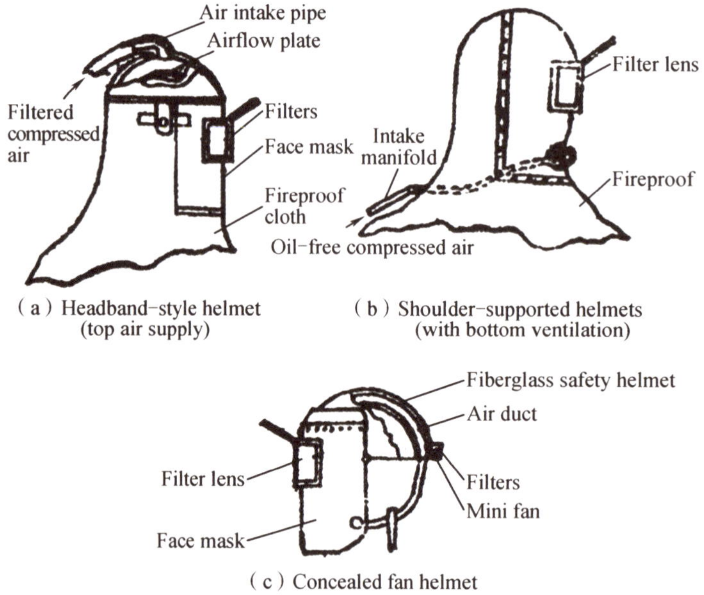

Fig. 1-2-4 Helmet-style Air Supply Mask

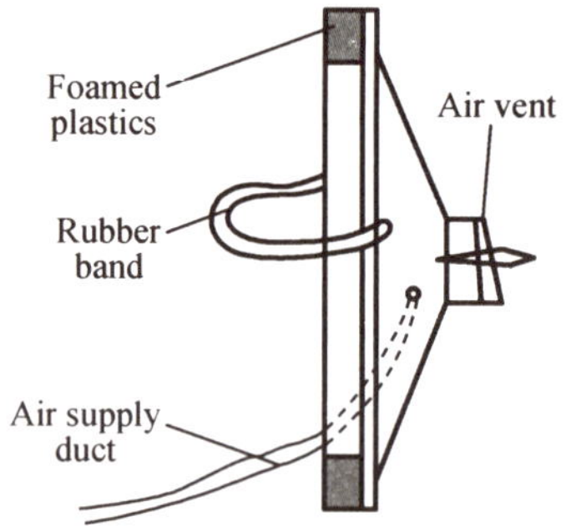

Fig. 1-2-5 Protective Mask

Task Assessment

1. The light that can cause welder's flash by welding arc radiation is ( ).

A. infrared B. ultraviolet C. visible D. purple

2. The visible light of welding arc radiation can cause ( ).

A. cataract B. dermatitis

C. welding flash burns D. photokeratitis

3. The predominant component in the composition of welding fume is the ( ) element.

A. Iron B. Silicon C. Manganese D. Calcium

4. The particle size of metal dust that is prone to cause the occupational disease "metal fume fever" is ( ) μm.

A. 0.01-0.02 B. 0.05-0.5 C. 0.6-0.9 D. 1.1-1.3

5. Under the stimulation of the welding arc's ( ), a significant amount of oxygen in the air is chemically altered, leading to the creation of ozone.

A. infrared B. intense visible light

C. long-wavelength ultraviolet D. short-wavelength ultraviolet

6. Nitrogen oxides are formed due to the ( ) effect of the welding arc, which causes the dissociation and recombination of oxygen and nitrogen molecules in the air.

A. high temperature B. visible light

C. ultraviolet D. purple light

7. The welding process that generates the highest concentration of carbon monoxide among various open arc welding methods is ( ).

A. shielded metal arc welding B. argon arc welding

C. CO_2 welding D. electroslag welding

8. China's health standards stipulate that the highest allowable concentration of ozone is ( ) mg/m^3.

A. 0.01 B. 0.05 C. 0.2 D. 0.3

9. The toxic gas that easily reacts with rubber and cotton fabrics is ( ).

A. nitrogen oxides B. carbon monoxide

C. hydrogen fluoride D. ozone

10. In welding arc radiation, ( ) has a strong destructive power on fibers.

A. ultraviolet B. visible light C. infrared D. purple

模块二
熔化极气体保护焊及应用

项目一　熔化极气体保护焊基础知识

【学习目标】

1. 理解气体保护焊的原理；
2. 掌握气体保护焊的分类方法；
3. 熟悉 CO_2 气体保护焊特点及应用。

任务1：理解气体保护焊的原理

气体保护焊是金属焊接中熔焊的一种。熔焊有其特殊性，那就是在焊接过程中，母材金属与填充金属都要经过高温熔化的过程，而在高温状态下的液体金属会与外界的气体及杂物产生物理的和化学的反应，这就会导致由填充金属与母材结合形成的焊缝金属产生质的变化，以致给焊接接头带来隐患。为了保证焊缝能达到预期的质量要求，关键的问题就是要保护好整个焊接区，以防有害气体及杂物侵入。

在熔焊中，采取的保护措施有三种：

第一种即采用焊条药皮。在电弧的高温下，焊条药皮会产生气体及形成熔渣，对整个焊接区形成渣-气保护环境，有效地保证了焊缝的质量。

第二种是利用电渣焊。这是一种焊接过程全部都在熔融状态的熔渣覆盖之下进行的焊接方法。

第三种是气体保护焊。气体保护焊的原理是依靠直接从喷嘴中送出的气流，在电弧周围形成局部的气体保护层，使电极端部、熔滴及熔池与空气机械隔离，从而保证了焊接过程的稳定，并获得高质量的焊缝。图 2-1-1 所示为熔化极气体保护焊示意图。

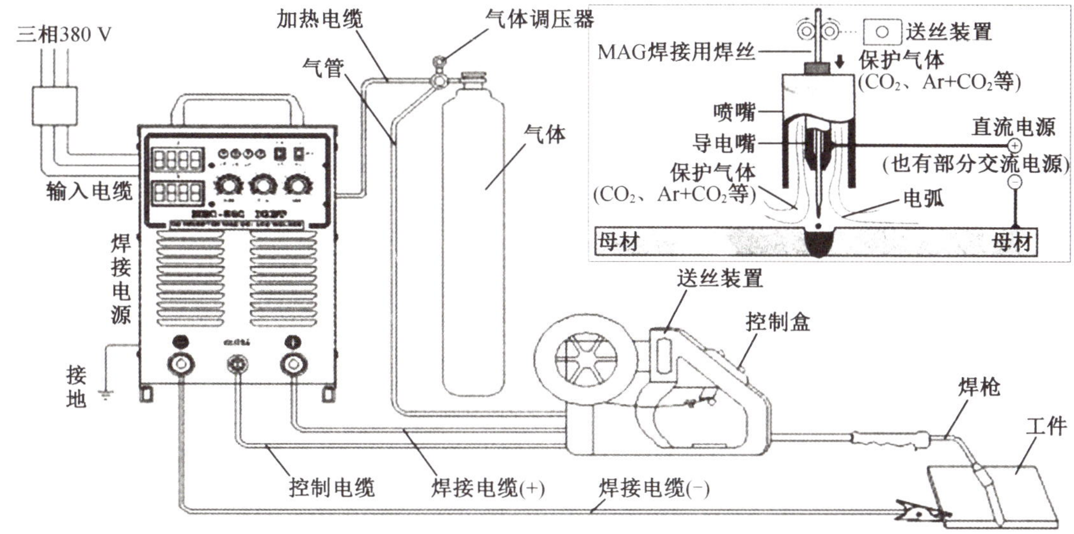

图 2-1-1　熔化极气体保护焊原理图

任务2：掌握气体保护焊的分类方法

气体保护焊的分类方法有三种。

1. 按保护气种类分类

根据气体种类不同，气体保护焊可分为氩弧焊、氦弧焊、氮弧焊、氢原子焊、CO_2 气体保护焊及混合气体保护焊等。

上述的保护气体中，Ar、He 是惰性气体，一般用于化学性质比较活泼的金属的焊接。Ar 保护效果好，使用最普遍；He 由于价格昂贵，且气体消耗量大，常与 Ar 等混合使用。

氮气(N_2)、氢气(H_2)是还原性气体。由于 N_2 不溶于铜，故用于铜及铜合金的焊接；H_2 则主要在氢原子焊中作为保护气体。此外，N_2、H_2 也常与其他气体混合使用。

CO_2 是氧化性气体。由于 CO_2 的来源丰富、成本低，因此应用也较广泛，主要用于碳素钢及合金钢的焊接。

混合气体就是在一种保护气体中加入适量的另一种(或几种)其他气体。由于混合气体能细化熔滴、增加电弧析出的热量及提高焊接质量，所以也被广泛采用。

各类合金常用的保护气体及焊接电极见表 2-1-1。

2. 按电极的形式分类

按不同的电极形式，气体保护焊可分为非熔化极气体保护电弧焊及熔化极气体保护电弧焊。

(1)非熔化极气体保护焊

非熔化极气体保护焊是指钨极惰性气体保护焊(简称 GTAW)，即使用不熔化的纯钨或活化钨(钍钨、铈钨等)作为电极，使用惰性气体做保护气体。

(2)熔化极气体保护焊

熔化极气体保护焊是指使用熔化电极的气体保护焊。其又按焊丝性能及结构的不同，分为实心焊丝及药芯焊丝气体保护焊两类。

表 2-1-1　各类合金常用的保护气体及焊接电极列表

适用的母材	保护气体	化学成分及其体积分数/%	气体化学性质	焊接电极种类
铝及其合金	Ar		惰性	熔化极、钨极
	Ar+He	He 10		
钛、锆及其合金	Ar			
	Ar+He	Ar 75;He 25		
铜及铜合金	Ar			
	Ar+He	Ar 50;He 50 或 Ar 30;He 70		
	N_2			熔化极
	$Ar+N_2$	Ar 80;N_2 20		
不锈钢及高强度钢	$Ar+O_2$	O_2 1~2	氧化性	
	$Ar+O_2+CO_2$	O_2 1~2;CO_2 5		
	Ar		惰性	钨极
碳钢及低合金钢	$Ar+O_2$	O_2 1~5 或 20	氧化性	熔化极
	$Ar+CO_2$	Ar 70~80		
	$Ar+O_2+CO_2$	O_2 5;CO_2 15		
	CO_2			
镍基合金	Ar		惰性	熔化极、钨极
	Ar+He	He 15~20		
	$Ar+H_2$	H_2<6	还原性	钨极

注:表中"体积分数"可用希腊字母 ψ(某物质的化学符号)(%)表示,如 Ar+He 的混合气体中,He 的体积分数为 10%,即可表示为 ψ(He)= 10%(或 0.10)。

①实心焊丝气体保护焊中有如下三种:

a. 熔化极惰性气体保护焊(MIG 焊),如 Ar 保护焊、He 保护焊及 Ar+He 保护焊等。

b. 富氩混合气体保护焊(MAG 焊),如 $Ar+O_2$、$Ar+CO_2$、$Ar+CO_2+O_2$ 保护焊等,具有氧化性气体的活性混合气体保护焊即属 MAG 焊。

c. CO_2 气体保护焊,包括 CO_2+O_2 气体保护焊,均属活性气体保护焊。

②药芯焊丝气体保护焊中有如下三种:

a. CO_2 气体保护焊。

b. CO_2+Ar 气体保护焊。

c. 自保护焊(由焊芯药粉中造气剂造气)。

3. 按操作方法分类

按操作方法不同,气体保护焊可分为手工气体保护焊、半自动及自动气体保护焊。

任务3：熟悉CO_2气体保护焊特点及应用

1. CO_2 气体保护焊一般过程

CO_2 气体保护焊是用 CO_2 作为保护气体，依靠焊丝与焊件之间产生的电弧来熔化金属的一种电弧焊方法。CO_2 气体的密度比空气大，受电弧加热分解后体积增大，所以在保护电弧和焊接熔池避免空气侵入方面，效果相当良好。CO_2 气体保护焊也称 CO_2 焊。

CO_2 气体保护焊一般过程如图 2-1-2 所示。直流电源的两极分别接在焊枪和焊件上。焊丝由焊丝盘经送丝机构带动通过焊枪不断地向电弧区域给送；同时，CO_2 气体以一定的压力和流量送入焊枪，在电弧和焊接熔池周围形成保护气流。随着焊枪的移动，熔化的焊丝和母材所组成的熔池金属冷却凝固而形成焊缝，从而将两焊件连成一个整体。

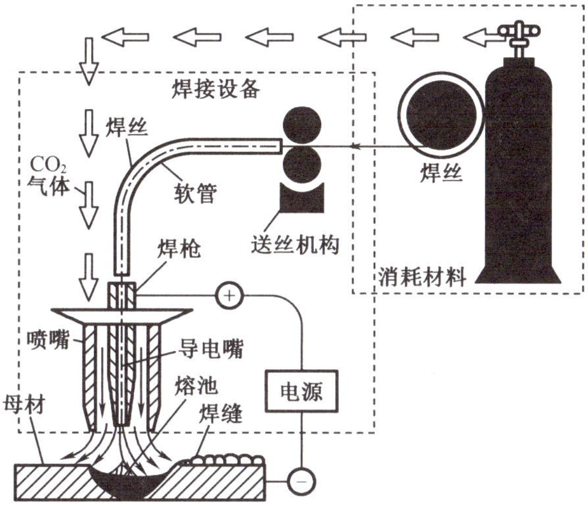

图 2-1-2　CO_2 气体保护焊的一般过程示意图

2. CO_2 气体保护焊的特点

CO_2 气体保护焊与其他焊接方法（如埋弧焊、焊条电弧焊等以渣保护为主的焊接方法）相比，具有以下优点。

（1）焊接成本低

CO_2 气体是酒精厂的副产品，来源广，价格低，而且消耗的焊接电能少，所以 CO_2 气体保护焊成本低，只有埋弧焊或焊条电弧焊的 40%～50%。

（2）生产率高

因使用细焊丝焊接，焊接电流密度高达 100～200 A/mm^2，使熔深增大，焊丝熔化率高，熔敷速度加快；另外，焊后没有焊渣，特别是在进行多层焊时，节省了清渣时间。所以此种方法的生产率通常比焊条电弧焊高 2～4 倍。

（3）抗锈能力强

在 CO_2 气体保护焊中，熔池具有剧烈的沸腾现象，有利于气体逸出；同时采用了高锰高硅型焊丝，使焊缝金属的还原作用大为增加，对铁锈敏感性大为降低。因此，焊缝中不易产生气孔，而且含氢量也很少，其强度和抗裂性能好。

(4)焊接变形小

由于电弧热量集中,加热面积小,焊速快,同时 CO_2 气流具有较大的冷却作用,因此焊接热影响区和焊件变形较小,特别适于焊接薄板。

(5)操作性能好

由于是明弧焊,可以看清电弧和熔池情况,能随时发现问题而加以调整,有利于实现机械化和自动化。

(6)适用范围广

CO_2 半自动焊具有手弧焊的灵活性,可实现全位置的焊接,并且对于薄板、中板甚至厚板(采用多层焊)都能焊接。

当然,CO_2 气体保护焊也有不足之处,主要表现在以下几个方面:

①金属飞溅较多,焊缝表面成形差;

②很难用交流电焊接,焊接辅助设备较多;

③不能在有风的位置施焊,否则容易出现气孔;

④不能焊接易氧化的金属材料。

3. CO_2 气体保护焊的应用

CO_2 气体保护焊是一种高效率、低成本的节能焊接方法,由于它本身所具有的特点,使得它可以广泛地用于多种材料的焊接,如不仅可用于焊接低碳钢、低合金钢,在对焊缝性能要求不高的情况下还可焊接耐热钢、不锈钢。CO_2 气体保护焊还可用于耐磨零件的堆焊、铸钢件的补焊以及异种金属材料的焊接。同时,CO_2 半自动焊可用于短焊缝、曲线焊缝和空间位置焊缝的焊接,也适于薄板的点焊和定位焊。长直缝和环缝则宜采用 CO_2 自动焊。CO_2 自动焊主要用于水平位置的焊接,在特殊装备的情况下,可以进行立焊和横焊。此外,CO_2 气体保护焊还可以用于水下焊接。因此,CO_2 气体保护焊在造船工业、汽车制造、工程机械及航空航天工业中都得到广泛的应用。

CO_2 气体保护焊根据应用场景的不同有多种分类方法。表 2-1-2 列出了按照焊丝直径、操作方法、特殊应用和新工艺对 CO_2 气体保护焊的分类。目前应用中,最常用的是根据焊丝形状(实心、药芯)对 CO_2 气体保护焊的分类。

表 2-1-2　CO_2 气体保护焊的应用分类

依据	分类
按焊丝形状	实心 CO_2 气体保护焊 药芯 CO_2 气体保护焊
按焊丝直径	细丝 CO_2 气体保护焊:焊丝直径≤1.2 mm 粗丝 CO_2 气体保护焊:焊丝直径≥1.6 mm
按操作方法	CO_2 自动焊 CO_2 半自动焊

表 2-1-2(续)

依据	分类
按特殊应用和新工艺	CO_2 气体保护电弧点焊 CO_2 气体保护垂直气电焊 CO_2 气体保护窄间隙焊 CO_2 气体保护振动堆焊
按保护形式	CO_2 与焊剂联合保护焊:CO_2+药芯焊丝 CO_2+实心焊丝带磁性焊剂 CO_2+O_2 或 CO_2+Ar 混合气体保护焊 双层气流保护焊

CO_2 气体保护焊通常按采用的焊丝直径来分类,当焊丝直径小于或等于 1.2 mm 时,称为细丝 CO_2 气体保护焊,主要采用短路过渡形式焊接薄板材料,用于薄板低碳钢和低合金钢结构零部件的焊接。当焊丝直径大于或等于 1.6 mm 时,称为粗丝 CO_2 气体保护焊,一般采用大电流和较高的电弧电压来焊接中厚板。

为了满足现代工业应用的需要,近十几年来 CO_2 气体保护焊得到迅速发展,在生产中除了常规的 CO_2 气体保护焊方法外,还派生出一些改进的方法,如 CO_2 电弧点焊、气电垂直自动焊、CO_2 保护窄间隙焊、CO_2 加其他气体(CO_2+O_2)的保护焊,以及 CO_2 气体与焊剂联合保护焊等。

任务考核

1. (　　)在国际上被公认为是焊接材料中最先进、发展最快的高科技技术之一,并将成为 21 世纪焊接材料的主导产品。

A. 药芯焊丝　　B. 实芯焊丝　　C. 不锈钢焊丝　　D. 铝焊丝

2. 实心焊丝的牌号用(　　)字母表示。

A. C　　B. Z　　C. H　　D. Y

3. 药芯焊丝的牌号用(　　)字母表示。

A. C　　B. Z　　C. H　　D. Y

4. 实心焊丝牌号“H”后面的一位数字或两位数字表示含(　　)量的万分之几。

A. S　　B. C　　C. N　　D. P

5. 药芯焊丝按焊丝断面可分为(　　)种。

A. 2　　B. 3　　C. 4　　D. 5

6. 药芯焊丝中细直径的焊丝是指直径为(　　)mm 以下的焊丝。

A. 1.0　　B. 1.2　　C. 2　　D. 2.5

7. 药芯焊丝牌号中第二个汉语拼音大写字母“J”表示(　　)。

A. 工具钢　　B. 结构钢　　C. 不锈钢　　D. 铸铁

8. 药芯焊丝牌号"J"后面的两位数字表示熔敷金属的(　　)等级。

A. 抗拉强度　　B. 抗压强度　　C. 疲劳强度　　D. 低温强度

9. 药芯焊丝牌号中短线"-"后的数字表示焊接时的保护方法,(　　)表示气保护。

A. 1　　B. 2　　C. 3　　D. 4

10. 实心焊丝为了防止焊丝表面生锈,同时改善导电性能以及减少送丝阻力,最好镀(　　)。

A. 铝　　B. 铜　　C. 镍　　D. 锡

Module Ⅱ

Gas Metal Arc Welding and Its Applications

Project Ⅰ　Basic Knowledge of Gas Metal Arc Welding

【Learning Objectives】

1. Understand the principle of gas shielded welding;
2. Master the classification method of gas shielded welding;
3. Familiar with the characteristics and applications of CO_2 gas shielded welding.

Task 1:Understand the Principle of Gas Shielded Welding

Gas shielded welding is a type of fusion welding in metal fabrication. Fusion welding has its uniqueness in that both the base metal and filler metal undergo a process of high-temperature melting during welding. However, the liquid metal at high temperature undergoes physical and chemical reactions with external gases and impurities, which can lead to qualitative changes in the weld metal formed by the combination of filler metal and base metal, thus presenting potential risks to welded joints. To ensure that the weld meets the expected quality requirements, the essential issue is to protect the entire welding area from harmful gases and impurities.

In fusion welding, there are three types of aforementioned protective measures:

The first type is similar to the electrode coating in shielded metal arc welding. Under the high temperature of the arc, the electrode coating generates gas and forms slag, creating a slag-gas protective environment for the entire welding area, effectively ensuring the quality of welds.

The second one is similar to electroslag welding, which is a welding method where the entire welding process takes place under the coverage of molten slag.

The third is gas shielded welding. The principle of gas shielded welding relies on the airflow directly emitted from the nozzle to form a localized gas protection layer around the arc. This isolates the electrode end, droplet, and molten pool from the surrounding air, ensuring welding process stability and the production of high-quality welds. Figure 2-1-1 depicts the schematic diagram of gas metal arc welding.

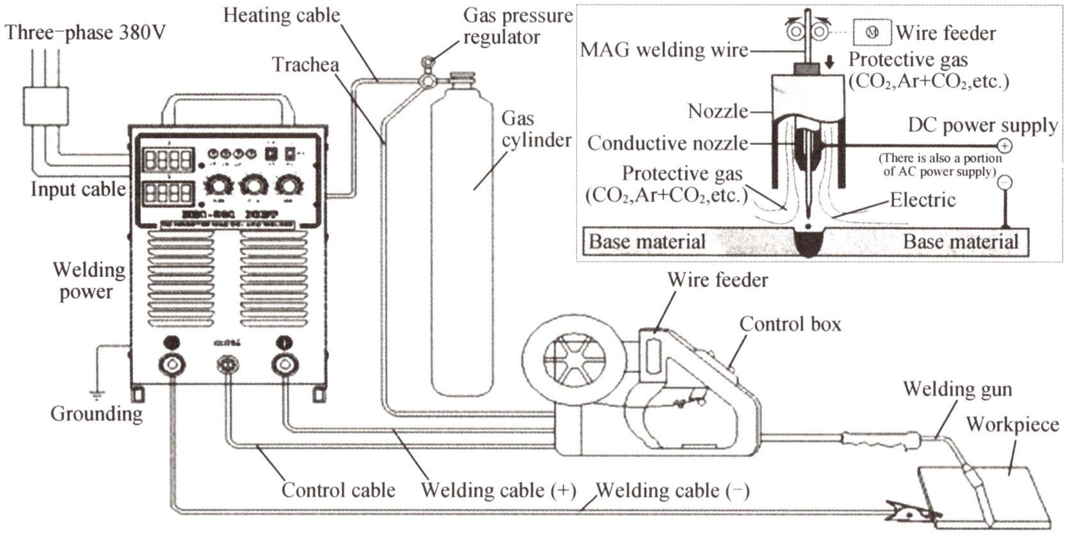

Fig. 2-1-1 Schematic Diagram of Gas Metal Arc Welding

Task 2:Master the Classification Method of Gas Shielded Welding

There are three classification methods for gas shielded welding.

1. Classification by type of shielding gas

It can be divided into argon arc welding, helium arc welding, nitrogen arc welding, hydrogen atomic welding, CO_2 gas shielded welding, and mixed gas shielded welding.

Among the aforementioned shielding gases, Ar and He are inert gases commonly used for welding chemically active metals. Ar provides a strong protective effect and is the most commonly used. He is often mixed with argon due to its high price and high gas consumption.

Nitrogen(N_2) and hydrogen(H_2) are reducing gases. Since nitrogen is insoluble in copper, it is used for welding copper and copper alloys. Hydrogen is primarily used as a shielding gas in atomic hydrogen welding. Additionally, nitrogen and hydrogen are often mixed with other gases.

CO_2 is an oxidizing gas. Due to its abundant sources and low cost, carbon dioxide gas is widely used, mainly for welding carbon steel and alloy steel.

Mixed gas refers to adding an appropriate amount of another (or several) different gases into a protective gas. It is widely used because mixed gas can refine molten droplets, increase the heat released from the arc, and improve welding quality.

The commonly used shielding gases and welding electrodes for various alloys are listed in the Table 2-1-1.

Table 2-1-1 List of Commonly Used Shielding Gases and Welding Electrodes for Various Alloys

Applicable base material	Protective gas	Chemical composition and volume fraction/%	Gas chemistry properties	Type of welding electrode
Aluminum and its alloys	Ar		Inertia	Molten electrode, tungsten electrode
	Ar+He	He 10		
Titanium, zirconium, and their alloys	Ar			
	Ar+He	Ar 75;He 25		
Copper and its alloys	Ar			
	Ar+He	Ar 50;He 50 or Ar 30;He 70		
	N_2			Molten electrode
	Ar+N_2	Ar 80;N_2 20		
Stainless and high-strength steel	Ar+O_2	O_2 1~2	Oxidizing properties	
	Ar+O_2+CO_2	O_2 1~2;CO_2 5		
	Ar		Inertia	Tungsten electrode
Carbon steel and low alloy steel	Ar+O_2	O_2 1~5 或 20	Oxidizing properties	Molten electrode
	Ar+CO_2	Ar 70~80		
	Ar+O_2+CO_2	O_2 5;CO_2 15		
	CO_2			
Nickel-based alloys	Ar		Inertia	Melted electrode, tungsten electrode
	Ar+He	He 15~20		
	Ar+H_2	H_2<6	Restorability	Tungsten electrode

Note: The "volume fraction" in the table can be represented by the Greek letter ψ (chemical symbol of a substance)(%). For example, if the volume fraction of He in the mixed gas of Ar+He is 10%, it can be expressed as ψ(He) = 10% (or 0.10).

2. Classification by electrode form

It can be classified into non-consumable electrode gas shielded arc welding and consumable electrode gas shielded arc welding.

(1) Non-consumable electrode gas shielded welding

Non-consumable gas metal arc welding refers to the gas tungsten arc welding (GTAW for short), which involves utilizing unmelted pure tungsten or activated tungsten electrodes (such as thorium tungsten, cerium tungsten, etc.) along with inert gas as the shielding gas.

(2) Gas metal arc welding

Gas shielded welding using a consumable electrode can be classified into two types based on the different properties and structures of welding wires: Solid wire gas shielded welding and flux-cored wire gas shielded welding.

①There are three types of gas-shielded arc welding using solid wire:

a. Metal inert gas welding (MIG welding), such as Ar welding, He welding, and Ar+He welding.

b. Argon-rich mixed gas shielded welding (MAG welding), such as $Ar+O_2$ welding, $Ar+CO_2$ welding, $Ar+CO_2+O_2$ welding, active mixed gas shielded welding with oxidizing gases belong to MAG welding.

c. CO_2 gas shielded welding, including CO_2+O_2 gas shielded welding, belongs to active gas welding.

②There are three types of flux-cored gas metal arc welding:

a. CO_2 gas shielded welding.

b. CO_2+Ar shielded welding.

c. Self-shielded welding (gas generated by gas generating agent in core powder).

3. Divide according to the operation method

It can be divided into manual gas shielded welding, semi-automatic gas shielded welding, and automatic gas shielded welding.

Task 3:Familiar with the Characteristics and Applications of CO_2 Gas Shielded Welding

1. General procedure of CO_2 gas shielded welding

CO_2 gas shielded welding is an arc welding process that utilizes CO_2 as a shielding gas to melt metal through the electric arc formed between the welding wire and the workpiece. CO_2 gas has a higher density than air, and its volume expands when decomposed by the heat of the arc. Thus, it effectively safeguards the arc and the welding pool against air infiltration. CO_2 gas shielded welding is also known as CO_2 welding.

The general process of CO_2 gas shielded welding is shown in Fig. 2-1-2. The two poles of the DC power supply are connected to the welding gun and the weldment respectively. The welding wire is continuously fed to the arc area through the wire feeding mechanism driven by the wire reel in the welding gun. Simultaneously, CO_2 gas is supplied to the welding gun at a certain pressure and flow rate to form a protective airflow around the arc and welding pool. With the movement of the welding gun, the molten pool metal, which consists of melted welding wire and base metal, cools and solidifies to form a weld, thereby connecting the two weldments into a unified whole.

2. Characteristics of CO_2 gas shielded welding

Compared to other welding methods such as submerged arc welding, electrode arc welding, and other slag-shielded welding methods, CO_2 gas shielded welding has the following advantages.

(1) Low welding cost

CO_2 gas is a by-product of alcohol factories, with a wide range of sources, low prices, and low welding power consumption. Therefore, the cost of CO_2 gas shielded welding is low, only

40%-50% of that of submerged arc welding or electrode arc welding.

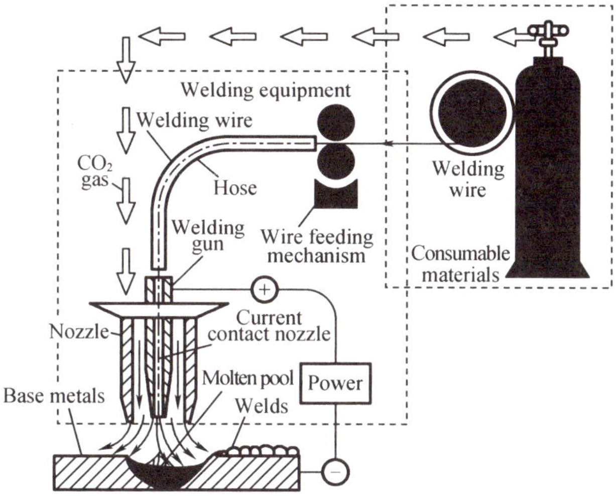

Fig. 2-1-2 Schematic Diagram of the General Process of CO_2 Gas Shielded Welding

(2) High productivity

Due to the use of fine welding wire, the welding current density can reach up to 100-200 A/mm^2, which increases the penetration depth. The melting rate of the welding wire is high, and the deposition speed is accelerated. In addition, there is no slag after welding, especially in multi-layer welding, which saves slag removal time. Therefore, the productivity of this method is usually 2-4 times higher than that of shielded metal arc welding.

(3) Strong rust resistance

In CO_2 gas shielded welding, the molten pool exhibits violent boiling, which facilitates gas escape. In addition, high manganese and high silicon type electrodes are used, significantly increasing the reduction effect of weld metal and reducing its sensitivity to rust. As a result, it is less prone to the formation of weld joint pores, and the hydrogen content is also very low, providing good strength and crack resistance.

(4) Small welding deformation

Due to the concentrated arc heat, small heating area, fast welding speed, and the cooling effect of CO_2 airflow, the deformation of the welding heat affected zone and weldment is minimal. This makes it particularly suitable for welding thin plates.

(5) Good operational performance

Due to the open arc welding process, the arc and molten pool are clearly visible, allowing for real-time problem detection and adjustment. This is beneficial for mechanization and automation.

(6) Wide application

CO_2 semi-automatic welding offers the flexibility of manual arc welding, enabling all-position welding. It can be used for thin plates, medium plates, and even thick plates (with multi-layer welding).

Of course, CO_2 gas shielded welding also has its limitations, primarily manifested in the following aspects:

①The main disadvantages are excessive metal splatter and poor weld surface formation;

②Welding with alternating current is difficult, and there are numerous auxiliary welding equipment required;

③Welding cannot be performed in windy locations, as it may lead to pore formation;

④Avoid welding metal materials that are prone to oxidation.

3. Application of CO_2 gas shielded welding

CO_2 gas shielded welding is an efficient and cost-effective energy-saving welding method. Its unique characteristics make it widely applicable in welding various materials. It can be used to weld not only low carbon steel and low alloy steel, but also heat-resistant steel and stainless steel when the weld performance requirements are not high. CO_2 gas shielded welding can also be used for surfacing wear-resistant parts, repairing steel castings, and welding dissimilar metal materials. Additionally, CO_2 semi-automatic welding is suitable for short welds, curved welds, space welds, as well as spot welding and tack welding of thin plates. For long straight welds and circumferential welds, CO_2 automatic welding should be adopted. CO_2 automatic welding is primarily used for horizontal welding, but with special equipment, it can also be performed vertically and horizontally. Furthermore, CO_2 gas shielded welding can be utilized for underwater welding. Therefore, CO_2 welding finds extensive applications in industries such as shipbuilding, automobile manufacturing, engineering machinery, and aerospace.

There are various classification methods for CO_2 gas shielded welding according to its application. Table 2-1-2 provides the classification of CO_2 gas shielded welding based on wire diameter, operation method, special application, and new process. Currently, the most commonly used classification for CO_2 gas shielded welding is based on the shape of electrodes and rods, namely solid core and flux-cored.

Table 2-1-2 Classification of Application for CO_2 Gas Shielded Welding

Basis	Classification
According to the shape of the welding wire	Solid-core CO_2 gas shielded welding Flux-core CO_2 gas shielded welding
According to the diameter of the welding wire	Fine wire CO_2 gas shielded welding: welding wire diameter ≤ 1.2 mm Coarse wire CO_2 gas shielded welding: welding wire diameter ≥ 1.6 mm
According to the operation method	CO_2 automatic welding CO_2 semi-automatic welding

Table 2-1-2(continued)

Basis	Classification
According to special applications and new processes	CO_2 gas shielded arc spot welding CO_2 gas shielded vertical electrogas welding CO_2 gas shielded narrow gap welding CO_2 gas shielded vibrating surfacing
In accordance with the form of protection	CO_2 and flux combined shielded welding: CO_2+ flux-cored wire CO_2+ solid wire with magnetic flux CO_2+O_2 or CO_2+Ar mixed gas shielded welding Double-layer gas shielded welding

CO_2 gas shielded welding is typically classified based on the diameter of the electrodes and rods used. When the diameter of the electrode and rod is less than or equal to 1.2 mm, it is referred to as fine wire CO_2 gas shielded welding. This technique primarily employs short-circuit transfer to join thin plate materials. It is mainly utilized for welding thin low carbon steel and low alloy steel structural components. When the diameter of the welding wire is more than or equal to exceeds 1.6 mm, it is referred to as thick wire CO_2 gas shielded welding. Generally, high current and elevated arc voltage are utilized for welding medium-thick plates.

In order to meet the needs of modern industrial applications, CO_2 gas shielded welding has experienced rapid development in the past decade. In addition to conventional CO_2 gas shielded welding methods, some improved methods have also emerged in production, including CO_2 arc spot welding, gas-electric vertical automatic welding, CO_2 shielded narrow gap welding, CO_2 combined with other gases (CO_2+ O_2) shielded welding, and CO_2 gas and flux combined shielded welding.

Task Assessment

1. (　　) is internationally recognized as one of the most advanced and rapidly developing high-tech technologies in welding materials, and it will become the leading product of welding materials in the 21st century.

A. Flux-cored wire　　B. Solid wire

C. Stainless steel wire　　D. Aluminum wire

2. The designation of solid wire is represented by the letter (　　).

A. C　　B. Z　　C. H　　D. Y

3. The identification of flux-cored wire is indicated by the letter (　　).

A. C　　B. Z　　C. H　　D. Y

4. The one or two-digit number following the solid wire designation "H" represents a fraction of ten thousandths of the content (　　).

A. S　　B. C　　C. N　　D. P

5. Flux-cored wires can be classified into (　　) types based on the cross section of the welding wire.

A. 2　　B. 3　　C. 4　　D. 5

6. The small-diameter flux cored wire refers to the wire with a diameter of (　　) mm or less.

A. 1.0　　B. 1.2　　C. 2　　D. 2.5

7. The second Chinese phonetic alphabet capital letter "J" in the designation of flux-cored wire represents (　　).

A. Tool steel　　B. Structural steel

C. Stainless steel　　D. Cast iron

8. The two digits following the grade "J" of flux-cored wire indicate the (　　) level of deposited metal.

A. Tensile strength　　B. Compressive strength

C. Fatigue strength　　D. Low-temperature strength

9. The number following the "-" in the designation of flux cored wire indicates the protection method used during welding, and (　　) indicates gas protection.

A. 1　　B. 2　　C. 3　　D. 4

10. In order to prevent rust formation on the surface of the welding wire, enhance conductivity, and reduce wire feeding resistance, it is advisable to plate (　　) solid wires.

A. Aluminum　　B. Copper　　C. Nickel　　D. Tin

项目二　CO_2气体保护焊设备选用、安装与调试

【学习目标】

1. 了解 CO_2 气体保护焊对设备的要求；
2. 掌握 CO_2 气体保护焊设备的组成；
3. 掌握 CO_2 气体保护焊设备的安装和调试方法。

任务1：了解CO_2气体保护焊对设备的要求

1. 综合工艺性能

要获得质量好的焊接接头，需要有综合工艺性能好的焊接设备，主要表现在：焊接引弧容易，电弧的自调节能力强，当弧长变化时，焊接电流的变化小，当干伸长变化时，产生的静态电压误差小，并且焊接参数调节方便，能够实现多种直径焊丝的焊接。

2. 良好的使用性能

使用过程中，焊枪轻巧，操作方便；送丝机构质量小，便于移动；供气系统工作顺畅；另外要求焊机维修方便；焊机有安全防护措施，确保使用安全。

3. 提高焊接过程稳定性的途径

送丝机构设计合理，焊接过程中确保匀顺送丝；电源的外特性选择合理，弧压反馈送丝焊机采用下降外特性电源，等速送丝焊机则选用平或缓降外特性电源。

任务2：掌握CO_2气体保护焊设备的组成

CO_2 焊所用的设备有半自动 CO_2 焊设备和自动 CO_2 焊设备。在实际生产中，由于船体结构的特点，半自动 CO_2 焊设备使用最为普遍，该设备主要由四部分组成，即焊接电源、送丝系统、焊枪及供气系统。图 2-2-1 所示为半自动 CO_2 气体保护焊设备组成系统图。自动 CO_2 焊设备仅多一套焊枪与焊件相对运动的机构，或者采用焊接小车进行自动操作。大电流 CO_2 焊设备还配有水冷却系统。

1. 焊接电源

(1)对焊接电源的要求

①具有平的或缓降的外特性曲线。电源输出电压和输出电流的关系叫作电源的外特性。当输出电流增加时，输出电压不变或缓慢降低的电源外特性叫作平特性或缓降特性。因为 CO_2 气体保护焊使用的焊丝直径小(通常小于 1.6 mm)，焊接电流大，电流密度比焊条电弧焊高 10 倍以上，电弧的静特性处于上升段(图 2-2-2)，所以要采用平特性或缓降特性的焊接电源(图 2-2-3)。采用平特性电源，由于短路电流大，容易引弧，不易粘丝；电弧拉长后，电流迅速减小，不容易烧坏焊丝嘴，且弧长变化时会引起较大的电流变化，电弧的自调节作用强，焊接参数稳定，焊接质量好。

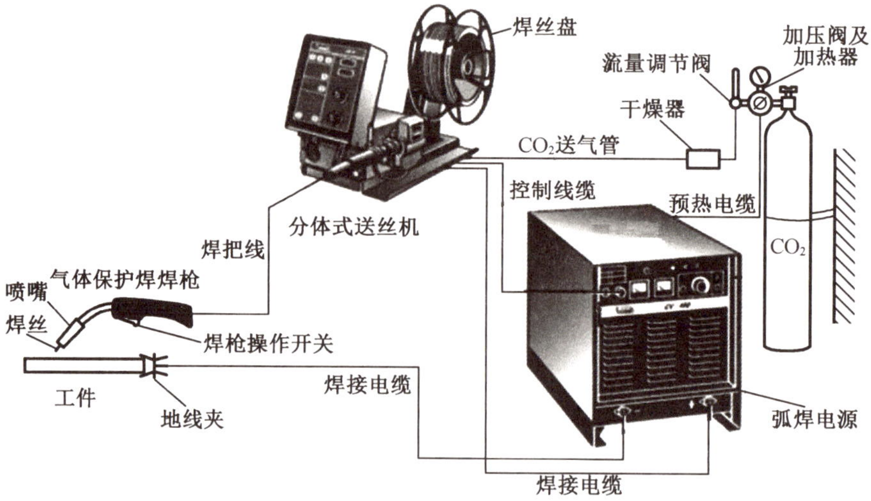

图 2-2-1　半自动 CO_2 气体保护焊设备组成系统图

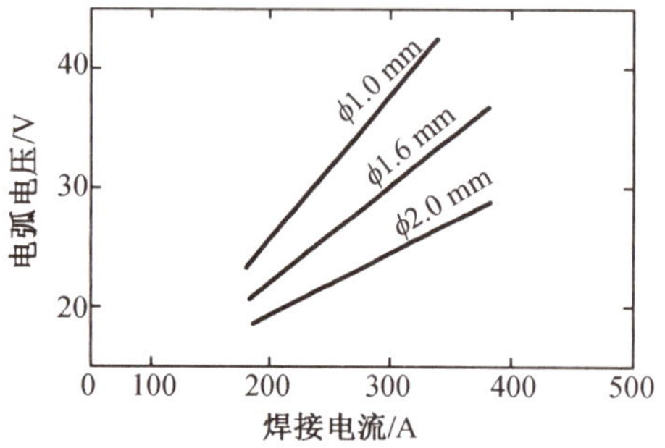

图 2-2-2　CO_2 气体保护焊电弧的静特性

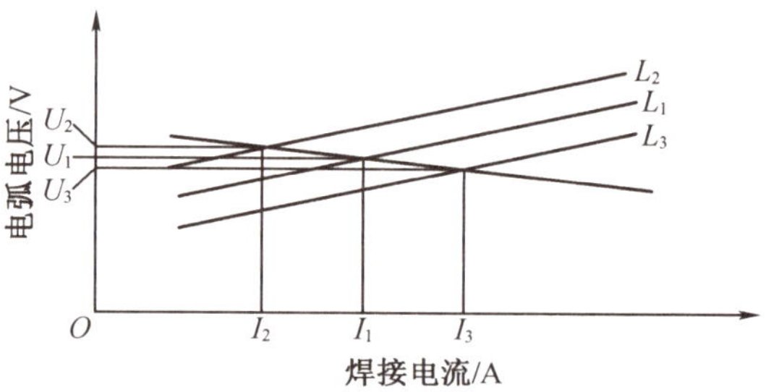

图 2-2-3　弧长变化时焊接电流的变化

设电弧稳定燃烧时弧长为 L_1，焊接电流为 I_1，电弧电压为 U_1。当某种原因使电弧变长到 L_2 时，焊接电流迅速减小为 I_2，焊丝熔化减慢，电弧长度变短，焊接电流增加，很快就恢复到 I_1。反之，若电弧变短至 L_3，则焊接电流迅速增加到 I_3，焊丝熔化加快，弧长增加，迫使焊接电流减小，很快恢复到 I_1。

②具有合适的空载电压。CO_2 气体保护焊机的空载电压一般为 38~70 V。

③具有良好的动特性。焊接过程中，焊丝与焊件之间会发生频繁的短路和重新引弧。如果焊机输出电流和电压不能迅速地适应电弧焊过程中的这些变化，电弧就不能稳定燃烧，甚至熄灭。焊机适应焊接电弧变化的特性称为焊接电源动特性。焊机动特性良好时，容易引弧，焊接过程稳定、飞溅小，操作时会感到电弧平静、柔软、富有弹性。

④合适的调节范围。能根据需要方便地调节焊接参数，满足生产需要。

(2)常见电源匹配型号

CO_2 气体保护焊平特性整流电源的型号是 ZP 型(磁放大器式)、ZP_3 型(动圈式)、ZPs 型(晶闸管式)、Z 型(抽头式)，适用于细丝焊。

CO_2 气体保护焊陡降特性整流电源的型号是 ZX 型(极管整流加饱和抗器)、ZX_5 型(晶闸管整流)，适用于粗丝焊。

同时具有两种特性的型号是 ZD 型(磁放大器式)、ZD_5 型(晶闸管式)。

气体保护焊因需要控制送丝等，其弧焊电源在通常的直流电源基础上还需要增加控制系统，因此在标准中为气体保护焊这类电源给出了专门的型号代码，如表 2-2-1 所示。图 2-2-4 所示的型号为 NBC-270 的电弧焊机就是半自动熔化极气体保护焊机。

表 2-2-1　熔化极气体保护焊机的型号符号代码表

产品名称	第一字母		第二字母		第三字母		第四字母	
	代表字母	大类名称	代表字母	小类名称	代表字母	附注特征	数字序号	系列序号
			Z	自动焊	省略	直流	省略	焊车式
							1	全位置焊车式
			B	半自动焊			2	横臂式
电弧焊机	N	MIG/MAG 焊机（熔化极惰性气体保护焊机/熔化极活性气体保护焊机）			M	脉冲	3	机床式
			D	点焊			4	旋转焊头式
			U	堆焊			5	台式
					C	CO_2 气体保护焊	6	焊机机器人
			G	切削			7	变位式

2. 送丝系统

熔化极气体保护焊一般采用半自动及自动气体保护焊，焊材一般为盘状焊丝，以便自动化送丝，因此需要有送丝机构。在 CO_2 气体保护焊中送丝系统是焊机的重要组成部分。送丝系统要能维持并保证送丝均匀和平稳，送丝机构应尽可能地结构简单和轻巧，并且维修及使用方便。送丝系统由送丝电机、送丝滚轮、压紧机构、送丝软管和减速器等组成。

图 2-2-4　半自动熔化极气体保护焊机

常用的送丝方式有三种：推丝式、拉丝式、推拉式，如图 2-2-5 所示。

（1）推丝式送丝系统

该方式由送丝滚轮将焊丝推入送丝软管，再经焊枪上的导电嘴送至电弧区。其结构简单，轻巧，是目前应用最广泛的一种形式，但是对送丝软管的要求较高且不宜过长，焊枪活动范围小，在 3~5 m。通常推送所用的焊丝直径在 0.8 mm 以上。目前，半自动 CO_2 气体保护焊多采用推丝式送丝方式。

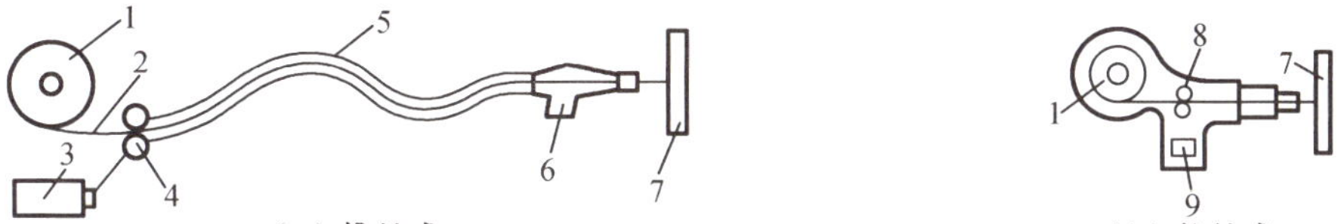

（a）推丝式　　（b）拉丝式

1—焊丝盘；2—焊丝；3—送（推）丝电动机；4—送（推）丝滚轮；5—送丝软管；
6—焊枪；7—焊件；8—送（拉）丝滚轮；9—送（拉）丝电动机。

图 2-2-5　送丝方式示意图

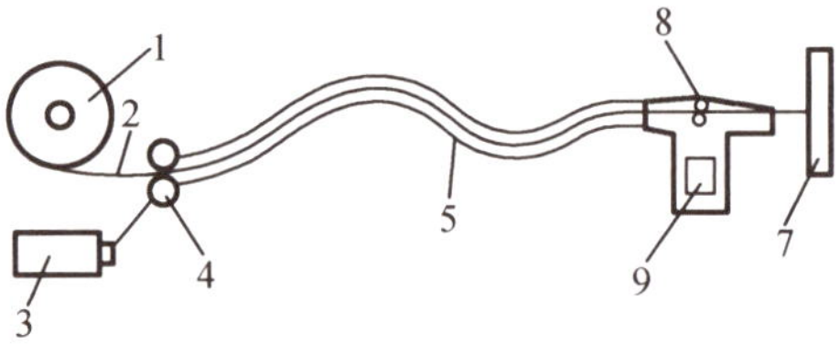

（c）推拉式

图 2-2-5(续)

(2)拉丝式送丝系统

该方式将送丝机构和焊丝盘都装在焊枪上。其焊枪结构复杂,比较笨重,但焊枪活动范围大,送丝均匀,适用于细丝(直径 0.5~0.8 mm)焊接。

(3)推拉式送丝系统

该方式由安装在焊枪中的拉丝电动机和送丝装置内的推丝电动机两者同步运转来完成。其结构复杂,送丝稳定,送丝软管可达 20~30 m,焊枪活动范围大。

CO_2 气体保护焊一般采用推丝式送丝系统,其电源与送丝机有一体机[图 2-2-6(a)]和分体机[图 2-2-6(b)]两种类型。

（a）

（b）

图 2-2-6　CO_2 气体保护焊一体机和分体机示意图

3. 焊枪及配件选配

焊枪的主要作用是向熔池和电弧区输送保护气流和稳定可靠地向焊丝导电。焊枪应结构紧凑,操作方便,连接件、易损件便于更换。半自动 CO_2 气体保护焊焊枪主要是推丝式的,也有少量是拉丝式的。推丝式焊枪按结构可分为鹅颈式、手枪式两种,冷却方式分气冷及水冷两种。

(1)鹅颈式气冷焊枪

推丝式焊枪中,常用的是鹅颈式焊枪,其操作较灵活,适用于平焊等位置的焊接。保护气体空冷是该式焊枪比较常用的方式。图 2-2-7 所示为典型鹅颈式气冷枪结构。

其主要部件有喷嘴、导电嘴(焊丝嘴)分流器、导管电缆。

①喷嘴

喷嘴是输送保护气体的出口,其内孔形状及内径的大小会直接影响到气体保护的效果,要求从喷嘴喷出的保护气能呈近似圆锥状的气层,笼罩在焊丝端部、电弧及熔池周围。喷嘴的形状多为圆锥筒形及圆柱筒形,如图 2-2-8 所示,以使 CO_2 气流从喷嘴中流出时有一定“挺度”的层流,可以对焊接电弧区起到良好的保护作用。喷嘴内孔的直径一般为 16~22

mm，最小不应小于12 mm，也不宜过大，以避免妨碍焊工操作视线及过多消耗保护气体。喷嘴应与导电部分绝缘，以免打弧。喷嘴常用导热性好、表面粗糙度好的紫铜或陶瓷材料制造，并在表面镀上一层铬，以增加表面硬度及光洁度，减少飞溅粘连和易于清除。为增强防护飞溅造成的危害，减少飞溅黏附在喷嘴上，焊前宜在喷嘴内外涂上飞溅防堵剂或硅油，以延长喷嘴使用寿命。目前常用的喷嘴以圆柱形居多。

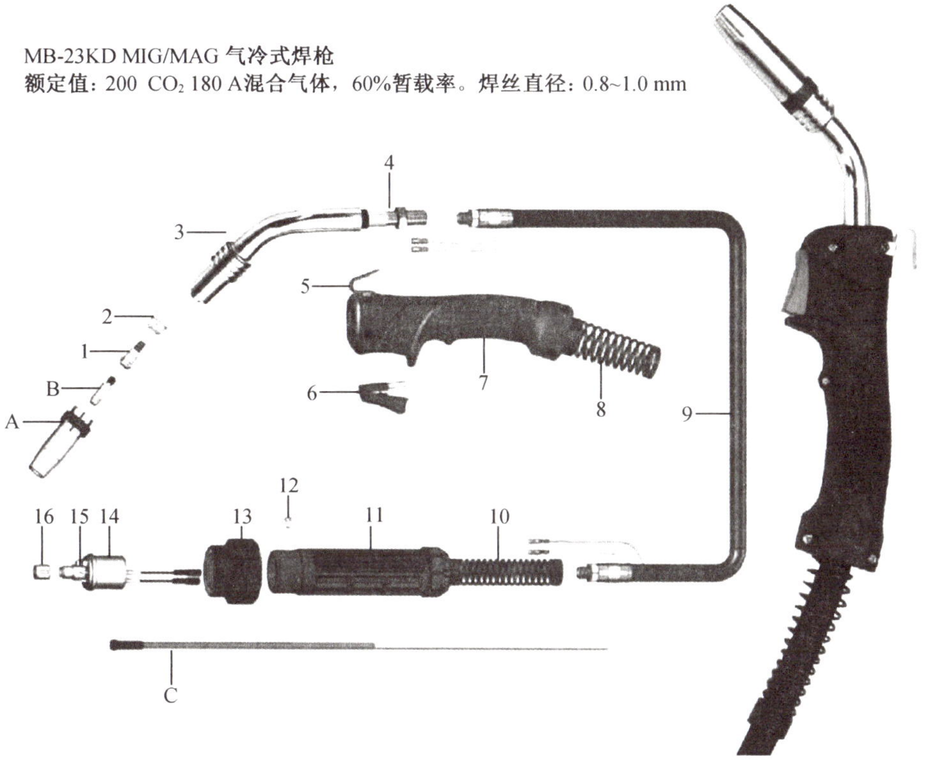

1—导电嘴座；2—分流器陶瓷；3—弯枪颈；4—六角螺母及管接头；5—挂钩；6—开关扳机；7—前枪壳；8—前弹簧护套；9—焊把线，电缆及气管总成（一般3~5 m）；10—后弹簧护套；11—后枪壳；12—螺钉；13—插头固定螺母；14—欧式插头（为集成式，也有分头式）；15—O形密封圈；16—螺母；A—各种口径喷嘴（锥筒形、直筒形）；B—导电嘴（各种规格、各种不同材质）；C—送丝软管。

图2-2-7　典型鹅颈式气冷焊枪结构图

（a）圆锥形　　（b）圆柱形

图2-2-8　喷嘴形状示意图

②导电嘴

导电嘴是直接传导焊接电流的零件，为保证导电性能良好、耐磨性能好、熔点高，一般用铜及铜合金（铬青铜、磷青铜）材料制成。图2-2-9所示为两种不同形状的导电嘴，分别用于细丝及粗丝焊丝［直径 $d<2$ mm时，$D=d+(0.1\sim0.3)$ mm；$d=2\sim3$ mm时，$D=$

d+(0.4~0.6)mm]。一般选用导电嘴的孔径应比焊丝大 0.2 mm 左右,这样既避免造成过大摩擦力,又避免焊丝端部出现剧烈的摆动。孔径过小,送丝阻力会较大地影响焊接过程的稳定;孔径过大,焊丝在孔内接触位置不固定,焊丝送出导电嘴后会偏移或摆动,使焊接过程不稳定,严重时会使焊丝与导电嘴起弧而黏结烧损。

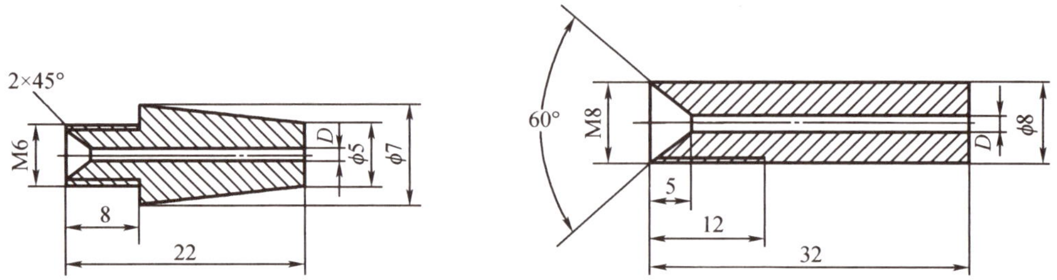

(a)用于细丝　　(b)用于直线>1.2 mm 的焊丝

图 2-2-9　导电嘴形状示意图(单位:mm)

鹅颈式焊枪对导电嘴的长度也有一定的要求,长度增加,导电性能变好,但送丝阻力也增加;长度太短,导电性能不好,尤其在磨损后会使焊接电弧不稳定。所以一般导电嘴长度应大于 25 mm。

③分流器

分流器的作用如同 TG 焊焊枪的"气体透镜",但结构、形状各不相同。分流器是用绝缘陶瓷制成的,在其圆形筒壁上有均匀分布的小孔,如图 2-2-10 所示,当由气瓶输出的保护气流经过分流器后,气流便会以稳定的层流状从喷嘴喷出,加强了保护效果。

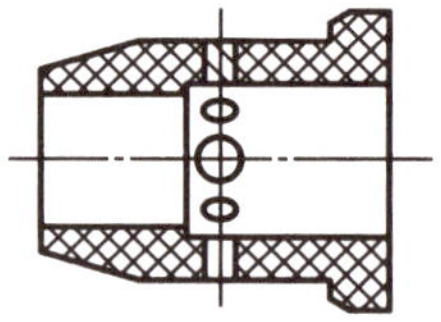

图 2-2-10　分流器形状示意图

④常见的两种接头方式

焊枪的接头有整体式(常称为欧式接头)和分体式两种,如图 2-2-11 所示。

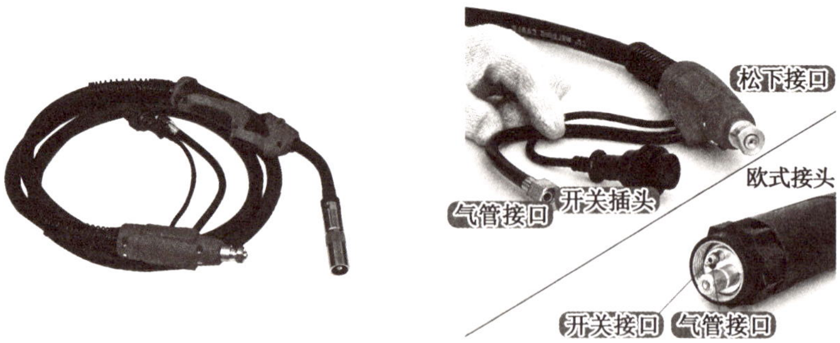

(a)　　(b)

图 2-2-11　焊枪及其接头

(2)手枪式焊枪

手枪式焊枪(图 2-2-12)的操作相对鹅颈式气冷焊枪要更灵活一些,但其成本也相对高一些。这种焊枪形似手枪,用来焊接除水平面以外的空间焊缝较方便。焊接电流较小时,焊枪采用自然方式冷却;当焊接电流较大时,采用水冷式冷却。

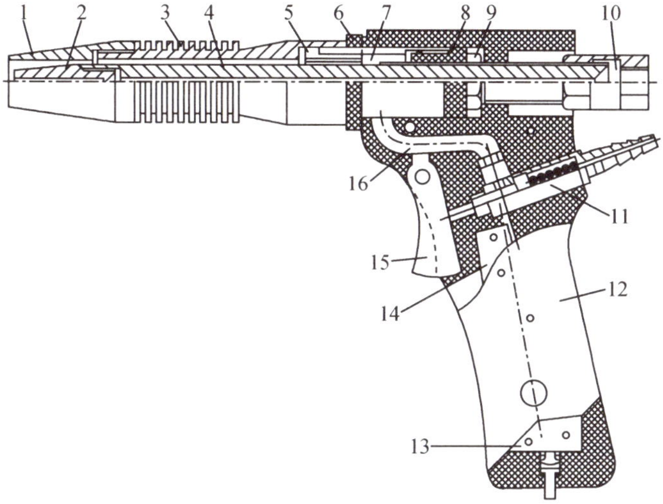

1—喷嘴;2—导电嘴;3-套筒;4—导电杆;5—分流环;6—挡圈;7—气室;8—绝缘圈;9—紧固螺母;10—锁紧螺母;11—球形气阀;12—枪把;13—退丝开关;14—送丝开关;15—扳机;16—气管。

图 2-2-12　手枪式焊枪示意图

4. 供气系统

供气系统的作用是将保存在钢瓶中呈液态的 CO_2 在需要时变成有一定流量的气态 CO_2。供气系统包括 CO_2 气瓶、预热器、干燥器、减压器和流量计及电磁气阀,如图 2-2-13 所示。

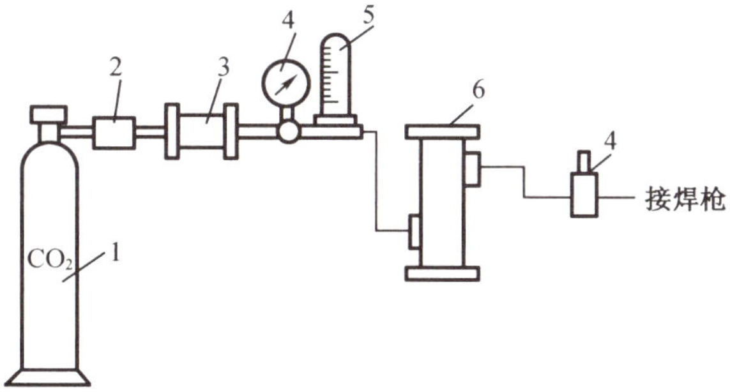

1—CO_2 气瓶;2—加热器;3—高压干燥器;4—气体减压表;5—气体流量计;6—低压干燥器;7—气阀。

图 2-2-13　供气系统示意图

(1)CO_2 气瓶

CO_2 气瓶涂铝白色,并用黑色标写有"液态二氧化碳"字样,用于贮存液态 CO_2。通常将焊接用的 CO_2 气体压缩成液态储存于容量为 40 L 的钢瓶内,每瓶可装 25 kg 液体 CO_2,约占钢瓶容积的 80%,其余 20%容积空间为瓶内液面的水蒸气、空气和 CO_2 气体三者的混合物,气瓶压力表指示的就是这部分气体的饱和压力,瓶内的压力随着外界温度的升高而增大,所以不能用压力表上的读数来估计瓶内液态 CO_2 的储量,因为压力表上的读数仅代表气体

CO_2 的压力，不代表液态 CO_2 的储量。如果要了解瓶内 CO_2 的余量，一般用称重法进行测量。0 ℃时，饱和气压为 3.63 MPa，20 ℃时，饱和气压为 5.72 MPa，30 ℃时，饱和气压为 7.48 MPa。由于 CO_2 气瓶瓶内压力随外界温度的升高而增大，所以 CO_2 气瓶不准靠近热源或置于烈日下暴晒，以防发生爆炸事故。

液态 CO_2 在大气压力下的沸点为-78 ℃，所以常温下容易蒸发。CO_2 气体中水气的含量与瓶中的压力有关，压力越小，水气越多，当压力小于 1 MPa 时，CO_2 气体中的含水量便大大增加，不能继续使用。为保证焊接质量，一般规定 CO_2 气体的纯度(体积分数)为 99.5%以上，含水量、含氮量均不得超过 0.1%。

液体 CO_2 中可溶解 0.05%(质量分数)的水，多余的水沉在瓶底，这些水与液态 CO_2 一起挥发后，将混入 CO_2 气体中进入焊接区。随着 CO_2 气体中水分的增加，焊缝金属中扩散氢含量也会增加，焊缝的塑性变差，同时还会增加气孔。

进行 CO_2 气体保护焊时，如果 CO_2 气体纯度不够，要采取措施来消除 CO_2 气体中的水分和空气。新装的 CO_2 气瓶应倒置 1~2 h，使密度大的水沉到瓶口部位，然后小心地打开瓶阀放出一部分液体，这样进行 2~3 次，每次间隔 30 min，就可以去除一部分水分。此外，使用前先将瓶内杂气放掉，一般放 2~3 min 即可，或者在供气管路中串联干燥器，以进一步减少 CO_2 气体中的水分。

在温度恒定的情况下，当气瓶中的 CO_2 全部挥发成气体后，瓶内压力才开始逐渐下降，使用钢瓶时，内部压力不能低于 0.7 MPa，CO_2 液体低于 0.7 MPa 时会形成干冰。CO_2 气瓶中气压降到 980 kPa 时，应该停止用于 CO_2 气体保护焊，因为这时 CO_2 气体中所含水分比饱和压力下增加 3 倍左右，如果继续作为 CO_2 气体保护焊的保护气体，将使焊缝产生气孔。

(2)预热器

当打开气瓶阀门时，液态 CO_2 挥发成气态，气化时要吸收大量的热量，从而使气体温度下降，为防止气体中的水分在气瓶出口处结冰，在减压前要将 CO_2 气体进行加热，即在供气系统中加入预热器。预热器的功率为 75~150 W。

(3)干燥器

干燥器用于吸收 CO_2 气体中的水分。干燥器有两种：一种是高压干燥器，在减压之前使用；另一种是低压干燥器，在减压之后使用。干燥器的选用主要根据气瓶中 CO_2 气体的纯度和对焊接质量的要求而定。可以选一个，也可以选两个。

(4)减压器及流量计

减压器是将高压的 CO_2 气体变为低压的气体并保持气体的压力在供气过程中稳定。流量计用于测量和控制气体的流量，常用的流量计一般与减压器、干燥器、预热器做成一体，如图 2-2-14 所示。

(5)电磁气阀

电磁气阀是用来控制保护气体的装置。

5. 控制流程

CO_2 气体保护焊的控制是对送丝系统、供气系统和焊接电源的控制，以及对焊件运转或焊接机头行走的控制。其控制流程如图 2-2-15 所示。

送丝控制系统是对送丝电动机的控制，即能够完成对焊丝的正常送进和停止动作，焊前对焊丝进行调整，在焊接过程中均匀调节送丝速度，并在网络波动时有补偿作用。

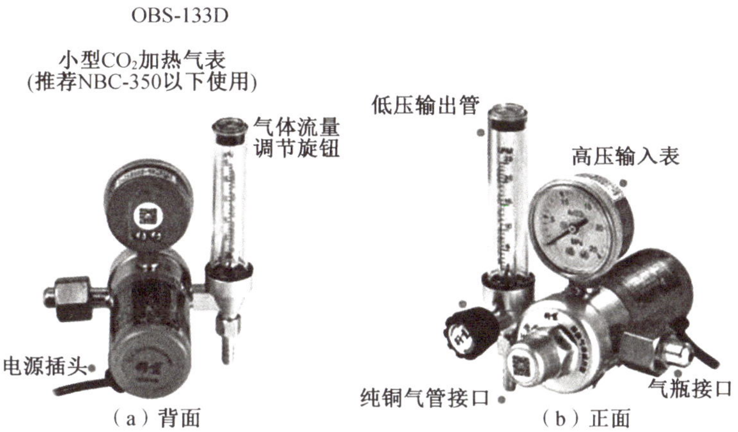

图 2-2-14　CO_2 加热减压流量调节气表

图 2-2-15　半自动熔化极 CO_2 气体保护焊的控制流程图

供气系统的控制分为三个步骤:第一步提前送气 1~2 s,这样可以排除引弧区周围的空气,保证引弧质量,然后引弧;第二步在焊接过程中保证气流均匀;第三步在收弧时滞后 2~3 s 断气,继续保护弧坑区熔化金属的凝固和冷却。

焊接电源的控制与送丝部分相关,引弧时,可在送丝同时接通焊接电源,也可在接通焊接电源后送丝。收弧时为了避免焊丝末端与熔池粘连而影响弧坑处的质量,应先停止送丝再切断焊接电源,有时还有延时切断焊接电源和焊接电流自动衰减的控制装置,以保护弧坑的质量。

任务3:掌握CO_2气体保护焊设备的安装和调试

1. 焊机的安装

(1)安装要求

①电源电压、开关、熔丝容量必须符合焊机铭牌上的要求,千万不能将额定输入电压为 220 V 的设备接在 380 V 的电源上。

②每台设备都用一个专用的开关供电,设备与墙距离应大于 0.3 m,保证通风良好。

③设备导电外壳必须接地线,地线截面面积必须大于 12 mm^2。

④凡需水路时须串联一个水压继电器,无水时可自动停电,以免烧毁焊接电源及焊枪。使用循环水箱的焊机,冬天应注意防冻。

⑤根据焊接电流的大小,正确选择电缆软线的截面规格。

当电焊钳软线允许压降为 4 V 时,电焊钳软线的截面规格可按表 2-2-2 选定。

(2)焊机的安装步骤

焊机安装前必须认真地阅读设备使用说明书,弄清基本要求后才能按下述步骤进行安装。

①查清电源的电压、开关和熔丝的容量。这些要求必须与设备铭牌上标明的额定输入

参数完全一致。

表 2-2-2　电焊钳软线截面规格的选定

电流/A	距离/m								
	20	30	40	50	60	70	80	90	100
100	30	38	38	38	38	38	38	50	50
150	30	38	38	38	50	50	60	80	80
200	38	38	38	50	60	80	80	100	100
250	38	50	50	60	80	100	100	125	125
300	38	50	60	80	100	100	125	125	—
350	38	50	80	80	100	125	—	—	—
400	38	60	80	100	125	—	—	—	—
450	50	80	100	100	—	—	—	—	—
500	50	80	100	100	—	—	—	—	—
550	50	80	100	125	—	—	—	—	—
600	80	100	125	—	—	—	—	—	—

②焊接电源的导电外壳必须可靠接地。

③用电缆将焊接电源输出端的负极和焊件接好，将正极与送丝机构接好。

注意，CO_2 气体保护焊通常都采用直流反接，可获得较大的熔深和生产效率。如果用于堆焊，为减小堆焊层的稀释率，最好采用直流正接，两根电缆的接法正好与上述要求相反。

④接好遥控盒插头，以便焊工能在焊接处灵活地调整焊接参数。

⑤将流量计至焊接电源及焊接电源至送丝机处的送气管道接好。

⑥将减压调压器上的预热器的电缆插头插至焊机插座上并拧紧（接通预热器电源）。

⑦将焊枪与送丝机接好。

⑧若焊机或焊枪需用水冷却，则需接好冷却水系统，冷却水的流量和水压必须符合要求。

⑨接好焊接电源至供电电源开关间的电缆，若焊机固定不动，焊机至开关这段电缆按要求应从埋在地下的钢管中穿过。若焊机需移动，最好采用截面合适和绝缘良好的四芯橡套电缆。

2. 焊机的调试

CO_2 气体保护焊设备的电路、气路和水路接通以后，为保证能正常地进行焊接操作，应立即对设备进行调试，焊接过程开始后不再调整。设备调试工作的一般流程如图 2-2-16 所示。

（1）闭合配电盘开关

闭合开关前应确认：焊接电缆的断面尺寸是否符合要求，焊接电缆与电缆接头是否绝缘，电源电压与焊机额定输入电压是否一致，三相输入电压是否平衡，然后在焊接电源开关切断的情况下，闭合电盘开关。

(2)闭合焊接电源开关

在焊枪开关切断的情况下,将焊机面板上的电源开关置于“开”的位置,电源指示灯亮,然后确认焊接电源内的风扇是否转动和转动方向(逆时针)是否正确。

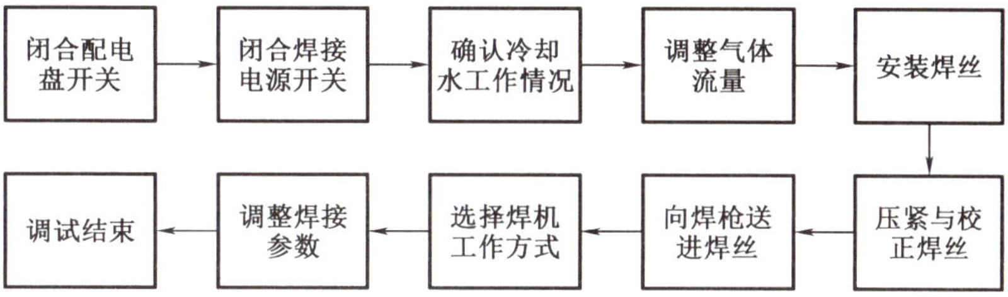

图 2-2-16　CO_2 气体保护焊设备调试工作的流程

(3)确认冷却水工作情况

有冷却水循环装置的焊机(焊接电流为 500 A 以上)需确认冷却水的工作状况,开放冷却水阀门后,冷却水循环侧水压开关动作,焊机上的水指示灯亮,水泵有轻微声音,最后确认水箱的回水管有水回流。

(4)调整 CO_2 气体流量

首先合上预热器开关,CO_2 气体预热器表面温度上升,然后打开气瓶,旋开低压调整手柄,此时气压表指示低压输出,注意要将输出压力调至 0.2~0.3 MPa 以上。将焊机面板上的供气开关置于“检查”位置,旋动流量计旋钮,调节气体流量到规定值,并注意有无漏气。最后将供气开关置于“焊接”位置,气路处于准备状态,一旦开始焊接,即按调好的流量供气。

(5)选择并安装焊丝

根据所使用的焊丝种类,将焊机面板上的焊丝按钮置于“药芯”或“实心”位置;根据焊丝直径的大小,将焊丝直径按钮置于相应的位置。将绕有焊丝的焊丝盘装在送丝机的安装轴上,并拧紧螺钉。抬起加压手柄,然后用钢丝钳将焊丝端头校直后,通过导向管将焊丝送到送丝轮的沟槽内,注意导向管应该与送丝轮的沟槽对正。送丝机通常有两只送丝轮,每只送丝轮上有两条沟槽,以适应不同直径焊丝的工作,此时应确认送丝轮沟槽大小与焊丝直径是否保持一致,安装正确时焊丝直径标号应朝向外侧。

(6)压紧与校正焊丝

首先确认焊丝是否送入送丝轮沟槽内,调节加压手柄对焊丝进行加压。在调节焊丝的压紧力过程中,若有压力刻度时,应按指定刻度调整压力;若无刻度时,压力调到焊丝不致在沟槽中滑动的程度,并能稳定地送丝。

(7)向焊枪送进焊丝

选择与焊丝相应的导电嘴,并把它可靠地拧紧在焊枪上,以使其可靠导电。按遥控器上的手动送丝按钮,直到焊丝头超过导电嘴端 15~20mm 。若没有手动送丝按钮,可直接按焊枪按钮送丝,应注意不要将焊丝与焊件碰上,以免打弧。

(8)选择焊机工作方式

使用焊机面板上的“收弧”转换按钮和焊枪开关,可进行以下两种焊接:

①无收弧控制时焊枪开关的操作:将“收弧”转换按钮处于“无”的位置处,按下焊枪开关,输气、通电、送丝,焊接工作进行,焊接时要始终按住焊枪开关。松开焊枪开关,停丝、断电、停气,焊接工作停止。

这种焊接主要应用于反复进行的定位焊、瞬时焊及薄板焊接。

②有收弧控制时焊枪开关的操作:将“收弧”转换按钮处于“有”的位置处,然后分别调节收弧电流和收弧电压旋钮使其约为正常焊接的2/3。按下焊枪开关,输气、通电、送丝,焊接工作开始;松开焊枪开关,焊接工作仍继续;再按下焊枪开关,这时焊接电流和电弧电压自行减小成收弧电流和收弧电压,便于收弧;最后,再松开焊枪开关,则停丝、断电、停气,焊接工作停止,填补了焊接结束时的弧坑。

在有收弧控制状态下,焊工在焊接时不需要按住焊枪开关,减轻了劳动强度。这种焊接适用于中厚板长焊缝的焊接。

(9)调整焊接参数

①将遥控盒上的焊接电流和电弧电压旋钮调整至预先选定的焊接电流和电弧电压刻度处。若焊接实现一元化调节时,只需调节遥控盒上的焊接电流旋钮至预先选定值,与其相应的电弧电压会自动给定。

②引燃电弧,并观察电流表和电压表读数与所选值是否相符,若不符,则再次调节输出旋钮至电流和电压读数相符为止。

③根据焊缝成形情况,用电压微调旋钮修正电弧电压值,直到焊缝宽度满意。

若焊缝较窄或两边熔合不太好,可适当增加电压,将微调旋钮按顺时针转动;若焊缝太宽或咬边,则降低电压,微调旋钮逆时针转动。

任务考核

1. 以下不属于 CO_2 气体保护焊设备的是(　　)。

A. 送丝机构　B. 焊剂漏斗　C. 焊枪　D. 气瓶

2. CO_2 气体保护焊送丝机构的送丝方式有(　　)。

A. 推丝式　B. 拉丝式　C. 推拉式　D. 以上都是

3. CO_2 气体保护焊的电源特性是(　　)。

A. 下降特性　B. 平特性

C. 上升特性　D. 平特性或下降特性

4. CO_2 焊用的 CO_2 气体纯度,一般要求不低于(　　)。

A. 99.5%　B. 99.9%　C. 99.95%　D. 99.99%

5. CO_2 气体保护焊最常出现的是(　　)气孔。

A. H_2　B. CO　C. N_2　D. O_2

6. CO_2 气瓶的瓶体温度不能超过(　　)。

A. 35 ℃　B. 40 ℃　C. 45 ℃　D. 50 ℃

7. CO_2 焊焊枪常用的喷嘴以(　　)为主。

A. 圆柱形　B. 圆锥形　C. 椭圆形　D. 梅花形

8. CO_2 气瓶涂(　　)。

A. 银灰色　B. 天蓝色　C. 白色　D. 铝白色

9. CO_2 气体保护焊机的空载电压一般为(　　)。

A. 16~45 V　B. 38~70 V　C. 110~220 V　D. 220~380 V

10. 喷嘴内孔的直径一般为(　　)mm。

A. 8~16　B. 10~16　C. 12~18　D. 16~22

Project Ⅱ Selection, Installation, and Commissioning of CO_2 Gas Shielded Welding Equipment

【Learning Objectives】

1. Understand the requirements of CO_2 gas shielded welding for equipment;
2. Master the composition of CO_2 gas shielded welding equipment;
3. Master the installation and debugging methods of CO_2 gas shielded welding equipment.

Task 1:Understand the Requirements of CO_2 Gas Shielded Welding Equipment

1. Comprehensive process performance

High-quality welded joints require welding equipment with excellent comprehensive process performance, which is primarily evident in: easy arc initiation, strong self-adjustment ability of the electric arc, minimal variation in welding current with changes in arc length, minimal static voltage error generated with changes in dry elongation, and convenient adjustment of welding parameters to accommodate welding wires of various diameters.

2. Good usability

During operation, the welding gun is lightweight and easy to handle; the wire feeder is compact and can be easily moved; the gas supply system operates smoothly; furthermore, the welding machine requires convenient maintenance; it is equipped with safety measures to ensure secure usage.

3. Ways to improve the stability of the welding process

The wire feeding mechanism is designed reasonably to ensure smooth wire feeding during welding. The external characteristics of the power supply are selected reasonably, and the arc voltage feedback wire feeder adopts a descending external characteristic power supply, while the constant speed wire feeder adopts a flat or gradually descending external characteristic power supply.

Task 2:Master the Composition of CO_2 Gas Shielded Welding Equipment

The equipment used for CO_2 welding consists of semi-automatic CO_2 welding equipment and automatic CO_2 welding equipment. In actual production, due to the characteristics of hull structure, semi-automatic CO_2 welding equipment is the most commonly used. This equipment mainly consists of four parts: Welding power supply, wire feeding system, welding gun, and gas supply system. Fig. 2-2-1 shows the system composition of semi-automatic CO_2 gas shielded welding equipment. Automatic CO_2 welding equipment only has an additional mechanism for relative movement between the welding gun and the weldment, or it adopts a welding trolley for automatic operation. High-current CO_2 welding equipment is also equipped with a water cooling system.

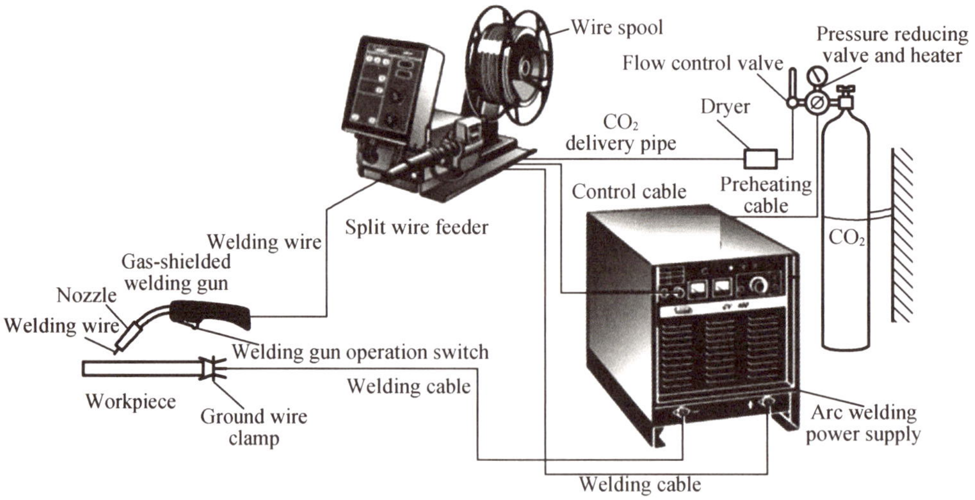

Fig. 2-2-1 Composition System Diagram of Semi-Automatic CO_2 Gas Shielded Welding Equipment

1. Welding power supply

(1) Requirements for welding power supply

①The relationship between the output voltage and current of a power supply is referred to as its external characteristic. When the output current increases, the power supply's external characteristic, in which the output voltage remains unchanged or decreases slowly, is called flat characteristic or ramp-down characteristic. Due to the small diameter of the welding wire used in CO_2 gas metal arc welding (usually less than 1.6 mm), the welding current is high, and the current density is more than 10 times higher than that of shielded metal arc welding. The static characteristic of the arc is in the rising stage (Fig. 2-2-2). Therefore, a welding power supply with flat or slow-drop characteristics should be used (Fig. 2-2-3). The adoption of a power supply with flat characteristics enables easy arc striking and prevents wire sticking due to the high short-circuit current. After the arc is elongated, the current decreases rapidly, reducing the likelihood of burning out the welding wire nozzle. Changes in arc length result in significant current fluctuations, and the arc exhibits a strong self-regulation effect. This ensures stable welding parameters and high welding quality.

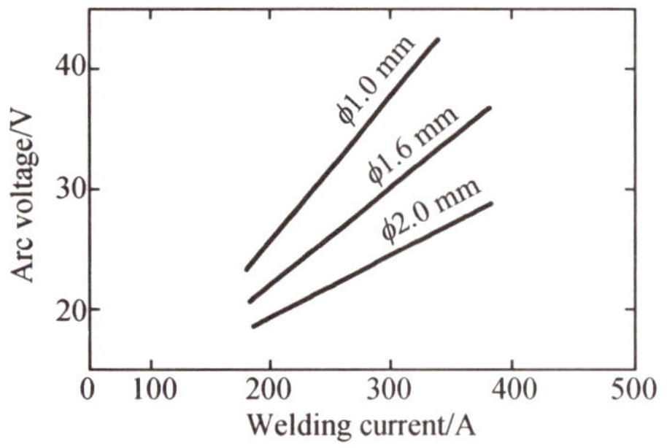

Fig. 2-2-2 Static Characteristics of CO_2 Welding Arc

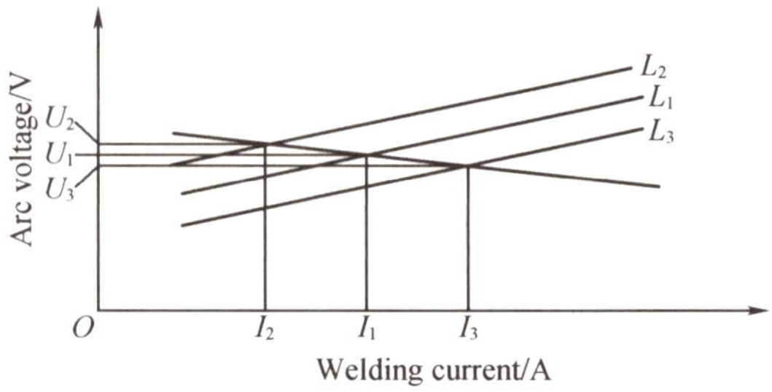

Fig. 2-2-3 Variation of Welding Current with Arc Length Change

When the arc is stably combusted, it is assumed that the arc length is L_1, the welding current is I_1, and the arc voltage is U_1. If for some reason the arc lengthens to L_2, the welding current rapidly decreases to I_2, which slows down the melting of the welding wire. As a result, the arc length becomes shorter and the welding current increases, quickly returning to I_1. Conversely, if the arc becomes shorter to L_3, the welding current rapidly increases to I_3, accelerating the melting of the electrode and rod. This causes the arc length to increase, forcing the welding current to decrease and quickly return to I_1.

②Have an appropriate no-load voltage. The no-load voltage of a CO_2 gas shielded welding machine is typically 38–70 V.

③Good dynamic characteristics. Frequent short circuits and re-strikes can occur between the wire and weldment during welding. If the output current and voltage of the welder cannot quickly adapt to these changes in the arc welding process, the arc will not burn stably or even extinguish. The characteristic that the welding machine adapts to the changes in the welding arc is called the dynamic characteristics of welding power. When the dynamic characteristics of welding are good, it is easy to strike an arc. The welding process is stable and spatter is minimal. During operation, the arc will be calm, smooth, and elastic.

④Appropriate adjustment range. The welding parameters can be conveniently adjusted as needed to meet production requirements.

(2) Common power supply model.

The models of flat characteristic rectifier power supply for CO_2 gas shielded welding are ZP (magnetic amplifier type), ZP_3 (moving coil type), ZPs (thyristor type), and Z (tapped type), which are suitable for fine wire welding.

The models of rectification power supply with steep drop characteristics for CO_2 gas shielded welding are ZX (electrode rectifier with saturable reactor) and ZX_5 (thyristor rectifier), which are suitable for thick wire welding.

Models with both characteristics are ZD (magnetic amplifier type) and ZD_5 (thyristor type).

To ensure control over wire feeding in gas shielded welding, the arc welding power supply must have a control system in addition to a common DC power supply. Therefore, this standard provides specific model codes for power supplies used in gas shielded welding, as shown in Table 2-2-1. The NBC-270 arc welder, depicted in Fig. 2-2-4, is a semi-automatic gas metal arc welding machine.

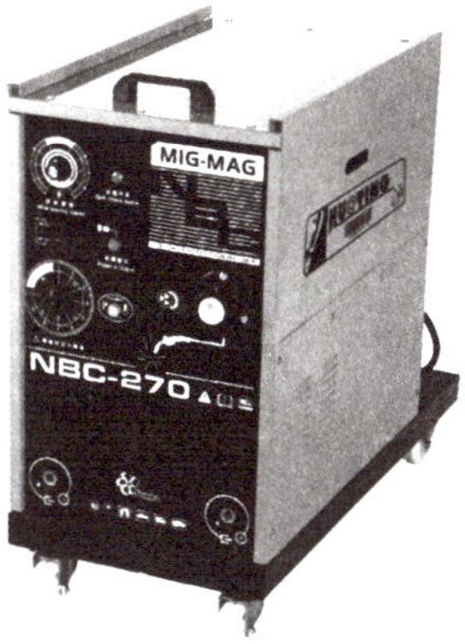

Fig. 2-2-4 Half-Automatic Gas Metal Arc Welding Machine

2. Wire feeding system

Semi - automatic and automatic gas shielded welding processes are generally employed for GMAW. The welding materials are usually shaped into disc-like welding wires to facilitate automated wire feeding, hence requiring a wire feeder. In CO_2 gas shielded arc welding, the wire feeding system plays a crucial role as an integral part of the welding machine. It should be capable of maintaining and ensuring consistent and stable wire feeding. The wire feeding mechanism should be designed to be as simple and lightweight in structure as possible, while also being convenient for maintenance and usage. The wire feeding system comprises a wire feeding motor, wire feeding roller, pressing mechanism, wire feeding hose, and reducer.

Table 2-2-1 Model Symbol Code for Gas Metal Arc Welding Power Supply

Product title	First letter		Second letter	
	On behalf of the letter	Category Name	Representative letter	Subcategory name
Arc welding machine	N	MIG/MAG welding machine (MIG/MAG welding machine)	Z	Automatic welding.
			B	Semi-automatic welding
			D	Spot welding
			U	Build-up welding
			G	Cutting
Product title	Third letter		Fourth letter	
	Representative letter	Note characteristics	Serial Number	Series number
Arc welding machine	Omit	Direct Current	Omit	Welding truck style
			1	All-position welding truck type
			2	Cross-arm type
	M	Pulse	3	Machine tool type
			4	Rotary welding head type
			5	Desktop
	C	CO_2 gas shielded welding	6	Welding robot
			7	Changed format

There are three common wire feeding methods: Push type, drawing type, and push-pull type, as illustrated in Fig. 2-2-5.

(1) Push-type wire feeding system

The welding wire is pushed into the wire feeding hose by the wire feeding roller and then sent to the arc zone through the current contact nozzle on the welding gun. Its structure is simple and lightweight, making it the most widely used form currently. However, it requires high standards for the wire feeding hose and should not be too long. The movement range of the welding gun is small, ranging from 3 to 5 m. Generally, the diameter of the welding wire used for pushing is above 0.8 mm. Currently, semi-automatic CO_2 gas shielded welding mostly adopts the push wire feeding mode.

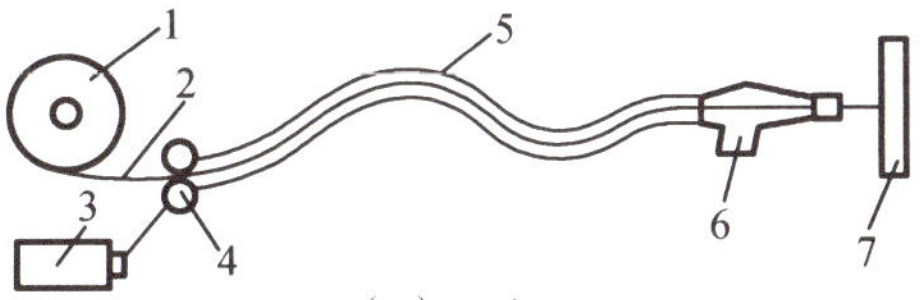

(a) Push type

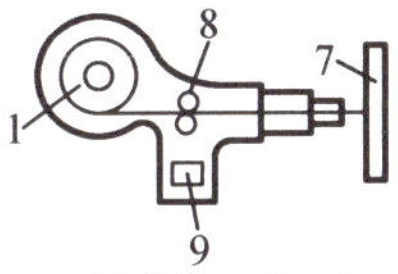

(b) Drawing type

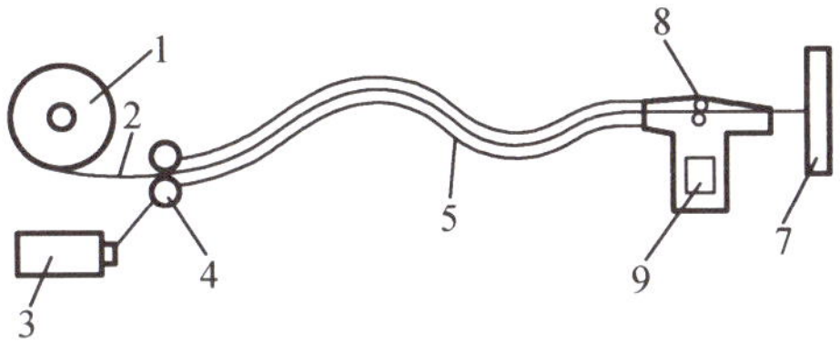

(c) Push-pull type

1—Wire spool; 2—Welding wire; 3—Wire feed (push) motor; 4—Wire feed (push) roller;
5—Wire feeding hose; 6—Welding gun; 7—Weldment; 8—Wire feeding roller; 9—Wire feeding motor.

Fig. 2-2-5 Schematic Diagram of Wire Feeding Mode

(2) Wire drawing type wire feeding system

Install the wire feeder and wire reel on the welding gun. The arc welding gun has a complex and relatively heavy structure, but it offers a wide range of motion and uniform wire feeding. It is suitable for welding thin wires with a diameter of 0.5-0.8 mm.

(3) Push-pull wire feeding system

It is completed by the synchronous operation of the wire drawing motor installed in the welding gun and the wire pushing motor in the wire feeder. The structure is complex, ensuring stable wire feeding with a wire feeding hose that can reach 20-30 m, and allowing the welding gun to have a large range of movement.

The wire feeding and delivery system is commonly used for CO_2 gas shielded welding. There are two types of power supply and wire feeder: Integrated machine [Fig. 2-2-6 (a)] and split machine [Fig. 2-2-6 (b)].

(a)

(b)

Fig. 2-2-6 Schematic Diagram of CO_2 Gas Shielded Welding Integrated Machine and Split Machine

3. Selection of welding gun and accessories

The primary function of the welding gun is to deliver protective airflow to the molten pool and arc zone, ensuring stable and reliable electrical conductivity to the welding wire. The welding gun should have a compact and user-friendly structure, with connectors that are easily replaceable. The semi-automatic CO_2 gas shielded welding gun is mainly of the push wire type, but there are also a few types that function through drawing. The push wire welding gun can be categorized into gooseneck and pistol types based on their structure, cooling methods include both air and water cooling.

(1) Gooseneck air-cooled welding gun

Among push-wire welding guns, the commonly used type is the gooseneck welding gun, which offers flexible operation and is suitable for flat welding and other positions. The common cooling method for this type of welding gun is air cooling with shielding gas. Fig. 2-2-7 below illustrates the structure of a typical gooseneck welding gun.

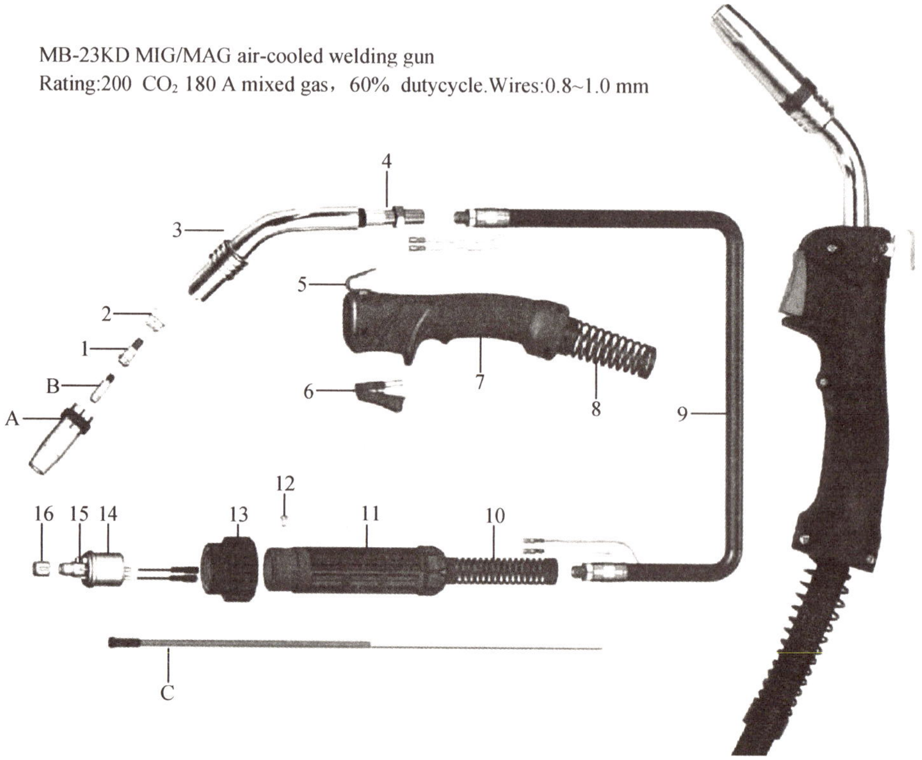

1—Conductive nozzle base; 2—Shunt ceramic; 3—Bent gun neck; 4—Hexagon nut and pipe joint; 5—Hook; 6—Switch trigger; 7—Front gun shell; 8—Front spring sheath; 9—Welding machine cable, cable and air pipe assembly (generally 3-5 m); 10—Rear spring sleeve; 11—Rear gun shell; 12—Screw; 13—Plug fixing nut; 14—European plug (integrated type, also tap type); 15—O-ring; 16—Nut; A—Nozzles of various calibers (conical cylinder shape and straight cylinder shape); B—Current contact nozzle (various specifications and different materials); C—Wire feeding hose.

Fig. 2-2-7 Schematic of the Structure of A Typical Gooseneck Air-cooled Welding Gun

Its main components are nozzle, contact tip (wire tip), shunt, and conduit cable.

①Nozzle

The nozzle is the outlet for conveying shielding gas, and its inner hole shape and inner diameter directly affect the effectiveness of gas shielding. It is required that the shielding gas ejected from the nozzle forms an approximately conical gas layer that covers the end of the welding wire, arc, and molten pool. The nozzle is mostly conical or cylindrical in shape, as shown in Fig. 2-2-8 below, to ensure that the carbon dioxide flows out from the nozzle with a laminar flow and certain stiffness, providing effective protection for the welding arc zone. The inner hole diameter of the nozzle is generally 16-22 mm, with a minimum diameter of 12 mm. The diameter should not be too large to obstruct the welder's line of sight or excessively consume protective gas. Nozzles should be insulated from conductive parts to prevent arcing. The nozzle is usually made of red copper or ceramic material with good thermal conductivity and surface roughness. It is chrome-plated for increased surface hardness and smoothness, reduced splash adhesion, and easy removal. To enhance protection against splash hazards and reduce splash adhesion to the nozzle, it is advisable to apply anti-splash agent or silicone oil inside and outside the nozzle before welding to prolong its service life. Currently, most commonly used nozzles are cylindrical in shape.

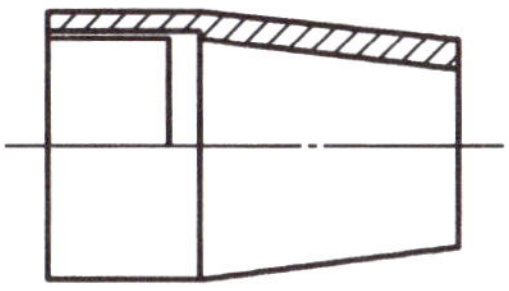

(a) Conical shape

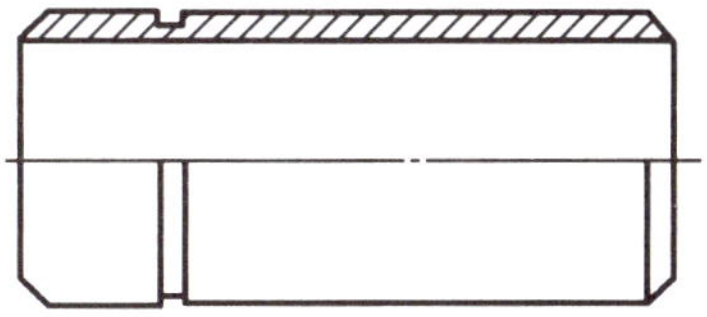

(b) Cylindrical shape

Fig. 2-2-8 Schematic Diagram of Nozzle Shape

②Conductive nozzle

The current contact nozzle is a component that directly conducts the welding current. In order to ensure good conductivity, excellent wear resistance, and a high melting point, it is typically made of copper and copper alloy materials (such as chromium bronze and phosphor bronze). The two different shapes of current contact nozzles shown in Fig. 2-2-9 are used for fine wire and thick wire electrodes respectively [when the diameter $d<2$ mm, $D=d+(0.1-0.3)$ mm; when $d=2-3$ mm, $D=d+(0.4-0.6)$ mm]. Generally, the aperture of the current contact nozzle should be approximately 0.2 mm larger than that of the welding wire to prevent excessive friction and significant wire swing at the end of welding. If the hole diameter is too small, it significantly affects the stability of the welding process due to higher wire feeding resistance. On the other hand, if the hole diameter is too large, the contact position of the welding wire within the hole will not be fixed, causing the wire to deviate or swing after passing through the current contact nozzle. This leads to an unstable welding process. In severe cases, it can result in arcing between the welding wire and the current contact nozzle, leading to bonding and burning.

There are also specific requirements for the length of the current contact nozzle. Increasing the length improves conductivity, but it also increases wire feeding resistance. If the length is too short, conductivity will be poor, especially after wear and tear, resulting in unstable welding arc. Therefore, the length of the current contact nozzle should generally be greater than 25 mm.

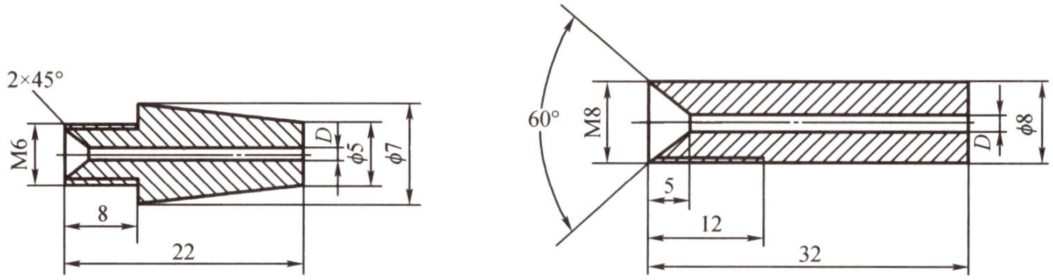

(a) For fine wire (b) For wires with a diameter larger than 1.2 mm

Fig. 2-2-9 Schematic Representation of Current Contact Tube Shape (Unit: mm)

③Splitter

The function of the shunt is similar to that of the "gas lens" in TG welding torch, but their structures and shapes are different. The shunt is made of insulating ceramics and has evenly distributed small holes on its cylindrical wall, as shown in Fig. 2-2-10. When the protective airflow outputted from the gas cylinder passes through the shunt, the airflow will be ejected from the nozzle in a stable laminar flow, thus enhancing the protection effect.

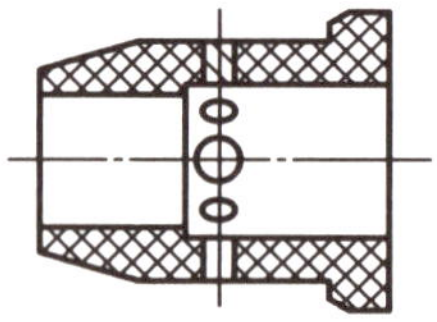

Fig. 2-2-10 Diverter Shape Schematic Diagram

④Two common joint types

The joint of the welding gun is divided into two types: Integral type (commonly known as European-style joint) and split type, as shown in the two categories depicted in Fig. 2-2-11 respectively.

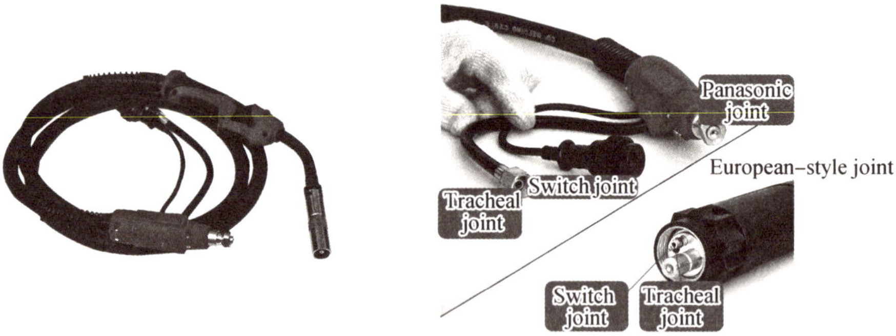

(a) (b)

Fig. 2-2-11 Welding Gun and Its Joint

(2) Pistol gun

The pistol-style welding gun (Fig. 2-2-12) is more maneuverable than the gooseneck air-cooled welding gun, but it has a relatively higher cost. This welding gun resembles a pistol and is convenient for welding in spaces other than horizontal surfaces. When the welding current is low, natural cooling should be used for the welding gun. When the welding current is high, a water-cooled welding gun should be used.

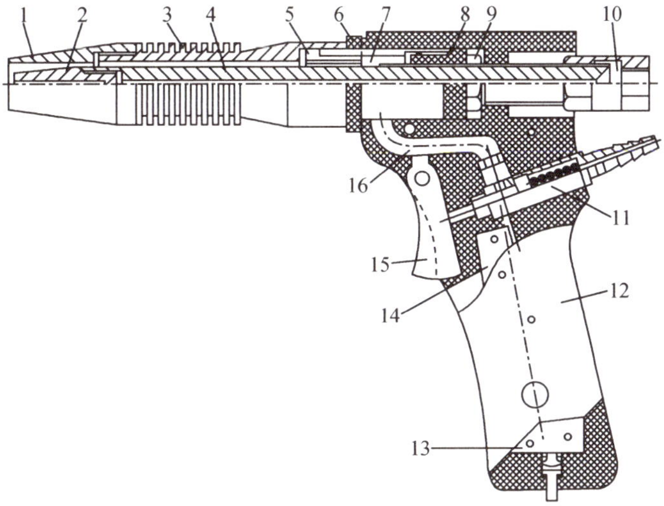

1—Nozzle; 2—Conductive nozzle; 3—Sleeve; 4—Conductive rod; 5—Shunt ring; 6—Retaining ring; 7—Gas chamber; 8—Insulation ring; 9—Fastening nut; 10—Locknut; 11—Ball valve; 12—Gun handle; 13—Wire withdrawal switch; 14—Wire feeding switch; 15—Trigger; 16—Air pipe.

Fig. 2-2-12 Pistol-style Welding Gun

4. Air supply system

The function of the gas supply system is to convert the liquid CO_2 stored in steel cylinders into gaseous CO_2 with a specific flow rate when required. The gas supply system consists of a CO_2 cylinder, preheater, dryer, pressure reducer, flowmeter, and solenoid valve, as shown in Fig. 2-2-13.

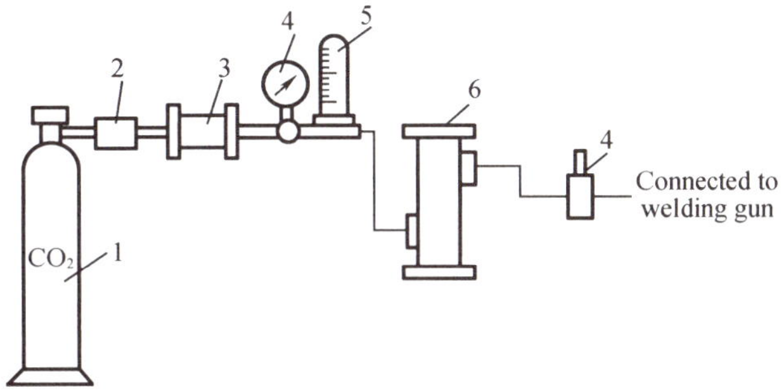

1—CO_2 gas cylinder; 2—Heater; 3—High-pressure dryer; 4—Gas pressure gauge; 5—Gas flow meter; 6—Low-pressure dryer; 7—Gas valve.

Fig. 2-2-13 Air Supply System Schematic Diagram

(1) CO_2 cylinder

The CO_2 cylinder is painted white with black lettering saying "LIQUID CARBON DIOXIDE", and it is used for storing liquid carbon dioxide. Generally, CO_2 gas for welding is compressed into a liquid state and stored in steel cylinders with a capacity of 40 L. Each cylinder can hold 25 kg of liquid CO_2, which accounts for approximately 80% of the cylinder volume. The remaining 20% volume is a mixture of water vapor, air, and CO_2 gas at the liquid level inside the cylinder. The pressure gauge on the cylinder indicates the saturation pressure of this gas mixture, and the pressure inside the cylinder increases with rising external temperature. Therefore, the pressure gauge reading cannot be used to estimate the amount of liquid CO_2 remaining in the cylinder, as it only represents the pressure of gaseous CO_2 and not the liquid CO_2 reserve. If you want to determine the remaining CO_2 in the cylinder, it is generally measured by weight. The saturation pressure is 3.63 MPa at 0 ℃, 5.72 MPa at 20 ℃, and 7.48 MPa at 30 ℃. When using the CO_2 cylinder, it should not be placed near a heat source or exposed to direct sunlight to prevent explosion accidents.

The boiling point of liquid CO_2 at atmospheric pressure is −78 ℃, making it easily evaporate at normal temperature. The moisture content in CO_2 gas is related to the pressure in the cylinder. The lower the pressure, the higher the moisture content. When the pressure is lower than 1 MPa, the moisture content in CO_2 gas significantly increases and renders it unfit for further use. To ensure welding quality, it is generally stipulated that the purity (volume fraction) of CO_2 gas must be above 99.5%, with water content and nitrogen content not exceeding 0.1%.

Liquid CO_2 can dissolve 0.05% (mass fraction) of water, and excess water will sink to the bottom of the cylinder. After evaporating together with liquid CO_2, this water will be mixed into CO_2 gas and enter the welding area. With the increase of moisture in the CO_2 gas, the content of diffusible hydrogen in the weld metal will also increase, making the weld less ductile and leading to an increase in the presence of pores.

During CO_2 gas shielded welding, if the purity of CO_2 is not sufficient, steps should be taken to eliminate moisture and air in CO_2. The newly installed CO_2 cylinder should be inverted for 1−2 h to allow the high-density water to sink to the mouth of the cylinder, and then carefully open the cylinder valve to discharge a portion of the liquid. By repeating this process 2 to 3 times at intervals of 30 min each time, some moisture can be removed. Additionally, before use, discharge the residual gas in the cylinder for approximately 2−3 min, or connect a dryer in series with the gas supply pipeline to further reduce the moisture in CO_2.

Under the condition of constant temperature, when all CO_2 in the cylinder volatilizes into gas, the pressure in the cylinder begins to gradually decrease. When using steel cylinders, the internal pressure should not be lower than 0.7 MPa. When carbon dioxide liquid is lower than 0.7 MPa, dry ice will be formed. When the air pressure in the CO_2 cylinder drops to 980 kPa, it should not be used for CO_2 gas shielded welding, because at this time, the moisture content in the CO_2 gas is about 3 times higher than that under saturation pressure. If it continues to be used as a shielding gas for CO_2 gas shielded welding, pores will occur in the weld joints.

(2) Heater

When the cylinder valve is opened, liquid carbon dioxide evaporates into a gaseous state and absorbs a significant amount of heat during the process of gasification, resulting in a reduction in gas temperature. To prevent moisture in the gas from freezing at the cylinder outlet, the carbon dioxide gas needs to be heated before being depressurized. This requires the addition of a preheater to the gas supply system. The power of the preheater should be 75−150 W.

(3) Dryer

The dryer is used to remove moisture from CO_2 gas. There are two types of dryers: One is a high-pressure dryer used before decompression, and the other is a low-pressure dryer used after decompression. The choice of dryer depends mainly on the purity of CO_2 gas in the cylinder and the welding quality requirements. You can choose one or both.

(4) Pressure regulator and flow meter

The pressure reducer is used to convert high-pressure carbon dioxide gas into low-pressure gas and maintain gas pressure stability during the gas supply process. The flowmeter is used for measuring and controlling gas flow. Commonly used flowmeters are typically integrated with pressure reducers, dryers, and preheaters, as shown in Fig. 2-2-14.

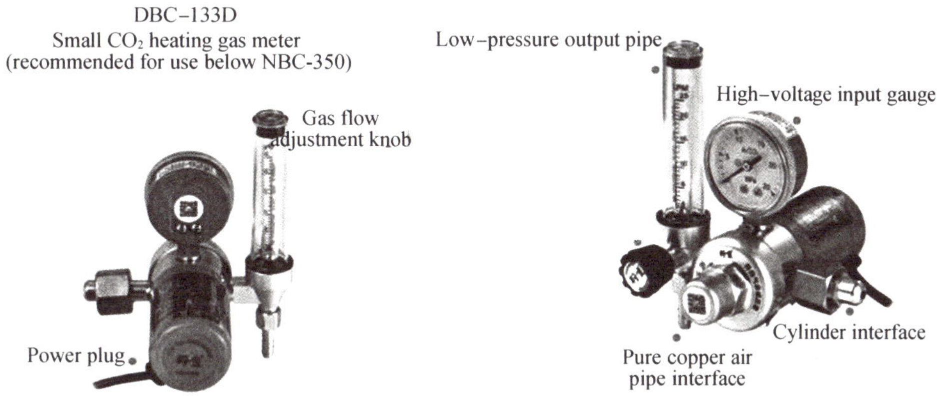

(a) Backside (b) Front

Fig. 2-2-14 CO_2 Heating and Decompression Flow Control Gas Meter

(5) Electropneumatic valve

It is a device used to regulate protective gases.

5. Control process

The control process of CO_2 gas metal arc welding involves control of the wire feeding system, gas supply system, welding power source, as well as the movement of the weldment or welding head. The control procedure is illustrated in Fig. 2-2-15 below.

Fig. 2-2-15 Flow Chart of Control Procedure for Semi-automatic CO_2 Gas Metal Arc Welding

The wire feeding control system controls the wire feeding motor, enabling it to perform the normal feeding and stopping actions of welding wires, make adjustments to the welding wires before welding, adjust the wire feeding speed uniformly during welding, and provide compensation when the network fluctuates.

The control of the air supply system is divided into three processes: The first step is to pre-supply air for 1-2 s, eliminating the air around the arc striking area, ensuring the quality of arc striking before igniting the arc; the second step is to maintain a uniform airflow during welding; and the third step is to cut off the air after 2-3 s when stopping the arc, continuing to protect the solidification and cooling of the molten metal in the crater area.

The control of welding power supply is related to wire feeding. During arc ignition, the welding power supply can be turned on simultaneously with wire feeding or after the welding power supply is turned on. To prevent adhesion between the end of the welding wire and the molten pool, which would affect the quality of the weld crater, it is necessary to stop wire feeding first and then cut off the welding power supply. Sometimes, there are control devices for delaying the disconnection of the welding power supply and automatically reducing the welding current to protect the quality of the weld crater.

Task 3:Master the Installation and Debugging Methods of CO_2 Gas Shielded Welding Equipment

1. Please provide the machine-translated phrase that needs refinement

(1) Installation requirements

①The power supply voltage, switch, and fuse capacity must meet the requirements stated on the welding machine's nameplate. Never connect a device with a rated input voltage of 220 V to 380 V power supply.

②Each equipment is powered by a dedicated switch, and there should be a distance of more than 0.3 m between the equipment and the wall to ensure proper ventilation.

③The conductive enclosure of the equipment must be grounded, and the cross-section of the grounding wire should be greater than 12 mm^2.

④When a water circuit is required, a water pressure relay must be connected in series. In the absence of water, the power can be automatically cut off to prevent damage to the welding power supply and welding gun. For welding machines using circulating water tanks, special attention should be given to preventing freezing during winter.

⑤The cross-section of the flexible cable should be selected correctly based on the welding current.

When the allowable voltage drop of the electrode holder flexible wire is 4 V, the cross section of the electrode holder flexible wire can be chosen based on Table 2-2-2.

Table 2-2-2 Selection of Cross-Section for Electrode Holder Flexible Wire

Current/A	Distance/m								
	20	30	40	50	60	70	80	90	100
100	30	38	38	38	38	38	38	50	50
150	30	38	38	38	50	50	60	80	80
200	38	38	38	50	60	80	80	100	100
250	38	50	50	60	80	100	100	125	125
300	38	50	60	80	100	100	125	125	—
350	38	50	80	80	100	125	—	—	—
400	38	60	80	100	125	—	—	—	—

Table 2-2-2(Continued)

Current/A	Distance/m								
	20	30	40	50	60	70	80	90	100
450	50	80	100	100	—	—	—	—	—
500	50	80	100	100	—	—	—	—	—
550	50	80	100	125	—	—	—	—	—
600	80	100	125	—	—	—	—	—	—

(2) Installation steps for welding machine

Before installing the welding machine, carefully read the equipment operation manual and fully understand the basic requirements before proceeding with the installation steps provided below.

①Make sure to verify the voltage of the power supply, as well as the capacity of the switches and fuses. These requirements must align precisely with the rated input parameters specified on the equipment's nameplate.

②The conductive enclosure of the welding power supply must be securely grounded.

③Connect the negative terminal of the welding power output to the workpiece using cables, and connect the positive terminal to the wire feeder.

Please ensure that CO_2 gas shielded welding typically uses direct current reverse polarity, which can achieve greater penetration and production efficiency. If used for surfacing, it is preferable to use direct current straight polarity to reduce the dilution rate of the surfacing layer. The connection of these two cables is exactly opposite to the requirements mentioned above.

④Connect the plug of the remote control box so that welders can adjust welding parameters flexibly at the welding position.

⑤Connect the air supply pipes from the flowmeter to the welding power source and from the welding power source to the wire feeder.

⑥Insert the cable plug of the preheater on the pressure reducing regulator into the welding machine socket and tighten it (connect the power supply of the preheater).

⑦Connect the welding gun to the wire feeder.

⑧If the welding machine or welding gun needs to be cooled with water, it is necessary to connect the cooling water system, and the flow rate and pressure of the cooling water must meet the requirements.

⑨Connect the cable between the welding power supply and the power switch. If the welding machine is fixed, the cable from the welding machine to the switch should pass through a steel pipe buried underground as required. If the welding machine needs to be moved, it is better to use a four-core rubber sheathed cable with a suitable cross-section and good insulation.

2. Welding machine commissioning

After connecting the circuit, gas path, and water path of the CO_2 gas shielded welding equipment, the equipment should be immediately commissioned to ensure proper welding operation. No further adjustments are required once the welding process starts. The general process of equipment commissioning is illustrated in Fig. 2-2-16.

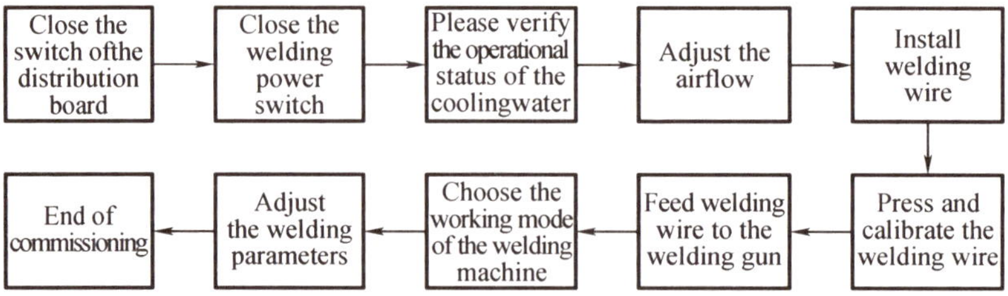

Fig. 2-2-16 Process for Commissioning CO_2 Gas Shielded Welding Equipment

(1) Close the switch of the distribution board

Before closing the switch, verify if the section size of the welding cable meets the requirements, if the welding cable and cable joint are insulated, if the power supply voltage is consistent with the rated input voltage of the welder, and if the three-phase input voltage is balanced. Afterwards, close the electric panel switch when the welding power switch is turned off.

(2) Close the welding power switch

When the welding gun switch is turned off, set the power switch on the welding machine panel to the "ON" position, ensuring that the fan in the welding power supply is rotating and that the rotation direction (counterclockwise) is correct.

(3) Confirm the working condition of the cooling water

For welding machines with cooling water circulation devices (welding current above 500 A), it is necessary to verify the operational status of the cooling water. After opening the cooling water valve, the water pressure switch on the cooling water circulation side will activate, the water indicator on the welding machine will illuminate, and the water pump will produce a slight sound. Finally, it is confirmed that there is water backflow in the return pipe of the water tank.

(4) Adjust the flow of CO_2 gas

First, close the preheater switch. The surface temperature of the CO_2 gas preheater will rise. Then open the cylinder and unscrew the low-pressure adjusting handle. At this time, the barometer will indicate a low-pressure output. Pay attention to adjusting the output pressure to above 0.2-0.3 MPa. Put the gas supply switch on the welding machine panel in the "CHECK" position, turn the knob of the flowmeter to adjust the gas flow to the specified value, and be mindful of any gas leakage. Finally, place the air supply switch in the "welding" position, and the gas circuit will be in a ready state. Once welding starts, air will be supplied at the adjusted flow rate.

(5) Selection and installation of welding wire

According to the type of welding wire used, place the welding wire button on the welding machine panel in the "flux-cored" or "solid core" position; according to the size of the welding wire diameter, place the welding wire diameter button in the corresponding position. Install the wire reel wound with welding wire on the installation shaft of the wire feeder and tighten the screws. Lift the pressure handle, straighten the welding wire end with a wire cutter, and feed the welding wire into the groove of the wire feeding wheel through the guide tube. Ensure that the guide tube is aligned with the groove of the wire feeding wheel. The wire feeder usually has two welding wire feeding rollers, each with two grooves to accommodate welding wires of different diameters. Verify that the groove size of the wire feeding roller matches the diameter of the welding wire, and when correctly installed, the diameter label of the welding wire should be facing outward.

(6) Clamp and adjust the welding wire

First, ensure that the welding wire is fed into the groove of the wire feeding wheel. Adjust the pressure handle to apply pressure to the welding wire. When adjusting the pressing force of the welding wire, if there is a pressure scale, adjust the pressure according to the specified scale; if there is no scale, adjust the pressure to a level where the welding wire does not slide in the groove and can be fed steadily.

(7) Feed the welding wire into the welding gun

Select the corresponding contact tip for the welding wire and securely fasten it onto the welding gun, ensuring reliable electrical conductivity. Press the manual wire feeding button on the remote controller until the welding head extends beyond the end of the current contact nozzle by 15–20 mm. If there is no manual wire feeding button, press the welding gun button directly to feed the wire. Be careful not to let the welding wire touch the weldment to avoid arcing.

(8) Select the working mode of the welding machine

The "Arc Stopping" changeover button and welding gun switch on the welder panel can be used to perform the following two types of welding:

①Operation of welding gun switch without arc stopping control: Turn the "Arc Stopping" toggle switch to the "Off" position, press the welding gun switch to initiate gas transmission, power supply, wire feeding, and welding. Hold down the welding gun switch throughout the welding process. Release the welding gun switch to stop wire feeding, power supply, and gas supply, and then stop welding.

This type of welding is primarily applied to repeated positioning welding, spot welding, and thin plate welding.

②Operation of welding gun switch with arc stopping control: Turn the "Arc Stopping" switch to the "On" position, and then adjust the arc stop current and voltage knobs respectively to approximately 2/3 of those for normal welding. Press the welding gun switch to initiate gas transmission, power-on, wire feeding, and welding. Release the welding gun switch to continue welding. Press the welding gun switch again to automatically reduce the welding current and arc voltage to the arc stop current and arc stop voltage for easy arc stopping. Finally, when the welding gun switch is released again, the wire, power, and gas supply will be stopped, and the welding work will cease to fill the arc crater at the end of welding.

In the state of arc extinguishing control, the welder does not need to hold down the switch of the welding gun during welding, which reduces labor intensity. This type of welding is suitable for long welds on medium-thick plates.

(9) Adjust the welding parameters

①Adjust the welding current and arc voltage knobs on the remote-control box to the predetermined welding current and arc voltage scales. If unified adjustment is achieved for welding, only the welding current knob on the remote-control box needs to be adjusted to a preset value, and the corresponding arc voltage will be automatically provided.

②Ignite the arc and observe whether the readings of the ammeter and voltmeter match the selected values. If not, adjust the output knob again until the current and voltage readings match.

③Based on the formation of the weld, adjust the voltage fine-tuning knob to correct the arc voltage value until the desired weld width is achieved.

If the weld is narrow or the fusion on both sides is not satisfactory, increase the voltage appropriately and turn the fine-tuning knob clockwise; if the weld is too wide or undercut, lower the voltage and turn the fine-tuning knob counterclockwise.

Task Assessment

1. Which of the following is not a CO_2 gas shielded welding equipment (　　).

A. Wire feeding mechanism　　B. Flux hopper

C. Welding torch　　D. Gas bottle

2. The wire feeding modes of the wire feeder for CO_2 gas shielded welding include (　　).

A. Silk-pushing type　　B. Silk-drawing type

C. Silk-push-pull type　　D. All of the preceding options

3. The power supply characteristics of CO_2 gas shielded welding are (　　).

A. Decreasing characteristic　　B. Flat characteristic

C. Increasing characteristic　　D. Flat or decreasing characteristic

4. The purity of CO_2 gas for CO_2 welding is generally required to be not lower than (　　).

A. 99.5%　　B. 99.9%　　C. 99.95%　　D. 99.99%

5. The most common occurrence in CO_2 gas shielded welding is the presence of (　　) pores.

A. H_2　　B. CO　　C. N_2　　D. O_2

6. The temperature of the CO_2 cylinder body should not exceed (　　).

A. 35 ℃　　B. 40 ℃　　C. 45 ℃　　D. 50 ℃

7. The commonly used nozzle of a CO_2 welding gun is mainly (　　).

A. Cylindrical　　B. Conical　　C. Oval　　D. Quincunx

8. The CO_2 cylinder is coated (　　).

A. Silver-gray　　B. Sky blue　　C. White　　D. Aluminum white

9. The no-load voltage of CO_2 gas shielded welding machine is generally (　　).

A. 16-45 V　　B. 38-70 V　　C. 110-220 V　　D. 220-380 V

10. The diameter of the nozzle's inner hole is typically (　　) mm.

A. 8-16　　B. 10-16　　C. 12-18　　D. 16-22

项目三　CO_2气体保护焊的焊接工艺

【学习目标】

1. 掌握 CO_2 气体保护焊焊前准备工艺要求；
2. 掌握 CO^2 气体保护焊焊接材料选用原则；
3. 掌握 CO_2 气体保护焊的工艺参数；
4. 掌握 CO_2 气体保护焊常见缺陷及控制措施。

CO_2 气体保护焊的焊接工艺涉及焊前准备和工艺参数两方面的设计和选定。

任务1：掌握CO_2气体保护焊焊前准备工艺要求

CO_2 气体保护焊的焊前准备工作包括接头和坡口设计，坡口加工，接头清理，焊接装配，工装及焊接设备调整、维护等。

1. 坡口设计

CO_2 气体保护焊细颗粒过渡时，电弧穿透力较强，熔深较大，容易烧穿，所以对焊前装配质量要求较严格。焊接坡口可以开得小一些，钝边可以适当大些，对接缝间隙一般不能超过 2 mm。如果用直径 1.6 mm 的焊丝，钝边尺寸可扩大到 4～6 mm，坡口角度可减小到 45°左右。

短路过渡时，熔深较浅，不能按细颗粒过渡的规范设计坡口。通常允许较小的钝边，甚至可以不留钝边。因为这时的熔池较小，搭桥性能良好，如果是对接接头，允许间隙为 3 mm，间隙大一些也不会烧穿，根部上下错边允许±1 mm。

采用细颗粒熔滴过渡焊接角焊缝时，考虑到其熔深特点，焊脚可以比焊条电弧焊时减小 10%～20%，这样可以进一步提高 CO_2 气体保护焊的效率，减少材料的消耗。不同板厚焊脚的尺寸见表 2-3-1。

表 2-3-1　不同板厚焊脚的尺寸　（单位：mm）

焊接方式	板厚			
	6	9	12	16
CO_2 气体保护焊	5	6	7.5	10
焊条电弧焊	6	7	8.5	11

2. 接头准备

焊接坡口可以剪切、刨边和气割加工。焊接装配前应仔细清除焊丝及被焊工件坡口附近的油、锈和水分。点固焊缝处应特别注意，该处积水易出现气孔，最好焊前用气体火焰预热一下，以便去除水分。

为了防锈，许多钢板表面都涂有油漆。这些油漆不一定都要去除，要看对焊接质量有无影响。有影响的油漆一定要去除，没有影响的油漆（如底漆）可以不除掉。

3. 焊接装配

装配的目的是防止焊接变形和维持预定的坡口。装配质量对焊接生产率与焊接质量影响很大。一般小尺寸的规则零件，常常采用夹具装配；大尺寸的焊接件一般都采用点固焊缝进行装配。点固焊缝对焊接质量影响很大，所以要特别引起重视。

点固方法可以采用细丝 CO_2 气体保护焊和优质焊条手工电弧焊，但禁止使用薄药皮焊条，因为易生成气孔。使用焊接夹具时，应注意磁偏吹现象。所以夹具的材质、形状、位置及焊接方向等均应注意。

点固焊缝的位置也很重要，应分布在焊缝的背面。如果不可能的话，建议焊一段短焊缝，焊接时此处就不要再焊了。点固焊缝的间距根据母材厚度决定，一般在 200~500 mm 范围内。点固焊缝的长度一般为 30~50 mm。

4. 设备维护

与焊条电弧焊不同的是，CO_2 气体保护焊都是自动焊或半自动焊，所以机械或电气部分出了故障就不能正常工作了。因此，对焊接设备要经常维护，尤其是焊前要重点检查如下几处：

①送丝机构。这是最容易出现故障的地方。应经常检查送丝滚轮压紧力是否合适，焊丝与导电嘴接触是否良好，送丝软管是否通畅。

②焊枪喷嘴的清理。CO_2 气体保护焊的飞溅较大，喷嘴上一般会被溅上许多飞溅金属，这将影响气体的保护效果。应采取一些防止飞溅黏附到喷嘴上的措施，如在喷嘴上涂硅油等。最常规的方法是采用机械清理，但要求喷嘴容易拆卸。

③工作场地要除尘，以便保持继电器或接触器触点的良好接触。如果触点烧损，应立即打磨干净或修复。

任务2：掌握CO_2气体保护焊焊接材料选用原则

CO_2 气体保护焊所用的焊接材料有焊丝和 CO_2 气体。

1. 焊丝的选用

CO_2 气体保护焊具体选用哪一种牌号的焊丝，应根据被焊金属材料的性质、焊接接头设计强度、焊缝质量要求、焊接施工条件（板厚、坡口形状、焊接位置、焊接条件、焊后热处理及焊接操作等）、成本等综合考虑。

焊丝选用要考虑的顺序如下。

（1）根据被焊结构的钢种选择焊丝

对于碳钢及低合金高强钢，主要是按“等强匹配”的原则，选择满足力学性能要求的焊丝。对于耐热钢和耐候钢，主要是侧重考虑焊缝金属与母材化学成分的一致或相似，以满足对耐热性和耐腐蚀性等方面的要求。

（2）根据被焊部件的质量要求（特别是冲击韧性）选择焊丝

与焊接条件、坡口形状、保护气体混合比等工艺条件有关，要在确保焊接接头性能的前提下，选择达到最大焊接效率及降低焊接成本的焊接材料。

(3)根据工件厚度及焊接位置选择焊丝

对应于被焊工件的板厚选择所使用的焊丝直径,确定所使用的电流值,参考各生产厂的产品介绍资料及使用经验,选择适合于焊接位置及使用电流的焊丝牌号。

焊丝的焊接工艺性能包括电弧稳定性、飞溅颗粒大小及数量、脱渣性、焊缝外观与形状等。对于碳钢及低合金钢的焊接(特别是半自动焊),主要是根据焊接工艺性能来选择焊接方法及焊接材料。

CO_2 气体保护焊所用的焊丝直径通常在 0.5~5 mm 范围内,在半自动焊时主要采用细焊丝(直径小于 1.6 mm)。焊丝表面有镀铜和不镀铜两种,镀铜的目的是防止焊丝生锈,有利于焊丝的储存与改善导电性。为了保证焊接质量,焊前必须对焊丝进行除油和除锈。

目前常用的 CO_2 气体保护焊焊丝直径为 0.6 mm、0.8 mm、1.0 mm、1.2 mm、1.6 mm、2.0 mm、2.4 mm 等。焊丝尺寸应保证有均匀的外径,公差为-0.025~0 mm。焊丝应具有一定的硬度和挺度,一方面防止焊丝被送丝滚轮压扁或压出深痕;另一方面要求焊丝从导电嘴送出后应有一定的挺直度。无论是推丝式、拉丝式或是推拉式送丝,都要求焊丝以冷拔状态供应,而不应采用退火焊丝。

2. CO_2 气体的选用

在 CO_2 气体保护焊中,除了自保护焊丝外,无论是实心焊丝还是药芯焊丝,均有一个与保护气体(介质)适当组合的问题。焊接用 CO_2 气体的性质见表 2-3-2。

表 2-3-2　焊接用 CO_2 气体的性质

气体名称	主要特征	在焊接中的应用
CO_2	化学性质稳定,不燃烧、不助燃,在高温时能分解为 CO 和 O_2,对金属有一定氧化性。能液化,流态 CO_2 蒸发时吸收大量热,能凝固成固态 CO_2,俗称干冰	焊接时配焊丝可作为保护气体,如 CO_2 气体保护焊和 CO_2+O_2、CO_2+Ar 等混合气体保护焊

由于 CO_2 气体的强氧化作用,焊丝合金过渡系数降低,熔敷金属成分与焊丝成分产生较大差异。保护气氛中 CO_2 气体所占比例越大,氧化性越强,合金过渡系数越低。因此,采用 CO_2 作为保护气体时,焊丝中必须含有足够量的脱氧合金元素,满足锰(Mn)、硅(Si)联合脱氧的要求,改善焊缝的组织和性能。

任务3:掌握CO_2气体保护焊的工艺参数

1. 工艺参数类别及选择条件

CO_2 气体保护焊通常采用短路过渡及细颗粒过渡工艺,工艺参数主要包括焊丝直径、焊接电流、电弧电压、直流回路电感值、焊接速度、焊丝伸出长度、焊枪角度及气体流量等。

大部分的焊接工艺参数直接影响着焊缝的形状尺寸。对于对接焊缝的尺寸,通常以熔深(H)、熔宽(B)和余高(a)三尺寸表示,熔宽与熔深之比称为焊缝成形系数($\varphi=B/H$),焊缝成形系数 φ 一般为 1.3~2。对于角焊缝尺寸,通常以焊脚(K)和焊喉(h)表示。一般角焊缝的外形要求是等腰三角形,这时焊脚和焊喉的关系是 $K=1.4h$ 或 $h=0.7K$。图 2-3-1 所示为焊缝的尺寸表示。

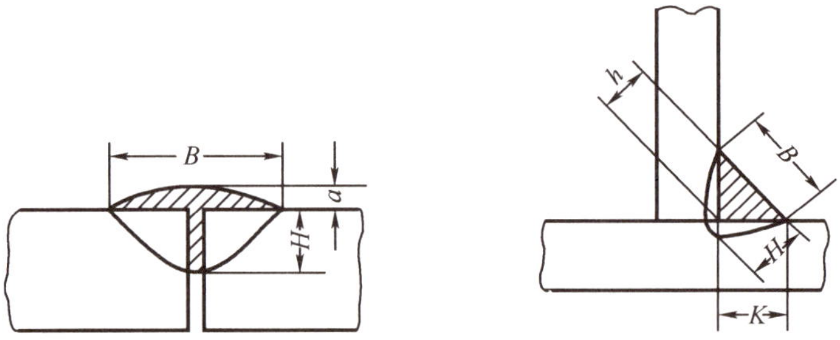

(a)对接焊缝　　(b)角焊缝

图 2-3-1　焊缝的尺寸表示

最佳的焊接工艺参数应满足以下几个条件：

①焊接过程稳定，飞溅最小；

②焊缝外形美观，没有烧穿、咬边、气孔和裂纹等缺陷；

③对两面焊接的焊缝，应保证一定的熔深，使之焊透；

④在保证上述要求的条件下，应具有最高的生产率。

2. 焊丝直径(d)

焊丝直径是一个重要的焊接工艺参数，更换焊丝直径，一则涉及焊接材料的供应，二则操作比较困难(要更换导电嘴、给送轮槽、弹簧软管及调整压力等)。如果生产中使用粗焊丝，则焊接电流相应增大，生产效率高，但焊缝成形较差。如果用同样的电流、电压及焊接速度，而焊丝直径变细，则焊缝的熔宽减小，熔深增大，余高略有提高。

选用焊丝直径主要考虑母材板厚、焊接接头及坡口形式、焊接空间位置(平、立、横、仰)及焊缝尺寸等因素。表 2-3-3 为焊丝直径与母材板厚的关系。

表 2-3-3　焊丝直径和母材板厚的关系　　(单位：mm)

<table>
<tr><th>板厚</th><th>0.6</th><th>0.8</th><th>1.2</th><th>1.6</th><th>2.0</th><th>2.3</th><th>3.2</th><th>4.0</th><th>4.5</th><th>6.0</th><th>9.0</th><th>12.0</th><th>16.0</th><th>20.0</th><th>>20.0</th></tr>
<tr><td rowspan="7">焊丝直径</td><td>0.6</td><td></td><td></td><td></td><td></td><td></td><td></td><td></td><td></td><td></td><td></td><td></td><td></td><td></td><td></td></tr>
<tr><td></td><td colspan="4">0.8</td><td></td><td></td><td></td><td></td><td></td><td></td><td></td><td></td><td></td><td></td></tr>
<tr><td></td><td colspan="7">0.9</td><td></td><td></td><td></td><td></td><td></td><td></td><td></td></tr>
<tr><td></td><td></td><td></td><td colspan="6">1.0</td><td></td><td></td><td></td><td></td><td></td><td></td></tr>
<tr><td></td><td></td><td></td><td></td><td colspan="11">1.2</td></tr>
<tr><td></td><td></td><td></td><td></td><td></td><td></td><td></td><td colspan="8">1.4</td></tr>
<tr><td></td><td></td><td></td><td></td><td></td><td></td><td></td><td></td><td></td><td colspan="6">1.6</td></tr>
</table>

由于 CO_2 气体保护半自动焊受到焊工移位的限制(焊速不能太高)，且焊丝给送速度最大只能达到 15 m/min 左右，因此细直径焊丝的允许焊接电流也是有限的，细直径焊丝用过大的焊接电流会造成熔深大、熔宽小，即焊缝成形系数(φ)过小，易产生气孔和热裂纹。考虑到这一点，通常在 300~500 A 以内的大电流范围焊接时，要使用直径 1.6 mm 焊丝，而直径 1.2 mm 焊丝可以用于 80~350 A 的场合。

另一方面，对于薄板用短路过渡焊接时，焊接电流在 100 A 以下的情况，焊丝直径越细，电弧越稳定，飞溅越小，这是使用直径 1.0 mm 以下焊丝的原因。但是直径 1.0 mm 以下焊丝的合适焊接电流范围比较狭窄，而直径 1.2 mm 和 1.6 mm 的焊丝能适用宽阔的焊接电流范围，工厂生产使用最多的是直径 1.2 mm 焊丝。

3. 焊接电流（I）

焊接电流决定着焊丝的熔化量和母材的熔化量。焊接电流越大，焊丝的熔化量也越多，两者基本上成正比；焊接电流越大，母材的熔化量越多，熔透深度越大。在相同的焊丝直径、电弧电压、焊接速度的条件下，增大焊接电流，母材熔化量会增多，而熔宽增加不多，所以熔深显著增加。同时焊丝熔化量增多，则焊缝的余高有所增加。

焊接电流选择的依据有母材的板厚、焊丝直径、焊缝空间位置、焊接接头及坡口形式，而主要依据是焊丝直径和焊缝空间位置。表 2-3-4 为焊接电流和焊丝直径之间的关系。

表 2-3-4　焊接电流和焊丝直径之间的关系

焊丝直径/mm	许用的焊接电流/A	较佳的焊接电流/A
0.6	30~90	40~70
0.8	50~120	60~100
0.9	60~150	70~120
1.0	70~180	70~120
1.2	80~350	90~180
1.6	110~500	140~200

通常情况下，增大焊接电流的同时，必须提高电弧电压。否则，焊缝的熔深剧增，熔宽略增，形成窄而深的焊缝，即焊缝成形系数（φ）变小，容易产生气孔和热裂纹。

4. 电弧电压（U）

电弧电压就是电弧的两极（焊丝和母材）之间的电压，它也是电弧长度的标志。电弧电压的高低直接影响着电弧稳定、熔滴过渡形式、飞溅及焊缝成形。电弧电压过高，电弧变长，熔滴过渡形式为滴状过渡而不是短路过渡，则电弧摇摆，且会发生大颗粒飞溅；电弧电压过低，电弧加热范围狭窄，熔宽变小，焊缝成形不良。电弧电压合适，短路过渡正常，电弧声音规律，这时的电弧状态是稳定的，飞溅是最小的。

在短路过渡正常的条件下，电弧电压的范围是不大的，约为 17~25 V。如果在这个范围内只增加电弧电压，而焊丝直径、焊接电流、焊接速度不变，这时由于电弧长度拉长，电弧活动范围会增大，即熔宽显著增大。由于焊接电流不变，焊丝熔化量近乎不变，熔敷金属量也不变，结果是由于熔宽增大而引起余高减小。关于熔深问题，分两种情况，在 21 V 以内，增大电弧电压（$d=1.2$ mm，$I=150$ A，$v=40$ cm/min），由于电弧热量增加，而引起熔深增大；超过 21 V 后，增大电弧电压，由于电弧拉长而使热利用率降低和熔宽增大，熔深反而减小。

根据前述可知，增大焊接电流同时，应适当增大电弧电压，即电压和电流匹配，其关系式为

$$I<250\ \text{A},\ U=(0.04I+16)\pm1.5\ \text{V}$$

$$I>250\ \text{A},\ U=(0.04I+20)\pm1.5\ \text{V}$$

例如：焊接电流 $I=150$ A，电弧电压 $U=0.04\times150+16=22$ V。

值得指出的是焊机上电压的读数是指焊接电源端输出的电压。输出电压（$U_{出}$）减去两

焊接电缆(接焊枪电缆和接焊件电缆)的电阻电压降,才等于电弧电压。例如,焊机输出电压表读数为21 V,而电弧电压仅有20.5 V,其中0.5 V为焊接电缆电阻电压降。如果焊接电缆加长,则电阻电压降还要增大。操作时电弧电压是否适合,要根据电弧的稳定性确定。

5. 电感(L)

在输出的焊接回路中,串接一个可调节的电感,一则可以调节短路电流增长速度,以实现电弧的稳定和飞溅的减小;二则可以调节短路过渡工作周期中的电弧燃烧时间,控制热量的分布以适应不同板厚焊件的需要。

焊接回路中的电感要根据焊丝直径、焊接电流及电弧电压来选定,表2-3-5为不同焊丝直径可选的电感。从表中可看出,细焊丝选用的电感小(短路频率高,短路电流增长速度快)。实际上可用的电感有一个相当大的范围。

表2-3-5　电感和焊丝直径

焊丝直径/mm	0.6	0.8	1.0	1.2
电感/mH	0.02~0.23	0.04~0.30	0.08~0.40	0.08~0.50

应当说明的是,当用不同类型的焊接电源时,其调节电感方法不完全相同,所选用的电感也可不一样。还有焊机通常不标明电感,所以焊工调节电感时,主要靠观察飞溅和焊缝成形情况,以及听电弧声音来判断。电弧声音柔和清晰连续而不夹杂,飞溅小,则可以认为电感是合适的。

6. 焊接速度(v)

焊接速度对焊缝的成形和焊接接头的性能都有很大的影响。在确定的焊丝直径、焊接电流及电弧电压条件下,加快焊接速度,单位长度焊接接头吸收电弧的热量减少,使熔深减小,熔宽也变窄;同时单位长度焊接接头上焊丝熔敷量减少,焊缝余高也有所减小,甚至会形成"蛇形"焊道,如图2-3-2所示。如果焊接速度过慢,会产生烧穿、焊瘤、咬边等缺陷。

选择焊接速度前,应先根据母材厚度、接头和坡口形式、焊缝空间位置对焊接电流和电弧电压进行调整,达到电弧稳定燃烧的要求,然后考虑焊道截面大小来选择焊接速度。焊道截面小,焊接速度要大;反之,焊速慢。CO_2气体保护半自动焊是手工操作的,当焊速小于0.25~0.3 cm/s时,因为焊工用手移动焊枪,易发生颤动,很难稳定匀速。当焊速大于1~1.3 cm/s时,用手移动焊枪难以对准焊缝线。随着焊速的增大,合适的电弧电压范围变小,并且会产生大颗粒飞溅和咬边,这时需要增大前倾角和降低电弧电压求得一些改善。CO_2气体保护半自动焊合适的焊接速度为0.5~1 cm/s。

7. 焊丝伸出长度($l_{伸}$)

焊丝伸出长度就是导电嘴末端至焊丝末端之间的距离,它和喷嘴至母材的距离有很密切的关系,如图2-3-3所示。抬高喷嘴,即使喷嘴和母材之间的距离增大,焊丝伸出长度也随之增大。

焊丝伸出长度也是焊丝进入电弧前的通电长度,对焊丝起着预热作用。所以在同一焊接电流情况下,如果焊丝伸出的长度较长,则焊丝预热作用大,熔化加快,导致焊丝熔化量增多。从另一个角度来说,焊丝给送速度一定时,如果焊丝伸出长度变长,则必须使用较小的焊接电流。

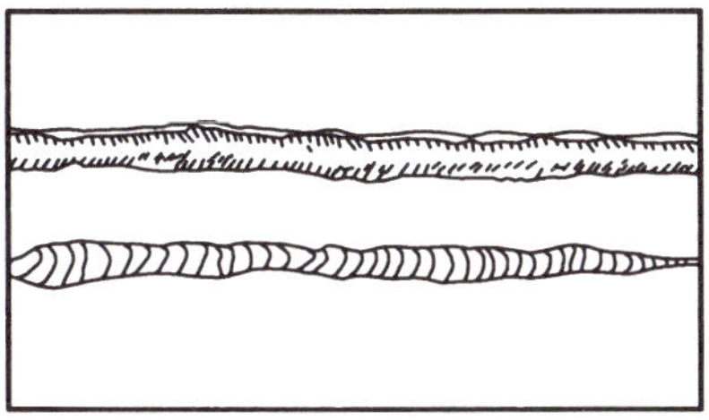

图 2-3-2　高速焊形成的“蛇形”焊道

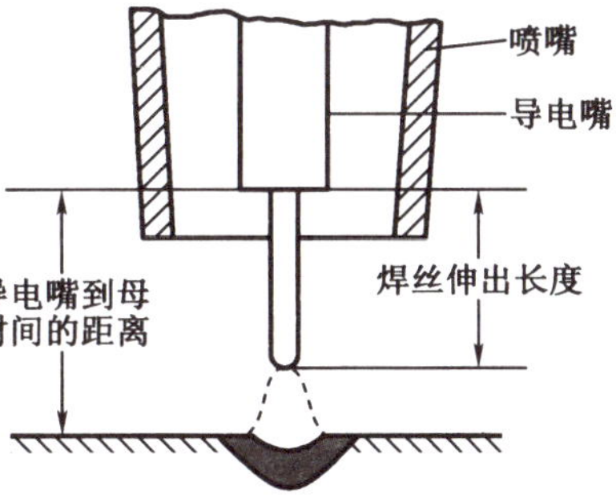

图 2-3-3　焊丝伸出长度

焊丝伸出长度对焊缝成形有较大的影响，如图 2-3-4 所示。焊丝伸出长度增加(其他焊接工艺参数不变)，使得焊丝刚性减小，易左右摇摆，引起电弧加热宽度增大，即熔宽增大，同时使熔深减小，余高也减小。过大的焊丝伸出长度，会使焊丝过热而成段熔断，飞溅也增大。同时焊丝伸出长度增大后，喷嘴和工件间的距离也增大，气体保护效果变差。过小的焊丝伸出长度，势必减小喷嘴和工件间的距离，这使得焊工观察电弧困难，喷嘴易被飞溅金属堵塞，如果操作不稳定，还会使得焊丝插入熔池中，使得电弧燃烧不稳定。

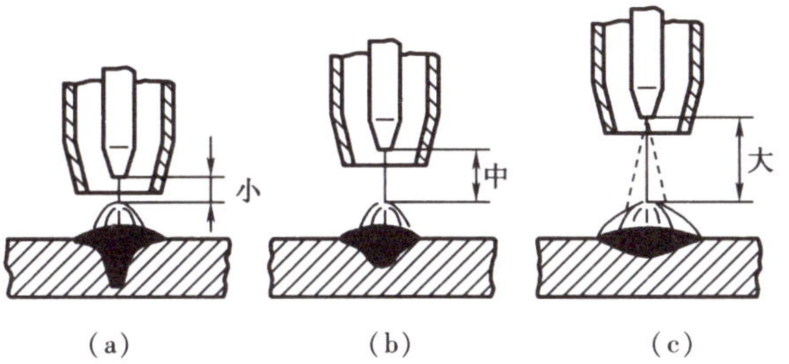

图 2-3-4　焊丝伸出长度对焊缝成形的影响

正常的焊丝伸出长度一般为焊丝直径的 10～12 倍，即 $l_{伸}\approx(10\sim12)d$。如果焊丝金属的电阻率高(如不锈钢焊丝)，预热作用强，这时应考虑选用较小的焊丝伸出长度。不同的材料，不同直径的焊丝，允许使用的焊丝伸出长度可参阅表 2-3-6。还有，当焊接电流增大时，即焊丝给送速度增大，这样焊丝的预热时间($l_{伸}/v_{给}$)也相应缩短，于是可以考虑增大焊丝伸出长度，图 2-3-5 所示为焊丝伸出长度和焊接电流之间的关系。

表 2-3-6　不同材料的焊丝伸出长度　(单位：mm)

焊丝直径	焊丝伸出长度	
	低合金钢焊丝 H08Mn2SiA	不锈钢焊丝 H06Cr19Ni9Ti
0.8	6～12	5～9
1.0	7～13	6～11
1.2	8～15	7～12

8. 焊枪倾角(θ)

大多数焊工是右手握焊枪操作的，而焊接方向可以向左或向右。CO_2 气体保护焊有两种方法操作：左焊法[图 2-3-6(a)]和右焊法[图 2-3-6(b)]。右焊法实际上是焊枪向焊接方向倾斜一个角度,又称后倾焊法;左焊法是焊枪向焊接方向相反方向倾斜一个角度,又称前倾焊法。

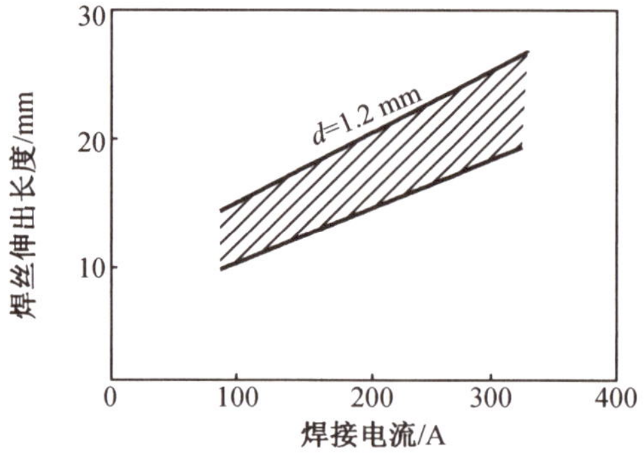

图 2-3-5 焊丝伸出长度和焊接电流之间的关系

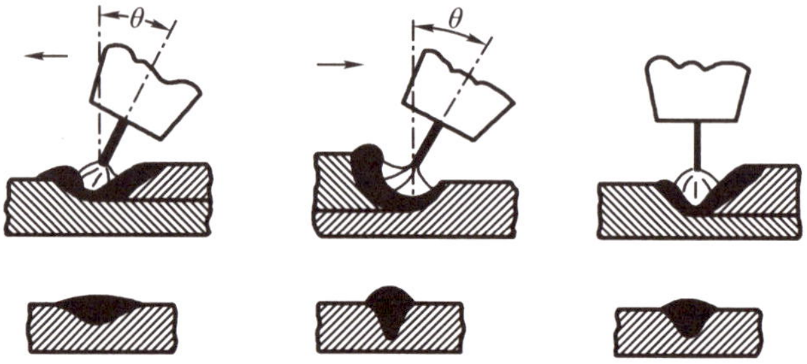

(a)左焊法 (b)右焊法 (c)无倾角

图 2-3-6 左焊法和右焊法对焊缝成形的影响

右焊法,由于电弧吹力将弧坑内的液体金属吹开,电弧可以进一步深入熔化母材,所以熔深增加,但熔宽减小。左焊法,电弧吹力作用使液体金属流向前方,这些液体金属阻碍了电弧进一步熔化母材,所以熔深浅,而熔宽大。右焊法和左焊法的比较见表 2-3-7。

表 2-3-7 右焊法和左焊法的比较

比较项目	右焊法	左焊法
焊道外形	余高大,形成窄焊道	余高小,形成较平坦的焊道
熔深	大	小
飞溅	小	大
小电流(100 A 以下)时的电弧稳定性	较稳定	略差些
接缝线可见度	接缝线被喷嘴所遮,可见度差	接缝线可见,焊丝能准确对准接缝

进行 CO_2 气体保护焊时,一般以左焊法为宜,而在焊接比较深的坡口时,左焊法难以保证焊透,这时就需要采用右焊法。

左焊法的倾角通常为 10°~20°,倾角过大易产生未焊透及严重飞溅。右焊法的倾角也是 10°~20°为宜,倾角过大时会使焊道变凸,甚至产生咬边,且飞溅也显著增加。

9. 保护气体流量(Q)

保护气体流量要确保良好的保护电弧和熔池的效果。气体保护效果不好,会产生大颗粒飞溅,电弧不稳定,焊缝易产生气孔。造成气体保护效果差的主要原因(图 2-3-7)有:①风的影响;②气体流量不足;③喷嘴和母材的距离太大;④气体流量过大造成紊流而使空气侵入;⑤喷嘴黏附飞溅等。其中风的影响最为严重,当风速超过 1.5 m/s 时,保护效果变差,影响焊接质量。

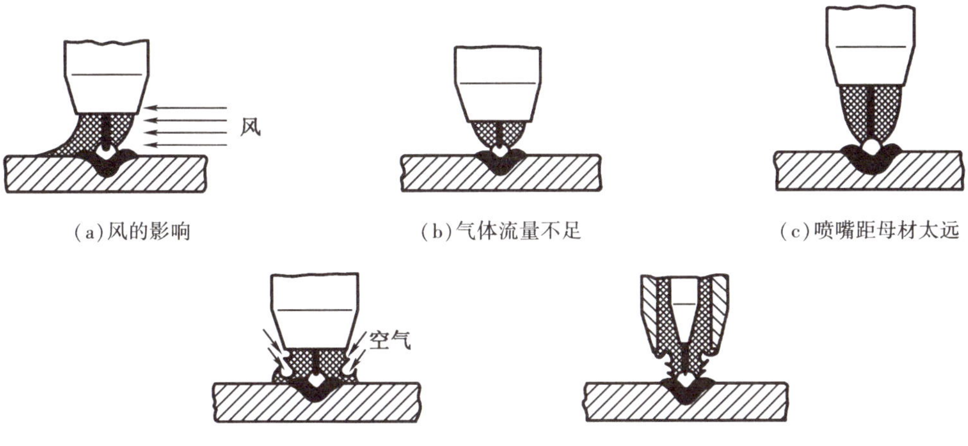

图 2-3-7　造成气体保护效果差的原因

在用电流 200 A 以下焊接薄板时,保护气体流量通常选 10~15 L/min;当室外风速较大时,应使用挡风装置,并加大保护气体流量。如果焊速加快,或焊丝伸出长度增大,则也应适当加大气体流量。

上述 CO_2 气体保护焊接工艺参数,其中大多数工艺参数对焊缝成形有较大的影响。当其中单项工艺参数变动时,对焊缝成形尺寸的影响见表 2-3-8。

表 2-3-8　各焊接工艺参数单项变动时对焊缝成形尺寸的影响

焊接工艺参数	d↑	I↑	U↑		v↑	$l_{伸}$↑
			<21 V	>21 V		
熔深	↓	↑↑	↑	↓	↓	↓
熔高	↑	↑	↑↑	↑↑	↓	↑
余高	↓	↑	↓	↓	↓	↓

注:↑增大;↓减小;↑↑显著增加。

除了焊接工艺参数对焊接质量有较大的影响外,还有电源外特性(它不是一个物理量,不能称为参数)也影响到电弧的稳定性及焊缝的熔深等。细丝 CO_2 气体保护焊普遍采用的是直流反接,即焊丝接正极,焊件接负极。这时电弧的稳定性比直流正接好,且飞溅较小(熔滴受到极点压力小),熔深大,焊缝含氢量低。相反,采用直流正接时(焊丝接负,焊件接正),焊丝的熔化系数大为提高,约为直流反接时的 1.6 倍,而熔深浅,飞溅增大。利用这个特点,直流正接用于堆焊、铸铁补焊和大电流高速 CO_2 气体保护焊。这对修补工作有利,并能提高生产率。

任务4:掌握CO_2气体保护焊常见缺陷及控制措施

1. 气孔

焊接开始前,必须正确地调整好保护气体的流量,使保护气体能均匀地、充分地保护好焊接熔池,防止空气渗入。如果保护不良,将使焊缝中产生气孔。引起保护不良的原因如下:

①CO_2 气体纯度低。含水或含氮气较多,特别是含水量太高时,整条焊缝上都有气孔。

②水冷式焊枪漏水。焊枪里面漏水,最容易产生气孔。

③没有保护气。焊前未打开 CO_2 气瓶上的高压阀或预热器未接通电源,就开始焊接。因为没有保护气,整条焊缝上都是气孔。

④有风。在保护气体流量合适时,因风较大,可将保护气体吹离熔池,保护不好,引起气孔,如图 2-3-8 所示。

⑤气体流量不合适。气体流量太小时,因保护区小,不能可靠地保护熔池(图 2-3-9);气体流量太大时产生涡流,将空气卷入保护区(图 2-3-10)。因此,气体流量不适宜会使焊缝中产生气孔。

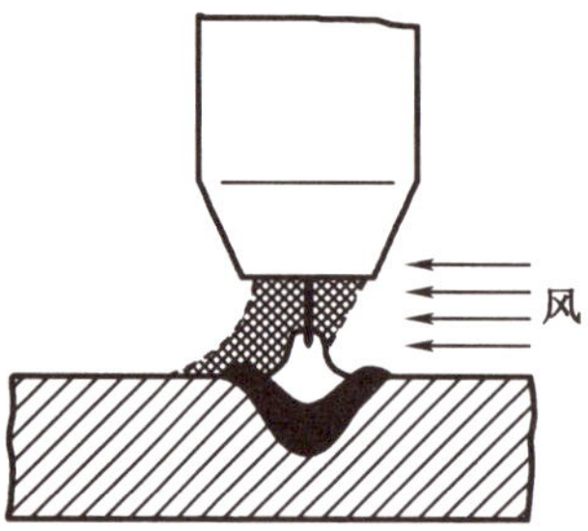

图 2-3-8　风的影响

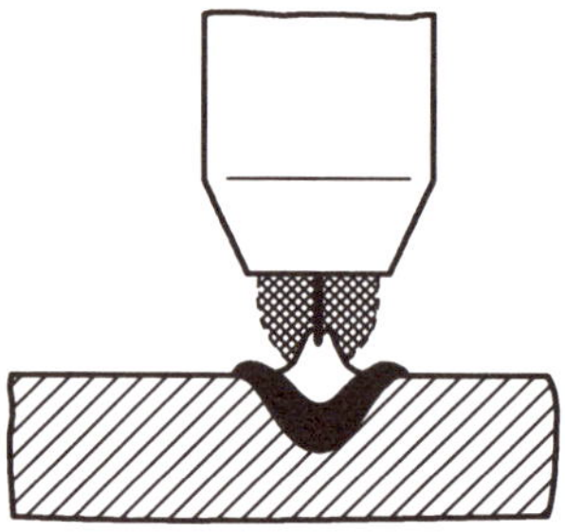

图 2-3-9　保护气流量太小

⑥喷嘴被飞溅堵塞。如图 2-3-11 所示,焊接过程中,喷射到喷嘴上的飞溅未及时除去,使保护气产生涡流,也会吸入空气,使焊缝产生气孔。焊接过程中必须经常清除喷嘴上的飞溅,并防止损坏喷嘴内圆的表面粗糙度。为便于清除飞溅,焊前最好在喷嘴的内表面喷一层防飞溅喷剂或涂一层硅油。

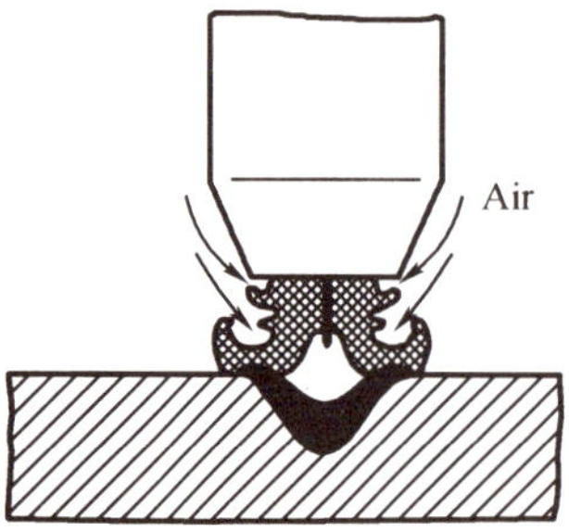

图 2-3-10　保护气流量太大

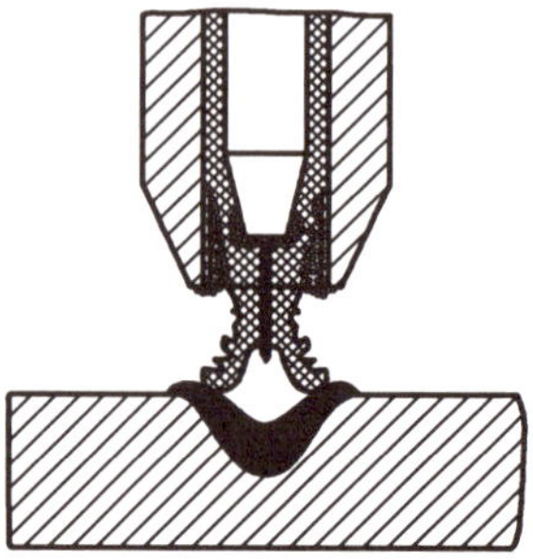

图 2-3-11　喷嘴被飞溅堵塞

⑦焊枪倾角太大。焊枪倾角太大(图 2-3-12)也会吸入空气,使焊缝中产生气孔。

⑧焊丝伸出长度太大或喷嘴位置太高。焊丝伸出长度太大或喷嘴位置太高时,保护效果不好,容易引起气孔,如图 2-3-13 所示。

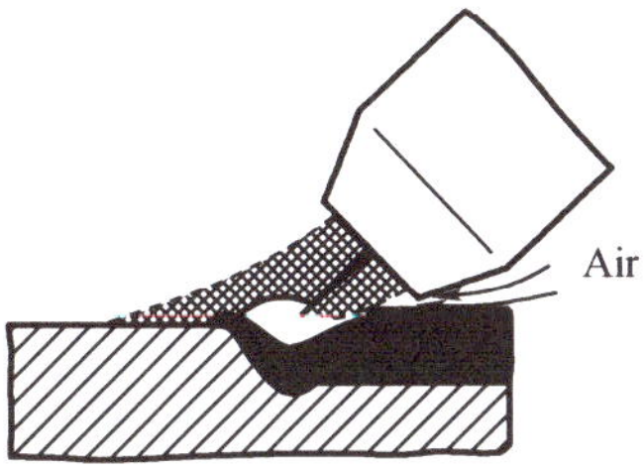

图 2-3-12　焊枪倾角太大

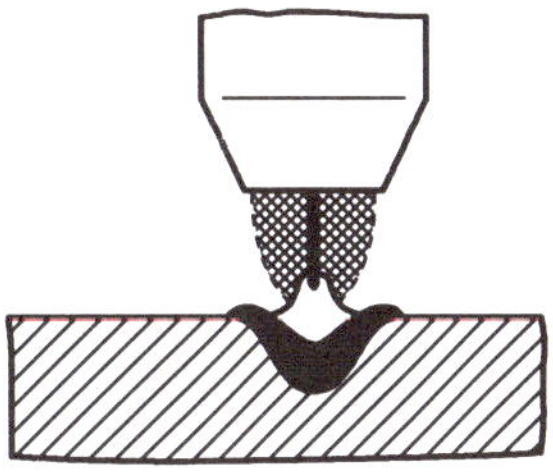

图 2-3-13　焊丝伸出长度太大

⑨弹簧软管内孔堵塞。弹簧软管内孔因被氧化皮或其他脏物堵塞,其前半段密封塑胶管破裂或进丝嘴处的密封圈漏气,保护气从焊枪的进口处外泄,使喷嘴处的保护气体流量减小,这也是产生气孔的重要原因之一。在这种情况下,往往能听到送丝机焊枪的连接处漏气的嘶嘶声,通常在整条焊缝上都是气孔,焊接时还可看到熔池中冒泡。

2. 未焊透

(1)坡口加工或装配不当

坡口太小、钝边太大、间隙太小、错边量太大都会引起未焊透,如图 2-3-14 所示。为防止未熔合,坡口角度以 40°~60°为宜。

(a)坡口太小

(b)钝边太大或间隙太小

(c)错边大

图 2-3-14　坡口加工或装配不当引起的未焊透

(2)打底焊道不好

打底焊道凸起太高,易引起未熔合,如图 2-3-15 所示。故打底时应控制焊枪的摆动幅度,保证打底焊道与两侧坡口面熔合好,才能覆盖好焊缝表面。

(a)　(b)

图 2-3-15　打底焊道引起的未熔合

(3)接头不好

接头处如果未修磨或引弧不当,易产生未熔合,如图 2-3-16 所示。为保证焊缝接头质量,要求将接头打磨成斜面,在最高处引弧并连续焊下去。

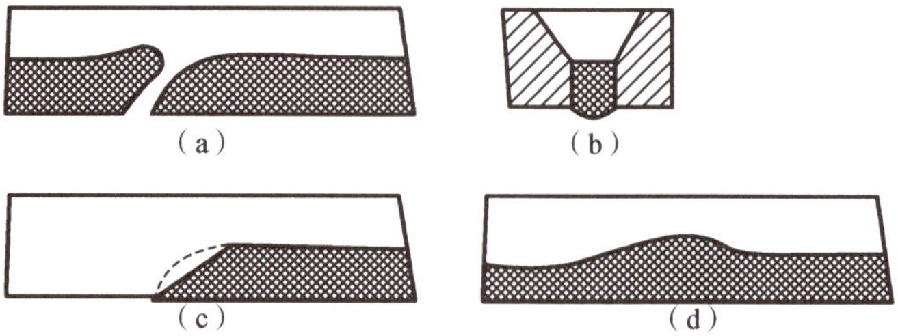

图 2-3-16　接头处的未熔合

(4)焊接参数不合适

平焊时,焊接速度太小,焊接电流过大,使熔敷系数过大,或焊枪的倾角 α 太大都会引起未焊透,如图 2-3-17、图 2-3-18、图 2-3-19 所示。为防止未焊透,必须根据熔合情况调整焊接速度,保证电弧位于熔池前部。

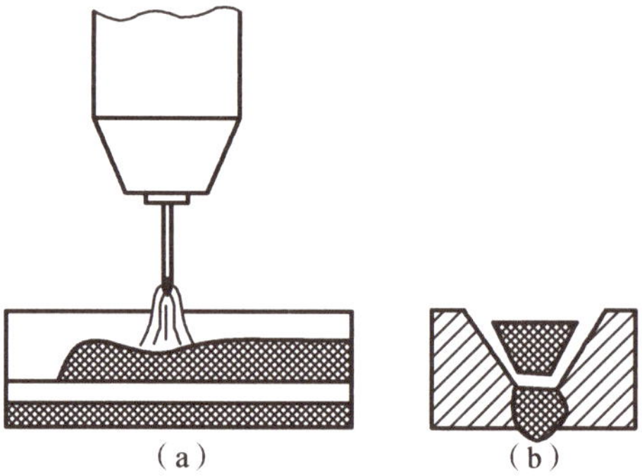

图 2-3-17　平焊时焊速太小或熔敷系数过大

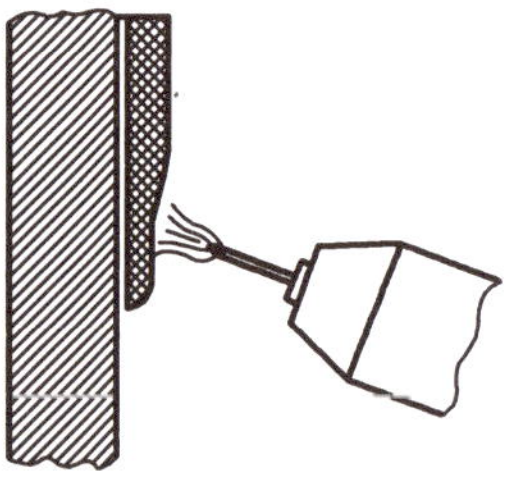

图 2-3-18　向下立焊时的未焊透

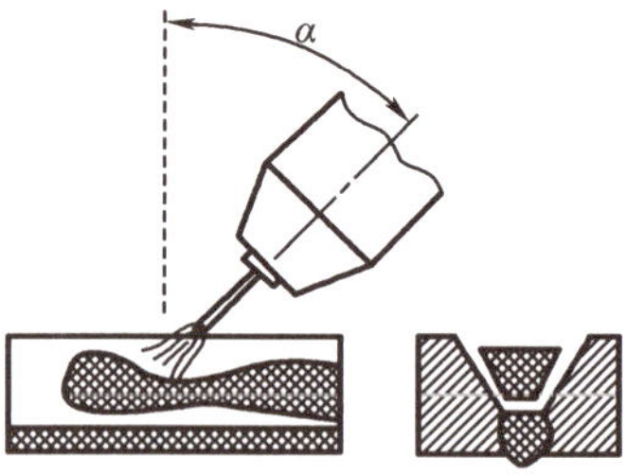

图 2-3-19　焊枪前倾角太大引起的未焊透

(5)电弧位置不对

电弧未对准坡口中心,或焊枪摆动时电弧偏向坡口的一侧,都会引起未焊透,如图 2-3-20 和图 2-3-21 所示。

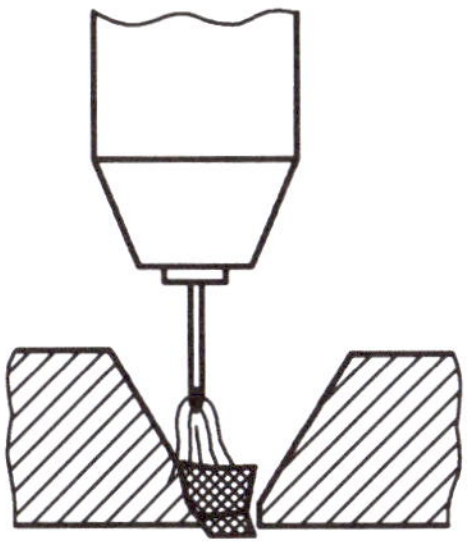

图 2-3-20 电弧未对中

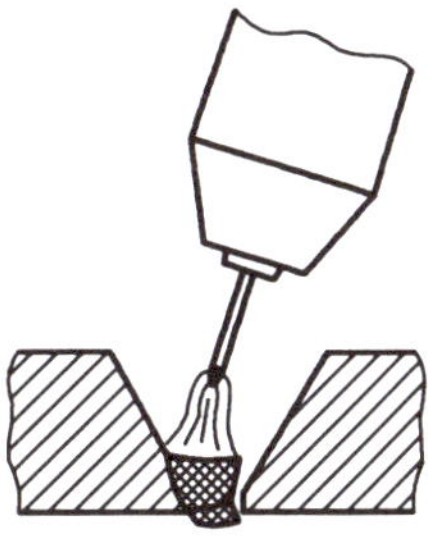

图 2-3-21 焊枪偏向一边

(6)位置限制

由于结构限制,使电弧不能对中或达不到坡口边缘,也会引起未焊透,如图 2-3-22 所示。

图 2-3-22 结构限制

任务考核

1. 焊丝的干伸长度应为焊丝直径的(　　)倍。

A. 2　　B. 5　　C. 8　　D. 10

2. 细丝 CO_2 焊普遍采用(　　)。

A. 直流反接　　B. 直流正接　　C. 交流反接　　D. 交流正接

3. CO_2 气体保护焊熔滴过渡产生飞溅有(　　)种形式。

A. 1　　B. 2　　C. 3　　D. 4

4. 采用(　　)可以减少飞溅。

A. 直流正接　　B. 直流反接　　C. 交流正接　　D. 交流反接

5. CO_2 气体保护焊正常飞溅率一般为(　　),当飞溅率达到 30%以上时就不能进行正常焊接了。

A. 5%~10%　　B. 10%~15%　　C. 15%~20%　　D. 20%~25%

6. CO_2 焊短路过渡时,当选择的焊丝直径为 0.8 mm 时,其适宜的焊接电压和焊接电流为(　　)。

A. 17~19 V, 30~70 A　　B. 18~21 V, 50~100 A

C. 19~23 V, 90~200 A　　D. 22~26 V, 140~300 A

7. CO_2 焊细滴过渡时,当选择的焊丝直径为 1.2 mm 时,其焊接电流下限为(　　)。

A. 300 A　　B. 400 A　　C. 500 A　　D. 650 A

8. 短路过渡焊接常用焊丝直径为(　　)mm。

A. 0.2~0.6　　B. 0.4~0.8　　C. 0.6~1.2　　D. 1.2~2.0

9. CO_2 焊短路过渡在采用(　　)时形成的。

A. 粗焊丝、小电流和低电压　　B. 细焊丝、小电流和低电压

C. 细焊丝、大电流和低电压　　D. 细焊丝、大电流和高电流

10. CO_2 焊时，当焊接电流和电弧电压(　　)短路过渡的条件时，会出现颗粒状过渡形式。

A. 低于　　B. 高于　　C. 低于一定值的　　D. 高于一定值的

Project Ⅲ CO_2 Gas Shielded Welding Process

【Learning Objectives】

1. Master the preparation process requirements before CO_2 gas shielded welding;
2. Master the principles of selecting welding materials for CO_2 gas shielded welding;
3. Master the process parameters of CO_2 gas shielded welding;
4. Master the common defects and control measures of CO_2 gas shielded welding.

The welding process of CO_2 gas shielded arc welding involves the design and selection of both pre-welding preparation and process parameters.

Task 1:Master the Preparation Process Requirements before CO_2 Gas Shielded Welding

Preparation for CO_2 gas shielded welding includes the following steps: Joint and groove design, groove processing, joint cleaning, welding assembly, adjustment, and maintenance of tooling and welding equipment.

1. Groove design

During the transition of fine particles in CO_2 gas shielded welding, the arc penetration force is strong, the fusion depth is large, and it is easy to burn through. Therefore, strict requirements are placed on the assembly quality before welding. The welding groove can be made smaller, and the root face can be appropriately larger. Generally, the gap between butt joints should not exceed 2 mm. If a welding wire with a diameter of 1.6 mm is used, the root face size can be expanded to 4-6 mm, and the groove angle can be reduced to approximately 45°.

In the case of short-circuit transfer, the fusion depth is shallow and the groove cannot be designed according to the specification for fine particle transfer. It is generally permissible to have a smaller or even no root face. At this time, the molten pool is small and the bridging performance is good. If it is a butt joint, a clearance of 3 mm is allowed. A larger clearance will not result in burn through, and the upper and lower misalignment of the root is allowed to be ±1 mm.

When using fine particle droplet transfer welding for fillet welds, considering its penetration characteristics, the leg can be reduced by 10%-20% compared to shielded metal arc welding. Refer to Table 2-3-1 for the dimensions of leg in different plate thicknesses. This further enhances the efficiency of CO_2 gas shielded welding and reduces material consumption.

Table 2-3-1 Dimensions of Weld Leg with Different Plate Thickness (Unit: mm)

Welding method	Plate thickness			
	6	9	12	16
CO_2 gas shielded welding	5	6	7.5	10
Shielded metal arc welding	6	7	8.5	11

2. Joint preparation

The welding groove can be processed by cutting, edging, and gas cutting. Oil, rust, and moisture near the groove of the welding wire and welded workpiece should be carefully removed before welding assembly. Special attention should be given to the tack-welding seam, as accumulated water can lead to porosity. It is preferable to preheat with a gas flame before welding to eliminate moisture.

For rust prevention, many steel plates are coated with paint. These paints may not necessarily need to be removed, depending on their impact on welding quality. Coatings that have an impact must be removed, while coatings that have no impact (such as primer) may be left as is.

3. Welding and assembly

The purpose of assembly is to prevent welding deformation and maintain the predetermined groove. The quality of assembly has a significant impact on welding productivity and welding quality. Generally, small-sized regular parts are often assembled using fixtures, while large-sized weldments are usually assembled by tack welding. The tack weld has a significant influence on welding quality, so it requires special attention.

Fine wire CO_2 gas shielded welding and high-quality electrode manual arc welding can be used for spot welding, but thin coating electrodes are prohibited because they tend to generate pores. When using welding jigs, attention should be paid to the phenomenon of magnetic deflection blow. Therefore, the material, shape, position, and welding direction of the fixture should all be taken into consideration.

The positioning of tack welds is also crucial and should be located on the reverse side of the weld. If this is not feasible, it is recommended to weld a short section and refrain from further welding at that point during the process. The spacing between tack welds is determined based on the thickness of the base metal, typically within the range of 200-500 mm. The length of tack welds is generally between 30-50 mm.

4. Equipment maintenance

Different from shielded metal arc welding, CO_2 gas shielded welding is automatic or semi-automatic welding, so it cannot function properly if there is a mechanical or electrical failure.

Therefore, it is necessary to frequently maintain the welding equipment, especially focusing on the following areas before welding:

①Wire feeding mechanism. It is the most prone to failure. Frequently check whether the pressing force of the wire feeding roller is appropriate, whether the contact between the welding wire and the current contact nozzle is good, and whether the wire feeding hose is unobstructed.

②Cleaning the welding gun nozzle. The spattering in CO_2 gas shielded welding is relatively high, and a significant amount of splatter metal is usually splashed onto the nozzle, which will affect the effectiveness of the gas shielding. Measures should be taken to prevent splatters from adhering to the nozzle, such as applying silicone oil onto it. The most common method is mechanical cleaning, but it requires the nozzles to be easily detachable.

③Dust removal should be carried out at the workplace. Please refine the machine-translated phrase so as to maintain good contact of relay or contactor contacts. If the contact is burnt, it shall be polished or repaired immediately.

Task 2:Master the Principles of Selectiing Welding Materials for CO_2 Gas Shielded Welding

The welding materials used for CO_2 gas shielded welding are welding wire and CO_2 gas.

1. Selection of welding wire

The selection of a specific brand of welding wire for CO_2 gas shielded welding should be comprehensively considered based on the nature of the welded metal material, design strength of the welded joint, weld quality requirements, welding construction conditions (plate thickness, groove shape, welding position, welding condition, post-weld heat treatment, and welding operation, etc.), cost, etc.

The order to consider for selecting welding wires is as follows.

(1) The selection of welding wire shall be based on the steel type of the welded structure

For carbon steel and low-alloy high-strength steel, the principle of "equal strength matching" is primarily employed to choose welding wire that meets the mechanical property requirements. For heat-resistant steel and weathering steel, emphasis is mainly placed on the consistency or similarity of chemical composition between the weld metal and base metal to meet the requirements for heat resistance and corrosion resistance.

(2) Welding wire shall be selected according to the quality requirements of welded parts (especially impact toughness)

It is related to welding conditions, groove shape, shielding gas mixing ratio, and other process conditions. On the premise of ensuring the performance of welded joints, select welding materials that achieve maximum welding efficiency and reduce welding costs.

(3) Select welding wire according to the thickness of the workpiece and welding position

Choose the diameter of welding wire that corresponds to the plate thickness of the welded workpiece, determine the current value to be used, and refer to the product introduction data and usage experience of each manufacturer to select the appropriate grade of welding wire for the welding position and current used.

The welding process performance of electrodes and rods includes arc stability, size and quantity of splatter particles, slag removal, weld appearance and shape, etc. For the welding of carbon steel and low alloy steel (especially semi-automatic welding), the choice of welding method and materials mainly depends on the welding process performance.

The diameter of welding wire used in CO_2 gas shielded welding is typically within the range of 0.5-5 mm. Fine welding wires (with a diameter less than 1.6 mm) are mainly utilized in semi-automatic welding. There are two types of welding wire surfaces: Copper-plated and non-copper-plated. Copper plating serves the purpose of preventing rusting of the welding wire, making it easier to store and improving its conductivity. To ensure welding quality, it is necessary to remove oil and rust before welding.

The commonly used diameters for CO_2 gas shielded welding wires are: 0.6 mm, 0.8 mm, 1.0 mm, 1.2 mm, 1.6 mm, 2.0 mm, 2.4 mm, etc. The welding wire should have a uniform outer diameter with a tolerance of -0.025-0 mm. The welding wire should have a certain level of hardness and stiffness. On one hand, it is required to prevent the welding wire from being flattened or leaving deep marks due to the wire feeding roller. On the other hand, the welding wire should remain straight after being discharged from the contact nozzle. Whether it is push wire, pull wire, or push-pull wire feeding, the welding wires should be supplied in a cold drawn state instead of annealed wires.

2. Selection of CO_2 gas

In CO_2 gas shielded welding, apart from self-shielded wire, there is a challenge of ensuring proper compatibility with the shielding gas (medium) for both solid wire and flux cored wire. Refer to Table 2-3-2 for the characteristics of CO_2 gas used for welding.

Table 2-3-2 Properties of CO_2 Gas for Welding

Gasname	Keyfeatures	Application in welding
CO_2	It possesses stable chemical properties, does not burn or support combustion, can decompose into CO and O_2 at high temperatures, and exhibits certain oxidizing properties towards metals. It can be liquefied. Gaseous CO_2 absorbs a substantial amount of heat upon evaporating and solidifies into solid carbon dioxide, commonly known as dry ice	Welding wire can be used as a shielding gas during welding, such as CO_2 gas shielding welding and mixed gas shielding welding with CO_2+O_2 and CO_2+Ar

Due to the strong oxidizing effect of CO_2 gas, the alloy transfer coefficient of the welding wire decreases, resulting in significant differences in the composition between the deposited metal and the welding wire. The higher the proportion of CO_2 in the protective atmosphere, the greater the oxidizing ability and the lower the alloy transfer coefficient. Therefore, when using CO_2 as the shielding gas, the welding wire must contain sufficient deoxidizing alloying elements to meet the requirements of combined deoxidization of manganese (Mn) and silicon (Si), and to improve the structure and performance of the welds.

Task 3: Master the Process Parameters of CO_2 Gas Shielded Welding

1. Process parameter category and selection conditions

CO_2 gas shielded welding typically employs the short-circuit transition and fine particle transition processes. The main process parameters include: Welding wire diameter, welding current, arc voltage, DC circuit inductance value, welding speed, welding wire extension length, welding gun angle, and gas flow rate, etc.

Most of the welding process parameters directly affect the shape and size of welds. For the size of butt welds, it is usually expressed using three dimensions: Penetration (H), width (B), and reinforcement (a). The ratio of width to penetration is called the weld form coefficient ($\varphi = B/H$), which is generally between 1.3 and 2. As for fillet weld sizes, they are typically represented by the leg (K) and throat (h). Generally, fillet welds are required to have an isosceles triangle shape. In this case, the relationship between the leg and throat of the weld is: $K=1.4h$ or $h=0.7K$. Fig. 2-3-1 illustrates the dimensional representation of welds.

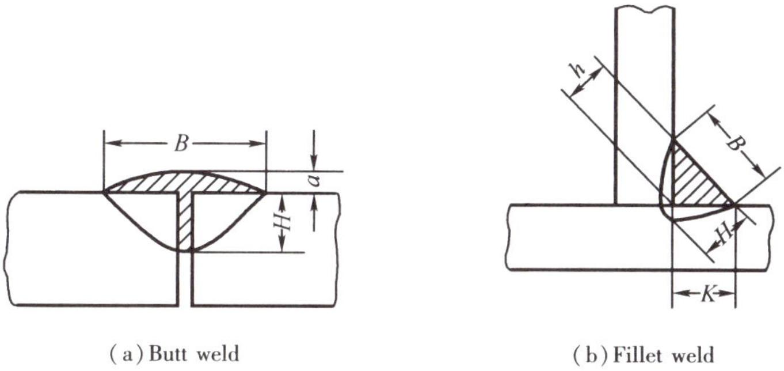

Fig. 2-3-1 Representation of Weld Dimensions

The optimal welding process parameters should meet the following conditions:

①The welding process is stable with minimal splattering;

②The weld appearance should be aesthetically pleasing and free from defects such as burn-through, undercut, pores, and cracks;

③For welds made on both sides, a certain level of fusion depth should be ensured to achieve complete penetration;

④While ensuring the above requirements, it should have the highest productivity.

2. Wire diameter (d)

The diameter of the welding wire is an essential welding process parameter. Changing the diameter of the welding wire involves two steps: First, it requires the supply of welding materials, and second, it can be challenging to modify the diameter of the welding wire (by replacing the contact tube, feed pulley groove, spring hose, and adjusting pressure). If thick welding wire is used during production, the welding current will increase proportionally, resulting in high production efficiency but poor weld formation. When the same current, voltage, and welding speed are used, and the electrode and rod diameter become thinner, the weld width decreases, the penetration increases, and there is a slight increase in excess weld metal.

When selecting the diameter of welding wire, factors such as base metal plate thickness, welded joint and groove form, welding position (flat, vertical, horizontal, and overhead), and weld size should primarily be considered. Table 2-3-3 illustrates the correlation between welding wire diameter and base metal plate thickness.

Table 2-3-3 Relationship between Welding Wire Diameter and Base Metal Plate Thickness (Unit: mm)

<table>
<tr><th>Plate thickness</th><th>0.6</th><th>0.8</th><th>1.2</th><th>1.6</th><th>2.0</th><th>2.3</th><th>3.2</th><th>4.0</th><th>4.5</th><th>6.0</th><th>9.0</th><th>12.0</th><th>16.0</th><th>20.0</th><th>>20.0</th></tr>
<tr><td rowspan="7">Wire diameter</td><td>0.6</td><td></td><td></td><td></td><td></td><td></td><td></td><td></td><td></td><td></td><td></td><td></td><td></td><td></td><td></td></tr>
<tr><td></td><td colspan="4">0.8</td><td></td><td></td><td></td><td></td><td></td><td></td><td></td><td></td><td></td><td></td></tr>
<tr><td></td><td colspan="7">0.9</td><td></td><td></td><td></td><td></td><td></td><td></td><td></td></tr>
<tr><td></td><td></td><td></td><td colspan="6">1.0</td><td></td><td></td><td></td><td></td><td></td><td></td></tr>
<tr><td></td><td></td><td></td><td></td><td colspan="11">1.2</td></tr>
<tr><td></td><td></td><td></td><td></td><td></td><td></td><td></td><td colspan="8">1.4</td></tr>
<tr><td></td><td></td><td></td><td></td><td></td><td></td><td></td><td></td><td></td><td colspan="6">1.6</td></tr>
</table>

Due to the limitation of welder displacement (the welding speed cannot be too high) in CO_2 gas shielded semi-automatic welding, and the maximum wire feeding speed can only reach about 15 m/min, the allowable welding current for thin-diameter electrodes and rods is also limited. Excessive welding current for thin-diameter electrodes and rods will result in a large fusion depth and small fusion width, meaning that the weld form coefficient (φ) is too small, which is prone to pores and thermal cracks. Considering this, a welding wire with a diameter of 1.6 mm is usually used for welding within a large current range of 300-500 A, and a welding wire with a diameter of 1.2 mm can be used for currents ranging from 80-350 A.

On the other hand, in short-circuit transfer welding of thin plates, when the welding current is below 100 A, the smaller the wire diameter, the more stable the arc and the less spatter. This is why a wire with a diameter of 1.0 mm or less is used. However, the suitable welding current range for wires with a diameter below 1.0 mm is relatively narrow, while wires with a diameter of 1.2 mm and 1.6 mm can be used in a wide range of welding currents. Among them, the most widely used in factory production is the wire with a diameter of 1.2 mm.

3. Welding current (I)

The welding current determines the amount of welding wire and base metal that melts. The higher the welding current, the more the electrode and rod will melt, which is essentially in direct proportion. Additionally, the higher the welding current, the more the base metal will melt, resulting in greater penetration depth. Under the same conditions of welding wire diameter, arc voltage, and welding speed, increasing the welding current will increase the amount of base metal melting, while the weld width will not increase significantly. As a result, the penetration depth increases significantly. Furthermore, when the amount of welding wire melting increases, the surplus height of the weld joint also increases.

The selection of welding current is based on the plate thickness of the base metal, electrode diameter, weld spatial position, welded joint, and groove form, primarily focusing on electrode diameter and weld spatial position. Table 2-3-4 presents the correlation between welding current and electrode diameter.

Table 2-3-4 Relationship between Welding Current and Wire Diameter

Wire diameter/mm	Allowable welding current/A	Optimal welding current/A
0.6	30-90	40-70
0.8	50-120	60-100
0.9	60-150	70-120
1.0	70-180	70-120
1.2	80-350	90-180
1.6	110-500	140-200

Generally, while increasing the welding current, the arc voltage must be increased. Otherwise, the weld penetration will significantly increase, and the weld width will slightly increase, resulting in a narrow and deep weld. This will cause the weld formation coefficient (φ) to decrease, making it prone to the generation of pores and hot cracks.

4. Arc voltage (U)

Arc voltage is the voltage between the two poles of an arc (welding wire and base metal), which also indicates the length of the arc. The arc voltage directly affects arc stability, droplet transition form, splashing, and weld formation. If the arc voltage is too high, the arc will elongate and droplet transition rather than short-circuit transition will occur, causing the arc to swing and large particles to splash. If the arc voltage is too low, the heating range of the arc will be narrow, resulting in a smaller weld width and poor weld formation. Appropriate arc voltage ensures normal short-circuit transition and regular arc sound. At this point, the arc state is stable, and splashing is minimized.

Under normal short-circuiting transfer conditions, the arc voltage range is small, approximately 17-25 V. If only the arc voltage is increased within this range, while the diameter of the welding wire, welding current, and welding speed remain unchanged, the active range of the arc will increase due to the extended arc length, resulting in a significant increase in weld width. Since the welding current remains unchanged, the amount of electrode and rod melting is almost unchanged, as is the amount of deposited metal. Consequently, the weld reinforcement decreases due to the increased weld width. The penetration can be divided into two cases. If the arc voltage (d=1.2 mm, I=150 A, v=40 cm/min) is increased within 21 V, the penetration will increase due to the increase in arc heat. If the arc voltage exceeds 21 V, the penetration will decrease due to the reduction in heat utilization rate and the increase in weld width caused by arc elongation.

It can be seen from the above that while increasing the welding current, the arc voltage should be appropriately increased, i. e. the voltage and current should be matched, and their relational expression are

$$I<250\ \text{A}, U=(0.04I+16)\pm1.5\ \text{V}$$

$$I>250\ \text{A}, U=(0.04I+20)\pm1.5\ \text{V}$$

For example: Welding current I=150 A, arc voltage $U=0.04\times150+16=22$ V.

It should be noted that the voltage reading on the welding machine refers to the output voltage of the welding power supply terminal. The arc voltage is equal to the output voltage (U_{out}) minus the resistance voltage drop of two welding cables (welding gun cable and weldment cable). For example, if the output voltage meter reading of the welding machine is 21 V, the arc voltage is only 20.5 V, with 0.5 V being the resistance voltage drop of the welding cable. If the welding cable is lengthened, the resistance voltage drop will increase. The suitability of the arc voltage during operation depends on the stability of the arc.

5. Inductance (L)

In the welding circuit output, an adjustable inductor is connected in series. It serves two purposes: Firstly, it can regulate the growth rate of short-circuit current in order to achieve arc stability and reduce spattering; secondly, it can adjust the burning time of the arc during the short-circuit transition working cycle and control the distribution of heat to meet the requirements of welded joints with varying plate thicknesses.

The selection of inductance in the welding circuit should be based on the diameter of electrodes and rods, welding current, and arc voltage. Table 2-3-5 presents the available inductance options for different electrode and rod diameters. It can be observed from the table that the inductance for fine welding wire is small (resulting in high short-circuit frequency and rapid growth of short-circuit current). There is a considerable range of practically feasible inductance values.

Table 2-3-5 Inductance and Welding Wire Diameter

Wire Diameter/mm	0.6	0.8	1.0	1.2
Inductance/mH	0.02-0.23	0.04-0.30	0.08-0.40	0.08-0.50

It should be noted that when different types of welding power sources are used, the methods for adjusting inductance are not exactly the same, and the selected inductance may also be different. Additionally, the welder typically does not indicate the inductance value. Therefore, when the welder adjusts the inductance value, they primarily rely on observing the spatter and weld formation, as well as listening to the arc sound. If the arc sound is soft, clear, and continuous without inclusions, and the spatter is minimal, it can be considered that the inductance is appropriate.

6. Welding Speed (v)

The welding speed has a significant impact on the shape of welds and the performance of welded joints. When the welding speed is increased under specific conditions of welding wire diameter, welding current, and arc voltage, the heat absorbed by the electric arc per unit length of the welded joint decreases, resulting in reduced penetration and narrower weld width. Additionally, the deposited amount of welding wire on the welded joint per unit length decreases, leading to a decrease in excess weld metal height and even the formation of a "snake-shaped" weld bead, as shown in Fig. 2-3-2. On the other hand, if the welding speed is too slow, defects such as burn-through and weld beading may occur, as well as undercut defects.

Before selecting the welding speed, the welding current and arc voltage should be adjusted according to the thickness of the base metal, joint and groove form, and weld spatial position in order to meet the requirements of stable arc combustion. Then, the welding speed should be selected by considering the size of the pass section. If the weld pass section is small, the welding speed should be high; otherwise, the welding speed should be slow. CO_2 gas shielded semi-automatic welding is manually operated. When the welding speed is less than 0.25-0.3 cm/s, it is difficult to maintain a constant speed because the welder moves the arc welding gun by hand, which can cause vibrations. When the welding speed is greater than 1-1.3 cm/s, it is difficult to align the welding gun with the weld line by hand. As the welding speed increases, the suitable arc voltage range decreases, and there may be splashing and undercutting of large particles. In such cases, it is necessary to increase the rake angle and reduce the arc voltage for some improvement. The suitable welding speed for semi-automatic CO_2 gas shielded arc welding is 0.5-1 cm/s.

7. Length of wire extension for welding (l_{ext})

The extension length of the welding wire refers to the distance between the end of the contact tube and the end of the welding wire. This distance is closely related to the distance from the nozzle to the base metal, as shown in Fig. 2-3-3. When the nozzle is raised, i.e. when the distance between the nozzle and the base metal increases, the extension length of the welding wire also increases.

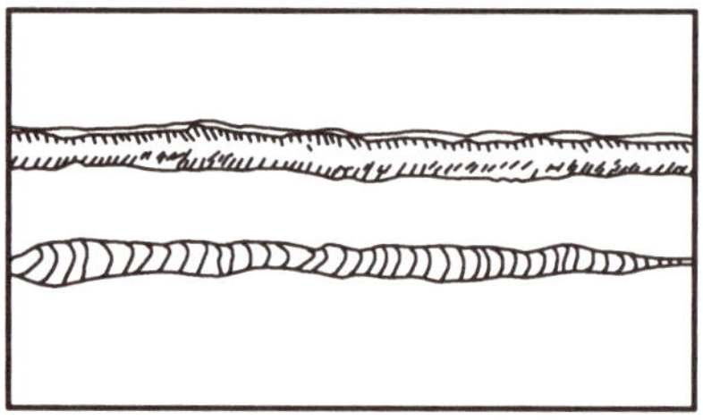

Fig. 2-3-2 "Serpentine" Weld Bead Formed by High-speed Welding

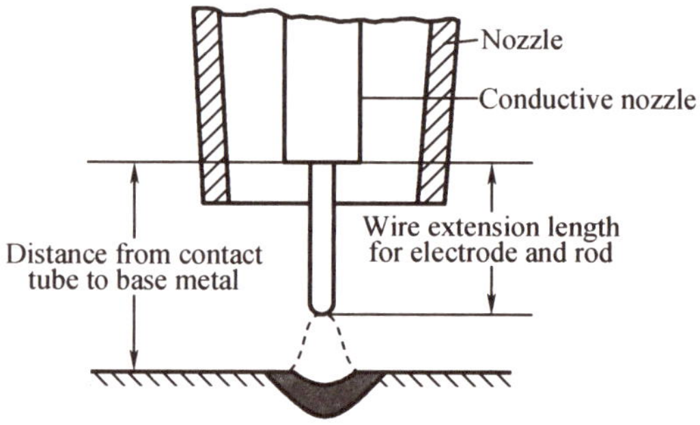

Fig. 2-3-3 Welding Wire Extension Length

The length of the wire extension is also the length energized before the wire enters the arc, which serves as a preheating function for the wire. Therefore, under the same welding current, if the electrode and rod protrude longer, the preheating effect of the electrode and rod will be greater, leading to accelerated melting and increased melting amount of the electrode and rod. From another perspective, when the wire feeding speed remains constant, a smaller welding current must be used if the wire extension length becomes longer.

The extension length of the welding wire has a significant impact on the formation of the weld, as illustrated in Fig. 2-3-4. Increasing the extension length of the welding wire (with other welding process parameters unchanged) reduces the stiffness of the wire, causing it to sway from side to side easily. This leads to an increase in arc heating width, i. e., the width of the fusion zone, while the penetration and excess weld metal decrease. Excessive extension length of the welding wire can cause overheating and fusion into sections, as well as an increase in spattering. Additionally, when the extension length of the welding wire increases, the distance between the nozzle and the workpiece also increases, resulting in poor gas protection effect. Conversely, if the extension length of the welding wire is too small, it will inevitably reduce the distance between the nozzle and the workpiece, making it difficult for welders to observe the arc. The nozzle is more likely to be blocked by spattered metal. Furthermore, unstable operation can cause the welding wire to be inserted into the molten pool, resulting in unstable arc combustion.

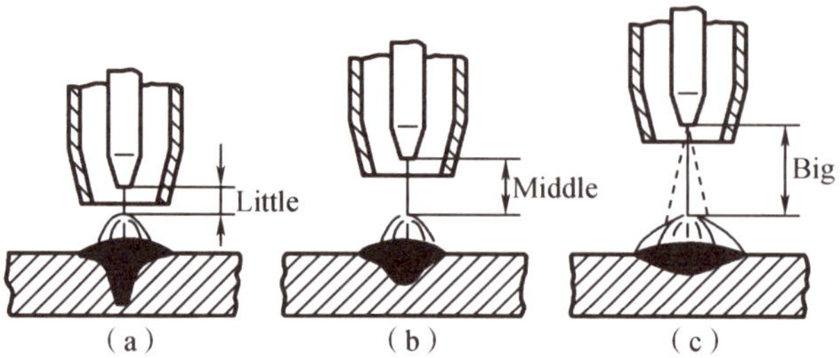

Fig. 2-3-4 Impact of Weld Wire Extension Length on Weld Formation

The normal extension length of electrodes and rods is generally considered to be 10–12 times the diameter of the electrode and rod, $l_{ext} \approx (10-12)d$. If the resistivity of the welding wire metal is high (such as stainless steel welding wire) and there is a strong preheating effect, a smaller extension length of the welding wire should be considered. The allowable extension length of electrodes and rods for different materials and diameters can be found in Table 2-3-6. Additionally, when the welding current increases, meaning the wire feeding speed increases, the preheating time (l_{ext}/v_{feed}) of the electrode and rod will also be shortened accordingly. Therefore, it can be considered to increase the extension length of the electrode and rod, as shown in Fig. 2-3-5.

Table 2-3-6 Extension Length of Electrodes and Rods for Different Materials Unit: (mm)

Wirediameter	Extension length of electrodes	
	Low alloy steel welding wire H08Mn2SiA	Stainless steel welding wire H06Cr19Ni9Ti
0.8	6–12	5–9
1.0	7–13	6–11
1.2	8–15	7–12

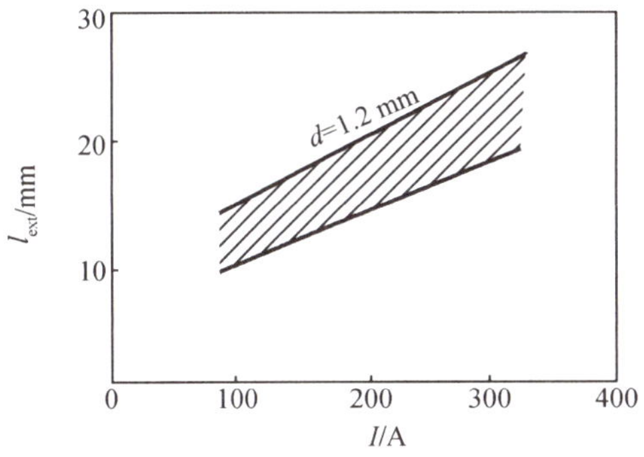

Fig. 2-3-5 Relationship between Welding Wire Extension Length and Welding Current

8. Welding gun inclination angle (θ)

Most welders operate with the welding gun held in their right hand, and the welding direction can be either left or right. There are two methods of CO_2 gas shielded welding: The left welding method [Fig. 2-3-6(a)] and the right welding method [Fig. 2-3-6(b)]. The right welding method involves tilting the arc welding gun at an angle towards the welding direction, also known as backward welding. The left welding method, on the other hand, involves tilting the arc welding gun at an angle opposite to the welding direction, also known as forward inclined welding.

For right welding, the liquid metal in the arc crater is blown away by the force of the arc blowing, allowing the arc to penetrate further and melt the base metal. As a result, the penetration increases but the width decreases. For left welding, the arc blowing force causes the liquid metal to flow forward. These liquid metals hinder the arc from further melting the base metal, resulting in shallow fusion depth and large fusion width. Refer to Table 2-3-7 for a comparison between right welding and left welding.

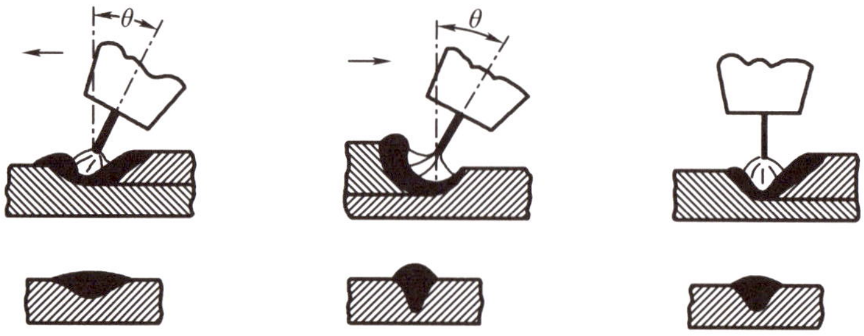

(a) Left welding (b) Right welding (c) No tilt angle

Fig. 2-3-6 Influence of Left Welding and Right Welding on Weld Formation

Table 2-3-7 Comparison between Right Welding and Left Welding

Comparison items	Right welding	Left welding
Weld bead profile	Large reinforcement, forming narrow weld bead	The reinforcement is small, forming a relatively flat weld bead
Deep fusion	Large	Little
Splash	Little	Large
Arc stability at low current (below 100 A)	Relatively stable	A little worse
Visible seam line	The stitching line is concealed by the nozzle, leading to limited visibility	The seam line is visible, and the welding wire can be accurately aligned with the joint

For CO_2 gas shielded welding, the left welding method is preferred. However, when welding a deep groove, it is difficult to ensure penetration with the left welding method, so the right welding method should be used.

The inclination angle for left welding is usually 10° - 20°. If the inclination angle is too large, insufficient penetration and significant spattering may occur. The inclination angle for right welding should also be 10°-20°. If the inclination angle is too large, the weld bead will become convex, potentially leading to undercutting and a significant increase in spattering.

9. Shielding gas flow (Q)

The flow rate of shielding gas should ensure a good protective arc and molten pool effect. If the gas protection effect is not good, it will result in large particles splashing, unstable arc, and easily formed pores in the welds. The main reasons for poor gas protection effect (Fig. 2-3-7) include: ①influence of wind; ②insufficient gas flow; ③excessive distance between nozzle and base metal; ④air intrusion due to turbulence caused by excessive gas flow; ⑤adhesion and splashing of nozzle, etc. The impact of wind is the most severe. When the wind speed exceeds 1.5 m/s, the protection effect becomes poor and affects the welding quality.

When welding thin plates with a current below 200 A, the recommended flow rate of protective gas is usually 10-15 L/min. In case of high outdoor wind speed, a wind shield should be used and the flow rate of protective gas increased before welding. If the welding speed is increased or the extension length of the electrode and rod is increased, the gas flow rate should also be appropriately increased.

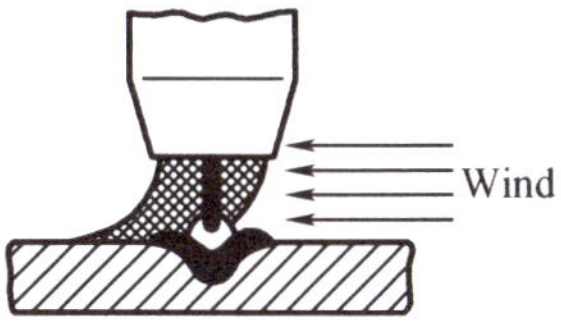

(a) Wind influence

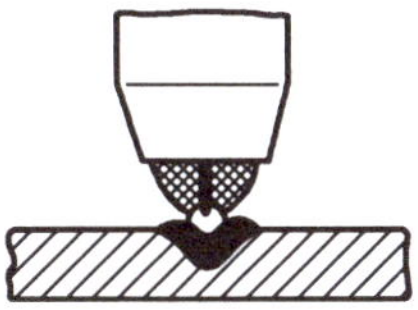

(b) Flow rate too small

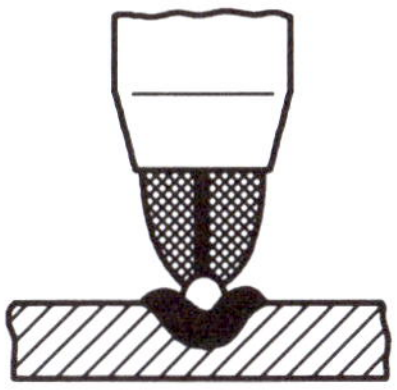

(c) Nozzle too far from base metal

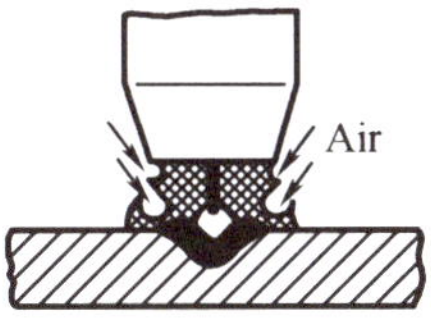

(d) Excessive flow rate

(e) Nozzle adhesion and splashing

Fig. 2-3-7 Reasons for Inadequate Gas Protection

Among these several CO_2 gas shielded welding process parameters, most of them have a significant influence on the formation of weld seams. Please refer to Table 2-3-8 for the impact of individual process parameter changes on the size of weld formation.

Table 2-3-8 The Impact of Individual Changes in Welding Procedure Parameters on the Shape and Size of Welds

Welding process parameters	d↑	I↑	U↑		v↑	l_{ext}↑
			<21 V	>21 V		
Deep fusion	↓	↑↑	↑	↓	↓	↓
Fusion height	↑	↑	↑↑	↑↑	↓	↑
Reinforcement	↓	↑	↓	↓	↓	↓

Note: ↑ increased; ↓ decreased; ↑↑ substantially increased.

In addition to the significant impact of welding process parameters on welding quality, there are also external characteristics of the power supply (which is not a physical quantity and cannot be referred to as a parameter) that also affect arc stability and weld penetration. Fine wire CO_2 gas shielded welding commonly employs direct current reverse polarity, where the welding wire is connected to the positive electrode and the workpiece is connected to the negative electrode. In this case, the arc stability is better than that of direct current straight electrode, resulting in less spatter (with lower pressure on droplets), greater penetration depth, and lower hydrogen content in the weld. Conversely, when DC positive polarity is adopted (welding wire connected to the negative electrode and workpiece connected to the positive electrode), the melting coefficient of the welding wire significantly increases, about 1.6 times higher than that of DC negative polarity.

However, shallow penetration depth and increased spatter are observed in this case. Utilizing this characteristic, direct current positive polarity is used for surfacing welding, cast iron repair welding, and high-current high-speed CO_2 gas shielded welding. This is advantageous for repair work and enhances productivity.

Task 4:Master the Common Defects and Control Measures in CO_2 Gas Shielded Welding

Before starting the welding process, the flow rate of the protective gas must be correctly adjusted to ensure that the welding pool is evenly and fully protected, preventing any air infiltration. Insufficient protection can result in the formation of porosity in the weld. The reasons for inadequate protection are as follows:

①Low purity of CO_2 gas. When there is a high amount of water or nitrogen, especially when the water content is too high, there are gas pores throughout the entire weld.

②Water leakage of water-cooled welding torch. Leakage inside the welding gun is most likely to cause gas pockets.

③No protective gas. Before welding, the high-pressure valve on the CO_2 cylinder must not be opened, nor should the preheater be powered on. If there is no shielding gas, the entire weld will be filled with pores.

④Windy. When the flow rate of the protective gas is appropriate, it can be blown away from the molten pool due to strong wind, resulting in poor protection and the formation of pores, as shown in Fig. 2-3-8.

⑤Incorrect gas flow. When the flow rate is too low, the small protection area cannot reliably shield the molten pool (Fig. 2-3-9); when the flow rate is too high, vortex will be generated and air will be drawn into the protection area (Fig. 2-3-10). Hence, improper gas flow can lead to the formation of weld porosity.

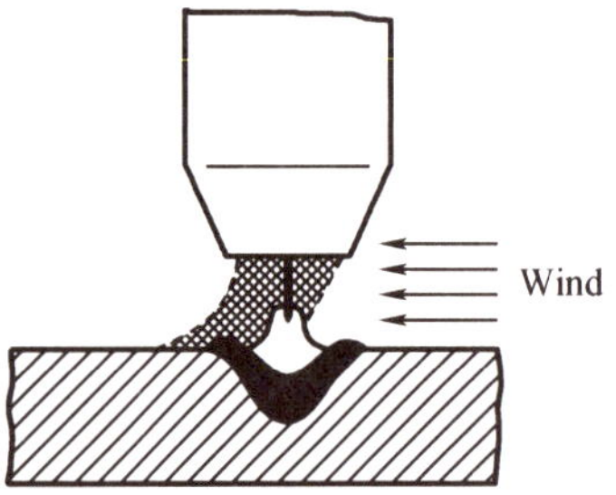

Fig. 2-3-8 Wind Influence

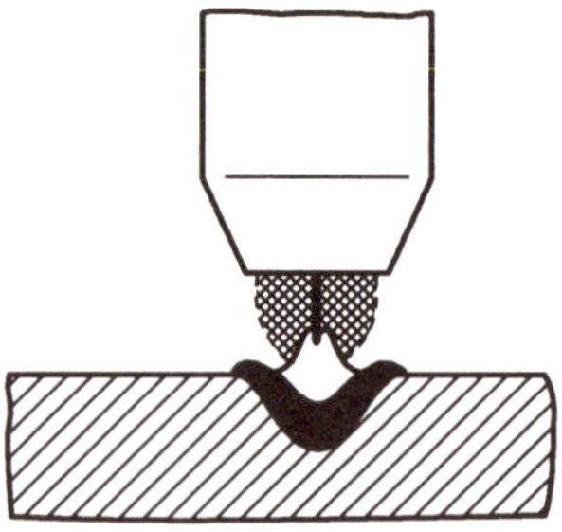

Fig. 2-3-9 Insufficient Protective Gas Flow

⑥The nozzle is obstructed by splashing. As shown in Fig. 2-3-11, during the welding process, if the spatter sprayed on the nozzle is not removed promptly, it will result in vortex formation of the shielding gas, which may also draw in air and cause pores in the weld joint. It is necessary to frequently remove the spatter on the nozzle during welding and prevent damage to the surface roughness of the inner circle of the nozzle. To facilitate the removal of spatter, it is recommended to spray a layer of anti-splash spray or apply a coat of silicone oil on the inner surface of the nozzle before welding.

⑦The welding gun tilt angle is too large. If the welding gun is inclined at too steep an angle (Fig. 2-3-12), air will also be drawn in, resulting in porosity in the weld.

⑧The wire extension length is too large or the nozzle position is too high. When the extension length of the welding wire is too long or the nozzle position is too high, inadequate protection can easily result in the formation of pores, as illustrated in Fig. 2-3-13.

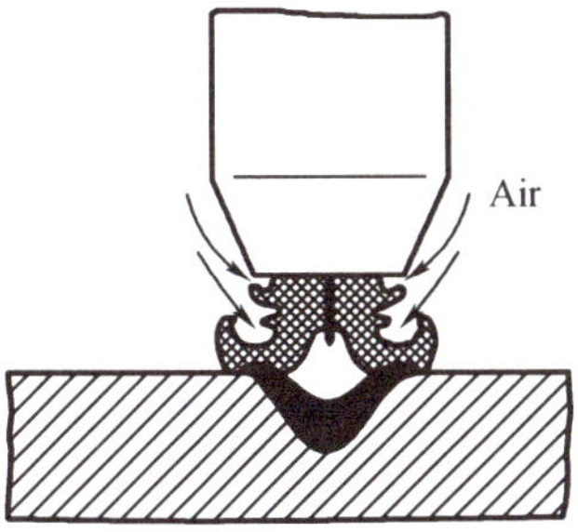

Fig. 2-3-10 Excessive Gas Flow for Protection

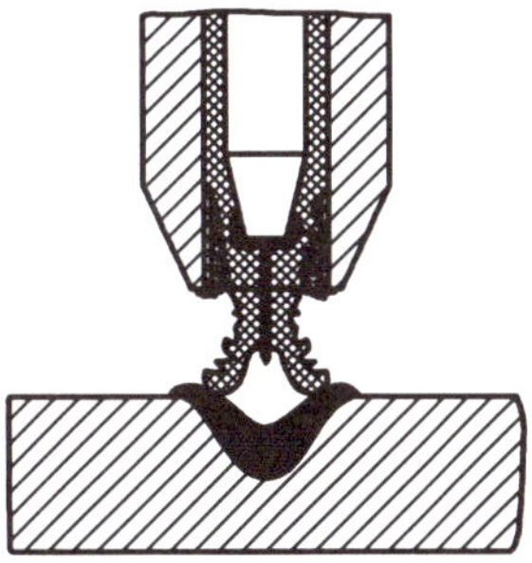

Fig. 2-3-11 Nozzle Blocked by Splashing

Fig. 2-3-12 Excessive Inclination Angle of Welding Gun

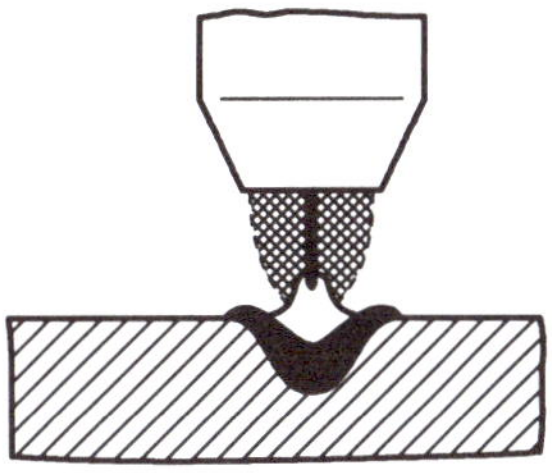

Fig. 2-3-13 Excessive Protruding Length of Welding Wire

⑨The inner hole of the spring hose is blocked. The inner hole of the spring hose is blocked by oxide skin or other dirt, and the sealing plastic tube in its front half section is broken or the sealing ring at the wire inlet nozzle leaks air, resulting in the leakage of protective gas from the welding gun's inlet. This reduces the flow rate of protective gas at the nozzle, which is also one of the important reasons for the formation of pores. In this case, you can often hear the hiss of air leakage at the joint of the wire feeder welding gun. Usually, there are pores throughout the weld, and bubbling can also be observed in the molten pool during welding.

2. Insufficient penetration

(1) Improper groove preparation or assembly

Too small bevel, too large blunt edge, too small gap, and too large misalignment will result in incomplete penetration, as shown in Fig. 2-3-14. To prevent incomplete fusion, the bevel angle should be 40°-60°.

(2) Bad bottom weld

The bulge of the backing weld bead is too high, which can easily cause incomplete fusion, as shown in Fig. 2-3-15. Therefore, the swing amplitude of the welding gun should be controlled during backing to ensure proper fusion between the backing weld pass and the groove surfaces on both sides, covering the weld surface.

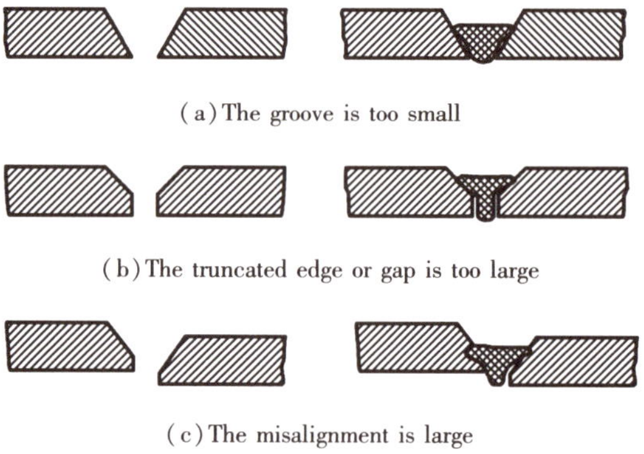

Fig. 2-3-14 Incomplete Welding Penetration Caused by Improper Groove Processing or Assembly

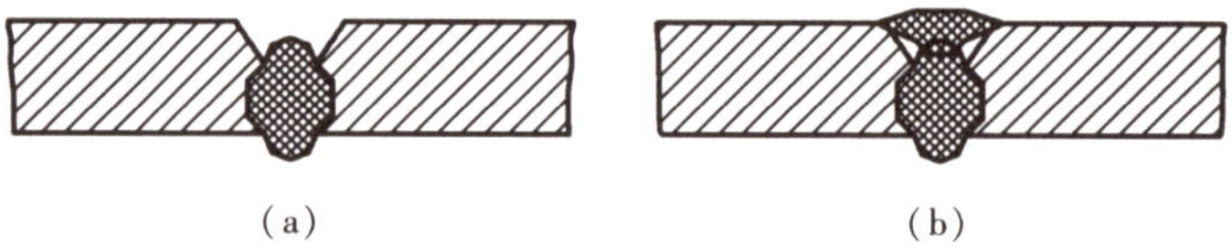

Fig. 2-3-15 Incomplete Fusion Caused by Underlying Weld Bead

(3) The joint is not good

If the joint is not polished or the arc strike is improper, incomplete fusion may occur at the joint as shown in Fig. 2-3-16. To ensure the quality of welded joints, it is necessary to polish the joints into inclined planes, strike the arc at the highest point, and continuously weld them.

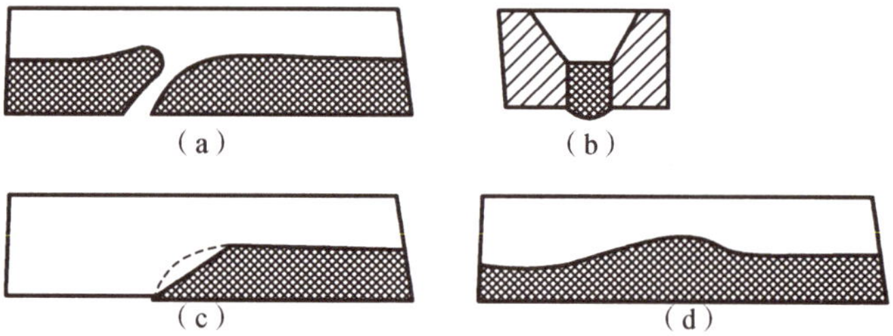

Fig. 2-3-16 Incomplete Fusion at Joints

(4) Improper welding parameters

In the case of flat welding, incomplete penetration can be caused by insufficient welding speed, excessive welding current, excessive deposition coefficient, or excessive inclination angle a of the arc welding gun, as illustrated in Fig. 2-3-17, Fig. 2-3-18, and Fig. 2-3-19. To prevent incomplete penetration, it is necessary to adjust the welding speed based on the fusion condition, ensuring that the arc is positioned at the front of the weld pool.

(5) Incorrect arc position

Incomplete penetration may occur if the arc is not aligned with the groove center or if it deviates to one side of the groove when the welding gun swings, as illustrated in Fig. 2-3-20 and Fig. 2-3-21.

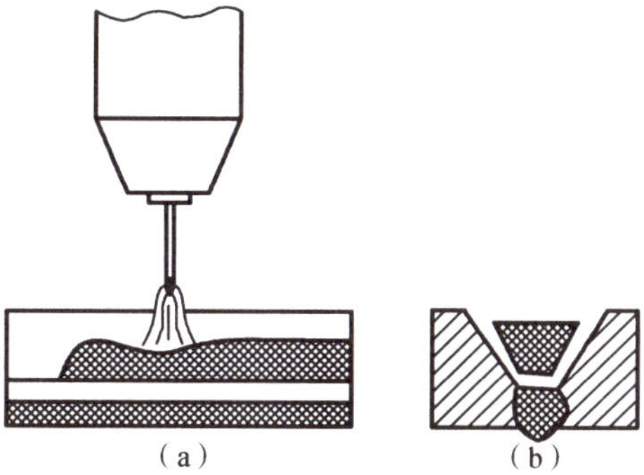

Fig. 2-3-17 Welding Speed is too Low or Deposition Coefficient is too High for Flat Welding

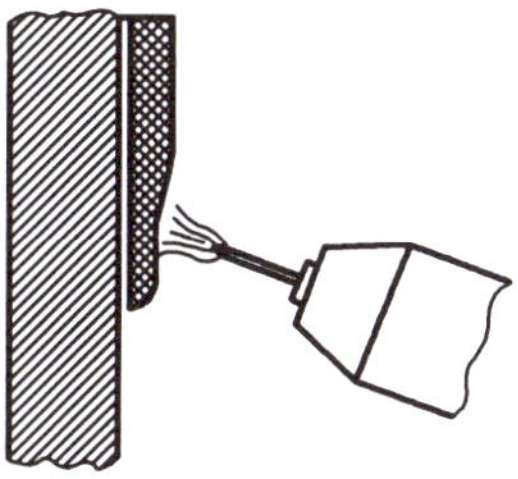

Fig. 2-3-18 Incomplete Penetration during Downward Vertical Welding

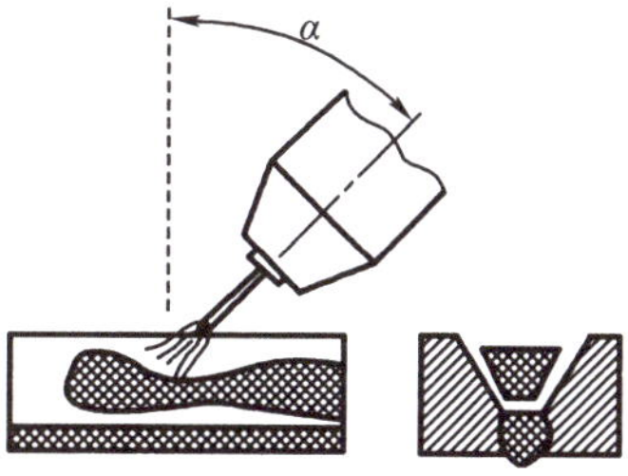

Fig. 2-3-19 Incomplete Penetration Caused by Excessive Front Angle of Welding Gun

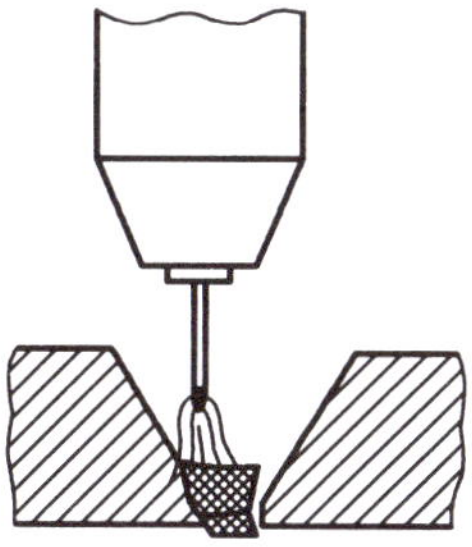

Fig. 2-3-20 Arc Misalignment

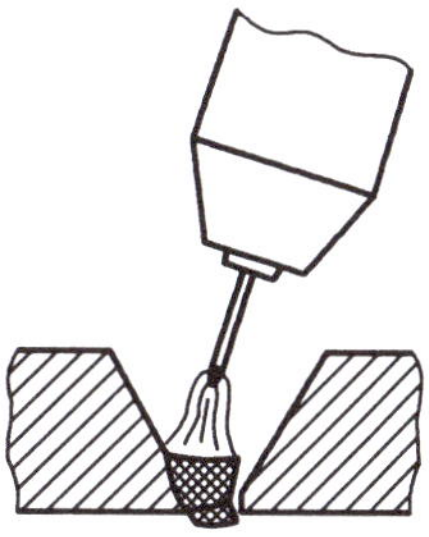

Fig. 2-3-21 Welding Gun Deviated to One Side

(6) Location Restrictions

Due to structural limitations, the arc cannot be aligned with the center or reach the edge of the groove, which will also result in incomplete penetration, as depicted in Fig. 2-3-22.

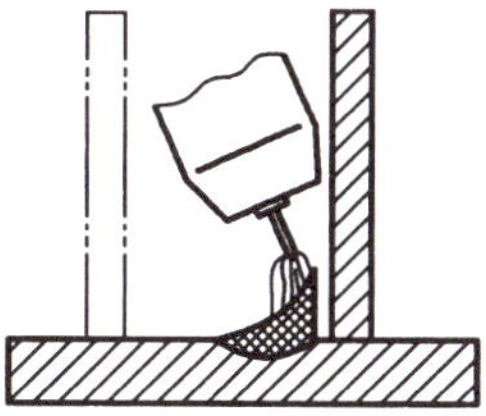

Fig. 2-3-22 Structure Limit

Task Assessment

1. The dry extension length of the welding wire shall be (   ) times the diameter of the welding wire.

A. 2   B. 5   C. 8   D. 10

2. Fine wire CO_2 welding commonly uses (   ).

A. Reverse DC connection   B. Straight DC connection

C. Reverse AC connection   D. Straight AC connection

3. There are (   ) forms of spatter caused by droplet transfer in CO_2 gas shielded welding.

A. 1   B. 2   C. 3   D. 4

4. Spatter can be reduced by using (   ).

A. DC positive connect   B. DC reverse connect

C. AC positive connect   D. AC reverse connect

5. The normal spatter rate for CO_2 gas shielded welding is generally (   ), and when the spatter rate exceeds 30%, normal welding cannot be carried out.

A. 5%–10%   B. 10%–15%   C. 15%–20%   D. 20%–25%

6. During short-circuit transition of CO_2 welding, when the selected electrode and rod have a diameter of 0.8 mm, the appropriate welding voltage and current are (   ).

A. 17–19 V, 30–70 A   B. 18–21 V, 50–100 A

C. 19–23 V, 90–200 A   D. 22–26 V, 140–300 A

7. During the droplet transfer of CO_2 welding, when the selected electrode and rod have a diameter of 1.2 mm, the lower limit of welding current is (   ).

A. 300 A   B. 400 A   C. 500 A   D. 650 A

8. The commonly used wire diameter for short-circuit transition welding is (   ) mm.

A. 0.2–0.6   B. 0.4–0.8   C. 0.6–1.2   D. 1.2–2.0

9. The short-circuit transition of CO_2 welding is formed when (   ) is adopted.

A. Thick welding wire, small current and low voltage

B. Fine welding wire, small current and low voltage

C. Thin welding wire, high current and low voltage

D. Thin welding wire, high current and high voltage

10. In CO_2 welding, when the welding current and arc voltage (   ) are short-circuited for transition, a granular transfer form will occur.

A. Below   B. Above

C. Below a specific value   D. Above a specific value

项目四　CO_2气体保护焊的基本操作技术

【学习目标】

1. 掌握 CO_2 气体保护焊操作注意事项；
2. 掌握 CO^2 气体保护焊基本操作技术。

CO_2 气体保护焊的焊接质量取决于焊接过程的稳定性，而焊接过程的稳定性是由焊接设备、焊接设备的调整（焊接参数的调整）以及焊工的操作技术水平决定的，且在很大程度上是决定于焊工的操作技术水平。

任务1：掌握CO_2气体保焊操作时注意事项

1. 正确的持枪姿势

焊工只有掌握了正确的持枪姿势才能长时间、稳定地进行焊接，并能够切实保证生产。正确的持枪姿势如图 2-4-1 所示，并应满足以下条件：

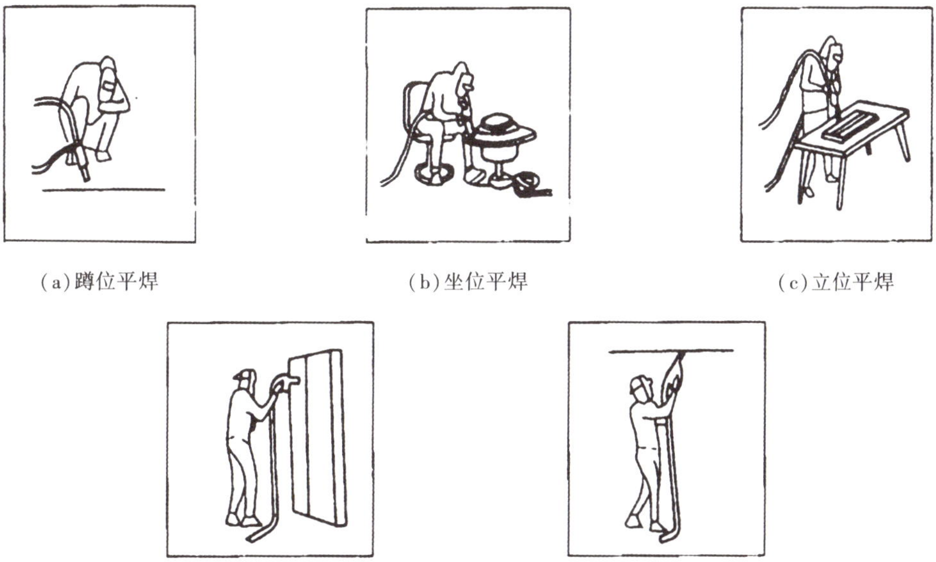

（a）蹲位平焊　（b）坐位平焊　（c）立位平焊　（d）站位立焊　（e）站位仰焊

图 2-4-1　正确的持枪姿势

①操作时用身体的某个部位承担焊枪的质量，通常手臂都处于自然状态，手腕能灵活带动焊枪平移或转动，以不感到累为宜。

②在焊接过程中，软管电缆最小的曲率半径应大于 300 mm，以便在焊接时可随意拖动焊枪。

③在焊接时应能维持焊枪倾角不变,并能清楚、方便地观察熔池。

④将焊丝机构放在合适的地方,以保证焊枪能在需要焊接的范围内自由移动。

2. 保持焊枪与焊件合适的相对位置

在 CO_2 气体保护焊的焊接过程中,必须使焊枪与焊件间保持合适的相对位置。主要是正确控制焊枪与焊件间的倾角和喷嘴角度。当焊枪与焊件间位置合适时,焊工既能方便地观察熔池,控制焊缝形式,又能可靠地保护熔池,防止出现缺陷。

合适的相对位置因焊缝的空间位置和接头的形式不同而异,这在实际操作时将再做介绍。

3. 保持焊枪匀速向前移动

在焊接过程中,焊工可根据焊接电流的大小、熔池的形状、焊件的熔合情况、装配间隙、钝边大小等情况,调整焊枪向前移动的速度,但在整个焊接中需保持焊枪匀速向前运动。

4. 焊枪横向摆幅一致

为了控制焊缝的熔宽和焊接质量,在焊接时必须使焊枪在一定范围内作摆幅一样的摆动,如图 2-4-2 所示。焊枪的摆动形式及应用范围见表 2-4-1。

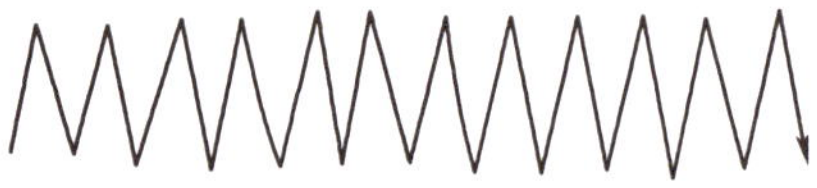
(a)锯齿形

(b)月牙形

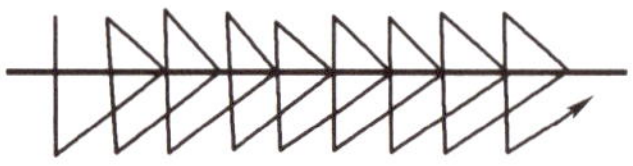
(c)正三角形

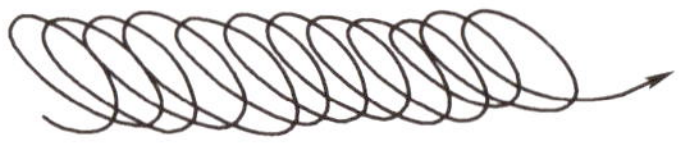
(d)斜圆圈形

图 2-4-2 CO_2 半自动焊时焊枪的几种摆动方式

表 2-4-1 焊枪的摆动形式及应用范围

摆动形式	用途	摆动形式	用途
直线往复式	薄板及中厚板打底焊	划圈式	平角焊或多层焊时的第一层
锯齿式	坡口小时及中厚板打底焊	月牙式	坡口大时

为了减小焊接热影响区和焊接变形,一般不采用大的横向摆动来获得宽焊缝,而提倡采用多层多道焊来焊接厚板。

任务2:掌握CO_2气体保护焊基本操作技术

1. 操作技术

CO_2 气体保护焊的基本操作与焊条电弧焊一样,都是由引弧、收弧、接头、摆动等过程组成的。焊接过程由于焊丝自动送进,只需维持弧长不变,并根据熔池情况摆动和移动焊枪就行了,因此,CO_2 气体保护焊的操作比较容易掌握。

(1)引弧

CO_2 气体保护焊与焊条电弧焊引弧的方法稍有不同。其不采用划擦法,主要是碰撞引弧，但引弧时不必抬起焊枪。具体步骤如下：

①引弧前先按遥控盒上的点动开关或按焊枪上的控制开关，点动送出一段焊丝，焊丝长度小于喷嘴与焊件间应保持的距离，超长部分或焊丝端部出现球状应剪去，如图 2-4-3 所示，喷嘴到焊缝的距离要尽量短，但最小距离不要小于 10 mm，中间填充焊、盖面焊时焊嘴到工件焊缝距离稍大些最大距离可达到 15 mm。

②将焊枪按要求（保持合适的倾角和喷嘴高度）放在引弧处，注意此时焊丝端部与焊件未接触，喷嘴高度由焊接电流决定，如图 2-4-4 所示。

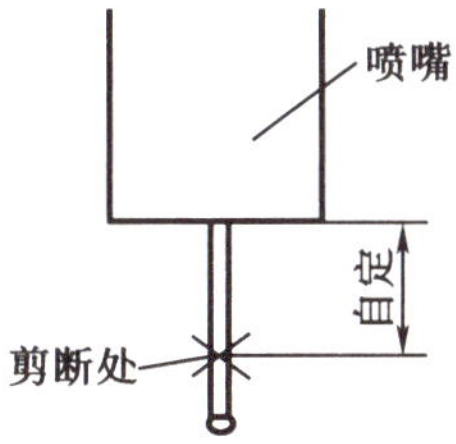

图 2-4-3　引弧前剪去超长的焊丝

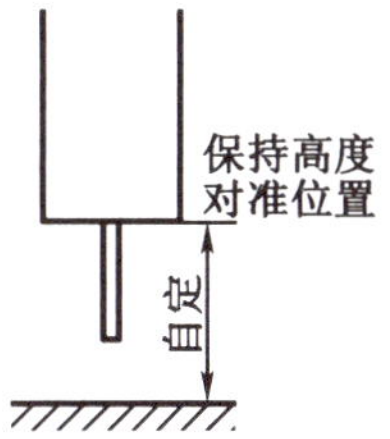

图 2-4-4　准备引弧

引弧时的焊丝端不可先与焊件接触，否则极可能在接通焊接电流时，焊丝因短路爆断会产生较大飞溅，致导电嘴堵塞，甚至使焊丝与导电嘴粘住，将电弧直接引向导电嘴。由于半自动 CO_2 焊多用于细丝焊，采用等速送丝的方式，不能像由弧压反馈自动调速埋弧焊焊机那样自动引弧，因此在引弧前要将焊丝头与焊件间的距离保持在 2～3 mm。若操作不熟练时，最好双手持枪。

③按焊枪上的控制开关，焊机自动提前送气，延时接通焊接电源，并保持高电压、慢送丝，当焊丝碰撞焊件短路后，自动引燃电弧。

当短路时，焊枪有自动顶起的倾向，如图 2-4-5 所示，故引弧时要稍用力向下压焊枪，保持喷嘴与焊件的间距，防止因焊枪抬起太高导致电弧熄灭。

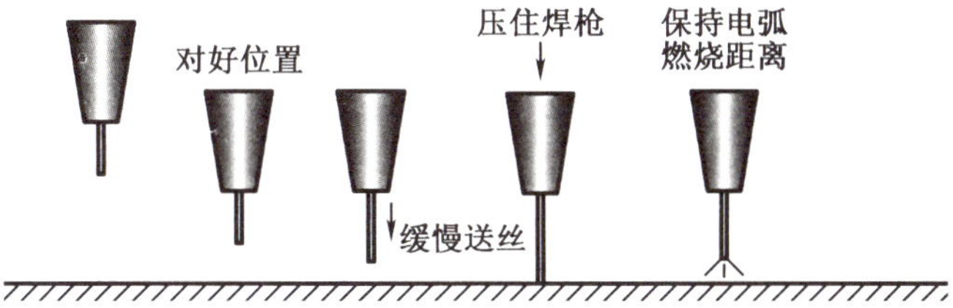

图 2-4-5　引弧过程

（2）焊接

引燃电弧后，通常都采用左向焊法。在焊接过程中，焊工的主要任务是保持焊枪合适的倾角和喷嘴高度，沿焊接方向尽可能均匀移动，当坡口较宽时，为保证两侧熔合好，焊枪还要作横向摆动。

焊工必须能够根据焊接过程的情况，判断焊接参数是否合适。像焊条电弧焊一样，焊工主要依靠在焊接过程中观察到的熔池情况、电弧的稳定性、飞溅的大小及焊缝成形的好坏调整焊接参数。

当焊丝直径不变时，实际上使用的焊接参数只有两组。其中一组焊接参数用来焊薄板或打底焊道,另一组焊接参数用来焊中厚板或盖面焊。

①焊薄板或打底焊的焊接参数。这组焊接参数的特点是焊接电流小,电弧电压较低,熔滴过渡为短路过渡。当采用多元控制的焊机进行焊接时,电弧电压与焊接电流相匹配是关键。对于直径为0.8 mm、1.0 mm、1.2 mm的焊丝,短路过渡时的电弧电压在20 V左右。当采用一元控制的焊机进行焊接时,如果选用小电流,控制系统会自动选择合适的低电压,焊工只需根据焊缝成形情况稍加修正,就能保证短路过渡。

②焊接中厚板的填充层和盖面层的焊接参数。这组焊接参数的焊接电流和电弧电压都较大,这时熔滴过渡主要以细颗粒过渡为主,它具有飞溅小、电弧较平稳的特点。

(3)收弧

焊接结束前必须收弧,若收弧不当容易产生弧坑,并出现弧坑裂纹(火口裂纹)、气孔等缺陷。操作时可以采取以下措施:

①如CO_2气体保护焊机有弧坑控制电路时,当焊枪在收弧处停止前进,同时接通此电路,焊接电流与电弧电压自动变小,待熔池填满时断电。

②若焊机没有弧坑控制电路时,或因焊接电流小没有使用弧坑控制电路时,在收弧处焊枪停止前进,并在熔池凝固时,反复断弧、引弧几次,直至弧坑填满为止。操作时动作要快,若熔池已凝固才收弧,则可能产生未熔合及气孔等缺陷。

但不论采用哪种方法收弧,操作中均需特别注意,收弧时焊枪除停止前进外,不能抬高喷嘴,即使弧坑已填满,电弧已熄灭,也要让焊枪在弧坑处停留几秒后才能移开。因为灭弧后,控制线路仍保证延迟送气一段时间,以保证在熔池凝固时能得到可靠的保护。若收弧时抬高焊枪,则容易因保护不良而引起缺陷。

(4)接头

CO_2气体保护焊不可避免地要接头,为保证接头质量,应按下述步骤操作:

①将待接接头处用角向磨光机打磨成斜面,如图2-4-6所示。

②在斜面顶部引弧,引燃电弧后将电弧移至斜面底部,转一圈返回引弧处后再继续向左焊接,如图2-4-7所示。应当指出,在引燃电弧后向斜面底部移动时,要注意观察熔孔,若未形成熔孔则接头处背面焊不透;若熔孔太小,则接头处背面产生缩颈;若熔孔太大,则背面焊缝太宽或出现烧穿。

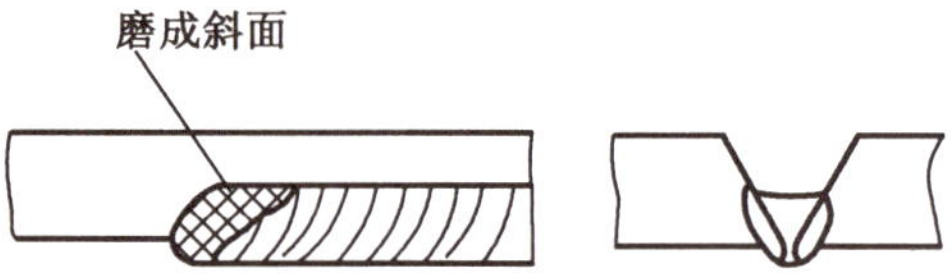

图2-4-6　接头处的准备

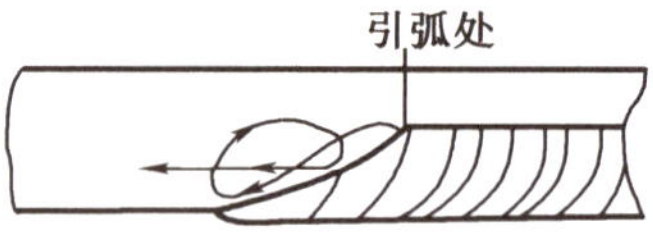

图2-4-7　接头处的引弧操作

(5)定位焊

由于CO_2气体保护焊电弧的热量较焊条电弧焊大,要求定位焊缝有足够的强度。通常定位焊缝都不磨去,仍保留在焊缝中,在焊接过程中很难全部重熔,因此应保证定位焊缝的质量。定位焊缝既要熔合好,余高又要合适,还不能有缺陷,要求焊工像正式焊接那样焊定位焊缝。定位焊缝的长度和间距应符合下述规定。

①中厚板对接时的定位焊缝如图2-4-8所示。焊件两端应装引弧、收弧板。

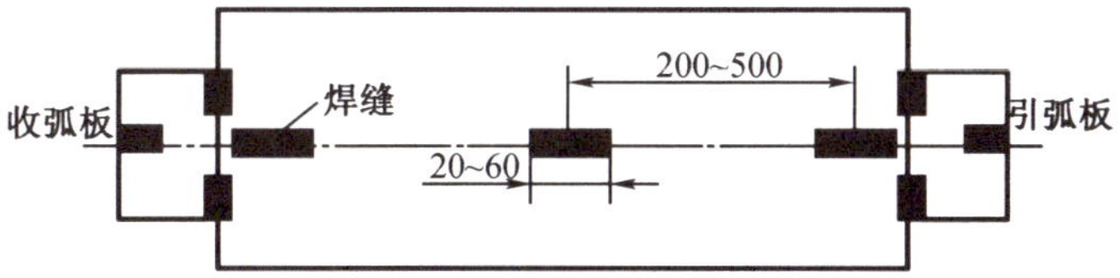

图 2-4-8　中厚板对接时的定位焊缝(单位:mm)

②薄板对接时的定位焊缝可参照图 2-4-9 所示。

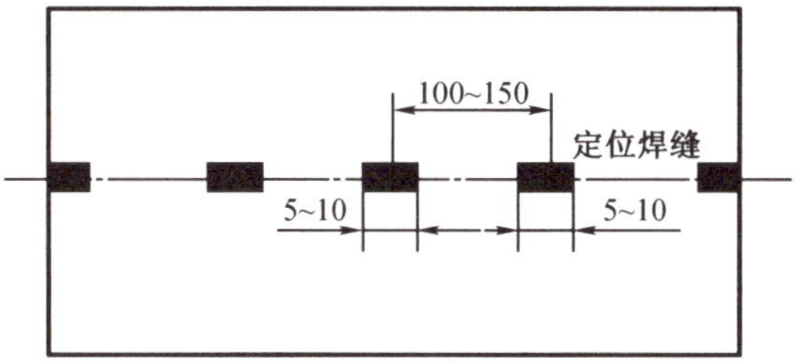

图 2-4-9　薄板对接时的定位焊缝(单位:mm)

2. 操作训练

根据基本操作要领进行熔化极气体保护焊基础操作回顾性实操训练。

任务考核

1. 向上立角焊时,焊枪的焊角为(　　)宜用月牙形。

A. 5°~9°　B. 7°~10°　C. 8°~12°　D. 10°~15°

2. 向上立角焊时,焊枪的焊角为(　　)宜用三角形。

A. 5°~9°　B. 7°~10°　C. 8°~12°　D. 10°~15°

3. 向上立角焊时,焊枪的焊角为 7°~10°宜用(　　)。

A. 月牙形　B. 人字形　C. 三角形　D. 圆形

4. CO_2 焊采用填充焊时,焊枪与焊缝后侧的倾角应为(　　　)。

A. 60°~35°　B. 70°~75°　C. 80°~85°　D. 90°~95°

5. CO_2 焊采用定位焊时,定位焊缝长度为(　　)mm,焊件留出(　　)的反变形。

A. 10~15,5°~6°　B. 12~15,5°~6°

C. 10~15,6°~8°　D. 12~15,6°~8°

6. 倾斜角度越大,飞溅就越多。通过实践证明,焊枪前倾或后倾最好不超过(　　),最大能不超过(　　)。

A. 10°,15°　B. 15°,20°　C. 20°,25°　D. 25°,30°

7. 当板厚大于 20 mm 时,则宜采用开坡口角焊,坡口角为(　　)。

A. 35°~40°　B. 40°~45°　C. 45°~50°　D. 50°~55°

8. 对接管水平固定位置向上焊接时,焊条的角度应随着焊接位置的变化而变化,但焊接位置中没有(　　)。

A. 平焊　B. 立焊　C. 横焊　D. 仰焊

9. 对接管水平固定位置向上焊接(　　)进行。

A. 按整圆　　B. 分两个半圆　　C. 分四个半圆　　D. 分六个半圆

10. 焊前在坡口两侧(正,反面)(　　)范围内除锈,去污,

A. 10 mm　　B. 20 mm　　C. 30 mm　　D. 420 mm

任务操作

根据基本操作要领进行熔化极气体保护焊基础操作回顾性实操训练。

Project Ⅳ Basic Operation Techniques of CO_2 Gas Shielded Welding

【Learning Objectives】

1. Master the precautions for CO_2 gas shielded welding operation;
2. Master the basic operation techniques of CO_2 gas shielded welding.

The quality of CO_2 gas shielded welding depends on the stability of the welding process, which is determined by the welding equipment, adjustment of welding parameters, and the skill level of the welder, and to a large extent, it depends on the welder's skill level.

Task 1:Master the Precautions for CO_2 Gas Shielded Welding Operation

1. Correct gun holding posture

Only when the welder masters the correct gun holding posture can they perform welding for extended periods of time and ensure effective production. The correct gun holding posture is illustrated in Fig. 2-4-1, and the following conditions must be met.

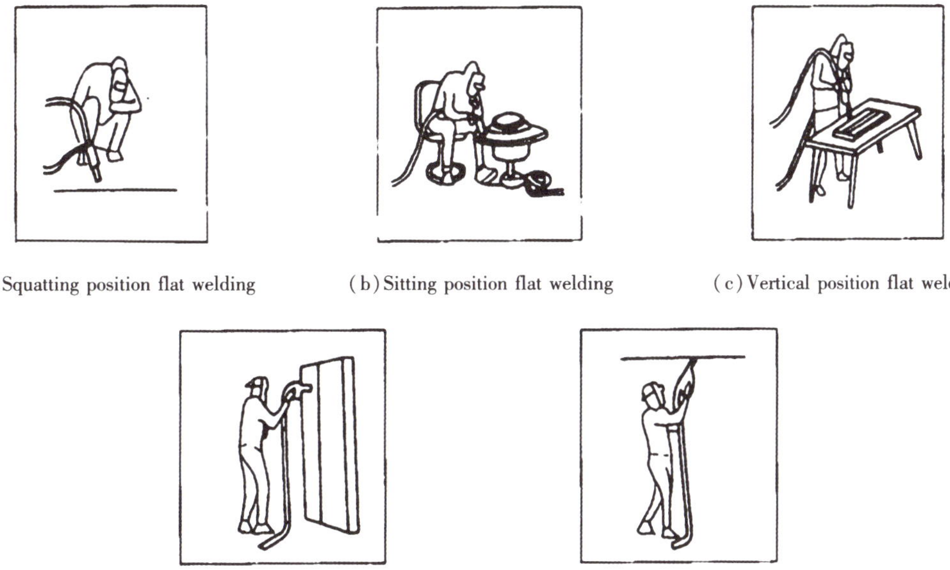

(a) Squatting position flat welding (b) Sitting position flat welding (c) Vertical position flat welding

(d) Standing position vertical welding (e) Standing position overhead welding

Fig. 2-4-1 Proper Gun Handling Posture

①During operation, a certain part of the body supports the weight of the welding gun. Usually, the arm remains in a natural state and the wrist can move flexibly to drive the welding gun for translation or rotation, in order to avoid feeling tired.

②During welding, the minimum bending radius of the hose cable should be greater than 300 mm, allowing for free movement of the welding gun during welding.

③The inclination angle of the welding gun should remain unchanged during welding, enabling clear and convenient observation of the molten pool.

④Position the welding wire mechanism in a suitable location to ensure that the welding gun can move freely within the welding range.

2. Keep the welding gun and weldment in the appropriate relative position

During CO_2 gas shielded welding, it is necessary to maintain the appropriate relative position between the welding gun and the weldment. This is mainly achieved by accurately controlling the inclination angle and nozzle angle between the welding gun and the weldment. When the positioning between the welding gun and the weldment is suitable, the welder can conveniently observe the molten pool, control the weld formation, and reliably protect the molten pool to prevent defects.

The suitable relative position varies depending on the spatial position of the weld and the form of the joint, which will be further explained during actual operation.

3. Keep the welding torch moving forward at a constant speed

During the welding process, welders can adjust the forward movement speed of the arc welding gun based on factors such as the welding current, shape of the molten pool, fusion of the weldment, assembly gap, and root face size. However, it is necessary to maintain a constant forward movement speed of the arc welding gun throughout the entire welding process.

4. The sideways swing of the welding gun shall be consistent

To ensure control over the width of the weld and welding quality, it is necessary for the arc welding gun to swing within a specific range, as demonstrated in Fig. 2-4-2. Refer to Table 2-4-1 for the swing patterns and application scope of the welding gun.

Fig. 2-4-2 Various Swing Modes of the Welding Gun During CO_2 Semi-automatic Welding

Table 2-4-1 Swing Form and Application Scope of Welding Gun

Oscillating form	Purpose	Oscillating form	Usage
Linear reciprocating	Backing welding of thin and medium -thick plates	Circular type	First layer in case of flat fillet or multi-layer welding
Sawtooth	Backing welding of small groove and medium-thick plate	Crescent	When the groove is large

To reduce the heat-affected zone and welding deformation, it is generally recommended to use multiple layers and passes for welding thick plates instead of employing wide transverse weaving to obtain a broader weld.

Task 2:Master the Basic Operation Techniques of CO_2 Gas Shielded Welding

1. Basic operating techniques

The basic operation of CO_2 gas shielded welding is the same as that of SMAW, which includes arc striking, arc extinguishing, joint formation, and swinging. In the welding process, due to the automatic feeding of welding wire, it is only necessary to maintain a consistent arc length and swing and move the welding gun according to the condition of the molten pool. Therefore, mastering the operation of CO_2 gas shielded welding is relatively easy.

(1) Arc striking

The arc initiation methods of CO_2 gas shielded welding and shielded metal arc welding are slightly different. It does not use the scratching method, but primarily initiates the arc through collision. However, lifting the welding gun is unnecessary during arc initiation. The specific steps are as follows: [specific steps are not provided].

①Before striking the arc, press the jog switch on the remote control box or the control switch on the welding gun to send out a short section of welding wire. The length of the welding wire should be shorter than the distance between the nozzle and the welded object. Cut off any excess length or ball shape at the end of the welding wire, as shown in Fig. 2-4-3. The distance from the nozzle to the weld joint should be kept as short as possible, but the minimum distance should not be less than 10 mm. During intermediate fill welding and cosmetic welding, the distance from the welding tip to the weld joint of the workpiece should be slightly larger, and the maximum distance can reach 15 mm.

②Place the welding gun at the specified arc striking position, ensuring the correct inclination angle and nozzle height. It is important to keep in mind that the end of the welding wire should not touch the weldment at this stage. The nozzle height should be adjusted based on the welding current, as illustrated in Fig. 2-4-4.

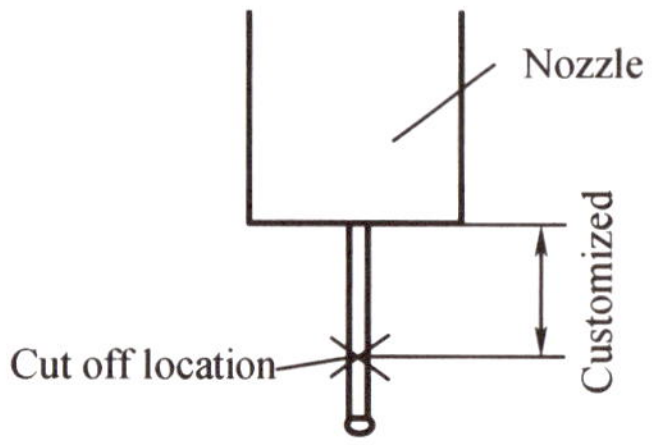

Fig. 2-4-3 Trimming Excessively Long Welding Wire Before Arc Ignition

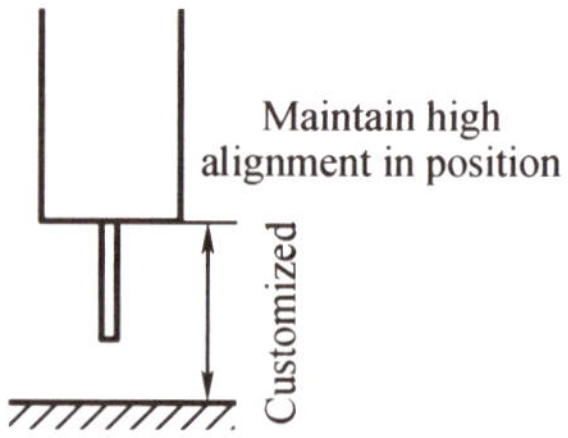

Fig. 2-4-4 Preparing for Arc Ignition

During arc striking, the welding wire end should not come into contact with the weldment first. Otherwise, there is a high possibility that when the welding current is turned on, the welding wire will burst due to a short circuit, causing large splashes. This can lead to blockage of the contact tube, or even sticking between the welding wire and the contact tube, resulting in the arc directly hitting the contact tube. Since semi-automatic CO_2 welding is mainly used for fine wire welding, it cannot automatically initiate the arc like an automatic submerged arc welding machine with arc voltage feedback for automatic speed regulation. Therefore, the distance between the welding wire end and the weldment should be kept within 2 – 3 mm before arc striking. If the operator is not skilled, it is better to hold the gun with both hands.

③Press the control switch on the welding gun to automatically supply gas in advance. The welding power supply will be delayed and will maintain high voltage and slow wire feeding. When the welding wire collides with the weldment, it will automatically ignite the arc.

When a short circuit occurs, the welding gun tends to automatically lift up, as shown in Fig. 2-4-5. Therefore, when striking an arc, the welding gun should be pressed down with slight force to maintain the distance between the nozzle and the weldment in order to prevent the arc from extinguishing due to excessive lifting of the welding gun.

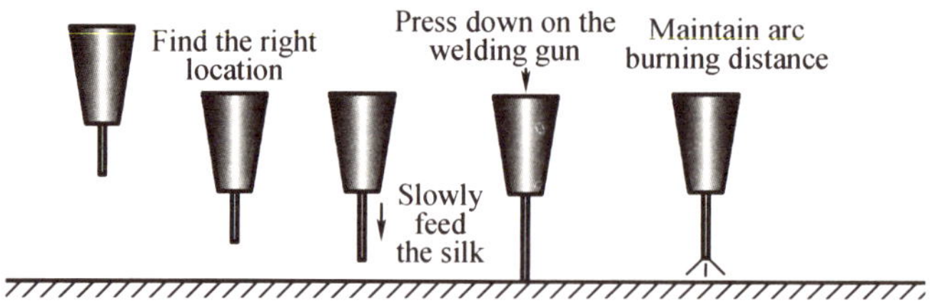

Fig. 2-4-5 Arc Ignition Process

(2) Welding

After igniting the arc, the left-hand welding method is usually employed. During the welding process, the main task of welders is to maintain the welding gun at an appropriate inclination angle and nozzle height, and move it as evenly as possible along the welding direction. When the groove is wide, the welding gun should also swing laterally to ensure good fusion on both sides.

The welder needs to determine whether the welding parameters are suitable based on the welding process. For instance, in shielded metal arc welding, the welder primarily adjusts the welding parameters based on the observed molten pool condition, arc stability, spatter size, and the quality of weld seam formation.

When the electrode and rod diameter remain constant, only two sets of welding parameters are actually employed. One set is utilized for welding thin plates or backing weld beads, while the other set is used for welding medium-thick plates or cosmetic welds.

①Welding parameters for welding thin plates or backings: This set of welding parameters is characterized by small welding current, low arc voltage, and short-circuit transfer. When using a multi-control welding machine, it is crucial to match the arc voltage with the welding current. For electrodes with diameters of 0.8 mm, 1.0 mm, and 1.2 mm, the arc voltage during short-circuit transfer is approximately 20 V. When using a single-control welding machine, if a small current is selected, the control system will automatically select an appropriate low voltage, and the welder only needs to make slight adjustments based on the weld formation to ensure short-circuit transfer.

②Welding parameters for filling layer and capping layer in welding medium-thick plates: This set of welding parameters requires relatively large welding current and arc voltage. At this stage, the droplet transfer is mainly fine particle transfer, characterized by minimal spattering and a stable arc.

(3) Arc stopping

Arc suppression must be performed before the completion of welding. Improper arc suppression can easily result in defects such as craters, crater cracks, and porosity. The following measures can be implemented during operation.

①If the CO_2 gas shielded welding machine has an arc crater control circuit, when the welding gun stops advancing at the arc stopping position and this circuit is activated, the welding current and arc voltage will automatically decrease, and the power supply will be cut off when the molten pool is filled.

②If there is no arc crater control circuit for the welder, or the arc crater control circuit is not utilized due to low welding current, stop advancing the welding gun at the arc stopping place, and repeat arc breaking and arc striking several times when the molten pool solidifies until the arc crater is filled. The actions should be executed swiftly. If the arc is extinguished after the molten pool has solidified, defects such as incomplete fusion and air pockets may occur.

However, regardless of the method used for arc termination, special attention must be paid during operation. During arc termination, the welding torch should not raise the nozzle unless it stops moving forward. Even if the arc crater has been filled and the arc has been extinguished, the welding torch can only be removed after staying at the arc crater for a few seconds. This is because after arc extinguishing, the control circuit still ensures a delayed gas supply to ensure reliable protection when the molten pool solidifies. Raising the welding torch during arc termination can easily cause defects due to poor protection.

(4) Connector

Joints are unavoidable in CO_2 gas shielded welding. To ensure the quality of the joints, the steps below should be followed.

①Grind the joint to be connected into an inclined plane using an angle grinder, as shown in Fig. 2-4-6.

②Strike the arc at the top of the inclined plane, move the arc to the bottom of the inclined plane after striking it, make one loop and return to the arc strike point before continuing welding to the left, as shown in Fig. 2-4-7. It should be noted that when igniting and moving the arc to the bottom of the inclined plane, attention should be paid to observing the formation of a melt hole. If no melt hole is formed, the joint on the backside cannot be thoroughly welded; if the melt hole is too small, necking occurs on the backside of the joint; if the melt hole is too large, the backside weld seam becomes too wide or burnt through.

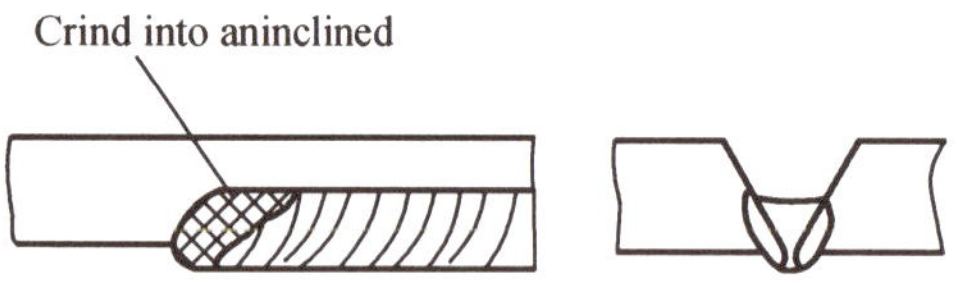

Fig. 2-4-6 Joint Preparation

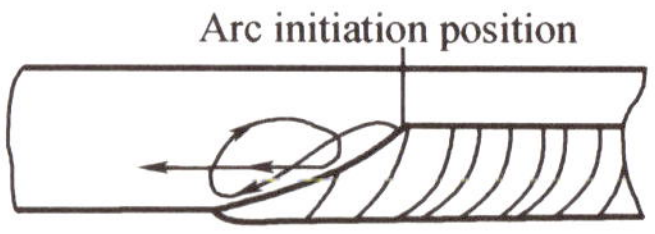

Fig. 2-4-7 Arc Striking Operation at Joint

(5) Spot welding

Due to the higher heat generated by the CO_2 gas shielded welding arc compared to SMAW, it is necessary to ensure sufficient strength in the tack weld. Generally, tack welds are not ground off and remain in the welds. It is difficult to remelt all of them during welding, so the quality of tack welds must be ensured. The tack welds should not only be well fused but also have appropriate reinforcement and no defects. Welders are required to weld the tack welds just like formal welding. The length and spacing of tack welds should meet the following requirements.

①The positioning weldment during butt joint of moderately thick plates is shown in Fig. 2-4-8. Both ends of the weldment should have run-on and run-off plates installed.

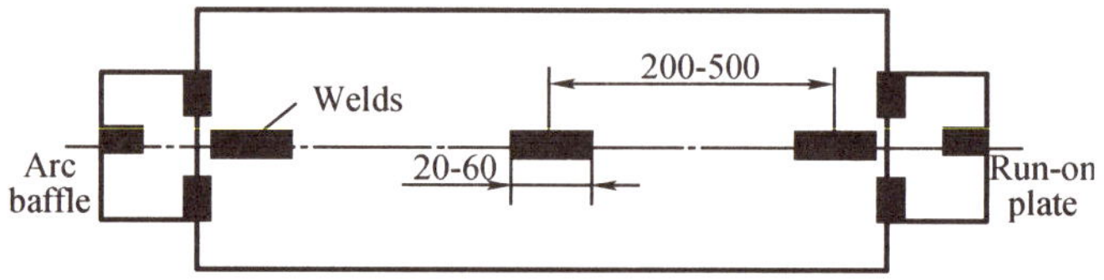

Fig. 2-4-8 Position Weld for Butt Joint of Medium and Thick Plates (Unit: mm)

②The alignment weld seam during butt joint of thin plates can be referred to in Fig. 2-4-9.

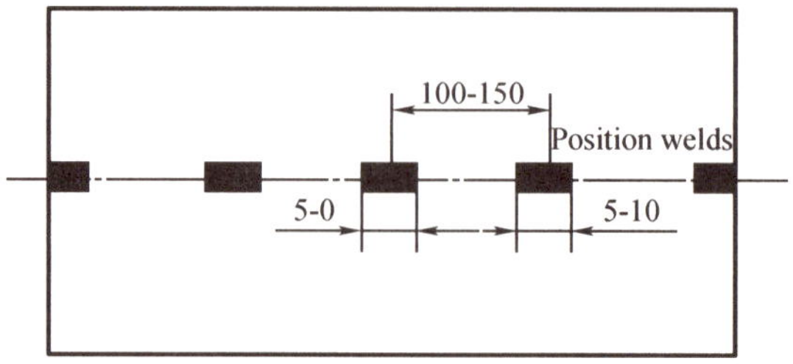

Fig. 2-4-9 Position Weld in Thin Plate Butt Joint (Unit: mm)

2. OperationTraining

Participate in a practical training course on the basic operation of gas metal arc welding based on the essentials of basic operation.

Task Assessment

1. For upward vertical fillet welding, the welding gun's angle should be ( ), and a crescent-shaped electrode should be used.

A. 5°-9° B. 7°-10° C. 8°-12° D. 10°-15°

2. For upward vertical fillet welding, the welding gun should be positioned at an angle ( ) and a triangular shape should be used.

A. 5-9 mm B. 7-10 mm C. 8-12 mm D. 10-15 mm

3. For upward vertical fillet welding, the welding gun should have a welding angle of 7 to 10 degrees ( ).

A. Moon-shaped B. Chevron C. Triangle D. Round

4. When CO_2 welding is used for filling welding, the inclination angle between the welding gun and the back side of the weld should be ( ).

A. 60°-35° B. 70°-75° C. 80°-85° D. 90°-95°

5. When tack welding is adopted for CO_2 welding, the length of tack weld shall be ( ) mm, and ( ) allowance shall be left for the weldment to prevent deformation.

A. 10-15, 5°-6° B. 12-15, 5°-6°

C. 10-15, 6°-8° D. 12-15, 6°-8°

6. The larger the inclination angle, the more splashes will occur. It has been proven through practice that the forward or backward inclination of the welding gun should not exceed ( ), and the maximum should not exceed ( ).

A. 10°, 15° B. 15°, 20° C. 20°, 25° D. 25°, 30°

7. When the plate thickness is greater than 20mm, it is advisable to use groove fillet welding, with a groove angle of ( ).

A. 35°-40° B. 40°-45° C. 45°-50° D. 50°-55°

8. When welding the butt-jointed pipe in a horizontal fixed position upwards, the angle of the electrode should vary with the welding position, without any exceptions ( ) in the welding position.

A. Flat welding B. Vertical welding

C. Horizontal welding D. Overhead welding

9. The butt joint pipe shall be welded upward in the horizontally fixed position ( ).

A. according to the whole circle B. divided into two semicircles

C. divided into four semicircles D. divided into six semicircles

10. Before welding, remove rust and dirt from both sides (front and back) of the groove ( ).

A. 10 mm B. 20 mm C. 30 mm D. 420 mm

Task Operation

Participate in a retrospective hands-on training on the fundamental operation of gas metal arc welding based on the essential operating principles.

项目五　板对接平焊CO_2气体保护焊

【学习目标】

1. 分析板对接平焊 CO_2 气体保护焊的技术要求；
2. 掌握板对接平焊 CO_2 气体保护焊的焊前准备；
3. 掌握板对接平焊 CO_2 气体保护焊的焊接操作；
4. 掌握板对接平焊 CO_2 气体保护焊的焊后处理与检查。

任务1：分析板对接平焊CO_2气体保护焊的技术要求

图 2-5-1 为常见板对接平焊试件装配图及技术要求。

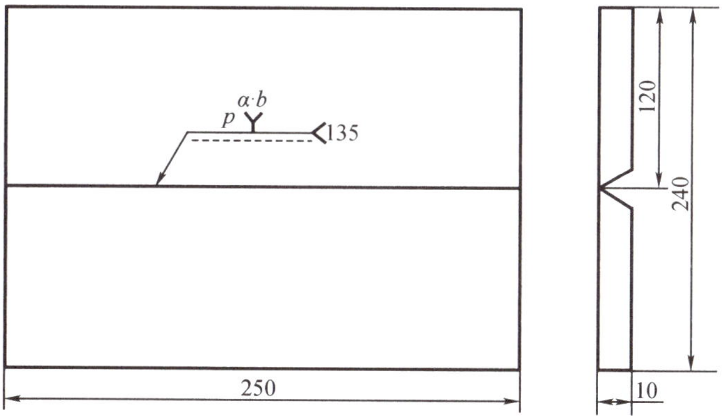

技术要求
1. 单面焊双面成形。
2. 坡口为 60°坡口角的 V 形带钝边坡口。
3. 根部间隙和钝边尺寸自定。
4. 错边≤1.2 mm。
5. 角变形<3°。
6. 不允许有咬边。
7. 不允许有未焊透。
8. 不允许有裂纹、气孔、夹渣。
9. 焊缝余高≤1+0.15b。

图 2-5-1　Q235B 板对接平焊单面焊双面成形焊件图(单位:mm)

CO_2 气体保护焊在很多金属结构生产中应用广泛，特别是平对接单面焊双面成形技术，更是值得学习，CO_2 气体保护焊单面焊双面成形工艺采用连续击穿焊法进行，连续击穿焊法是在焊接过程中利用 CO_2 气体保护焊电弧热量集中、穿透能力强的特点，直接熔透坡口根部，使坡口根部两侧各熔化 1~2 mm，这样就在熔池前沿形成了一个大于装配间隙的熔孔。焊接时，一部分熔敷金属过渡到焊缝根部及背面，另外大部分熔敷金属则在正面与母材金属形成熔池。当焊枪向前移动时，表面张力使熔融的金属向熔孔后方流动，冷却时，熔孔在电弧后方锁闭，熔池不断冷却结晶最终形成完全熔透的正、反面焊缝。

本单元以实际工程中常用的低碳钢材质为例介绍板对接平焊熔化极气体保护焊的焊前准备、焊接操作和焊后处理与检查等任务实施流程。

任务2：掌握板对接平焊CO_2气体保护焊的焊前准备

1. 焊件准备及坡口清理

根据任务单要求，准备 10 mm×120 mm×250 mm 尺寸的 Q235B 材质焊件两块，单边开

30°V 形坡口。

焊缝上的油、锈、水、漆、氧化皮、灰尘、油污、毛刺等杂物可以引起焊接缺陷，比如气孔、夹渣、未熔合等，所以应通过清理措施将这些对焊接有害因素清除干净。清理的范围一般为坡口面及坡口边缘上下两侧 15~20 mm 范围，并露出金属光泽，如图 2-5-3 所示，并打磨出 0.5~1.0 mm 的坡口钝边。

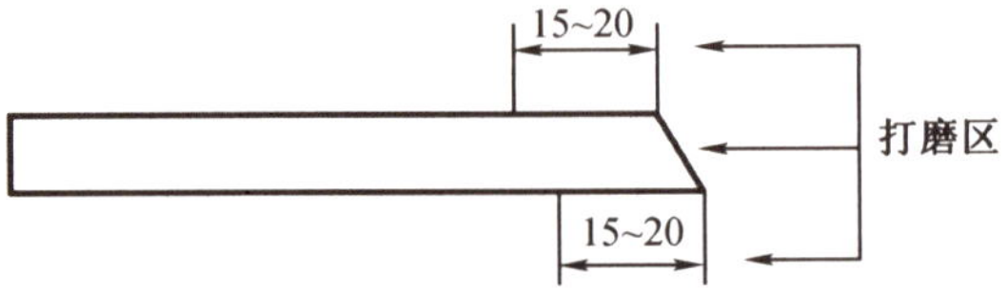

图 2-5-3　接头打磨区域示意图(单位:mm)

2. 焊接工艺参数确定

结合本任务母材 Q235B 的焊接特性和板厚来看，选择直径 1.2 mm 的 ER50-6 焊丝，保护气体为 CO_2 气体，纯度高于 99.5%，采用三层三道来焊接，具体焊接工艺参数见表 2-5-1。

表 2-5-1　焊接工艺参数

焊接层次	焊丝型号	焊丝直径/mm	焊接电流/A	焊接电压/V	保护气体流量/(L/min)	焊丝伸出长度/mm	电源极性
打底层	ER50-6	1.2	90~110	18~20	12~15	10~15	直流反接
填充层			120~140	20~22	12~15	10~15	
盖面层			140~160	21~23	12~15	10~15	

多层焊是指熔敷两个以上的焊层来完成整条焊缝所进行的焊接，多层焊包括多层单道焊和多层多道焊，如图 2-5-4 所示，一层焊缝可以由若干道焊道组成，如果坡口角度小，熔敷一道就可以是一层，即为单道焊，当坡口角度较大时，熔敷两道及以上焊道才能组成一层焊缝，就是多道焊。多层焊是焊接大厚壁结构常用的方法，较之相同情形下采用单层焊，可以减少热输入量、减小变形、降低产生缺陷的概率。多层多道焊还可以提高焊缝金属的质量，特别是塑性，这是因为后层(后道)焊缝对前层(前道)焊缝具有热处理作用，相当于对前层(前道)焊缝进行了一次正火热处理，因而改善了二次组织。单次焊层的热处理作用只达 3~5 mm，如果每层焊道厚度超过 6 mm，热处理效果差，焊缝金属组织质量就不高。

(a)多层焊　　(b)多层多道焊

图 2-5-4　多层焊、多层多道焊剖面示意图

通常板厚≤6 mm 时,采用 I 形坡口对接平焊,采用双面焊时,正面采用直线运条,稍慢,电流较小;背面也采用直线运条,焊接电流稍大,速度稍快。

板厚>6 mm 时,采用其他形式坡口对接平焊,可采用多层焊或多层多道焊。焊接打底层,特别是单面焊双面成形时,为保证背面焊缝质量,常使用较小的焊接电流;焊接填充层时,为了提高效率、保证熔合良好,常使用较大的焊接电流;焊接盖面层时,为防止咬边和保证焊缝成形,使用的焊接电流应比填充层稍小些。

多层多道焊电流调节特点:打底焊电流<盖面焊电流<填充焊电流。盖面焊电流要大于打底焊。

3. 装配定位

装配定位需考虑到焊接变形的因素,以便在装配定位时给予一定的补偿修正。

将两块钢板水平放工装台上,两端对齐装配成对接接头,装配时焊件始焊端根部间隙设置为 3.2 mm,结束端为 4.0 mm,采取和打底相同的工艺参数在两端进行点固焊,焊点长度为 10~15 mm,起始端厚度为 3~4 mm,结束厚度为 7~8 mm,错边量不大于 1.2 mm,反变形预留量为 3°~5°,如图 2-5-5 所示。点焊后应将焊点渣壳敲掉并打磨至金属光泽,呈斜坡状,以便于接头。

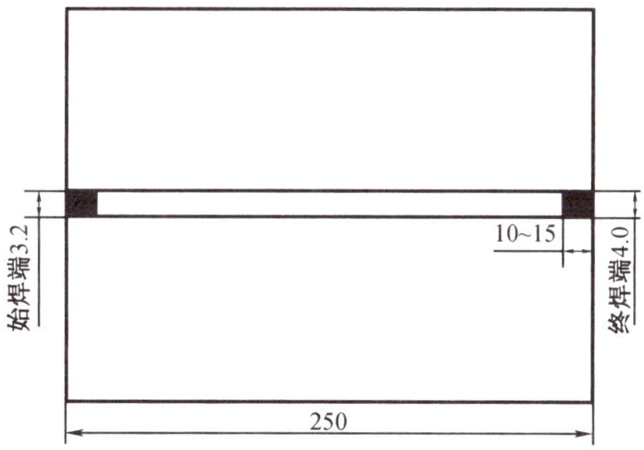

图 2-5-5　装配定位焊位置示意图(单位:mm)

任务3:掌握板对接平焊CO_2气体保护焊的焊接操作

工程中常用的 10 mm 厚板件对接时,焊接层次常有三层三道和四层四道焊的做法,操作方法类似,这里介绍更加常见的三层三道焊。

将焊件固定在操作台上,水平放置,焊件高度一般到操作者脚踝处(蹲姿焊),间隙小的一端放置右侧,采用左向焊法,焊丝与板件之间夹角为 70°~80°,与焊缝方向成 90°,如图 2-5-6 所示。

1. 打底焊

①在距离焊件右端定位焊缝约 20 mm 处坡口的一侧引弧,并迅速拉回到端部定位焊点上稍作停留,然后按照设置好的焊接参数开始向左焊接,采用锯齿形或月牙形运条法沿坡口两侧做小幅度横向摆动并在坡口两侧稍作停留,控制电弧在离坡口底边 2~3 mm 处,当坡口底部熔孔直径为 3~4 mm 时,转入正常焊接。

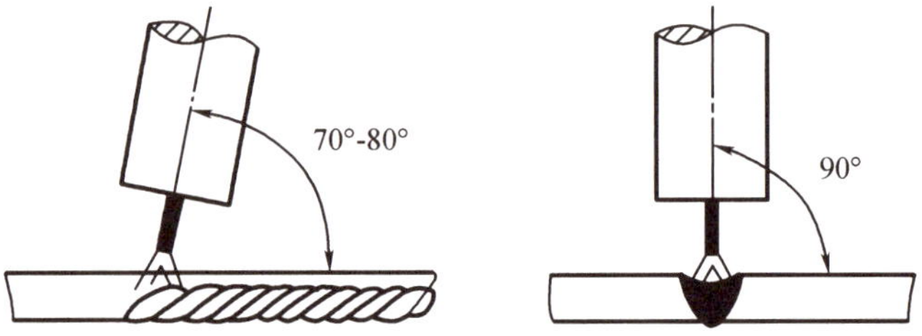

图 2-5-6　焊枪角度示意图

②焊接过程中,焊枪始终对准焊缝中心线,并在坡口两侧稍作停留 0.5～1 s,避免产生咬边缺陷。焊枪在摆动时,注意观察熔孔直径要比间隙大 0.5～1 mm,并随时根据熔孔直径和间隙的变化,调整焊枪摆动的幅度和焊接速度,尽可能保证熔孔直径不变,并保持焊道平整,以获得宽窄和高低均匀的反面焊缝。焊完后清理焊道表面熔渣及飞溅。

③喷嘴高度要严格控制,保证电弧在距坡口根部 2～3 mm 处燃烧,使打底焊缝厚度保持在不超过 4 mm,同时这样的喷嘴高低也不会遮挡操作者视线,从而能观察熔池边缘熔合情况,又能够起到保护熔池的作用。

④收弧时要特别注意,一定要填满弧坑,防止产生弧坑裂纹。

2. 填充焊

①彻底清理打底层焊渣,铲除接头高点和焊瘤,使打底层焊道平整。

②按照设置好的焊接参数,在距离焊件右端 20 mm 处引弧,快速拉到最右端并压低电弧稍作停顿,待形成熔池,采用锯齿形或月牙形向左摆动焊接。焊枪的横向摆动幅度要稍大于打底层焊道,运条时左右两侧稍作停留,注意熔池两侧的熔合情况,电弧前移步伐为 1/2～2/3 熔池大小,保证焊道表面平整且稍有下凹,并使填充层的高度低于母材表面 1～1.5 mm,以免烧化坡口棱边,导致盖面层产生咬边或焊偏现象,如图 2-5-7 所示。

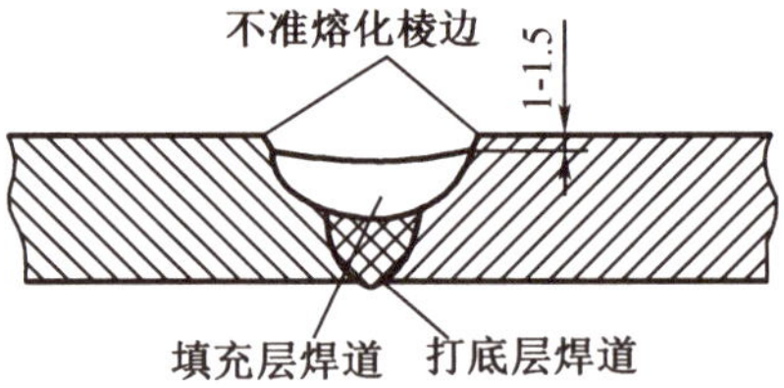

图 2-5-7　填充层焊道要求

3. 盖面焊

①彻底清理打底层焊渣,调节工艺参数到预先选好的盖面焊挡位。

②盖面层的焊接与填充层焊接方法基本相同,采用锯齿形或月牙形运条方法,从右向左焊接,焊枪摆动幅度要比填充焊大一些,尽量保持焊接速度均匀,避免盖面层焊道中间凹陷,焊丝摆动到坡口两侧时,焊丝对准坡口棱边,不要超过棱边,形成熔池后熔化棱边 0～1 mm。

③收弧时一定要填满弧坑,并且收弧弧长要短,以免产生弧坑裂纹。

任务4:掌握板对接平焊CO_2气体保护焊焊后处理与检查

1. 焊缝清理

焊件焊接完毕后,用敲渣锤、钢丝刷等清理掉焊缝上的焊渣、飞溅物等,或用砂纸重新打磨一遍焊缝外观,不得存在焊渣、焊点、毛刺等,焊缝应光滑、平整,应保证焊件的“边齐、面平”, 包括焊件上开口边缘的垂直平行度,但不能破坏焊缝原始表面。

2. 焊缝质量检测

(1) 焊缝外观检测

焊后对焊缝表面质量进行检测，肉眼观察或用低倍放大镜检查焊缝表面是否有气孔、裂纹、咬边等缺陷，用钢直尺、钢角尺、焊缝检验尺对焊缝进行外观质量和外观成形尺寸检测。常规具体检测条目及要求参考表 2-5-2。

表 2-5-2　焊缝目视检测的项目参考表

检测项目	检测部位	质量要求	备注
清理质量	所有焊缝及其两侧 25 mm 范围内	无焊渣、飞溅及阻碍检测的附着物	
几何形状	焊缝与母材连接处	焊缝完整不得有漏焊，连接处应圆滑过渡	
	焊缝形状和尺寸急剧变化的部位	焊缝高低、宽窄及结晶焊缝波纹应均匀	可用焊接检测尺等测量
伤痕补焊	母材机械划伤部位	伤痕部位不应有明显棱角和沟槽，伤痕深度不超过有关标准规定	

(2) 焊缝尺寸不符合要求的类型及原因

焊缝尺寸不符合要求的类型包括焊缝超高、超宽、过窄、高低差过大，焊缝过渡到母材不圆滑，焊缝粗、外形高低不平，焊缝加强高度过低或过高，焊缝宽度不一等，角焊缝单边或下陷量过大等均为焊缝尺寸不合要求，其原因是：

①焊件坡口角度不当或装配间隙不均匀。

②焊接电流过大或过小，焊接规范选用不当。

③焊接速度不均匀，焊枪角度不当。

(3) 焊缝检测常用评分标准

对焊件按规范进行焊后处理与检测评分，板对接焊缝外观常用评分标准见表 2-5-3，分值总分以 60 分计算，可以根据实际情况修改，常用内部质量评分标准见表 2-5-4，外观(正、背)成形评判标准见表 2-5-5。

表 2-5-3　板对接焊缝外观评分表

检查项目	评判标准及得分	评判等级				自测数据	自评分数	教师测量	教师评分	备注
		Ⅰ	Ⅱ	Ⅲ	Ⅳ					
焊缝余高	尺寸标准/mm	≤2	>2，≤3	>3，≤4	<0 或>4					
	得分标准/mm	4 分	3 分	2 分	0 分					
焊缝高度差	尺寸标准/mm	≤1	>1，≤2	>2，≤3	>3					
	得分标准/mm	8 分	4 分	2 分	0 分					

表 2-5-3(续)

检查项目	评判标准及得分	评判等级				自测数据	自评分数	教师测量	教师评分	备注
		Ⅰ	Ⅱ	Ⅲ	Ⅳ					
焊缝宽度	尺寸标准/mm	17~19	16~20	15~22	<15 或 >22					
	得分标准/mm	4 分	2 分	1 分	0 分					
焊缝宽度差	尺寸标准/mm	≤1 .5	>1.5,≤2	>2,≤3	>3					
	得分标准/mm	8 分	4 分	2 分	0 分					
咬边	尺寸标准/mm	无咬边	深度≤0.5		深度>0.5					
	得分标准/mm	12 分	长度每 5 mm 扣 2 分		0 分					
正面成形	标准	优	良	中	差					
	得分标准	8 分	6 分	4 分	0 分					
背面成形	标准	优	良	中	差					
	得分标准	6 分	4 分	2 分	0 分					
背面凹度	尺寸标准	≤0.5	>0.5,≤1	>1,≤2	长度>30					
	得分标准	2 分	1 分	0 分	0 分					
背面凸度	尺寸标准/mm	≤2	>2,≤3	>1						
	得分标准/mm	2 分	1 分	0 分						
角变形	尺寸标准/mm	≤1	>1,≤3	>3,≤5	>5					
	得分标准/mm	4 分	2 分	1 分	0 分					
错边量	尺寸标准/mm	≤0.5	>0.5,≤1	>1						
	得分标准/mm	2 分	1 分	0 分						
外观缺陷(裂纹、气孔、咬边、弧坑凹坑、夹渣、未熔合等)记录										

表 2-5-4　板对接焊缝内部质量评分标准

考核项目	考核要求	评分要求	自查数据	自评得分	教师检查	教师评分	备注
焊缝内部质量检查	焊件的射线检测按 GB/T 3323.1—2019 标准评定	Ⅰ级片无缺陷不扣分,Ⅰ级片有缺陷扣 5 分,Ⅱ级片扣 10 分,Ⅲ级片扣 15 分,Ⅳ级片扣 20 分					

表 2-5-5　焊缝外观(正、背)成形评判标准

优(10分)	良(8分)	中(6分)	差(5分)	自查数据	自评得分	教师检查	教师评分
成形美观,焊缝均匀、细密,高低宽窄一致	成形较好,焊缝均匀、平整	成形尚可,焊缝平直	焊缝弯曲,高低、宽窄相差明显				
焊件综合得分							

注:1. 若焊件未完成焊接,表面有修补痕迹及焊缝正反面有裂纹、夹渣、气孔、未熔合缺陷,则该件按0分处理。
2. 试板两端20 mm内的缺陷不计。

3. 工位工具清理点检与评分

完工后对工位按6S标准进行清理清扫整顿,并做好记录,按表2-5-6进行评分。

表 2-5-6　完工后工位环境点检整理评分表

序号	点检内容		点检	评分标准	自评得分	教师评分	检查记录
1	防护用品整理	电弧焊工作服:无破损,整理规范	□合格　□不合格	0.5			
2		劳保鞋:无破损,整理规范	□合格　□不合格	0.5			
3		脚盖:无破损,整理规范	□合格　□不合格	0.5			
4		焊接手套:无破损,整理规范	□合格　□不合格	0.5			
5		面罩:无破损,遮光镜片无破损无油污;紧固无晃动,整理规范	□合格　□不合格	0.5			
6		护目镜:无破损,整理规范	□合格　□不合格	0.5			
7	焊接设备、用具	电源开关:电压指示正常、接线紧固无破损、电流保护复位正常	□合格　□不合格	0.5			
8		电焊机:进线接线正确、牢固无破损;电压电流指示正常,调节正常,摆放规范	□合格　□不合格	0.5			
9		焊把与输出电缆:输出电缆接线正确、牢固、无破损,焊把无破损、接线牢固无外露、操作灵活,整理规范	□合格　□不合格	0.5			
10		护目镜:完好,整理规范	□合格　□不合格	0.5			
11		开坡口工具:锉刀——手柄牢固、纹齿正常;角磨机——无破损,能正常使用,整理规范	□合格　□不合格	0.5			

表 2-5-6(续)

序号	点检内容		点检	评分标准	自评得分	教师评分	检查记录
12	焊接设备、用具	除渣工具:敲渣锤、锤子手柄牢固,錾子、钢丝刷无缺损,整理规范	□合格 □不合格	0.5			
13		焊条保温桶:无破损,能合盖,保温良好,整理规范	□合格 □不合格	0.5			
14		焊缝检测尺:无损坏,刻度线清晰,操作灵活,能正确调零,整理规范	□合格 □不合格	0.5			
15	作业环境	有无未熄灭火种	□合格 □不合格	0.5			
16		灭火器:齐全,整理规范	□合格 □不合格	0.5			
17		隔断:整理规范	□合格 □不合格	0.5			
18		工位卫生清扫,整理规范	□合格 □不合格	0.5			
19		焊条材料整理规范	□合格 □不合格	0.5			
20		作业指示警示牌:醒目,正确放置	□合格 □不合格	0.5			

任务考核

1. 一般情况下,10 mm 厚工件板对接平焊时应单边开(　　)V 形坡口。

A. 30°　　B. 45°　　C. 50°　　D. 60°

2. 板对接工件焊缝坡口处应进行打磨清理,清理范围一般为坡口面及坡口边缘上下两侧(　　)mm 范围。

A. 5~10　　B. 10~15　　C. 15~20　　D. 20~25

3. 10 mm 厚工件板对接平焊时,坡口应打磨或加工(　　)mm 的钝边。

A. 0　　B. 0.5~1.0　　C. 1.0~1.5　　D. 1.5~2.0

4. 12 mm 厚工件板对接平焊装配时,焊件始焊端和结束端的根部间隙常常设置为(　　)mm。

A. 3.2、4.0　　B. 0、2.0　　C. 1.0、2.5　　D. 2.5、3.2

5. CO_2 气体保护焊板对接平焊时,常采用(　　)焊法。

A. 左　　B. 右　　C. 前　　D. 后

6. CO_2 气体保护焊板对接平焊时,焊枪与板件之间夹角常用角度为在打底层施焊时,可采用(　　)角度摆动焊丝。

A. 45°~60°　　B. 50°~70°　　C. 70°~80°　　D. 80°~90°

7. CO_2 气体保护焊对低碳钢进行平焊,在打底层施焊时,可采用(　　)摆动焊丝。

A. 月牙形或锯齿形　　B. 直线　　C. 画圈形　　D. 反月牙形

8. CO_2 气体保护焊对低碳钢进行平焊,在填充层施焊时,保持焊道表面低于母材表面(　　)mm 左右,不能熔化坡口的棱边。

A. 1~1.5　　B. 1.5~2　　C. 2~2.5　　D. 2.5~3

9. CO_2 气体保护焊对低碳钢进行平焊，在盖面层施焊时，焊丝摆动到坡口两侧时，焊丝对准坡口棱边，不要超过棱边，形成熔池后熔化棱边(　　)mm。

A. -1　　B. 0　　C. 1~2　　D. 0~1

10. 焊缝尺寸不符合要求的原因是(　　)。

A. 焊件坡口角度不当或装配间隙不均匀

B. 焊接电流过大或过小，焊接规范选用不当

C. 焊接速度不均匀，焊枪角度不当

D. 以上都是

任务操作

按任务要求和流程顺序进行任务实施训练，焊后能够根据焊缝检查要求进行自检和进行工位工具整理，训练后进行考核，并按检测要求进行评分。

Project Ⅴ Plate Butt Joint Flat Welding Using CO_2 Gas Shielded Welding

【Learning Objectives】

1. Analysis the technical requirements of CO_2 gas shielded welding for board butt welding;
2. Master the pre welding preparation of CO_2 gas shielded welding for flat welding of board joints;
3. Master the welding operation of CO_2 gas shielded welding for board butt welding;
4. Master the post weld treatment and inspection of CO_2 gas shielded welding for board butt welding.

Task 1:Analysis the Technical requirements of CO_2 Gas Shielded Welding for Board Butt Welding

Figure 1-5-1 shows the assembly drawing and technical requirements for common plate butt joint flat welding test pieces.

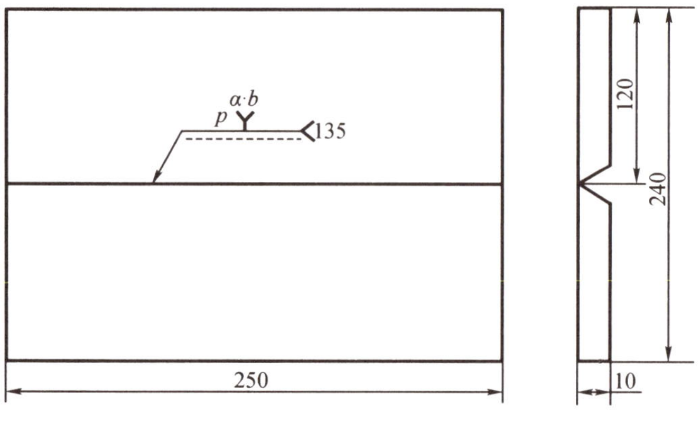

Technical requirements

1. Single-side welding double-side forming.
2. V - shape groove with a groove angle of 60°.
3. Self-determined root gap and root face size.
4. Misalignment ≤1.2 mm.
5. Angular deformation < 3°.
6. Undercut is not allowed.
7. Incomplete penetration is not allowed.
8. Cracks, pores, and slag inclusion are not allowed.
9. Weld reinforcement ≤1+0.15b.

Figure 2-5-1 Single-side Welding Double-side Forming Weldment Using Q235B Plate Butt Joint Flat Welding(Unit:mm)

CO_2 gas shielded welding is widely used in the production of various metal structures, particularly in flat butt single-side welding double-side forming techniques, which are worth studying. The single-side welding double-side forming process of CO_2 gas shielded welding adopts the continuous breakdown welding method. This method utilizes the concentrated arc heat and strong penetration ability of CO_2 gas shielded welding to directly penetrate the groove root, melting 1-2 mm on both sides of the groove root respectively. As a result, a melt hole larger than the assembly clearance is formed at the front edge of the molten pool. During welding, a portion of the deposited metal transfers to the root and back of the weld, while most of the deposited metal forms a molten pool with the base metal on the front side. As the welding gun moves forward, the surface tension causes the molten metal to flow behind the melt hole. During cooling, the melt hole is sealed behind the arc, and the molten pool continuously cools and solidifies to ultimately form fully penetrated front and back welds.

This unit uses low carbon steel commonly used in practical engineering as an example to introduce the task implementation process of platebutt joint flat welding GMAW, including pre-welding preparation, welding operation, post-weld treatment, and inspection.

Task 2:Master the Pre Welding Preparation of CO_2 Gas Shielded Welding for Flat Welding of Board Joints

1. Weldment preparation and groove cleaning

Prepare two Q235B weldments with a dimension of 10 mm×120 mm×250 mm and a 30° V-shape groove on one side according to the requirements of the task list.

Oil, rust, water, paint, oxide skin, dust, oil stains, burrs, and other impurities on the weld can cause welding defects such as pores, slag inclusion, incomplete fusion, etc. Therefore, these detrimental factors to welding must be removed through cleaning measures. The cleaning range is generally 15-20 mm on the groove surface and the upper and lower sides of the groove edge, revealing a metallic luster, as shown in Figure 2-5-3. Additionally, the groove root face should be polished to a depth of 0.5-1.0 mm.

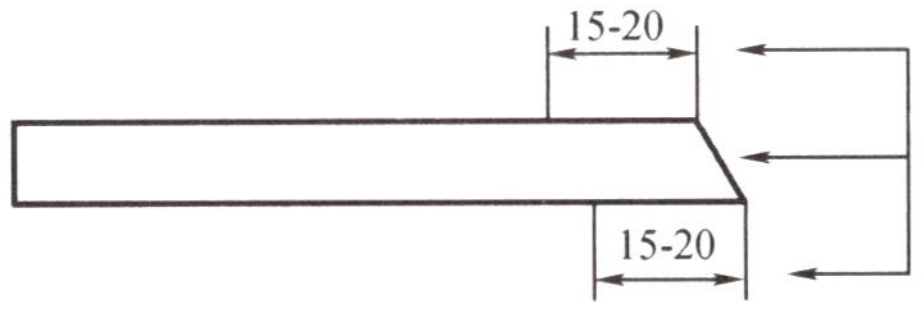

Figure 2-5-3 Schematicdiagram of Joint Grinding Area(Unit:mm)

2. Determination of welding process parameters

Considering the welding characteristics and plate thickness of base metal Q235B in this task, a diameter of 1.2 mm ER50-6 welding wire is selected. The protective gas used is CO_2 gas with a purity greater than 99.5%. Three layers and threebeads are employed for welding. Refer to Table 2-5-1 for specific welding process parameters.

Table 2-5-1 Welding Process Parameters

Welding layer	Type of welding wire	Welding wire diameter/mm	Welding current/A	Welding voltage/V	Shield gas flow rate (L/min)	Wire extension length/mm	Power supply polarity
Backing layer	ER50-6	1.2	90-110	18-20	12-15	10-15	DC reverse polarity
Filling layer			120-140	20-22	12-15	10-15	
Covering layer			140-160	21-23	12-15	10-15	

Multi-layer welding refers to the process of depositing more than two welding layers to complete the entire weld. It includes both multi-layer single-bead welding and multi-layer multi-bead welding, as shown in Figure 2-5-4. A layer of weld can consist of several beads. If the groove angle is small, a single bead can be deposited, which is called single-bead welding. When the groove angle is large, two or morebeads can be deposited to form a layer of weld, known as multi-bead welding. Multi-layer welding is a common method used for welding large thick-walled structures. Compared to single-layer welding under the same conditions, it can reduce heat input, deformation, and the probability of defects. Multi-layer and multi-bead welding can also improve the quality of the weld metal, especially its plasticity. This is because the back layer (back bead) weld has a heat treatment effect on the front layer (front bead) weld, similar to a normalizing heat treatment, thereby improving the secondary structure. The heat treatment effect of a single welding layer is only 3-5 mm. If the thickness of each weld bead exceeds 6 mm, the heat treatment effect is poor, leading to lower quality of the weld metal structure.

(a) Multi-layer welding　　(b) Multi-layer and multi-bead welding

Figure 2-5-4 Profile of Multi-layer and Multi-bead Welding

Generally, when the plate thickness is ≤6 mm, I-shape groove butt welding is used. When double-side welding is used, linear electrode manipulation is adopted on the front side, which is slightly slower and has a smaller current. Linear electrode manipulation is also adopted on the backside, which has slightly larger current and faster welding speed.

When the plate thickness is greater than 6mm, other forms of groovebutt joint flat welding should be adopted, and multi-layer welding or multi-layer and multi-bead welding can be used. When welding the backing layer, especially when single-side welding double-side forming is performed, a small welding current is often used to ensure the quality of the back weld. When welding the filling layer, a large welding current is often used to improve efficiency and ensure good fusion. When welding the covering layer, the welding current used should be slightly smaller than that of the filling layer to prevent undercut and ensure proper weld formation.

Current regulatory characteristics of multi-layer and multi-bead welding: backingwelding current < covering welding current < filling welding current. The covering welding current should be greater than that of backing welding.

3. Assembly and positioning

The factors of welding deformation should be considered for assembly positioning, in order to provide certain compensation and correction during assembly positioning.

Place two steel plates horizontally on the fixture table, align both ends and assemble them into butt joints. During assembly, set the root gap at the initial welding end of the weldment to

3.2 mm and that at the final end to 4.0 mm. Carry outpositioning welding at both ends using the same process parameters as backing. The length of the welding spot is 10–15 mm, the thickness of the initial end is 3–4 mm, the thickness of the final end is 7–8 mm, the misalignment should not exceed 1.2 mm, and the allowance for anti-deformation is 3°–5°. As shown in Figure 2-5-5. After spot welding, the slag shell of the welding spot should be knocked off and polished to a metallic luster in a slope shape to facilitate jointing.

Task 3:Master the Welding Operation of CO_2 Gas Shielded Welding for Board Butt Welding

When butt welding commonly used 10 mm-thick plates in engineering, the welding process often includes three-layer and three-bead welding or four-layer and four-bead welding. The operation methods are similar. Here we will introduce the more common three-layer and three-bead welding.

Fix the weldment on the operating table and place it horizontally. The height of the weldment is generally up to the operator's bare foot (welding in a squatting position). Place the end with a small gap on the right side. Adopt the left-hand welding method. The included angle between the welding wire and the plate is 70°–80°, and it forms a 90° angle with the direction of the weld, as shown in Figure 2-5-6.

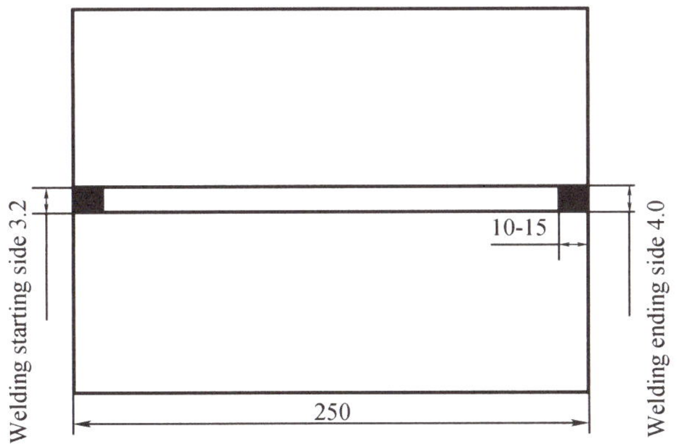

Figure 2-5-5 Schematic Diagram of Assembly Positioning Welding Locations (Unit: mm)

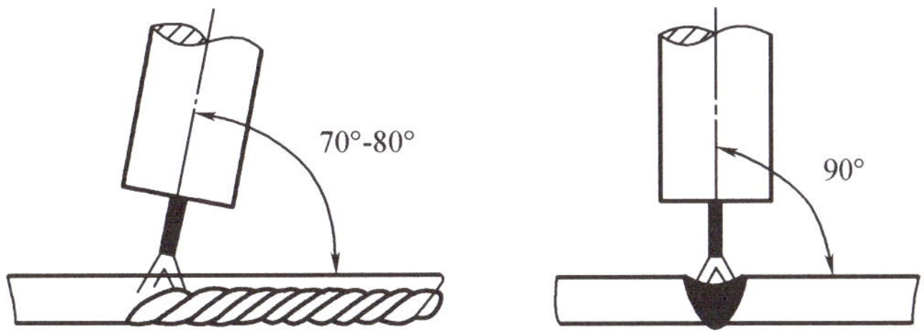

Figure 2-5-6 Welding Gun Angle Illustration

1. Backing welding

①Strike the arc on one side of the groove about 20 mm away from thepositioning weld at the right end of the weldment, and quickly pull it back to the positioning weld at the end for a short stay. Then start welding to the left according to the set welding parameters. Use a zigzag or crescent electrode moving method to make small transverse swings on both sides of the groove and stay on both sides of the groove. Control the arc at about 2–3 mm away from the bottom edge of the groove. When the diameter of the melting hole at the bottom of the groove is 3–4 mm, proceed to normal welding.

②During welding, the welding gun should always align with the weld centerline and remain on both sides of the groove for 0.5–1 second to prevent undercut defects. When the arc welding gun swings, observe that the diameter of the melting hole is 0.5–1mm larger than the gap. Adjust the amplitude and welding speed of the arc welding gun as needed according to changes in the diameter and gap of the melting hole to ensure that the diameter of the melting hole remains unchanged as much as possible and maintain a flat weld bead to achieve a reverse weld with uniform width and height. Clean slag and splashes from the weld bead surface after welding.

③The nozzle height must be strictly controlled to ensure that the arc burns at a distance of 2–3 mm from the root of the groove, maintaining a backing weld thickness not exceeding 4mm. Simultaneously, this nozzle height should not obstruct the operator's vision, enabling observation of fusion at the edge of the molten pool and providing protection.

④Special attention should be paid during arcending and the arc pit must be filled to prevent cracks from forming in the pit.

2. Filler welding

①Thoroughly clean the backinglayer welding slag, remove joint high points and overlaps to make the backing weld bead smooth.

②According to the set welding parameters, strike the arc 20 mm from the right end of the weldment. Quickly pull down the rightmost end and press down the arc briefly. When a molten pool is formed, use the zigzag or crescent – shape swing welding method towards the left. The transverse swing amplitude of the arc welding gun should be slightly larger than that of the backing weld bead. When manipulating the electrode, pause on both sides and pay attention to fusion on both sides of the molten pool. The forward moving pace of the arc should be about 1/2–2/3 of the size of the molten pool to ensure a flat and slightly concave surface of the weld bead, with the height of the filling layer being 1–1.5 mm lower than that of the base metal surface, to avoid burning groove edges, resulting in undercut or weld misalignment on the covering layer, as shown in Figure 2-5-7.

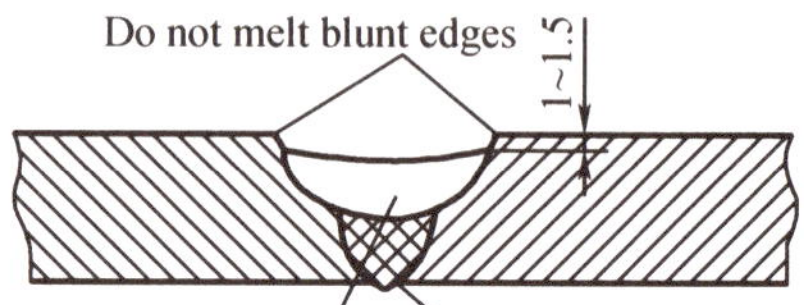

Figure 2-5-7 Requirements for Weld Bead of Filling Layer (Unit: mm)

3. Covering welding

①Thoroughly clean thebacking layer welding slag and adjust the process parameters to the pre-selected covering welding gear.

②The welding method for the covering layer is essentially the same as that for the filling layer. The zigzag or crescent electrode movement method is used, welding from right to left. The swing amplitude of the arc welding gun should be larger than that of the filling weld. The welding speed should be kept as uniform as possible to prevent depression in the middle of the covering layer weld bead. When the welding wire swings to both sides of the groove, it should align with and not exceed the groove's edge. After a molten pool is formed, the edge should be melted by 0–1 mm.

③The arc crater must be filled during arcending, and the arc ending length should be short to prevent the formation of crater cracks.

Task 4:Master the Post Weld Treatment and Inspection of CO_2 Gas Shielded Welding for Board Butt Welding

1. Weld seam cleaning

After the weldment is welded, remove any welding slag and splatter on the weld using a slag hammer, wire brush, etc. , or re-polish the weld's appearance with an emery cloth. There should be no presence of welding slag, welding spots, or burrs. The weld should be smooth and flat. The "flush edge and flat surface" of the weldment should be ensured, including the vertical parallelism of the upper opening edge of the weldment, but the original surface of the weld should not be damaged.

2. Weld seam quality inspection

(1) Weld appearance inspection

After welding, the surface quality of the welds should be examined. The presence of defects such as pores, cracks, and undercut on the weld surface should be visually inspected or checked using low-power magnifying glasses. The appearance quality and dimensions of the welds should be assessed using steel rulers, steel squares, and weld inspection rules. Refer to Table 2-5-2 for specific routine test items and requirements.

Table 2-5-2 Reference Table for Visual Inspection Items of Welds

Test item	Tested part	Quality requirement	Annotations
Cleaning quality	All welds and their sides within a 25 mm range	No welding slag, splashing, or attachments that hinder inspection	
Geometric shape	Weld and base metal joint	The weld joint shall be complete without solder skips, and the connection shall be smooth	
	Parts with abrupt changes in weld shape and size	The weld height, width and crystalline weld ripples shall be uniform	A welding inspection ruler can be used for measurements
Scar repair welding	Mechanical scratched part of the base material	There should be no obvious edges and grooves in the damaged area, and the depth of the scar should not exceed the relevant standard requirements	

(2) Types and causes of weld size not meeting the required specifications

The nonconforming weld dimensions, which do not meet the requirements, include excessive height, excessive width, excessive narrowness, significant height difference, unsmooth transition from weld to base metal, coarse appearance, uneven height, too low or too high reinforcement height of weld, unequal width of weld, unilateral fillet weld or excessive subsidence, and so on. These are all due to the following reasons: .

①Improper groove angle or uneven assembly clearance of the weldment.

②The welding current is either too high or too low, and the choice of welding specifications is inappropriate.

③The welding speed is inconsistent and the angle of the welding gun is improper.

(3) Common Scoring Criteria for Weld Inspection

Post-weld treatment and testing scoring are conducted for welded components according to specifications. Refer to Table 2-5-3 for common scoring criteria for the appearance of butt welds on plates, with a total score of 60 points calculated, which can be adjusted based on actual circumstances. Refer to Table 2-5-4 for common scoring criteria for internal quality, and Table 2-5-5 for scoring criteria for overall inspection of weld appearance (front and back).

2. Defects within 20 mm at both ends of the test plate are not taken into account

(3) Workstation tool cleaning inspection and scoring

After completion, clean and organize the workstations according to the 6S standard, make records, and evaluate according to Table 2-5-6.

Table 2-5-3 Scoring System for the Appearance of Plate Butt Weldsmm

Inspection Items	Evaluation criteria and score	Judgment level				Self-test data	Self-assessment score	Teacher evaluation	Teacher's score	Comments
		Ⅰ	Ⅱ	Ⅲ	Ⅳ					
Weld Seam Height	Sizing standard/mm	≤2	>2, ≤3	>3, ≤4	<0 或>4					
	Score	4	3	2	0					
Welding seam height difference	Sizing standard/mm	≤1	>1, ≤2	>2, ≤3	>3					
	Score	8	4	2	0					
Weld width	Sizing standard/mm	17-19	16-20	15-22	<15 or >22					
	Score	4	2	1	0					
Weld seam width difference	Sizing standard/mm	≤1.5	>1.5, ≤2	>2, ≤3	>3					
	Score	8	4	2	0					
Bite-edge	Sizing standard/mm	No edge biting	Depth≤0.5		Depth>0.5					
	Score	12	2 points will be deducted for every 5mm in length.		0					
Front Forming	Standards	Great	Good	Average	Bad					
	Score	8	6	4	0					
Back molding	Standards	Great	Good	Average	Bad					
	Score	6	4	2	0					
Backconcavity	Sizing standard/mm	≤0.5	>0.5, ≤1	>1, ≤2	Length >30					
	Score	2	1	0	0					

Table 2-5-3 (Continued)

Inspection Items	Evaluation criteria and score	Judgment level				Self-test data	Self-assessment score	Teacher evaluation	Teacher's score	Comments
		Ⅰ	Ⅱ	Ⅲ	Ⅳ					
Backconvexity	Sizing standard/mm	≤2	>2, ≤3	>1						
	Score	2	1	0						
Angular distortion	Sizing standard/mm	≤1	>1, ≤3	>3, ≤5	>5					
	Score	4	2	1	0					
Inaccuracy of edge deviation	Sizing standard/mm	≤0.5	>0.5, ≤1	>1						
	Score	2	1	0						
Appearance defects (crack, pore, edge biting, arc pit, inclusion of slag, incomplete fusion, and other defects) defect records										

Table 2-5-4 Internal Quality Scoring Criteria for Plate Butt Welding

Assessment Items	Assessment Requirements	Scoring Requirements	Self-inspection data	Self-assessment score	Teacher inspection	Teacher's rating	Remarks
Inside of weld quality inspection	The radiographic testing of weldments shall be carried out according to the GB/T 3323. 1—2019 standard assessment	No deduction for Grade I film without defects, 5 points deducted for defective Grade I film, 10 points deducted for Grade II film, 15 points deducted for Grade III film, and 20 points deducted for Grade IV film					

Table 2-5-5 Evaluation Criteria for Weld Appearance (Front and Back) Forming

Excellent (10 points)	Good (8 points)	Average (6 points)	Average (6 points)	Self-inspection data	Self-evaluation score	Teacher inspection	Teacher's score
Beautiful appearance, uniform and fine welds, consistent height and width	Good formation, uniform and flat welds	The shaping is acceptable, and the weld joint is straight	The weld is bent, with obvious differences in height and width				
Comprehensive weldment score							

Note: If the weldment is not properly welded, with repair marks on the surface and cracks, slag inclusions, pores, and incomplete fusion defects on both sides of the weld seam, the workpiece shall be scored 0.

Table 2-5-6 Scoring for Spot Check and Arrangement of Station Environment after Completion

Serial number	Spot check contents		Spot check	Grading standards	Self-evaluation score	Teacher's score	Inspection records
1	Sorting protective articles.	Arc welding work clothes: undamaged, neatly arranged.	□Qualified □Unqualified	0.5			
2		Safety shoes: undamaged, arranged in a standardized manner.	□Qualified □Unqualified	0.5			
3		Foot cover: undamaged, neatly arranged.	□Qualified □Unqualified	0.5			
4		Welding gloves: They must be free from any damage and neatly organized.	□Qualified □Unqualified	0.5			
5		Face shield: no damage, lens for light shielding is free from damage and oil stains; it is securely fastened without shaking, and neatly arranged.	□Qualified □Unqualified	0.5			
6		Goggles: undamaged and neatly organized.	□Qualified □Unqualified	0.5			
7	Welding equipment and tools	Power switch: Voltage indication is normal, wiring is securely fastened without damage, and current protection reset is normal.	□Qualified □Unqualified	0.5			
8		Electric welding machine: The incoming wiring is correct, secure, and undamaged; the voltage and current indicators are normal, properly adjusted, and placed in a standardized manner	□Qualified □Unqualified	0.5			

Table 2-5-6(continued 1)

Serial number	Spot check contents		Spot check	Grading standards	Self-evaluation score	Teacher's score	Inspection records
9	Welding equipment and tools	Welding handle and output cable: The connection of the output cable should be correct, firm, and undamaged. The welding handle should be undamaged, the connection should be firm without any exposed parts, the operation should be flexible, and the arrangement should be standardized	□Qualified □Unqualified	0.5			
10		Goggles: intact and properly organized	□Qualified □Unqualified	0.5			
11		Beveling tools: file-with a sturdy handle and regular teeth; angle grinder - undamaged, can be used normally, and arranged in a standardized manner	□Qualified □Unqualified	0.5			
12		Slag removal tools: The slag hammer and hammer handle are sturdy, the chisel and wire brush are defect - free, and the arrangement is standardized	□Qualified □Unqualified	0.5			
13		Insulation barrel for welding rods: undamaged, closable, providing excellent thermal insulation and organized in a standardized manner	□Qualified □Unqualified	0.5			

Table 2-5-6 (continued 2)

Serial number	Spot check contents		Spot check	Grading standards	Self-evaluation score	Teacher's score	Inspection records
14	Welding equipment and tools	Weld inspection ruler: undamaged, clear scale lines, flexible operation, accurate zero adjustment, and standardized arrangement	□Qualified □Unqualified	0.5			
15	Operating environment	Is there any kindling that has not been extinguished	□Qualified □Unqualified	0.5			
16		Fire extinguishers: fully equipped and organized in a standardized manner	□Qualified □Unqualified	0.5			
17		Partition: organized systematically	□Qualified □Unqualified	0.5			
18		Clean and organize the workstation in a standardized manner	□Qualified □Unqualified	0.5			
19		Welding Rod Material Sorting Guidelines	□Qualified □Unqualified	0.5			
20		Caution signs for operation instructions: prominently displayed and correctly positioned	□Qualified □Unqualified	0.5			

Task Assessment

1. Generally, (　　) single-side V-shape grooves shall be opened during plate butt joint flat welding of 12mm-thick workpieces.

A. 30°　　B. 45°　　C. 50°　　D. 60°

2. The weld groove of the plate butt joint workpiece should be polished and cleaned, and the cleaning range is generally (　　) mm above and below the groove surface and groove edge.

A. 5-10　　B. 10-15　　C. 15-20　　D. 20-25

3. For plate butt joint flat welding of 12mm-thick workpieces, the groove shall be polished or processed with (　　) mm root face.

A. 0　　B. 0.5-1.0　　C. 1.0-1.5　　D. 1.5-2.0

4. When assembling 12 mm-thick workpieces using plate butt joint flat welding, the root gap between the starting end and the ending end of the weldment is typically set to (　　) mm.

A. 3.2, 4.0　　B. 0, 2.0　　C. 1.0, 2.5　　D. 2.5, 3.2

5. The (　　) welding method is often used for plate butt joint flat weldingusing CO_2 gas shielded welding.

A. Left　　B. Right　　C. Front　　D. Rear

6. For plate butt joint flat welding using CO_2 gas shielded welding, the commonly used angle between the welding gun and plates adopts the backing welding, (　　) angle swing welding is used.

A. 45°-60°　　B. 50°-70°　　C. 70°-80°　　D. 80°-90°

7. CO_2 gas shielded welding is used for flat welding of low carbon steel. (　　) swing welding wire can be used for the backing layer welding.

A. Crescent or sawtooth shape　　B. Straight line

C. Circular shape　　D. Reverse crescent shape

8. CO_2 gas shielded welding is used for flat position welding of low carbon steel. When welding the filling layer, keep the weld bead surface about (　　) mm lower than the base metal surface and do not melt the edge of the groove.

A. 1-1.5　　B. 1.5-2　　C. 2-2.5　　D. 2.5-3

9. CO_2 gas shielded welding is used for flat position welding of low carbon steel. When welding on the covering layer, when the welding wire swings to both sides of the groove, it should align with the edge of the groove and should not exceed it. The edge should be melted by (　　) mm after a molten pool is formed.

A. -1　　B. 0　　C. 1-2　　D. 0-1

10. The reason for the weld size not meeting the requirements is (　　).

A. Improperweldment groove angle or uneven assembly clearance

B. Excessive or insufficient welding current and improper selection of welding specifications.

C. Uneven welding speed and improper angle of welding gun

D. All of the above

Task Operation

Carry out task implementation training according to task requirements and process sequence. After welding, carry out self-inspection and sort out station tools according to weld inspection requirements. After training, conduct assessment and score according to testing requirements.

项目六　板对接立焊CO_2气体保护焊

【学习目标】

1. 分析板对接立焊 CO_2 气体保护焊的技术要求；
2. 掌握板对接立焊 CO_2 气体保护焊的焊前准备；
3. 掌握板对接立焊 CO_2 气体保护焊的焊接操作；
4. 掌握板对接立焊 CO_2 气体保护焊的焊后处理与检查。

任务1：分析板对接立焊CO_2气体保护焊的技术要求

图 2-6-1 为常见板对接平焊试件装配图及技术要求。

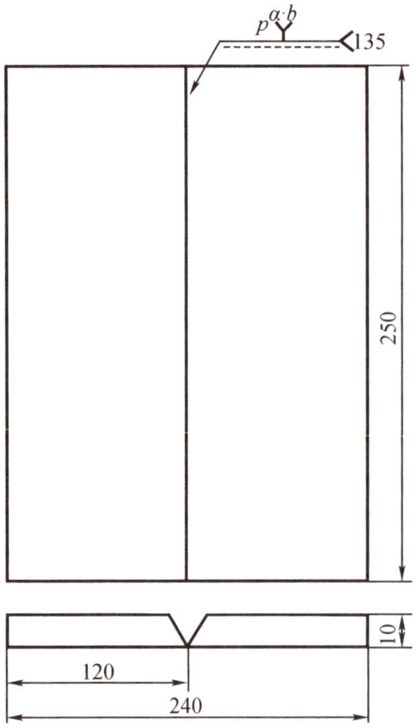

技术要求

1. 坡口为 60°坡口角的 V 形带钝边坡口。
2. 根部间隙和钝边尺寸自定。
3. 错边≤0.5 mm。
4. 角变形<3°。
5. 不允许有咬边。
6. 不允许有未焊透。
7. 不允许有裂纹、气孔、夹渣。
8. 焊缝余高≤1+0.15*b*。

图 2-6-1　Q235B 板对接立焊焊焊件图(单位:mm)

板对接立焊时，液态金属受重力作用易下淌，因此，很难保证焊道表面平整，为防止液态金属下淌，采用立向上焊，且采用比板对接平焊稍小的焊接电流，焊枪摆动频率稍快，使熔池小而薄。

本单元以实际工程中常用的低碳钢材质为例介绍板对接立焊熔化极气体保护焊的焊前准备、焊接操作和焊后处理与检查等任务实施流程。

任务2：掌握板对接立焊CO_2气体保护焊的焊前准备

1. 焊件准备及坡口清理

根据任务单要求，准备 10 mm×120 mm×250 mm 尺寸的 Q235B 材质焊件两块，单边开 30°V 形坡口。

焊缝上的油、锈、水、漆、氧化皮、灰尘、油污、毛刺等杂物可以引起焊接缺陷，比如气孔、夹渣、未熔合等，所以应通过清理措施将这些对焊接有害因素清除干净。清理的范围一般为坡口面及坡口边缘上下两侧 15~20 mm 范围，并露出金属光泽，并打磨出 0.5~1.0 mm 的坡口钝边，具体如项目五中图 2-5-3 所示。

2. 焊接工艺参数确定

结合本任务母材 Q235B 的焊接特性和板厚来看，选择直径 1.2 mm 的 ER50-6 焊丝，保护气体为 CO_2 气体，纯度高于 99.5%，采用三层三道来焊接，具体焊接工艺参数见表 2-6-1。

表 2-6-1　焊接工艺参数

焊接层次	焊丝型号	焊丝直径/mm	焊接电流/A	焊接电压/V	保护气体流量/(L/min)	焊丝伸出长度/mm	电源极性
打底层	ER50-6	1.2	90~110	18~20	12~15	12~15	直流反接
填充层			120~140	20~22	12~15	12~15	
盖面层			110~120	18~20	12~15	12~15	

3. 装配定位

装配定位需考虑到焊接变形的因素，以便在装配定位时给予一定的补偿修正。

将两块钢板水平放工装台上，两端对齐装配成对接接头，装配时焊件始焊端根部间隙设置为 3.2 mm，结束端为 4.0 mm，采取和打底相同的工艺参数在两端进行点固焊，焊点长度为 10~15 mm，起始端厚度为 3~4 mm，结束厚度为 7~8 mm，错边量不大于 1.2 mm，反变形预留量为 3°~5°。点焊后应将焊点渣壳敲掉并打磨至金属光泽，呈斜坡状，以便于接头。

任务3：掌握板对接立焊CO_2气体保护焊的焊接操作

板对接立焊时，操作者要选择适合的高度位置固定焊件。由于焊枪和焊把线较重，所以焊枪的握持要选择一种较为省力的方式，以减少焊接过程中手的疲劳程度，有利于控制焊接质量。焊接过程中要根据装配间隙和熔池温度的变化及时调整焊枪的角度、摆动幅度和焊接速度，控制熔池和熔孔的尺寸，保证正反两面成形良好。

将焊件固定在操作台上，焊缝垂直装夹，焊缝面向操作者，焊件高度一般和操作者膝盖同等高度（蹲姿焊），间隙小的一端放置下侧，采用立向上焊法，如图 2-6-2 所示。

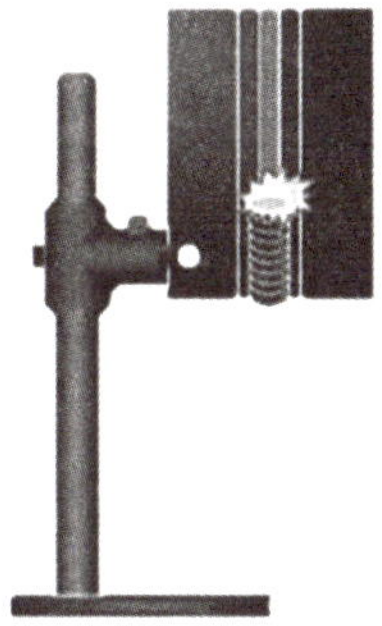

图 2-6-2　安装固定示意图

10 mm 厚板件的焊接层次常有三层三道和四层四道焊的做法，即为打底一层、填充一层或两层、盖面一层，如图 2-6-3 所示，为四层四道焊。二者操作方法类似，这里介绍三层三道焊。

焊接时焊枪角度均为与板件之间夹角为90°,与立焊缝下端方向成70°~90°,如图2-6-4所示,焊枪角度从起焊至焊完应尽量保持一致。

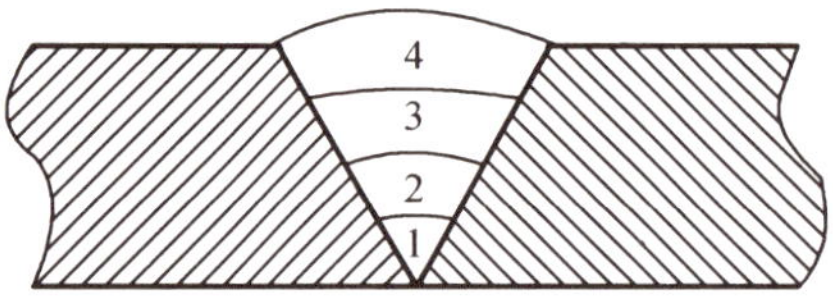

图2-6-3　焊接层次示意图

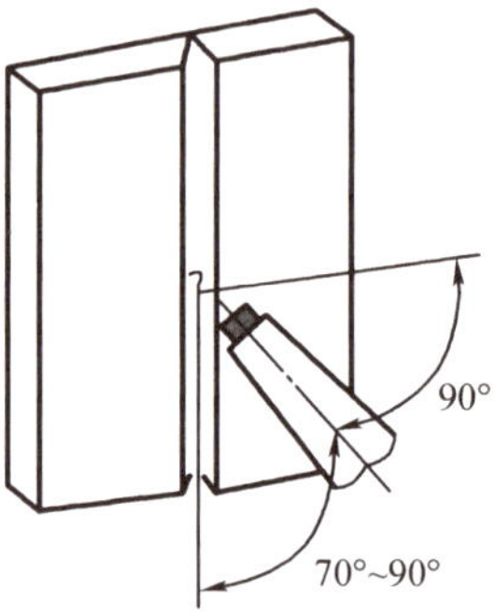

图2-6-4　立向上焊法焊枪角度

1. 打底焊

①打底焊时,按确定的工艺卡调试好焊接工艺参数,检查、清理导电嘴和喷嘴,并在喷嘴上涂防飞溅剂,并先按动焊枪开关,检查送丝是否正常。

②起焊时,在焊件下端定位焊点上引燃电弧,并控制电弧在距离底边2~3 mm处燃烧,然后以小锯齿形向上摆动焊枪施焊,当电弧运动到定位焊缝与坡口根部连接处时,用电弧将坡口根部击穿,产生熔孔后,转入正常施焊。

③正常施焊时,采用锯齿法左右摆动焊枪,电弧始终在坡口内做小幅度横向摆动,如图2-6-5所示。始终保持焊丝在熔池前缘,摆动时中间稍快,两侧稍作停顿,依靠电弧在坡口两侧的停留时间,保证坡口两侧熔合良好,一般使熔孔直径比间隙大0.5~1 mm,使打底层焊接道两侧与坡口结合处稍下凹,焊道表面平整,防止穿丝,如图2-6-6所示。如熔孔太大时,可适当加快摆动,并加宽摆幅,以使散热面积加大。

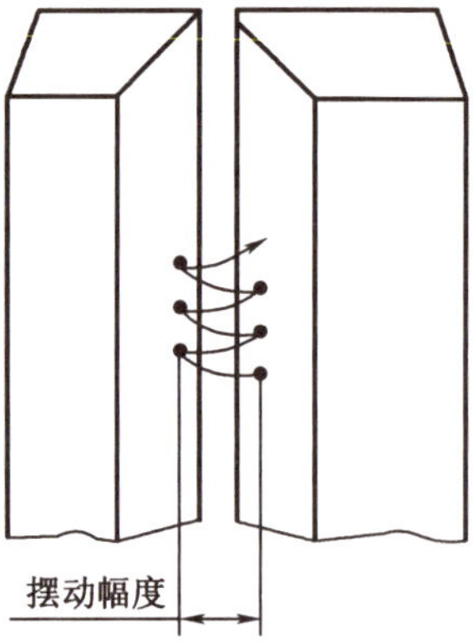

图2-6-5　打底焊摆动轨迹示意图

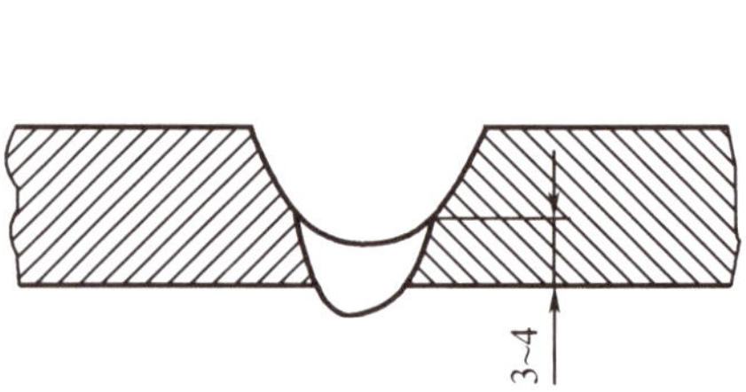

图2-6-6　底层焊道示意图

④焊接时应根据间隙和熔孔直径的变化调整横向摆动幅度和焊接速度,尽可能维持熔孔直径不变,以获得宽窄和高低均匀的反面焊缝,保证打底层厚度不超过4 mm。随着焊接的进行,焊枪向上移动,注意焊枪与焊件的角度应保持不变。焊枪向上运动时,操作者的手

臂也要随之上移，否则焊至上方时焊枪与下方夹角会减小，焊丝会穿过间隙，造成穿丝。

⑤当焊丝用完，或者由于送丝机、焊枪出现故障需要中断施焊时，焊枪不能马上离开熔池，应先稍停顿，如可能应将电弧移向坡口侧再停弧，以防产生气孔和缩孔。

⑥接头前用角向磨光机将弧坑焊道打磨成缓坡形，操作时焊丝的端部对准缓坡的 最高点，然后引弧，以锯齿形摆动焊丝，将焊道缓坡处覆盖，当电弧到达缓坡最低处时即可转入正常施焊。CO_2 气体保护焊的接头方法与焊条电弧焊有所不同，电弧燃烧到原熔孔处时，不需压低电弧形成新的熔孔，而只用它的熔深就可将接头接好。

2. 填充焊

①施焊填充层前，应将打底层焊道和试件表面的飞溅物清理干净，焊道局部凸起处打磨平整。

②按设定的填充规范调整好焊接工艺参数，焊枪角度与打底层焊接时相同，运丝方法可采用锯齿形运丝法、圆圈形运丝法和反月牙形运丝法进行施焊，电弧摆动不要太快，要稍慢而稳，摆幅比焊接打底层时稍宽，电弧在坡口两侧稍作停留，保证焊道两侧熔合良好，焊道表面平整。填充层焊道一般比坡口边缘要低 1.5~2 mm，并确保不熔化坡口棱边，确保盖面操作时可以以坡口棱边为参照物，保证焊缝宽窄一致，整齐划一。

a. 锯齿形运丝法：在焊件下端引弧后电弧运动稍慢，起预热作用，待形成熔池后，电弧向另一侧摆动，摆到打底层焊道与坡口边缘的夹角处时稍作停留，以便两侧熔合良好。采用锯齿形运丝法焊接填充层需焊两层，各层焊接速度较快，焊道温度低，表面光亮美观，容易掌握。

b. 圆圈形运丝法：这种运丝法因为散热面积较大，应用较大的电流和电压（如用直径为 1.2 mm 的焊丝，焊接电流为 120~140 A，电弧电压为 20~22 V），电流小时波纹不光滑，成形不美观。立焊圆圈形运丝法可以看作向前的反月牙运动加横向锯齿形运动。起焊时电弧以较慢的速度作横向摆动，较慢的速度起预热作用，同时可以使起焊处稍厚一些，注意两侧应熔合好，此运动完成后，电弧沿熔池的上缘作反月牙运动，目的是保证熔池与两侧夹角处及前一层充分熔合，电弧运动至坡口一侧稍停后，以直线形向另一侧运动，此时电弧位于熔池下缘，其目的是增加熔池的厚度，同时保证焊道的平整。这种运条方法类似三角形运条，只是三角形上面的角是圆弧过渡的，就是上圆下直。圆圈形运丝法焊接速度较慢，焊道及熔池温度较高，焊后焊道颜色较暗，不是很美观。其优点是熔合很好，一次可以焊出较厚的焊层，生产率高。采用这种运丝法时，填充层只需焊一层。

c. 反月牙形运丝法：焊接电流和电弧电压同圆圈形运丝法，焊接时电弧沿熔池前部边缘作反月牙形移动，但较圆圈形运丝法要慢，注意电弧在两侧坡口应适当停留，以使两侧熔合良好。电弧运动速度不能太快，否则熔池温度低，成形不光滑，中间可能会出现凹陷。反月牙形运丝法一次可以焊出较厚的焊层，熔合好，成形美观，方法简单，生产率高。采用这种运丝法，填充层也只需焊一层。本任务即采用这种运丝方法进行。

3. 盖面焊

①施焊盖面层前，应清理前层焊道和飞溅物，清理喷嘴上的飞溅物，并在喷嘴上涂硅油。

②按设定的盖面规范调整好焊接工艺参数，焊枪角度与施焊打底层时相同。施焊盖面层用锯齿形运丝法，焊丝横向摆动幅度比焊填充层要大，在坡口两侧应稍作停留，以填满坡口。停顿时间以焊缝与母材圆滑过渡、焊缝余高不超过标准为宜。焊丝横向摆动时，应注

意控制摆动间距，使之均匀合适，间距不宜过大，否则易产生咬边，焊缝表面也不美观。收弧时应注意填满弧坑，防止产生弧坑裂纹。

③盖面焊时要注意：保持焊嘴高度，焊接熔池边缘应超过坡口棱边0.5~1.5 mm，并防止产生咬边。收弧时一定要 填满弧坑，并且收弧弧长要短，以免产生弧坑裂纹。

任务4：掌握板对接立焊CO_2气体保护焊的焊后处理与检查

同教学项目五。

任务考核

1. 一般情况下，10 mm 厚工件板对接平焊时应单边开(　　)V 形坡口。

A. 30°　　B. 45°　　C. 50°　　D. 60°

2. 板对接工件焊缝坡口处应进行打磨清理，清理范围一般为坡口面及坡口边缘上下两侧(　　)mm 范围。

A. 5~10　　B. 10~15　　C. 15~20　　D. 20~25

3. 10 mm 厚工件板对接平焊时，坡口应打磨或加工(　　)mm 的钝边。

A. 0　　B. 0.5~1.0　　C. 1.0~1.5　　D. 1.5~2.0

4. 12 mm 厚工件板对接平焊装配时，焊件始焊端和结束端的根部间隙常常设置为(　　)mm。

A. 3.2、4.0　　B. 0、2.0　　C. 1.0、2.5　　D. 2.5、3.2

5. 板对接立焊CO_2气体保护焊所用电流一般比板对接平焊时(　　)。

A. 大　　B. 一样　　C. 小　　D. 大小不定

6. 立向上焊时焊枪角度与板件之间夹角为90°，与立焊缝下端方向成(　　)，焊枪角度从起焊至焊完应尽量保持一致。

A. 70°~90°　　B. 10°~20°　　C. 30°~40°　　D. 0°

7. 立焊打底焊起焊时，在焊件下端定位焊点上引燃电弧，并控制电弧在距离底边(　　)mm 处燃烧。

A. 2~3　　B. 0~1　　C. 3~4　　D. 0

8. 打底焊时，始终保持焊丝在熔池前缘，摆动时中间稍快，两侧稍作停顿，依靠电弧在坡口两侧的停留时间，保证坡口两侧熔合良好，一般使熔孔直径比间隙大(　　)mm。

A. 2~3　　B. 0~1　　C. 3~4　　D. 0.5~1

9. 填充层焊道比坡口边缘要低(　　) mm，并确保不熔化坡口棱边，为施焊盖面层打好基础

A. 2~3　　B. 0~1　　C. 3~4　　D. 1.5~2

10. 盖面焊时要注意保持焊嘴高度，焊接熔池边缘应超过坡口棱边(　　)mm，并防止产生咬边。

A. 2~3　　B. 0~1　　C. 3~4　　D. 0.5~1.5

任务操作

按任务要求和流程顺序进行任务实施训练，焊后能够根据焊缝检查要求进行自检和进行工位工具整理，训练后进行考核，并按检测要求进行评分。

Project Ⅵ Plate Butt Joint Vertical Welding Using CO_2 Gas Shielded Welding

【Learning Objectives】

1. Analysis the technical requirements of CO_2 gas shielded welding for board butt welding;
2. Master the pre welding preparation of CO_2 gas shielded welding for board butt welding;
3. Master the welding operation of CO_2 gas shielded welding for board butt welding;
4. Master the post weld treatment and inspection of CO_2 gas shielded welding for board butt welding.

Task 1:Analysis the Technical Requirements of CO_2 Gas Shielded Welding for Board Butt Welding

Figure 2-6-1 shows the assembly diagram and technical specifications of common plate buttjoint flat welding test pieces.

During plate butt joint vertical welding, the liquid metal easily flows downward due to gravity. Therefore, ensuring a smooth weld bead surface is difficult. To prevent the liquid metal from flowing down, upward vertical welding is adopted with a slightly smaller welding current than that used forplate butt joint flat welding. The swing frequency of the arc welding gun is slightly faster, resulting in a small and thin molten pool.

This unit uses commonly used low carbon steel in practical engineering as an example to explain the task implementation process of plate butt joint vertical welding GMAW, including preparation before welding, welding, and post-weld treatment and inspection.

Task 2:Master the Pre Welding Preparation of CO_2 Gas Shielded Welding for Board Butt Welding

1. Weldment preparation and groove cleaning

Prepare two Q235B weldments with a size of 10 mm×120 mm×250 mm and a 30° V-shape groove on one side, in accordance with the requirements of the task list.

Oil, rust, water, paint, oxide skin, dust, oil stain, burr, and other debris on the weld can cause welding defects, such as porosity, slag inclusion, incomplete fusion, etc. Therefore, these harmful factors to welding should be removed through cleaning measures. The cleaning range is generally 15-20 mm on the upper and lower sides of the groove surface and groove edge, with a metallic luster exposed, and 0.5-1.0 mm groove root face polished, as shown in Figure 2-5-3.

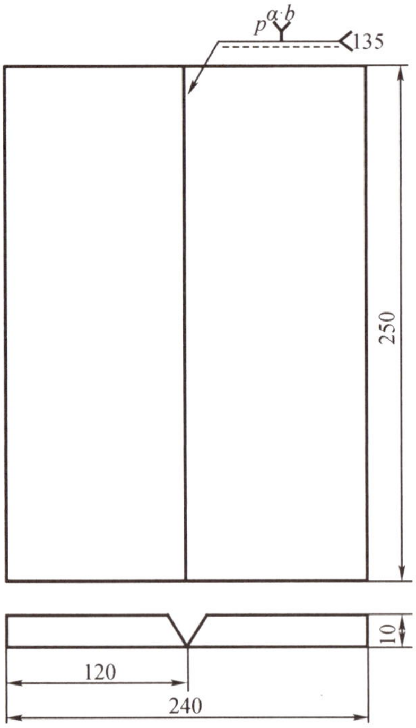

Technicalrequirements

1. V-shape groove with a groove angle of 60° and a root face.
2. Self-determined root clearance and root face size.
3. Misalignment≤0. 5 mm.
4. Angular deformation <3°.
5. No undercut is permitted.
6. Incomplete penetration is not allowed.
7. Cracks, porosity, and slag inclusion are not allowed.
8. Weld reinforcement≤1+0. 15*b*.

Figure 2-6-1 Q235B Weldment Using Plate Butt Joint Vertical Welding(Unit:mm)

2. Determination of welding process parameters

Considering the welding characteristics and plate thickness of base metal Q235B in this task, we have selected ER50-6 welding wire with a diameter of 1. 2 mm. The protective gas used is CO_2 gas with a purity higher than 99. 5%. We are using a three-layer and three-bead welding technique. The specific welding process parameters are shown in Table 2-6-1.

Table 2-6-1 Welding Process Parameters

Welding layer	Welding wire model	Welding wire diameter/mm	Welding current/A	Welding voltage/V	Shield gas flow rate /(L/min)	Welding wire extension length/mm	Power supply polarity
Backing layer			90-110	18-20	12-15	12-15	
Filling layer	ER50-6	1. 2	120-140	20-22	12-15	12-15	DC reverse polarity
Covering layer			110-120	18-20	12-15	12-15	

3. Assembly and positioning

The factors of welding deformation should be considered for assembly positioning in order to provide certain compensation and correction during assembly positioning.

Place two steel plates horizontally on the tooling table, aligning both ends to assemble them into butt joints. Set the root gap at the starting end of the weldment as 3. 2 mm and at the ending end as 4. 0 mm. Use the same process parameters as the backing forpositioning welding at both ends. The length of the welding spot is 10-15 mm. The starting end has a thickness of 3-4 mm, while the ending end has a thickness of 7–8 mm. The misalignment should not exceed 1.2 mm, and the anti-deformation allowance should be 3°–5°. After spot welding, knock off the slag shell of the welding spot and polish it to a metallic luster in a sloped shape to facilitate jointing.

Task 3:Master the Welding Operation of CO_2 Gas Shielded Welding for Board Butt Welding

During theplate butt joint vertical welding, the operator should fix the weldment at an appropriate height. Since the welding gun and welding wire are relatively heavy, a labor-saving method should be chosen for holding the welding gun to reduce hand fatigue during welding and facilitate control of welding quality. During welding, the angle, swing amplitude, and welding speed of the arc welding gun should be adjusted in a timely manner according to changes in assembly clearance and molten pool temperature, and the sizes of the molten pool and melting hole should be controlled to ensure a well-formed front and back side.

Fix the workpiece on the operating table, clamping the welding seam vertically and facing the operator. The height of the workpiece is generally the same as that of the operator's knee (welding in a squatting position). Place the end with a small gap on the lower side and use the vertical upward welding method, as shown in Figure 2-6-2.

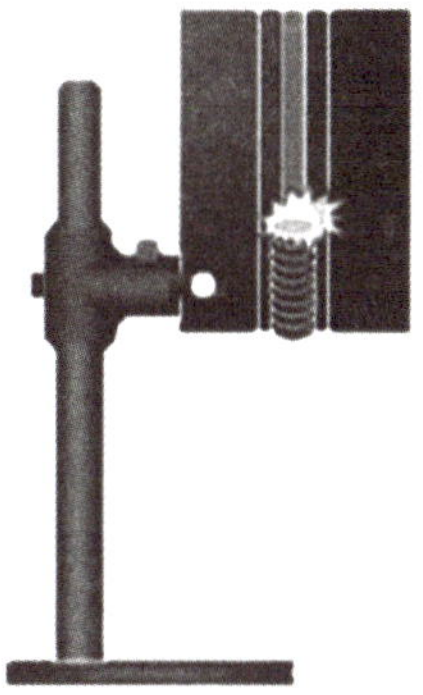

Figure 2-6-2 Diagram of Installation and Fixing

The welding layers of 10 mm thick plates often involve three-layer and three-bead welding and four-layer and four-bead welding, namely, a priming layer, a filling layer or two layers, and a covering layer, as shown in Figure 2-6-3, which represents four-layer and four-bead welding. The operation methods of the two are similar, and three-layer and three-bead welding is introduced here.

During welding, the angle of the arc welding gun is 90 degrees with the plate and 70°–90° degrees with the lower end direction of the vertical weld, as shown in Figure 2-6-4. The angle of the arc welding gun should be consistently maintained from the beginning to the end of welding.

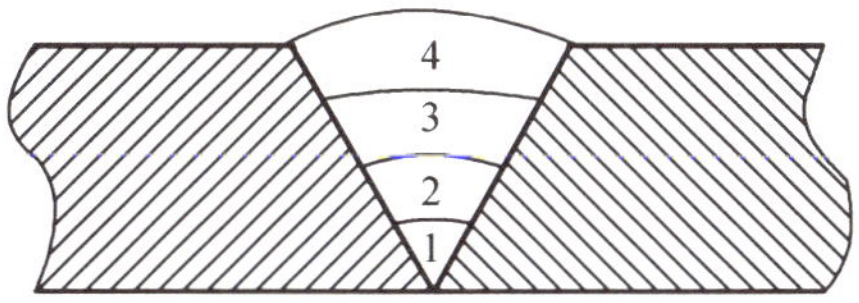

Figure 2-6-3 Schematic Diagram of Welding Layer

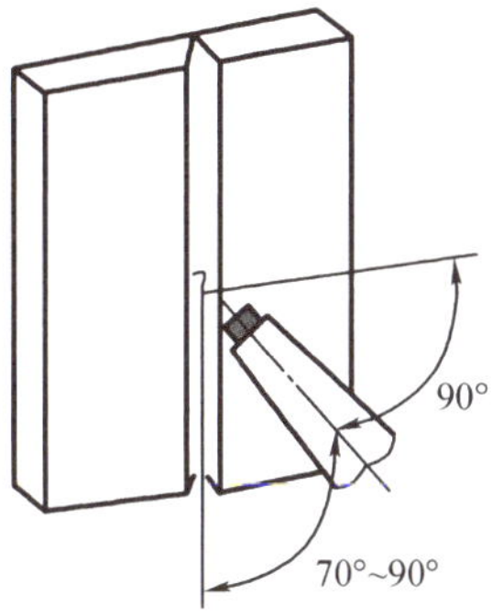

Figure 2-6-4 Angle of Welding Gun for Vertical Upward Welding

1. Backing welding

① During backing welding, adjust the welding process parameters according to the determined process card, check and clean the current contact nozzle and nozzle, apply anti-splash agent on the nozzle, and press the switch of the welding gun first to check whether wire feeding is normal.

②When starting welding, ignite the arc on thepositioning weld at the lower end of the weldment, and control the arc to burn 2-3 mm away from the bottom edge. Then swing the welding gun upward in a small sawtooth shape for welding. When the arc moves to the joint between the positioning weld and the groove root, use the arc to break down the groove root. After a melting hole is generated, turn to normal welding.

③During normal welding, swing the welding gun left and right by sawtooth method. The arc always swings laterally in a small range in the groove, as shown in Figure 2-6-5. The welding wire shall always be kept at the front edge of the molten pool. When swinging, it is slightly faster in the middle and a slight pause on both sides. Depending on the residence time of the arc on both sides of the groove, good fusion on both sides of the groove can be ensured. Generally, the diameter of the melt hole is 0.5-1 mm larger than the gap, so that the joint between both sides of the backing layer weld bead and the groove is slightly concave, and the surface of the weld bead is flat to preventburn-through, as shown in Figure 2-6-6. If the melting hole is too large, the swing can be accelerated appropriately and widened to increase the heat dissipation area.

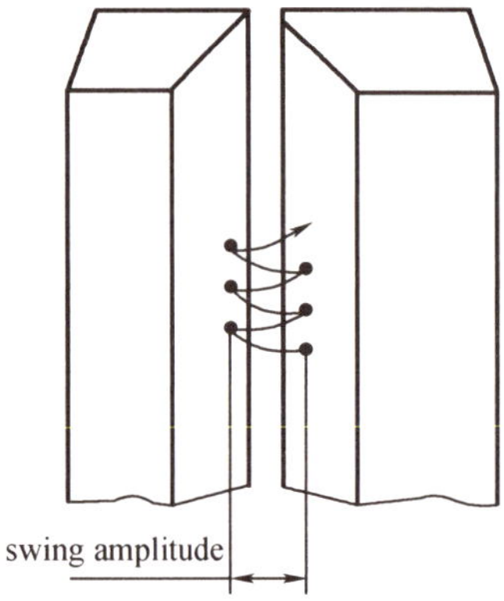

Figure 2-6-5 Schematic Diagram of Backing Welding Swing Track

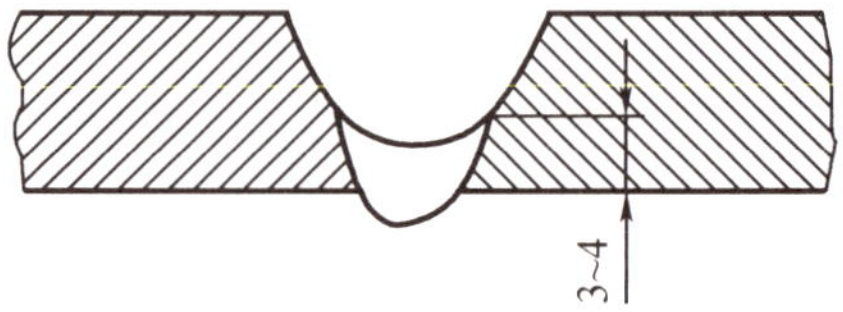

Figure 2-6-6 Schematic Diagram of Backinglayer Bead

④During welding, adjust the transverse swing amplitude and welding speed according to changes in gap and weld hole diameter. Maintain a consistent weld hole diameter to achieve a reverse weld with uniform width and height. Ensure that the thickness of the backing layer does not exceed 4 mm. As welding progresses, the arc welding gun moves upwards. Note that the angle between the arc welding gun and the weldment should remain unchanged. When the welding gun moves upward, the operator's arm should also move upward. Otherwise, when it is welded to the top, the included angle between the welding gun and the bottom will decrease, and the welding wire willpass through the gap, resulting in burn-through.

⑤When the welding wire is used up or welding needs to be interrupted due to wire feeder and welding gun failure, the welding gun should not immediately leave the molten pool. It should be stopped for a while first. If possible, move the arc to the groove side and then stop to prevent the formation of air holes and shrinkage cavities.

⑥Before joining, use an angle grinder to polish the crater weld bead into a gentle slope shape. During operation, align the end of the welding wire with the highest point of the gentle slope, then strike the arc, and swing the welding wire in a zigzag motion to cover the gentle slope of the weld bead. When the arc reaches the lowest point of the gentle slope, normal welding can be started. The joining method of CO_2 gas shielded welding differs from shielded metal arc welding. When the arc burns to the original melt hole, there is no need to lower the arc to form a new melt hole, but only its penetration depth is used to connect the joint well.

2. Filling welding

①Clean up the splashes on the backing layer bead and the surface of the test piece before welding the filling layer, and polish any local bulges of the weld bead.

②Adjust the welding process parameters according to the set filling specifications. The angle of the arcing gun should be the same as when welding the backing layer. The wire transportation method for welding can be zigzag, circular, or anti-crescent. The arc swing should not be too fast, but slightly slow and stable. The swing amplitude should be slightly wider than when welding the backing layer. The arc should stay on both sides of the groove for a while to ensure good fusion and a smooth surface of the weld bead. The weld bead of the filling layer should generally be 1.5-2 mm lower than the groove edge, and the groove edge should not be melted in order to serve as a reference duringcovering operation and ensure consistent and neat weld width.

a. Zigzag wire conveying method: After striking an arc at the lower end of the weldment, the arc moves slowly for preheating. After a molten pool is formed, the arc swings to the other side and pauses briefly when it reaches the included angle between the backing layer bead and the groove edge to ensure proper fusion on both sides. Two layers are required for welding the filling layer using the zigzag wire conveying method. Each layer is welded at a fast speed, resulting in low weld bead temperature and a bright and beautiful surface, making it easy to master.

b. Circular wire conveying method: This method utilizes high current and voltage (for instance, if a welding wire with a diameter of 1.2 mm is used, the welding current ranges from 120-140 A and the arc voltage ranges from 20-22 V). Insufficient current results in uneven ripples and unsightly formation. The circular wire handling method for vertical welding can be seen as a forward anti-crescent movement combined with transverse zigzag movement. During the initial welding, the arc swings laterally at a slower speed for preheating. Simultaneously, the weld start can be slightly thicker. Note that both sides should fuse well. Once this movement is completed, the arc follows an anti-crescent motion along the upper edge of the molten pool to ensure complete fusion between the molten pool, the included angle on both sides, and the previous layer. After moving to one side of the groove and pausing momentarily, the arc moves straight to the other side. At this point, the arc is positioned at the lower edge of the molten pool, intended to increase its thickness while ensuring a smooth weld bead. This method resembles a triangle, but with rounded top angles and straight bottom angles. The circular wire transportation method exhibits slower welding speed, higher temperature of the weld bead and molten pool, and a darker color of the weld bead after welding, which is less aesthetically pleasing. However, its advantages include excellent fusion, the ability to weld thicker layers in one go, and high productivity. Only one layer of the filling layer needs to be welded when employing this wire conveying method.

c. Anti-crescent wire feeding method: The welding current and arc voltage are the same as those of the circular wire feeding method. During welding, the arc moves in an anti-crescent shape along the front edge of the molten pool, but at a slower speed compared to the circular wire feeding method. It is important to ensure that the electric arc stays properly at the grooves on both sides, allowing for a good fusion on both sides. The electric arc should not move too fast, otherwise, the temperature of the molten pool will be low, resulting in an uneven formation and possible depression in the middle. The anti-crescent wire feeding method enables welding of a thicker welding layer at once, with a good fusion, pleasing appearance, simple technique, and high productivity. This wire feeding method requires only one layer of fill metal to be welded. This task is performed using this wire feeding method.

3. Covering welding

①Before welding the covering layer, clean the previous weld bead and splashes, clean the splashes on the nozzle, and apply silicone oil to the nozzle.

②Adjust the welding process parameters according to the specified cover specification, and maintain the same angle of the welding gun as during welding the backing layer. Use a zigzag wire handling method for welding the covering layer. The transverse swing amplitude of the electrode and rod should be larger than that of the filling layer, and it should stay on both sides of the groove for a while to fill it completely. The dwell time should ensure a smooth transition between the weld and base metal and prevent excessive weld joint height. Pay attention to controlling the swing spacing of the welding wire to be uniform and appropriate when it swings transversely. The spacing should not be too large to prevent undercut and maintain a beautiful weld surface. During arcending, ensure the arc crater is filled to avoid the occurrence of arc crater cracks.

③During covering welding, pay attention to maintaining the height of thewelding tip. The edge of the welding pool should exceed the groove edge by 0.5-1.5 mm and prevent undercut. When ending the arc, always fill the crater and keep the length of arc ending short to avoid crater cracks.

Task 4:Master the Post Weld Treatment and Inspection of CO_2 Gas Shielded Welding for Board Butt Welding

Same as Project Ⅴ.

Task Assessment

1. Generally, (　　) single-side V-shape grooves shall be opened during plate butt joint flat welding of 10mm-thick workpieces.

A. 30° B. 45° C. 50° D. 60°

2. The weld groove of the plate butt joint workpiece should be polished and cleaned, and the cleaning range is generally ( ) mm above and below the groove surface and groove edge.

A. 5-10 B. 10-15 C. 15-20 D. 20-25

3. For plate butt joint flat welding of 10 mm-thick workpieces, the groove shall be polished or processed with ( ) mm root face.

A. 0 B. 0.5-1.0 C. 1.0-1.5 D. 1.5-2.0

4. When assembling 12 mm-thick workpieces using plate butt joint flat welding, the root gap between the starting end and the ending end of the weldment is typically set to ( ) mm.

A. 3.2, 4.0 B. 0, 2.0 C. 1.0, 2.5 D. 2.5, 3.2

5. The current used for plate butt joint vertical welding using CO_2 gas shielded welding is generally ( ) compared with that in plate butt joint flat welding.

A. Large B. Same C. Small D. Variable

6. During vertical upward welding, the angle between the welding gun and the plate shall be 90°, forming an angle of ( ) with the lower end direction of the vertical weld. The angle of the welding gun shall be maintained as consistent as possible from starting to ending.

A. 70°-90° B. 10°-20° C. 30°-40° D. 0°

7. During backing welding of vertical welds, the arc should be ignited on the positioning weld at the lower end of the weldment and controlled to burn at a distance of ( ) mm from the bottom edge.

A. 2-3 B. 0-1 C. 3-4 D. 0

8. During backing welding, always keep the welding wire at the front edge of the molten pool. When swinging, it is slightly faster in the middle and slightly paused on both sides. Depending on the residence time of the arc on both sides of the groove, ensure that both sides of the groove are well fused. Generally, the diameter of the melt hole is ( ) mm larger than the gap.

A. 2-3 B. 0-1 C. 3-4 D. 0.5-1

9. The weld bead of the filling layer shall be ( ) mm lower than the groove edge, and ensure that the groove edge is not melted to provide a solid foundation for welding the covering layer.

A. 2-3 B. 0-1 C. 3-4 D. 1.5-2

10. During covering welding, attention should be paid to maintaining the height of thewelding tip. The edge of the weld pool should exceed the groove edge by ( ) mm to prevent undercut.

A. 2-3 B. 0-1 C. 3-4 D. 0.5-1.5

Task Operation

Carry out task implementation training according to task requirements and process sequence. After welding, perform self-inspection and organize station tools based on weld inspection requirements. After training, conduct assessment and scoring according to testing requirements.

项目七　板对接仰焊CO_2气体保护焊

【学习目标】

1. 分析板对接仰焊 CO_2 气体保护焊的技术要求；
2. 掌握板对接仰焊 CO_2 气体保护焊的焊前准备；
3. 掌握板对接仰焊 CO_2 气体保护焊的焊接操作；
4. 掌握板对接仰焊 CO_2 气体保护焊的焊后处理与检查。

任务1：分析板对接仰焊CO_2气体保护焊的技术要求

图 2-7-1 为常见板对接仰焊试件装配图及技术要求。

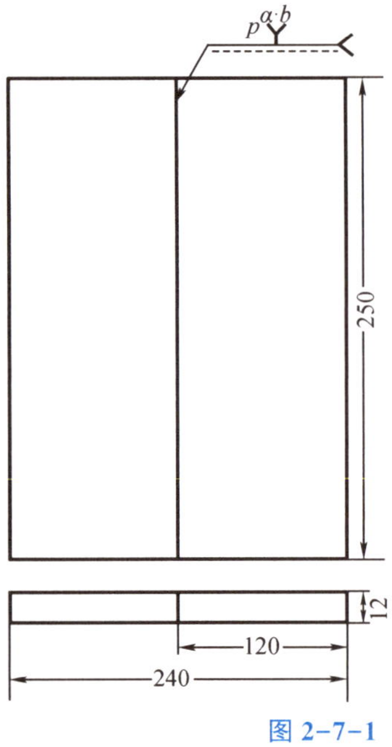

技术要求

1. 试件材质为 Q235B。
2. 接头形式为板-板对接接头，焊接位置为仰焊。
3. 焊接采取单面焊双面成形技术。
4. V 形坡口角度 $\alpha=60°\pm5°$，钝边 $p=0.5\sim1.0$ mm，根部间隙 $b=3.2\sim4.0$ mm。
5. 成形要求：焊缝表面无缺陷，焊缝波纹均匀，宽窄一致，高低平整，焊缝与母材圆滑过渡，焊后无变形，具体参照评分标准。

图 2-7-1　板对接仰焊焊件图(单位：mm)

仰焊单面焊双面成形是所有焊接位置中最难操作的一种。仰焊时，熔池倒悬在坡口内，液态金属受重力的作用极易下坠，从而易形成焊瘤，而在焊缝背面产生下凹等缺陷。在焊接过程中，熔池温度越高，焊接电弧越长，上述现象越严重，且易烫伤人，给焊工操作带来困难，飞溅物还易使焊枪喷嘴堵塞。操作时，焊工的位置应选好，以减少飞溅物的影响和便于操作。

本单元以此为例介绍低碳钢板对接仰焊熔化极气体保护焊的焊前准备、焊接操作和焊后处理与检查等任务实施流程。

任务2：掌握板对接仰焊CO_2气体保护焊的焊前准备

焊前准备任务常规实施路线：图样识读、焊件准备及坡口清理、焊接工艺参数确定、装配定位。

1. 焊件准备及坡口清理

（1）焊件准备

根据任务单要求：下料 10 mm×120 mm×250 mm 尺寸的 Q235B 材质焊件两块，并单边开 30°V 形坡口。

在焊接时为确保焊件能焊透，必须开一定形状的坡口。焊件厚度小于 6 mm 时，只需在接头处留一定的间隙（0～2.5 mm），就能保证焊透。但在焊较厚的焊件时，就需要在焊接前，把焊件接头处加工成一定的形状，以确保焊透。对接接头是采用最多的一种接头形式，这种接头常见的坡口形式有 V 形坡口或 Y 型坡口（也称带钝边 V 形坡口）。

Y 形坡口为什么需要带钝边呢？下面结合坡口的几何尺寸了解各部分的作用，Y 坡口的几何尺寸如图 2-7-2 所示。

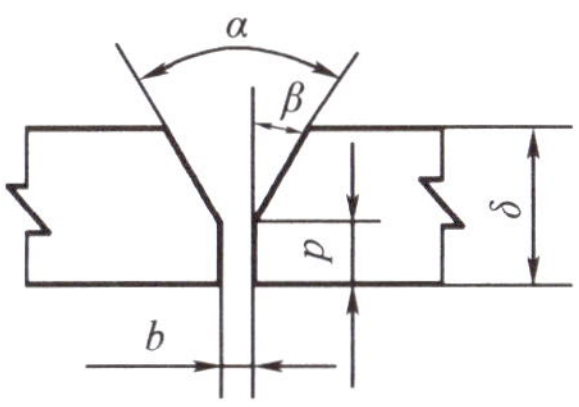

图 2-7-2　Y 形坡口尺寸示意图

①坡口面：待焊件上的坡口表面叫坡口面。

②坡口面角度和坡口角度：待加工坡口的端面与坡口面之间的夹角叫坡口面角度，用 β 表示；两坡口面之间的夹角叫坡口角度，用 α 表示。

③根部间隙：焊前在接头根部之间预留的空隙叫根部间隙，用 b 表示。其作用在于打底焊时能保证根部焊透。根部间隙又叫装配间隙。

④钝边：焊件开坡口时，沿焊件厚度方向未开坡口的端面部分叫钝边，用 p 表示。钝边的作用是防止根部烧穿，但钝边的尺寸要保证第一层焊缝能焊透。

⑤板厚：坡口的尺寸与板厚有关，用 δ 表示。常用板厚的坡口要素选择原则见表 2-7-1。

表 2-7-1　常用板厚单边 Y 形坡口的尺寸范围表

板厚 δ/mm	坡口角 α/(°)	钝边 p/mm	根部间隙 b/mm
6～26	40～60	1～4	0～4

（2）坡口清理

焊缝上的油、锈、水、漆、氧化皮、灰尘、油污、毛刺等杂物可以引起焊接缺陷，比如气孔、夹渣、未熔合等，所以应通过清理措施将这些对焊接有害因素清除干净。清理的范围一般为坡口面及坡口边缘上下两侧 15～20 mm 范围，并露出金属光泽，如图 2-7-3 所示，并打磨出 0.5～1.0 mm 的坡口钝边。

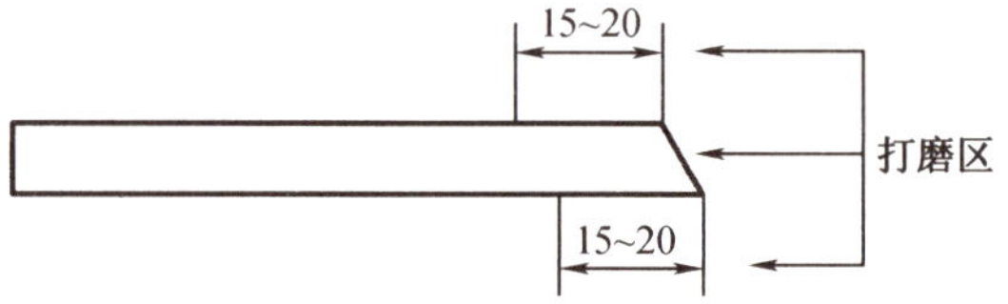

图 2-7-3　接头打磨区域示意图(单位:mm)

2. 焊接工艺参数确定

结合本任务母材 Q235B 的焊接特性和板厚来看,选择直径 1.2 mm 的 ER50-6 焊丝,保护气体为 CO_2 气体,纯度高于 99.5%,采用三层三道来焊接,具体焊接工艺参数见表 2-7-2。

表 2-7-2　焊接工艺参数

焊接层次	焊丝型号	焊丝直径/mm	焊接电流/A	焊接电压/V	保护气体流量/(L/min)	焊丝伸出长度/mm	电源极性
打底层	ER50-6	1.2	90~110	18~20	15~20	12~15	直流反接
填充层			130~150	20~22	15~20	12~15	
盖面层			120~140	20~22	15~20	12~15	

多层焊是指熔敷两个以上的焊层来完成整条焊缝所进行的焊接,多层焊包括多层单道焊和多层多道焊,如图 2-7-4 所示,一层焊缝可以由若干道焊道组成,如果坡口角度小,熔敷一道就可以是一层,即为单道焊,当坡口角度较大时,熔敷两道及以上焊道才能组成一层焊缝,就是多道焊。多层焊是焊接大厚壁结构常用的方法,较之相同情形下采用单层焊,可以减少热输入量、减小变形、降低产生缺陷的概率。多层多道焊还可以提高焊缝金属的质量,特别是塑性,这是因为后层(后道)焊缝对前层(前道)焊缝具有热处理作用,相当于对前层(前道)焊缝进行了一次正火热处理,因而改善了二次组织。单次焊层的热处理作用只达 3~5 mm,如果每层焊道厚度超过 6 mm,热处理效果差,焊缝金属组织质量就不高。

(a)多层焊　　(b)多层多道焊

图 2-7-4　多层焊、多层多道焊剖面示意图

通常板厚≤6 mm 时,采用 I 形坡口对接平焊,采用双面焊时,正面采用直线运条,稍慢,电流较小;背面也采用直线运条,焊接电流稍大,速度稍快。

板厚>6 mm 时,采用其他形式坡口对接平焊,可采用多层焊或多层多道焊。焊接打底层,特别是单面焊双面成形时,为保证背面焊缝质量,常使用较小的焊接电流;焊接填充层时,为了提高效率、保证熔合良好,常使用较大的焊接电流;焊接盖面层时,为防止咬边和保证焊缝成形,使用的焊接电流应比填充层稍小些。

多层多道焊电流调节特点：打底焊电流<盖面焊电流<填充焊电流。盖面焊电流要大于打底焊。

(3)装配定位

装配定位需考虑到焊接变形的因素，以便在装配定位时给予一定的补偿修正。

将两块钢板水平放工装台上，两端对齐装配成对接接头，装配时焊件始焊端根部间隙设置为 3.2 mm，结束端为 4.0 mm，采取和打底相同的工艺参数在两端进行点固焊，焊点长度为 10~15 mm，起始端厚度为 3~4 mm，结束厚度为 7~8 mm，错边量不大于 0.5 mm，反变形预留量为 3°~5°，如图 2-7-5 所示。点焊后应将焊点渣壳敲掉并打磨至金属光泽，呈斜坡状，以便于接头。

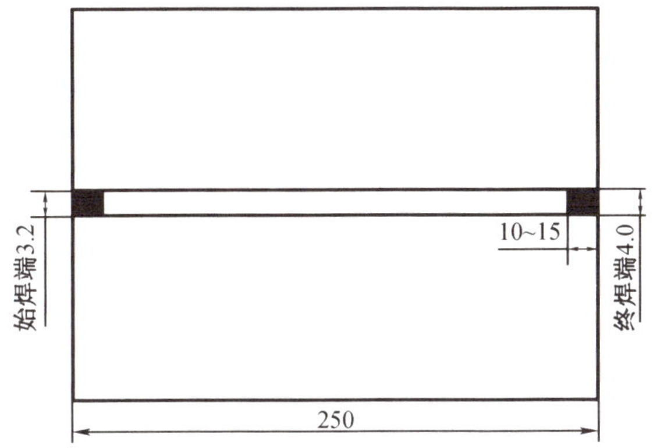

图 2-7-5　装配定位焊位置示意图(单位：mm)

任务3：掌握板对接仰焊CO_2气体保护焊的焊接操作

任务实施路线：10 mm 厚板件的焊接层次常有三层三道和四层四道焊的做法，操作方法类似，这里介绍三层三道焊。

1. 打底焊

将焊件固定在操作台上，焊缝水平装夹，焊缝面向地面，焊件高度适合操作者单膝跪地手臂上扬时操作舒服的位置，间隙小的一端放在起焊端，采取从远端向近端焊接的方法进行焊接。熔化极气体保护焊仰焊的操作要点如下：

①打底焊时，按确定的工艺卡调试好焊接工艺参数，检查、清理导电嘴和喷嘴，并在喷嘴上涂防飞溅剂，并先按动焊枪开关，检查送丝是否正常。

②打底焊时，焊枪角度如图 2-7-6 所示，焊枪角度从起焊至焊完应尽量保持一致。

③焊接时，在焊件间隙小的定位焊点上引燃电弧，并稍作停留预热 1~2 s，以小锯齿形摆动焊枪施焊，焊接过程中不能让电弧脱离熔池，以利用电弧吹力托住熔池金属，防止液态金属下淌，保证焊缝背面成形饱满。必须注意控制熔孔的大小，既要保证根部焊透，又要防止焊道背面下凹、正面下坠。打底层焊接时熔池金属重力与电弧吹力和表面张力对熔池的影响情况如图 2-7-7 所示。

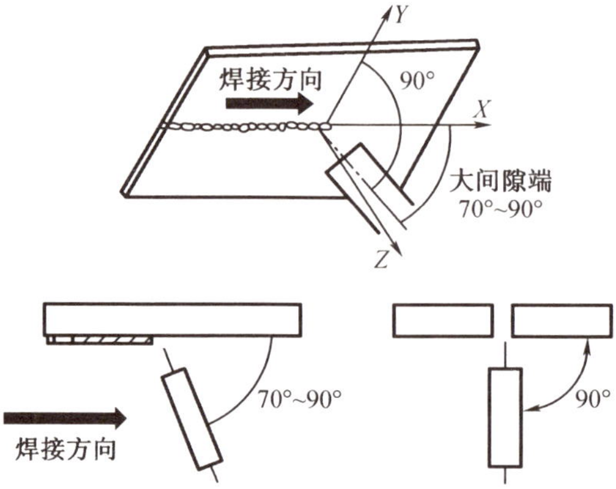

图 2-7-6　打底焊焊枪角度示意图

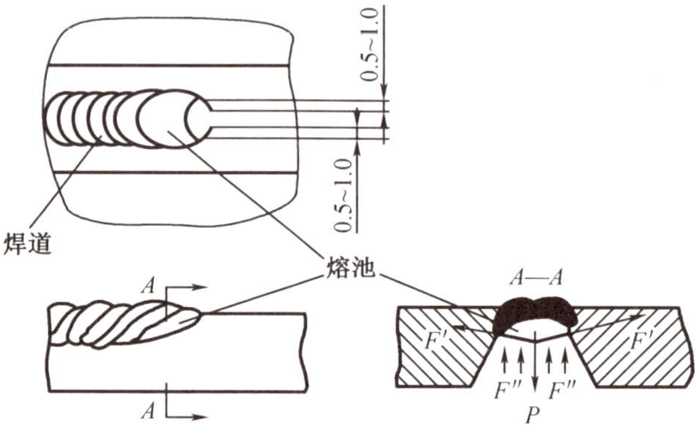

P—熔池金属重力；F′—表面张力；F″—电弧吹力

图 2-7-7　打底层焊接熔池情况

2. 填充焊

熔化极气体保护焊仰焊填充焊操作要点如下：

①焊前先清除、打磨打底焊道和坡口表面的飞溅和熔渣，并用角向砂轮机将局部凸起的焊道磨平。

②按设定的填充规范调整好焊接工艺参数进行焊接，焊枪与焊接前进方向的夹角控制在 80°～90°，运丝方法采用反月牙形运丝法，焊枪横向摆动幅度要比打底焊稍大，摆动时中间一带而过，坡口两侧稍加停顿，这样做为了保证熔池和坡口两侧温度均匀，有利于熔合和排渣，但也要控制好电弧在坡口两侧的停顿时间，既要保证焊道两侧熔合良好，又要防止焊道中间下坠。

③焊接时一定要采用短弧焊接，否则会出现气孔等缺陷，并且通过控制运丝方法，使焊道形成中间凹陷的形状，填充层焊道表面应距离焊件下表面 1.0 mm 左右，且不能熔化坡口的棱边，若有凹凸不平处要予以磨平，以便盖面焊时易于控制焊缝的平直度。

3. 盖面焊

熔化极气体保护焊仰焊盖面焊操作要点如下：

①施焊盖面层前，应清理前层焊道和飞溅物，清理喷嘴上的飞溅物，并在喷嘴上涂硅油。

②按设定的盖面规范调整好焊接工艺参数，焊枪角度与施焊填充层时相同。施焊盖面

层用反月牙形运丝法，焊丝横向摆动至坡口边线，在坡口两侧应稍作停留，以填满坡口，停顿时间以焊缝与母材圆滑过渡、焊缝余高不超过标准为宜。焊丝横向摆动时，应根据填充焊道的高度调整焊接速度，并注意控制摆动幅度均匀，使焊道平直、均匀，不产生两侧咬边、未熔合、焊瘤和中间下坠等缺陷。

任务4：掌握板对接仰焊CO_2气体保护焊的焊后处理与检查

同项目五。

任务考核

1. 根据含碳量的高低，碳素钢常分为高碳钢、(　　)碳钢、低碳钢

A. 锰　　B. 中　　C. 磷　　D. 非

2. 低碳钢的含碳量小于(　　)。

A. 0.25%　　B. 0.3%　　C. 0.35%　　D. 0.4%

3. 室温时，下列(　　)钢种的比重最大。

A. 低碳钢　　B. 中碳钢　　C. 高碳钢　　D. 合金钢

4. CO_2 气体保护焊焊接低碳钢时，板厚小于 6 mm，采用(　　)形坡口。

A. I　　B. V　　C. Y　　D. X

5. CO_2 气体保护焊对低碳钢进行仰焊，在打底层施焊时，可采用(　　)摆动焊丝。

A. 月牙形　　B. 锯齿形　　C. 画圈形　　D. 反月牙形

6. CO_2 气体保护焊对低碳钢进行仰焊，在填充层施焊时，保持焊道表面距离坡口棱边(　　)mm 左右，不能熔化坡口的棱边。

A. 1~1.5　　B. 1.5~2　　C. 2~2.5　　D. 2.5~3

7. CO_2 气体保护焊对低碳钢进行仰焊，在盖面层施焊时，可采用(　　)摆动焊丝。

A. 月牙形　　B. 锯齿形　　C. 圆圈形　　D. 反月牙形

8. 焊缝尺寸不符合要求的原因是(　　)。

A. 焊件坡口角度不当或装配间隙不均匀

B. 焊接电流过大或过小，焊接规范选用不当

C. 焊接速度不均匀，焊枪角度不当

D. 以上都是

9. 仰焊时，为了防止火星、熔渣造成灼伤，焊工可用(　　)的披肩、长袖套、围裙和脚盖。

A. 塑料　　B. 合成纤维织物　　C. 石棉物　　D. 棉物

10. CO_2 气体保护焊不能焊接(　　)。

A. 碳钢　　B. 合金钢　　C. 不锈钢　　D. 易氧化的有色金属

任务操作

按任务要求和流程顺序进行任务实施训练，焊后能够根据焊缝检查要求进行自检和进行工位工具整理，训练后进行考核，并按检测要求进行评分。

Project Ⅶ CO_2 Gas Shielded Welding for Board Buee Welding

【Learning Objectives】

1. Analysis the technical requirements of CO_2 gas shielded welding for board butt welding;
2. Master the pre welding preparation of CO_2 gas shielded welding for butt welding of boards;
3. Master the welding operation of CO_2 gas shielded welding for board butt welding;
4. Master the post weld treatment and inspection of CO_2 gas shielded welding for board butt welding.

Task 1:Analysis the Technical Requirements of CO_2 Gas Shielded Welding for Board Butt Welding

Fig. 2-7-1 displays the assembly drawing and technical specifications of commonly used plate butt overhead welding specimens.

Overhead single - side welding and double - side forming is one of the most challenging operations in all welding positions. During overhead welding, the molten pool is suspended upside down in the groove, and the liquid metal easily falls due to gravity, leading to the formation of weld beads and defects such as concavity on the back of the weld. In the welding process, the higher the temperature of the molten pool, the longer the welding arc becomes. This phenomenon is more severe and poses a scalding risk to individuals, making it difficult for the welder to operate. Splashes also tend to block the welding gun nozzle. Therefore, the welder's position should be carefully selected to minimize the impact of splashes and facilitate operation.

This unit uses this as an example to explain the implementation process of gas metal arc welding (GMAW) for overhead position butt welding of low carbon steel plates, including pre-welding preparation, welding operation, and post-weld treatment and inspection.

Task 2:Master the Pre Welding Preparation of CO_2 Gas Shielded Welding for Butt Welding of Boards

Conventional implementation route for pre - welding preparation tasks: interpretation of drawings, weldment preparation and groove cleaning, determination of welding process parameters, assembly positioning.

1. Preparation of weldment and cleaning of grooves

(1) Weldment preparation

According to the task requirements: Cut two Q235B welded pieces with dimensions of

10 mm×120 mm×250 mm and create a 30° V-shaped groove on one side.

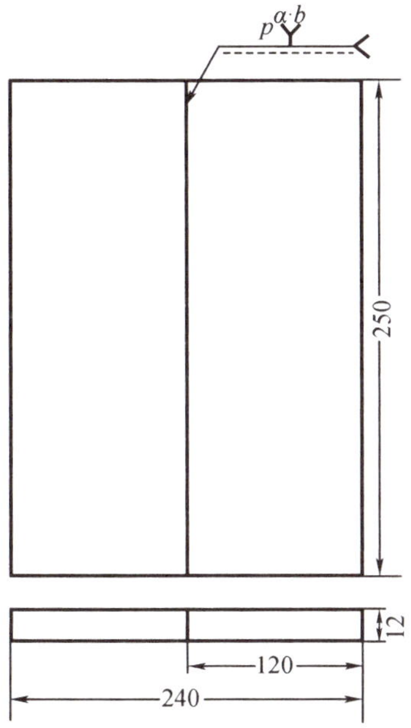

Technical requirements:

1. The test specimen is made of Q235B material.
2. The joint form is plate-to-plate butt joint, and the welding position is overhead welding.
3. Single - side welding and double - side forming technology should be adopted for welding.
4. V-shaped groove angle $\alpha=60°\pm5°$, root face $p=0.5-1.0$ mm, root gap $b=3.2-4.0$ mm.
5. Forming requirements: The weld surface must be free of defects, the weld ripples must be uniform, consistent in width, and flat in height. There must be a smooth transition between the weld and the base metal, and there should be no deformation after welding. Please refer to the scoring standard for details.

Fig. 2-7-1 Butt Joint Overhead Welding Assembly Plate (Unit: mm)

To ensure proper penetration during welding, a groove of a specific shape must be created. When the weldment thickness is less than 6mm, sufficient penetration can be achieved by maintaining a specific gap (0-2.5 mm) at the joint. However, when welding thicker weldments, the joint of the weldment needs to be processed into a specific shape before welding to ensure complete penetration. The butt joint is the most commonly used type, with V-shaped groove or Y-shaped groove (also known as V-shaped groove with truncated edge) being the typical groove types for this joint.

Why does the Y-groove need to have a blunt edge? The function of each part is understood by considering the geometric dimensions of the groove, as shown in Fig. 2-7-2.

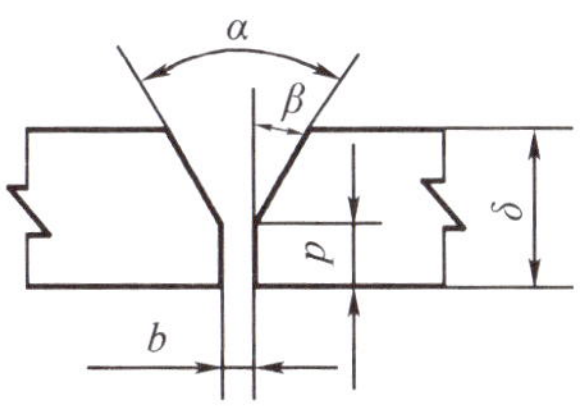

Fig. 2-7-2 Schematic Diagram of Y-shaped Groove Dimensions

①Groove face: The surface of the weldment to be welded is called the groove face.

②Groove face angle and groove angle: The angle between the end face of the groove to be processed and the groove face is called the groove face angle, represented by β; the angle between two groove faces is called the groove angle, represented by α.

③Root gap: The gap reserved between the joint roots before welding is called the root gap, represented by b. Its function is to ensure root penetration during backing welding. The root gap is also called the assembly clearance.

④Truncated edge: When the weldment is beveled, the end face part without a groove along the thickness direction of the weldment is called the truncated edge, represented by p. The function of the root face is to prevent root burn-through, but the size of the root face should ensure that the first layer of weld can be fully penetrated.

⑤Plate thickness: The size of the groove is related to the plate thickness and indicated by δ. The selection principles of groove elements for common plate thicknesses are shown in Table 2-7-1.

Table 2-7-1　Size Range of Unilateral Y-shaped Groove with Common Plate Thickness

Plate thickness δ/mm	Groove angle α/(°)	Blunt edge p/mm	Root gap b/mm
6~26	40~60	1~4	0~4

(2) Cleaning grooves

Oil, rust, water, paint, oxide skin, dust, oil stain, burr, and other impurities on the weld can lead to welding defects, such as porosity, slag inclusions, incomplete fusion, etc. Therefore, these harmful factors to welding should be removed through cleaning measures. The cleaning range generally includes a 15-20 mm area on the groove surface and the upper and lower sides of the groove edge, exposing a metallic luster as shown in Fig. 2-7-3. Additionally, the groove root face should be polished to a depth of 0.5-1.0 mm.

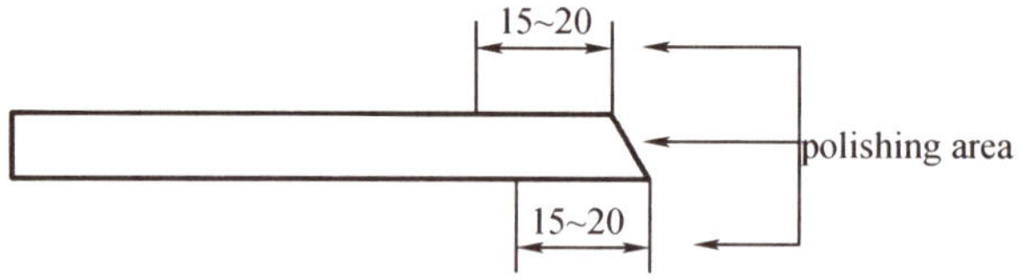

Fig. 2-7-3　Schematic Diagram of the Joint Grinding Area (Unit: mm)

2. Determination of welding process parameters

According to the welding characteristics and plate thickness of the base metal Q235B in this task, we have chosen ER50-6 welding wire with a diameter of 1.2 mm. The protective gas used is CO_2 gas with a purity higher than 99.5%. Three layers and three passes are used for welding. Please refer to Table 2-7-2 for specific welding process parameters.

Table 2-7-2　Welding Process Parameters

Welding level	Type of welding wire	Wire diameter /mm	Welding current/A	Welding voltage/V	Shielding gas flow rate (L/min)	Extension length of welding wire/mm	Power supply polarity
Base coat	ER50-6	1.2	90-110	18-20	15-20	12-15	DC reverse polarity
Filler layer			130-150	20-22	15-20	12-15	
Cover layer			120-140	20-22	15-20	12-15	

Multi-layer welding refers to the process of depositing more than two welding layers to complete the entire weld. It includes both multi-layer single-pass welding and multi-layer multi-pass welding, as illustrated in Fig. 2-7-4. A layer of weld can consist of multiple passes. If the groove angle is small, a single pass can be used to form a layer, known as single-pass welding. Conversely, if the groove angle is large, two or more passes are required to form a layer of weld, known as multi-pass welding. Multi-layer welding is a common technique employed in welding large thick-walled structures. Compared to single-layer welding under similar conditions, it can reduce heat input, deformation, and the likelihood of defects. Additionally, multi-layer and multi-pass welding can improve the quality of the weld metal, particularly its plasticity. This is because the back layer (back pass) weld functions as a heat treatment for the front layer (front pass) weld, similar to a normalizing heat treatment, thereby enhancing the secondary structure. The heat treatment effect of a single welding layer is only limited to 3-5 mm. When the thickness of each weld bead exceeds 6mm, the heat treatment effect diminishes and the quality of the weld metal structure is compromised.

(a) Multi-layer welding　　(b) Multi-layer and multi-pass welding

Fig. 2-7-4 Profile of Multi-layer and Multi-pass Welding

Usually, when the plate thickness is ≤ 6 mm, I-shaped groove butt flat welding is employed. When double-sided welding is used, linear electrode manipulation is applied on the front side, which is slightly slower and uses smaller current; linear electrode manipulation is also used on the backside, which has slightly higher current and faster welding speed.

When the plate thickness is > 6 mm, other forms of groove butt flat welding should be used, and multi-layer welding or multi-layer and multi-pass welding can be utilized. When welding the backing layer, especially during one-side welding and double-side forming, a lower welding current is often employed to ensure the quality of the back weld. When welding the filling layer, a higher welding current is typically used to increase efficiency and ensure good fusion. The welding current for the covering layer should be slightly smaller than that used for the filling layer to prevent undercut and ensure proper weld formation.

The current regulation characteristics of multi-layer and multi-pass welding are as follows: the backing current is less than the cosmetic current, which is less than the fill current. The current for cosmetic welding should be greater than that for backing welding.

3. Assembling and positioning

The factors of welding deformation should be taken into consideration for assembly positioning in order to provide certain compensation and correction during assembly positioning.

Place two steel plates horizontally on the tooling table and align both ends to assemble them into butt joints. During assembly, set the root gap at the initial welding end of the weldment as

3.2 mm and that at the final end as 4.0 mm. Adopt the same process parameters as backing for tack welding at both ends. The length of the welding spot is 10−15 mm, the thickness of the initial end is 3−4 mm, the thickness of the final end is 7−8 mm, the misalignment is not more than 0.5 mm, and the anti−deformation allowance is 3°−5°. As shown in Fig. 2−7−5. After spot welding, knock off the slag shell of the weld spot and polish it to a metallic luster in a slope shape to facilitate joining.

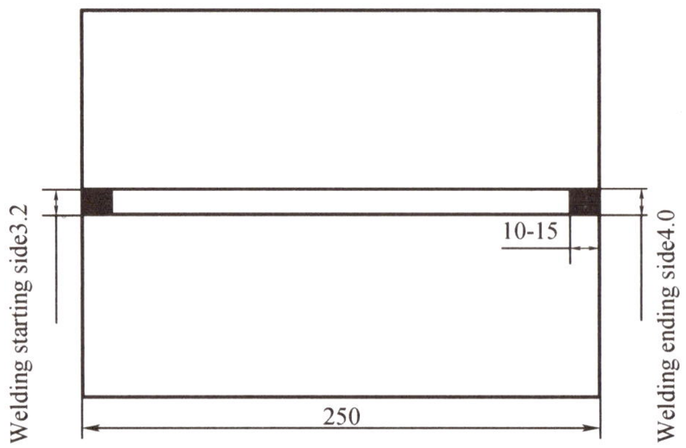

Fig. 2−7−5 Schematic Diagram Illustrating Tack Welding Positions during Assembly (Unit: mm)

Task 3: Master the Welding Operation of CO_2 Gas Shielded Welding for Board Butt Welding

Task implementation route: The welding process for 10 mm thick plates often includes three−layer and three−pass welding, as well as four−layer and four−pass welding. These methods have similar operation techniques. Here, we will focus on the three−layer and three−pass welding.

1. Underlying welding

Please ensure the weldment is securely fixed on the operating table, with the weld seam clamped horizontally and facing downwards. The height of the weldment should be suitable for the operator to comfortably operate while kneeling on one knee and raising their arm. Position the end with a small gap at the starting point, and carry out the welding from the far end to the near end. The key points for gas metal arc welding in an overhead position are as follows:.

①Adjust the welding process parameters according to the specified process card during back welding. Check and clean the current contact nozzle and nozzle, apply an anti−splash agent to the nozzle, and press the welding gun switch first to check if wire feeding is normal.

②The angle of the arc welding gun during back welding is shown in Fig. 2−7−6. It should be kept as consistent as possible from start to finish.

③During welding, the electric arc should be ignited at the tack welding spot with a small gap in the weldment, and preheated for a short duration of 1−2 s. The welding gun should be swung in a small zigzag pattern during welding. It is important to keep the electric arc in contact with the molten pool to support the metal and prevent liquid metal from flowing down, ensuring a complete formation of the weld on the backside. Attention should be given to controlling the size of the weld hole, ensuring complete penetration at the root while preventing sinking on the backside and falling on the front side. The influence of metal gravity, arc blowing force, and surface tension on the molten pool during backing layer welding is shown in Fig. 2-7-7.

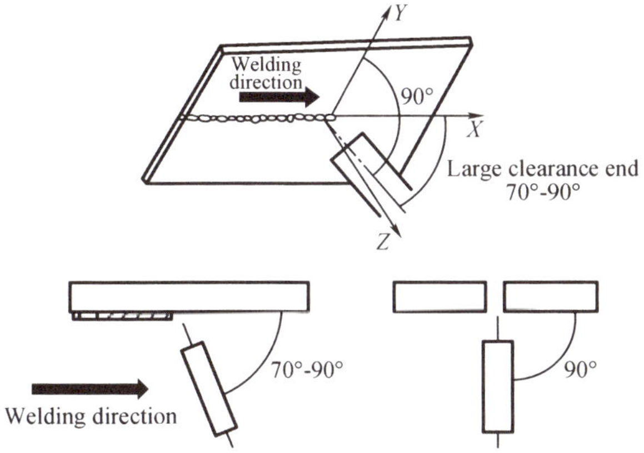

Fig. 2-7-6 Illustration of Welding Gun Angle for Backing Weld

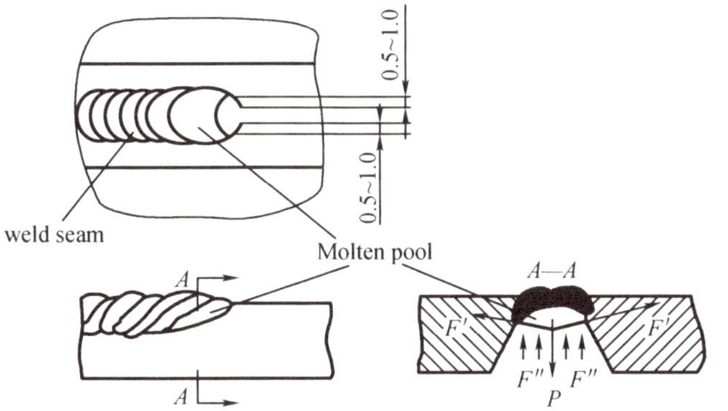

P—gravity of molten pool metal; *F'*—surface tension; *F''*—arc blowing force

Fig. 2-7-7 Backing Layer Weld Pool(Unit: mm)

2. Welding filler

The key points for gas metal arc welding (GMAW) overhead filling are as follows.

①Prior to welding, remove and polish the splashes and slag on the surface of the backing weld bead and groove. Use an angular grinder to flatten any raised weld bead locally.

②Adjust the welding process parameters according to the specified filling specifications for welding. The included angle between the arc welding gun and the direction of welding should be controlled within 80°-90°. Use the anti-crescent wire conveying method. The transverse swing amplitude of the arc welding gun should be slightly larger than that of the backing weld. During swinging, pass through the middle with a slight pause on both sides of the groove. This ensures uniform temperature of the molten pool and both sides of the groove, aiding fusion and slag discharge. However, the dwell time of the arc on both sides of the groove should also be well controlled to ensure good fusion on both sides of the weld bead and prevent sagging in the middle of the weld bead.

③Short arc welding must be used during welding to avoid defects such as pores. The weld pass should form a concave shape in the middle by controlling the wire transportation method. The surface of the fill layer weld pass should be approximately 1.0 mm away from the lower surface of the weldment, and the edge of the groove should not be melted. If there are any uneven areas, they should be intentionally made uneven to easily control the straightness of the weld during cosmetic welding.

3. Cover welding

The key points for gas metal arc welding (GMAW) in overhead position welding and cosmetic welding are as follows:

①Before applying the cover layer, clean the previous weld bead and splashes, clean the splashes on the nozzle, and apply silicone oil to the nozzle.

②Adjust the welding process parameters according to the specified cover specifications, and the angle of the welding gun should be the same as when welding the filling layer. The cover layer should be welded using the anti-crescent wire handling method. The welding wire should swing transversely to the edge line of the groove and pause on both sides of the groove for a while in order to fill it up. The pause time should ensure a smooth transition between the weld and the base metal, and the excess height of the weld should not exceed the standard. When the welding wire swings transversely, adjust the welding speed based on the height of the filling weld pass, and ensure even control of the swing amplitude to achieve a straight and uniform weld pass without defects such as undercut on both sides, incomplete fusion, overlap, and middle drop.

Task 4: Master the Post Weld Treatment and Inspection of CO_2 Gas Shielded Welding for Board Butt Welding

Same as Project Ⅴ.

Task Assessment

1. According to the carbon content, carbon steel is often divided into high-carbon steel, (　　) steel, and low-carbon steel.

A. Manganese　　B. Medium　　C. Phosphorus　　D. Non-

2. The carbon content of mild steel is less than (　　).

A. 0.25%　　B. 0.3%　　C. 0.35%　　D. 0.4%

3. The following steel grades (　　) have the highest specific gravity at room temperature.

A. Low carbon steel　　B. Medium carbon steel

C. High carbon steel　　D. Alloy steel

4. When CO_2 gas shielded welding is used to weld low carbon steel, a (　　) groove should be adopted if the plate thickness is less than 6mm.

A. I B. V C. Y D. X

5. CO_2 gas shielded welding is used for overhead position welding of low carbon steel. ( ) Swing welding wire can be used for backing layer welding.

A. Moon-shaped B. Sawtooth-shaped

C. Circular-shaped D. Inverted moon-shaped

6. CO_2 gas shielded welding is used for overhead welding of low carbon steel. When welding on the filling layer, keep the weld bead surface approximately ( ) mm away from the groove edge and avoid melting the groove edge.

A. 1-1.5 B. 1.5-2 C. 2-2.5 D. 2.5-3

7. CO_2 gas shielded welding is employed for overhead welding of low carbon steel. When welding on the cover layer, ( ) swing welding wire can be utilized.

A. Moon-shaped B. Sawtooth C. Round D. Inverse crescent

8. The reason for the inadequate weld size is ( ).

A. Improper weld groove angle or uneven assembly clearance

B. Welding current too high or too low, and improper selection of welding specifications

C. Uneven welding speed and improper angle of welding gun

D. All of the above

9. During overhead welding, in order to prevent burns caused by sparks and slag, welders can use ( ) shawls, long sleeves, aprons, and foot covers.

A. Plastic B. Synthetic fiber fabric

C. Asbestos D. Cotton

10. CO_2 gas shielded welding is prohibited ( ).

A. Carbon steel B. Alloy steel

C. Stainless steel D. Easily oxidized non-ferrous metal

Task Operation

Carry out task implementation training according to task requirements and process sequence. After welding, carry out self-inspection and sort out station tools according to weld inspection requirements. After training, conduct assessment and score according to testing requirements.

模块三

手工钨极氩弧焊及应用

项目一　钨极氩弧焊基础知识

【学习目标】

1. 理解惰性气体保护焊的原理及特点；
2. 理解钨极氩弧焊的工作原理、分类及特点；
3. 掌握钨极氩弧焊的设备；
4. 掌握钨极氩弧焊的焊接材料及工艺参数选择原则。

钨极惰性气体保护焊方法是利用惰性气体保护，用钨棒做电极的一种电弧焊焊接方法，由于我国常用氩气，所以常直接称为钨极氩弧焊（简称 TIG 焊），其他国家也常用氦气等，这里以钨极氩弧焊为例介绍，其他惰性气体原理和操作方法相类似。钨极氩弧焊焊接时由于钨极本身不熔化，只起发射电子产生电弧的作用，故也称非熔化极氩弧焊。焊接时，从喷嘴喷出的氩气形成一个厚而密的气体保护层隔绝空气，在氩气层流的包围之中，电弧在钨极和焊件之间燃烧，利用电弧产生的热量熔化待焊处和填充焊丝，把两块分离的金属连接在一起，从而获得牢固的焊接接头。目前主要用于焊接薄件或用于重要产品的打底焊。

任务1：理解惰性气体保护焊的原理及特点

1. 惰性气体保护焊的原理

惰性气体保护焊的焊接过程如图 3-1-1 所示。从焊枪喷嘴中喷出的惰性气体流，在焊接区形成厚而密的气体保护层而隔绝空气，同时，在电极与焊件之间燃烧产生的电弧热量使被焊处熔化，并填充或不填充焊丝将被焊金属连接在一起，获得牢固的焊接接头。

2. 惰性气体保护焊的特点

（1）焊缝质量较高

惰性气体可在空气与焊件间形成稳定的隔绝层，保证高温下被焊金属中合金元素不会氧化烧损，同时惰性气体不溶解于液态金属，故能有效地保护熔池金属，获得较高的焊接质量。

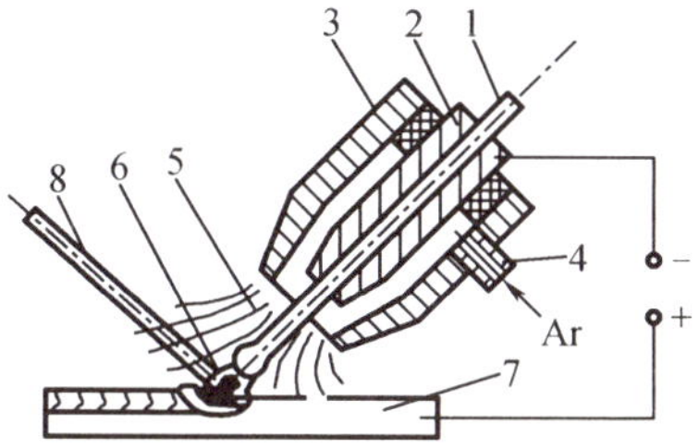

(a)非熔化极惰性气体保护焊

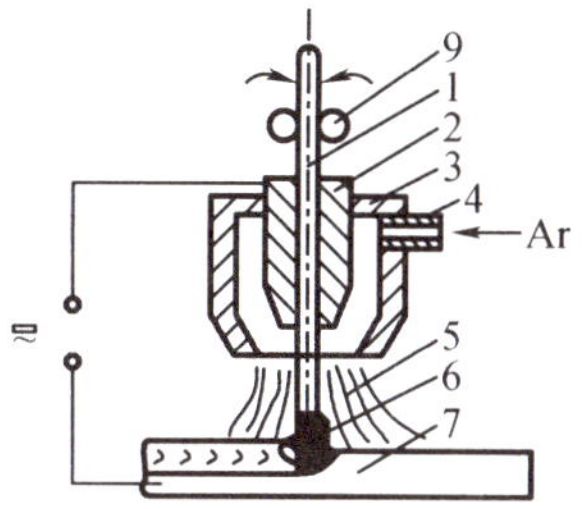

(b)熔化极惰性气体保护焊

1—焊丝或电极;2—导电嘴;3—喷嘴;4—进气管;5—惰性气体流;6—电弧;7—工件;8—填充焊丝;9—送丝辊轮。

图 3-1-1　惰性气体保护焊示意图

(2)焊接变形与应力小

由于惰性气体保护焊热量集中,电弧受惰性气体流的冷却和压缩作用,使热影响区窄,焊接变形和应力小,特别适宜于薄板的焊接。

(3)可焊的范围广

几乎所有的金属材料都可进行惰性气体保护焊。通常,多用于焊接不锈钢、铝、铜等有色金属及其合金,有时还用于焊接构件的打底焊。

(4)操作技术易于掌握

采用惰性气体保护无熔渣,且为明弧焊接,电弧、熔池可见性好,适合各种位置焊接,容易实现机械化和自动化。

任务2:理解钨极氩弧焊的工作原理、分类及特点

1. 惰性气体保护焊的分类和适用范围

惰性气体保护焊根据常用的电极材料可分为两种:一种是用只起发射电子产生电弧作用而自身不熔化的钨极作为电极,称为钨极(非熔化极)惰性气体保护焊;另一种是用即要填充焊缝也要发射电子产生电弧的焊丝作为电极,称为熔化极惰性气体保护焊,如图 3-1-1 所示;按其操作方式可分为手工、半自动和自动焊;若在惰性气体保护焊电源中加入脉冲装置又可分为钨极脉冲焊和熔化极脉冲焊。

由于氩气是常见常用的惰性气体,故常把惰性气体保护焊称为氩弧焊,以钨极为电极的非熔化极氩弧焊称为钨极氩弧焊(简称 TIG 焊),以焊丝为电极的称为熔化极氩弧焊(简称 MIG 焊)。氩弧焊的适用范围见表 3-1-1。

表 3-1-1　氩弧焊的适用范围

被焊材料	焊件厚度/mm	焊接方法	电源种类和极性
钛及钛合金	0.5~3.0 >2.0	钨极氩弧焊 熔化极氩弧焊	直流正接 直流反接
镁及镁合金	0.5~5.0 >2.0	钨极氩弧焊 熔化极氩弧焊	交流或直流反接 直流反接
铝及铝合金	0.5~4.0 >3.0	钨极氩弧焊 熔化极氩弧焊	交流或直流反接 直流反接

表 3-1-1(续)

被焊材料	焊件厚度/mm	焊接方法	电源种类和极性
铜及铜合金	>0.5 >3.0	钨极氩弧焊 熔化极氩弧焊	直流正接 直流反接
不锈钢、耐热钢	0.5~3.0 >2.0	钨极氩弧焊 熔化极氩弧焊	直流正接或交流 直流反接

惰性气体保护焊几乎可用于所有钢材、有色金属及其合金的焊接。但由于成本较高，目前主要用于焊接高合金钢材料、有色金属及其合金、难熔的活泼金属(钼、铌)等。此外还用于补焊、反面不加衬垫的打底焊。例如，造船生产中，手工钨极氩弧焊常用于重要管系(碳钢)焊接时的打底焊(单面焊双面成形)，以获得管内焊缝成形均匀、无熔渣、夹杂等缺陷的优质焊缝。

由于熔化极氩弧焊属于模块二的熔化极气体保护焊的一种，焊接操作技术类似，此处仅介绍非熔化极气体保护焊中常用的钨极氩弧焊方法。

2. 钨极氩弧焊的工作原理

钨极氩弧焊是利用钨极与焊件之间产生的电弧热，来熔化附加的填充焊丝或自动送给的焊丝(也可不加填充焊丝)及基体金属形成熔池而形成焊缝的。焊接时，氩气流从焊枪喷嘴中连续喷出，在电弧区形成严密的保护气层，将电极和金属熔池与空气隔离，以形成优质的焊接接头。钨极氩弧焊的工作原理如下图 3-1-2 所示。

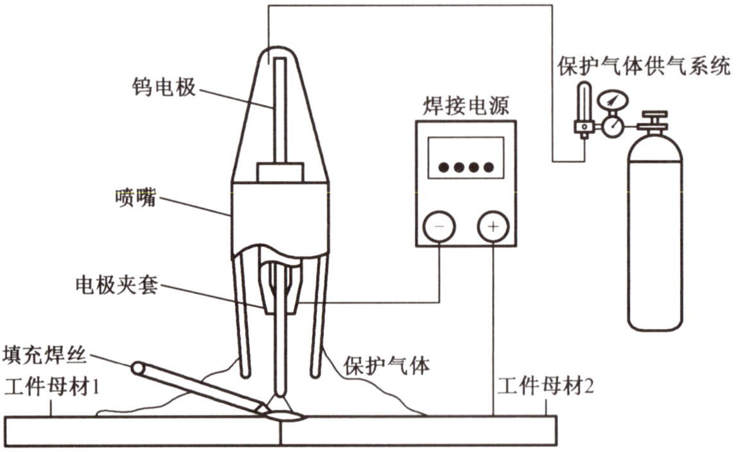

图 3-1-2　钨极氩弧焊工作原理图

3. 钨极氩弧焊的分类

钨极氩弧焊按所采用的电流种类，可分为直流钨极氩弧焊、交流钨极氩弧焊和脉冲钨极氩弧焊等。

钨极氩弧焊按其操作方式可分为手工钨极氩弧焊和自动钨极氩弧焊。

手工钨极氩弧焊时，焊工一手握焊枪，另一手持焊丝，随焊枪的摆动和前进逐渐将焊丝填入熔池之中,如图 3-1-3 所示。有时也不加填充焊丝,仅将接口边缘熔化后形成焊缝。在实际生产中,手工钨极氩弧焊应用最广。

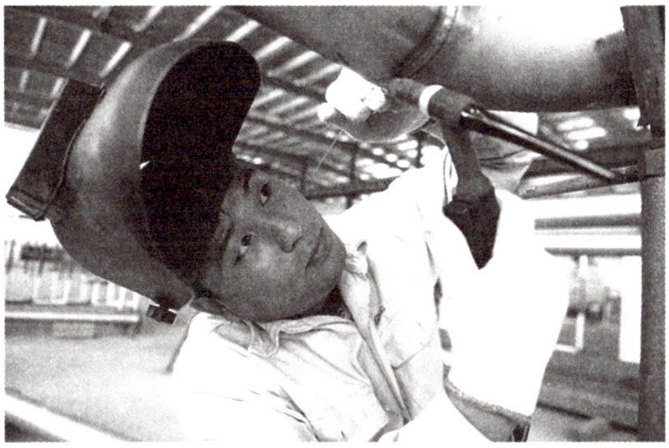

图 3-1-3　手工钨极氩弧焊

自动钨极氩弧焊是以传动机构带动焊枪行走,送丝机构尾随焊枪进行连续送丝的焊接方式,如图 3-1-4 所示。

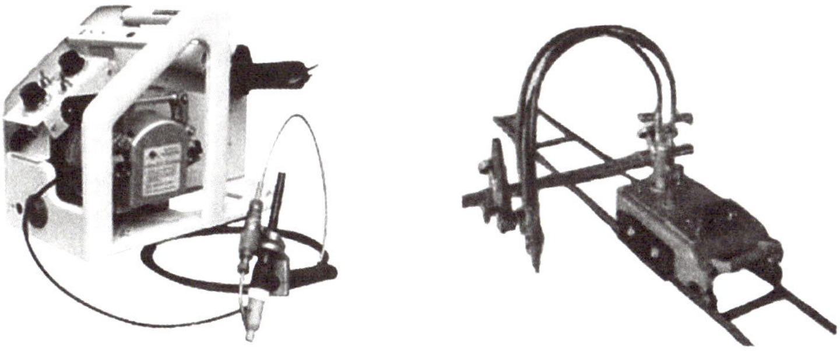

图 3-1-4　半自动钨极氩弧焊和自动钨极氩弧焊示意图

4. 钨极氩弧焊的特点

这类焊接方法的焊接过程具有良好的稳定性,易于获得质量优良的焊缝。

(1)钨极氩弧焊优点

与其他焊接方法相比,钨极氩弧焊具有如下优点:

①焊接过程稳定。氩弧燃烧非常稳定,而且焊接过程中钨棒不熔化,弧长变化干扰因素相对较少,因此焊接过程非常稳定。

②焊接质量好。氩气是一种惰性气体,它既不溶于液态金属,又不与金属发生任何化学反应;而且氩气容易形成良好的气流隔离层,有效地阻止氧、氮等侵入焊缝金属。

③适用面广。几乎可焊接所有金属及合金,适合于各种位置的焊接。

④适于薄板焊接、全位置焊接。即使是用几安培的小电流,钨极氩弧仍能稳定燃烧,而且热量相对较集中,因此可焊接 0.3 mm 的薄板;采用脉冲钨极氩弧焊电源,还可进行全位置焊接及不加衬垫的单面焊双面成形焊接。

⑤焊接过程易于实现自动化钨极氩弧焊的电弧是明弧,焊接过程参数稳定,易于检测

及控制，是理想的自动化乃至机器人化的焊接方法。

⑥焊接区无熔渣 焊工可清楚地看到熔池和焊缝成形过程。

(2)钨极氩弧焊缺点

①抗风能力差。钨极氩弧焊利用气体进行保护，抗侧向风的能力较差。侧向风较小时，可通过降低喷嘴至工件的距离，同时增大保护气体的流量来保证保护效果；侧向风较大时，必须采取防风措施。

②对工件清理要求较高。由于采用惰性气体进行保护，无冶金脱氧或去氢作用，因此为了避免气孔、裂纹等缺陷，焊前必须严格去除工件上的油污、铁锈等。

③生产率低。由于钨极的载流能力有限，尤其是交流焊时钨极的许用电流更低，因此钨极氩弧焊的熔透能力较低，焊接速度小。

任务3：掌握钨极氩弧焊的设备

手工钨极氩弧焊设备包括焊机、焊枪、供气系统、冷却系统、控制系统等部分，如图 3-1-5 所示。自动钨极氩弧焊设备除上述几部分外，还有送丝装置及焊接小车行走机构。

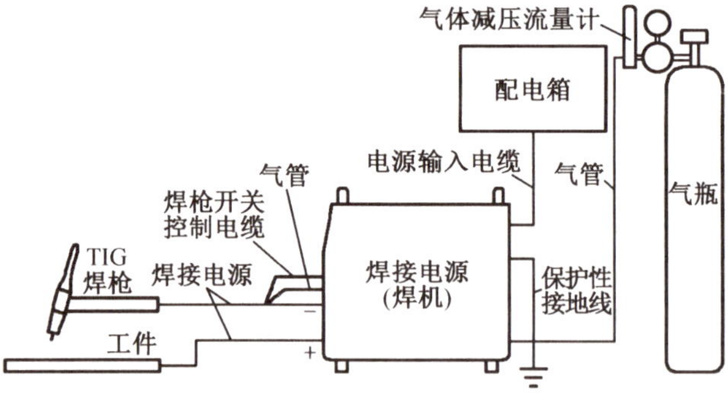

图 3-1-5 手工钨极氩弧焊设备组成

1. 钨极氩弧焊机

焊机包括焊接电源及高频振荡器、脉冲稳弧器、直流分量消除装置等。若采用焊条电弧焊的电源，则应配用单独的控制箱。直流钨极氩弧焊的焊机较为简单，直流焊接电源附加高频振荡器即可。

(1)焊接电源

钨极氩弧焊应选用具有陡降外特性的电源。一般焊条电弧焊的电源(如弧焊变压器、弧焊整流器等)都可用做手工钨极氩弧焊接电源，如图 3-1-6 所示。

钨极氩弧焊焊机按电源性质可分为直流钨极氩弧焊焊机、交流钨极氩弧焊焊机、交直流钨极氩弧焊焊机和脉冲钨极氩弧焊焊机。直流钨极氩弧焊焊机型号有 WS-250、WS-400 等，交流钨极氩弧焊焊机型号有 WSJ-300、WSJ-500 等，交直流钨极氩弧焊焊机型号有 WSE-150、WSE-400 等，脉冲钨极氩弧焊焊机型号 有 WSM-200、WSM 400 等。

(2)引弧及稳弧装置

由于氩气的电离能较高，难以电离，引燃电弧困难，但又不宜采用提高空载电压，因此，钨极氩弧焊必须使用高频振荡器来引燃电弧，如图 3-1-7 所示。对于交流电源，由于电流每秒经过零点 100 次,电弧不稳,故还需要使用脉冲稳弧器,以保证重复引燃电弧并稳弧。

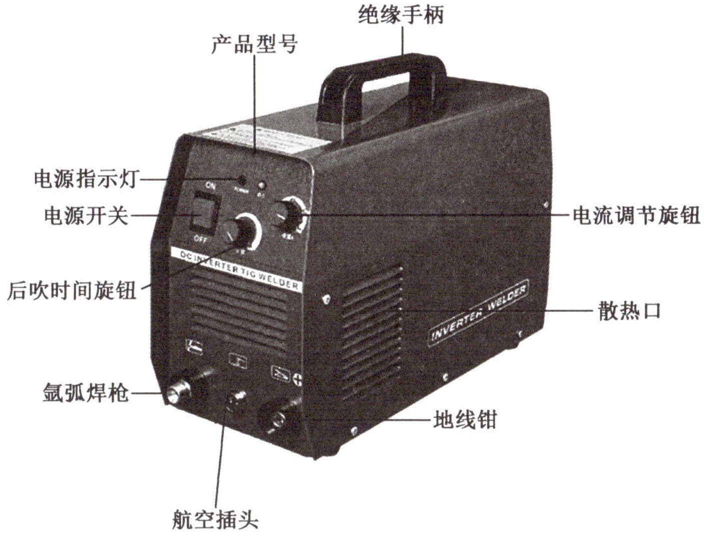

图 3-1-6　钨极氩弧焊接电源

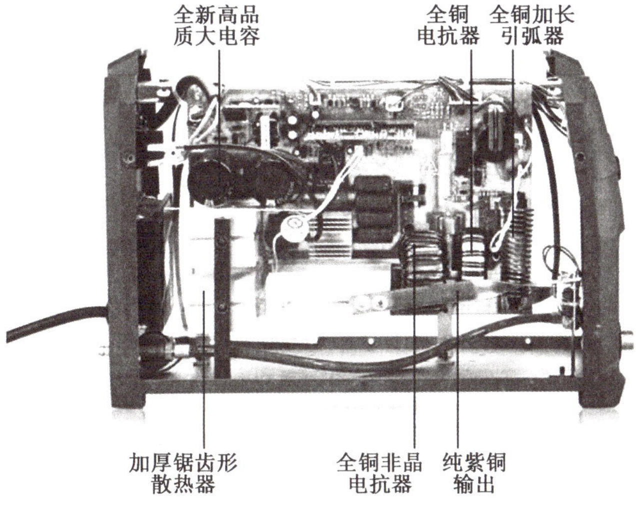

图 3-1-7　钨极氩弧焊接电源内部结构

高频振荡器是钨极氩弧焊设备中的专用引弧装置,它可在钨极和工件之间加入约 3 000 V 的高频电压,而这种焊接电源的空载电压只要在 65 V 左右即可达到钨极与焊件非接触而点燃电弧的目的。高频振荡器一般仅用于引弧,不用于稳弧,引燃电弧后马上切断。

脉冲稳弧器是施加一个高压脉冲而迅速引弧,并保持电弧连续燃烧,从而起到稳定电弧的作用。

(3) 直流分量及其消除

交流电焊接时,由于极性不断变化,会造成电流在正负半波不对称的现象,这在焊接铝及其合金时特别突出。这种正负半波不对称的电流,可以看成由两部分组成,一部分是真正的交流电,另一部分是叠加在交流部分上的直流电,这部分直流电称为直流分量。

直流分量的出现，一是减弱了“阴极破碎”作用，二是会使焊接变压器发热，甚至损坏设备。因此，交流钨极氩弧焊时必须消除直流分量。消除直流分量的常用方法是在焊接电路中串联电容。

(4)控制系统

钨极氩弧焊的控制系统是通过控制线路，对供电、供气、引弧与稳弧等各个阶段的动作程序实现控制。图 3-1-8 所示为交流手工钨极氩弧焊控制程序。

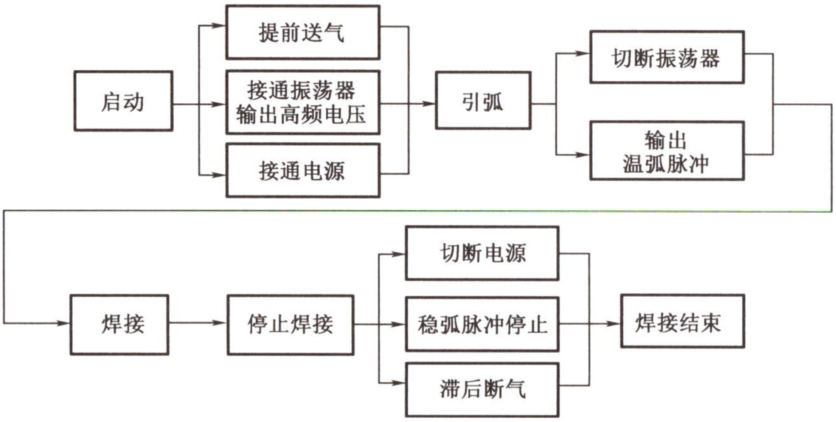

图 3-1-8　交流手工钨极氩弧焊控制程序流程图

2. 钨极氩弧焊枪

钨极氩弧焊焊枪的作用是夹持电极、导电和输送氩气流。钨极氩弧焊焊枪一般由枪体、喷嘴、电极夹持机构、电缆、氩气输入管、水管和开关及按钮等组成。钨极氩弧焊焊枪分为气冷式焊枪(QQ 系列)和水冷式焊枪(QS 系列)。气冷式焊枪使用方便，但限于小电流(150 A)焊接使用；水冷式焊枪适合大电流和自动焊接使用。QQ 系列气冷式钨极氩弧焊枪如图 3-1-9(a)所示，QS 系列水冷式焊枪如图 3-1-9(b)所示。

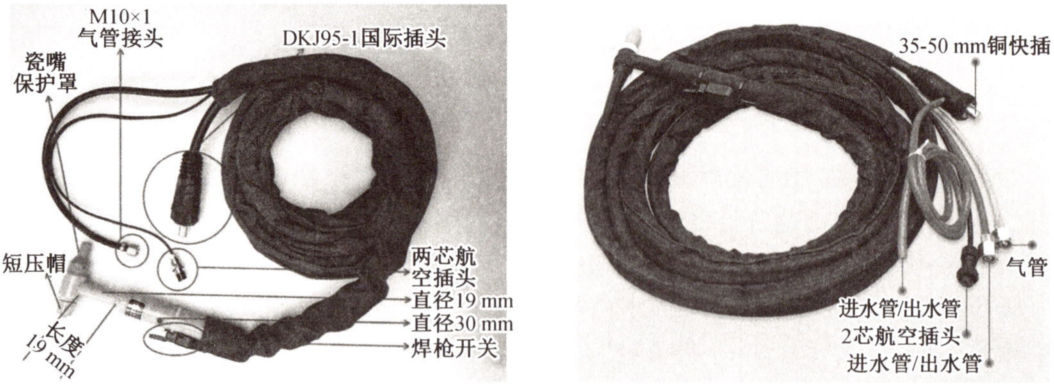

(a)气冷式　　(b)水冷式

图 3-1-9　钨极氩弧焊枪

水冷式钨极氩弧焊枪枪体的结构如图 3-1-10(a)所示,气冷式钨极氩弧焊枪枪体的结构如图 3-1-10(b)所示。

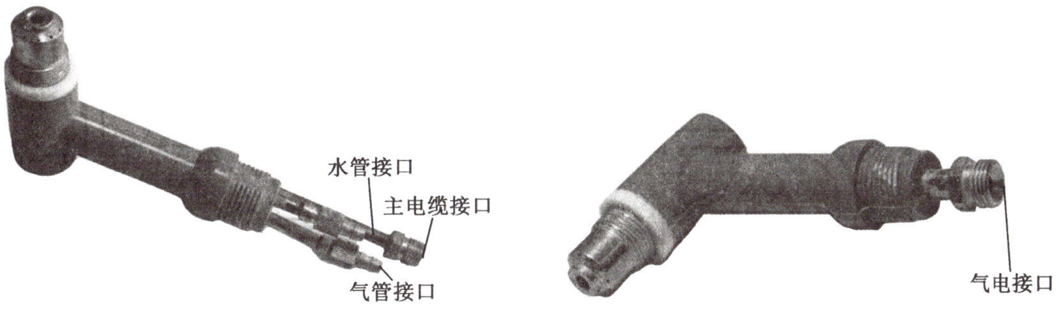

(a)气冷式　　(b)水冷式

图 3-1-10　钨极氩弧焊枪体座结构

钨极氩弧焊枪枪头部分的组合结构如图 3-1-11 所示。

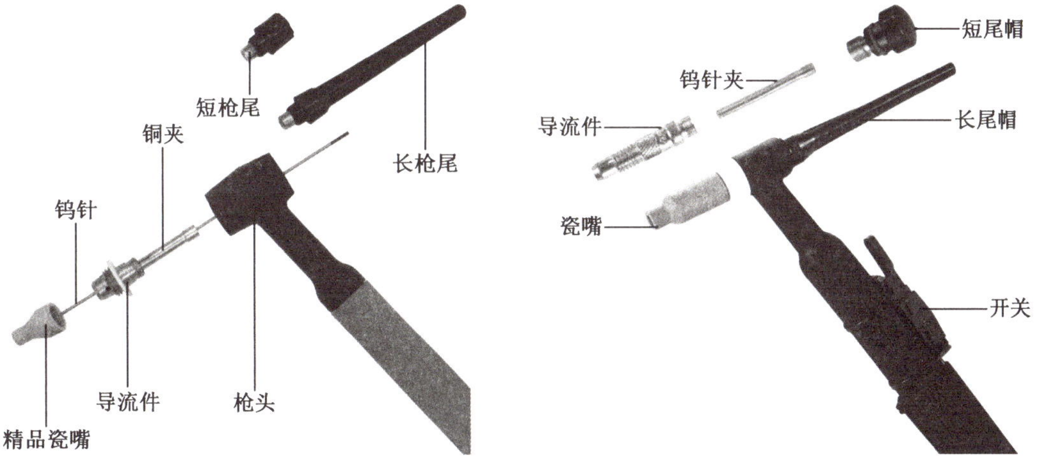

图 3-1-11　钨极氩弧焊枪枪头组合结构

3. 供气系统

钨极氩弧焊的供气系统由氩气瓶、减压器、流量计和电磁阀组成。氩气钢瓶外表涂为灰色,标有绿色“氩”或“氩气”字样,如图 3-1-12 所示。减压器用以减压和调压,流量计用来调节和测量氩气流量的大小,现常将减压器与流量计制成一体,称为氩气流量调节器,如图 3-1-13 所示。电磁阀是控制气体通断的装置。

4. 冷却系统

当选用的最大焊接电流在 150 A 以上时,必须通过水来冷却焊枪和电极。在冷却水接通并有一定压力后,才能启动焊接设备,通常在钨极氩弧焊设备中用水压开关或手动来控制水流量。

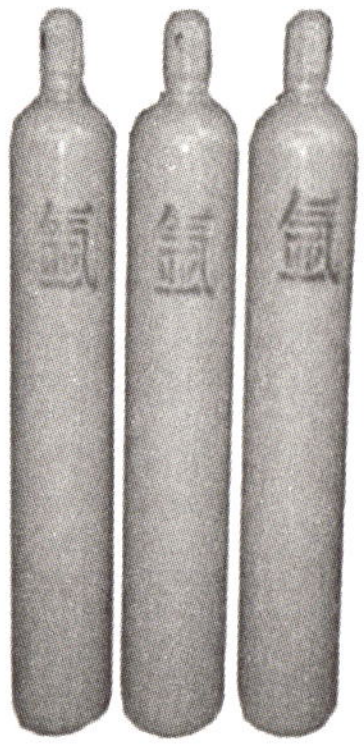

图 3-1-12　氩气瓶

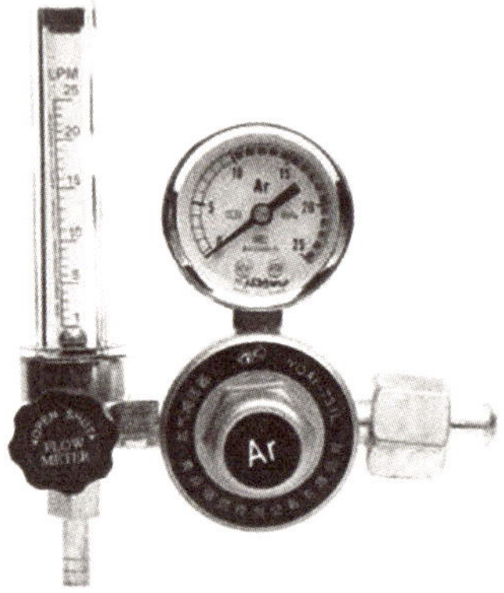

图 3-1-13　氩气流量调节器

任务4：掌握钨极氩弧焊的焊接材料及工艺参数选择原则

1. 钨极氩弧焊的焊接材料

钨极氩弧焊的焊接材料有钨针(钨极)、焊丝和保护气体。

(1)钨针(钨极)

钨极是钨极氩弧焊的电极材料，对电弧的稳定性和焊接质量有很大的影响。通常要求钨极具有电流容量大、施焊损耗小、引弧和稳弧性能好等优点，这主要取决于钨极的电子发射能力的大小。

①钨极的种类

钨极有纯钨极、钍钨极、铈钨极、锆钨极和镧钨极五种，目前常用的是前三种。

a. 纯钨极。纯钨极含钨 99.85%(质量分数)以上，熔点很高(为 3 390~3 479 ℃)，沸点也很高(约为 5 900 ℃)，不易熔化和蒸发，是使用最早的一种电极材料。但纯钨极发射电子的电压较高，要求焊机具有高的空载电压。另外，纯钨极易烧损，电流越大烧损越严重，因此目前很少使用。

b. 钍钨极。在纯钨极的基础上加入 1%~2%(质量分数)的氧化钍的钨极称为钍钨极。由于钨极棒内含有钍元素，使钨极发射电子的能力增加，具有电流承载能力较好、寿命较长且抗污染性能较好、容易引弧、所需的引弧电压小、电弧稳定性好等优点。其缺点是成本较高，钍钨极的粉尘具有微量的放射性，在磨削电极时，需注意防护。

c. 铈钨极。在纯钨极的基础上加入 2%(质量分数)的氧化铈的钨极称为铈钨极。它比钍钨极具有更大的优点，电弧细长，热量集中，电流密度可提高 5%~8%；烧损率低，寿命长，易引弧，电弧稳定，几乎没有放射性，是一种理想的电极材料，也是我国目前推广使用的钨极。铈钨极的优越性还表现在大电流焊接或等离子弧切割时，其损耗比小电流时更小。

②钨极的牌号、规格

a. 牌号。纯钨极的牌号是 W1、W2，纯度在 99.85%(质量分数)以上；钍钨极的牌号是 WTh-7、WTh-10、WTh-15；铈钨极的牌号是 WCe-5、WCe-13、WCe-20。

b. 规格。制造厂家按长度范围供给 76~610 mm 的钨极。常用钨极直径为 0.5 mm、1.0 mm、1.6 mm、2.0 mm、3.2 mm、4.0 mm 等。

为了方便使用，钨极的一端为了常涂有颜色，以便于识别，如图 3-1-14 所示。例如，钍钨极涂红色（代表含二氧化钍 2%），铈钨极涂灰色（代表含二氧化铈 2%），纯钨极涂绿色，天蓝色代表含 2%镧，蓝色代表含 2%钇，棕色代表含 4%锆。

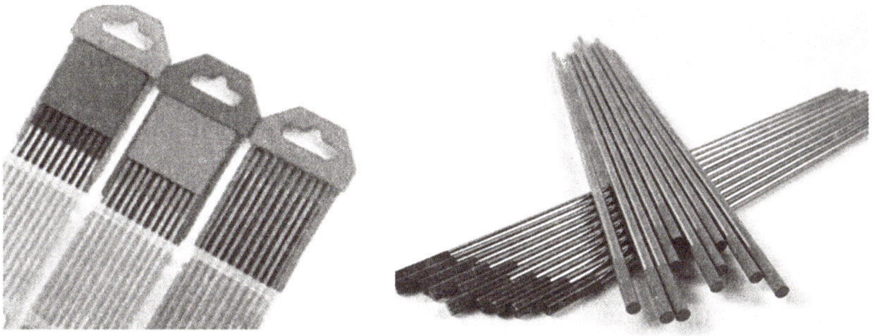

图 3-1-14　钨针示意图

铈钨极牌号举例如下：

WCe-20

- 20：氧化铈含量2%
- Ce：铈
- W：钨极

钨极应尽量选用铈钨极。存放钨极时，若数量较大，最好保存在铅盒中。

（2）焊丝

选择焊丝的原则是熔敷金属的化学成分或力学性能与被焊材料相当。氩弧焊用焊丝主要分钢焊丝和有色金属焊丝两大类。焊丝可按对应国际或国家标准选用，如中国国家标准 GB/T 8110《气体保护电弧焊用碳钢、低合金钢焊丝》和不锈钢焊丝可按 GB/T 20878《焊接用不锈钢焊丝》，国际标准常用 AWS。

焊接有色金属时一般采用与母材相当的焊丝，如铜及铜合金根据中国国家标准 GB/T 9460《铜及铜合金焊丝》，常用铜及铜合金焊丝的型号、成分及用途参见表 3-1-2。

表 3-1-2　常用铜及铜合金焊丝的型号、成分及用途

焊丝型号	焊丝牌号	名称	主要化学成分（质量分数，%）	熔点/℃	用途
SCu1898（CuSnl）	HS201	纯铜焊丝	Cu（≥98.0），Sn（≤1.0），Si（≤0.5），Mn（≤0.5）	1083	纯铜的气焊、氧弧焊及等离子弧焊等
SCu6560（CuSi3Mn）	HS211	青铜焊丝	Si（2.8～4.0），Mn（≤1.5），Zn（≤1.0），Sn（≤1.0），Fe（≤0.5），Pb（≤0.02），Al（≤0.01），其他（≤0.5），其余为 Cu	958	青铜的气焊、氩弧焊及等离子弧焊等

表 3-1-2(续)

焊丝型号	焊丝牌号	名称	主要化学成分(质量分数,%)	熔点/℃	用途
SCu4700 (CuZn40Sn)	HS221	黄铜焊丝	Cu(57~61),Sn(0.25~1.0),Pb(≤0.05),Al(≤0.01),其他(≤0.5),其余为 Zn	886	黄铜的气焊、氩弧焊及等离子弧焊等
SCu6800 (CuZn40Ni)	HS222	黄铜焊丝	Cu(56~60),Sn(0.8~1.1),Mn(0.01~0.50),Si(0.04~0.15),Fe(0.25~1.20),Ni+Co(0.2~0.8),Al(≤0.01),Pb(≤0.05),其他(≤0.5),其余为 Zn	860	
SCu6810A (CuZn40SnSi)	HS223	黄铜焊丝	Cu(58~62),Si(0.1~0.5),Sn(≤1.0),Mn(≤0.03),Fe(≤0.02),Al(≤0.01),Pb(≤0.03),其他(≤0.5),其余为 Zn	905	

(3)保护气体

①氩气的性质

氩气是一种无色、无味的单原子惰性气体,密度为空气的 1.4 倍。由于氩气比空气重,使用时不易漂浮散失,因此能在熔池上方形成较好的覆盖层,有利于起到保护焊缝金属的作用。另外,在用氩气保护焊接时,产生的烟雾较少,便于观察、控制熔池和电弧。

氩气既不与任何金属产生化学反应,也不溶解于金属中,因此可以避免焊缝金属中的合金元素的烧损及由此带来的其他焊接缺陷,使得焊接冶金反应变得简单和容易控制。

氩气的另一个应用特点是具有较低的热导率且是单原子气体,高温时不分解、不吸热,所以在氩气中燃烧的热量损失较少。在氩气中,电弧一旦引燃,燃烧就很稳定。在各种保护气体中,氩弧的稳定性最好,即使在低电压时也十分稳定。氩气对电弧的热收缩效应较小,即使氩弧长度稍有变化,也不会显著地改变电弧电压,因此电弧稳定,很适合手工焊。

②对氩气纯度的要求

氩气是制氧时的副产品,是通过分馏液化空气制取的。氩气的沸点介于氧、氮之间,因此制取时会残留一定量的其他杂质。若杂质含量过多,在焊接过程中不但影响对熔化金属的保护,而且易使焊缝产生气孔、夹渣等缺陷,并使钨极的烧损增加。按照现行有关标准的规定,氩气纯度应达到 99.99%才完全合乎焊接铝、钛等活泼金属的要求。焊接用氩气目前常有 99.99%及 99.999%两种纯度,均能满足各种材料的焊接要求,其成分要求见表 3-1-3。

③氩气的储运

氩气可在低于-184 ℃的温度下以液态形式储存和运送,但焊接时,氩气大多装入钢瓶中，供焊工使用。氩气瓶是一种钢质圆形高压容器，目前，我国常用氩气瓶的容积为 33 L、40 L、44 L，满瓶时的压力为 15 MPa，其外面涂成灰色，用绿色漆标以“氩气”二字。氩气瓶在使用中应直立放置，严禁敲击、碰撞等，也不得用电磁起重搬运机搬运，并防止日光暴晒。装运时，应戴好瓶帽，以免损坏接口螺纹。

表 3-1-3 焊接用氩气的成分要求 (%)

氩气纯度	N_2	O_2	H_2	C_nH_m	H_2O
≥99.99	<0.01	<0.015	<0.000 5	<0.001	30 mg/m^3
≥99.999	≤10^{-4}	≤10^{-5}	≤5~10^{-6}	10^{-5}	≤2~10^{-5}

2. 钨极氩弧焊工艺参数及选择

(1)钨极氩弧焊的工艺参数

钨极氩弧焊的工艺参数主要有电流的种类及极性、焊接电流、钨极直径及端部形状、保护气体流量等。对于自动钨极氩弧焊还包括焊接速度和送丝速度。当被焊接的材料确定之后，应通过工艺试验和工艺评定来确定工艺参数。

①焊接电流种类及极性

不同的电流种类及极性具有不同的工艺特点，适用于不同材料的焊接。因此，应首先根据工件的材料选择电流的种类及极性。钨极氩弧焊的焊接电流有三种，各种电流的适用范围如下。

a. 交流。交流焊接的熔深和熔宽比较适中，主要用于焊接铝、镁及其合金，焊接带氧化膜的铜。

b. 直流。直流焊接分为正接和反接。正接时工件热量约占 70%，钨极约占 30%。正极性几乎可以焊接所有的钢铁材料，反极性直流电很少采用。

c. 脉冲电流。脉冲电流能控制和改善熔深、焊缝成形，适用于特殊位置的焊接。

不同金属材料对钨极氩弧焊电流种类及极性的选用见表 3-1-4。

表 3-1-4 不同金属材料对钨极氩弧焊电流种类及极性的选用

被焊金属		直流		交流
		正极性	反极性	
低碳钢	0.4~0.8 mm	优	不推荐	好①
	0.8~3.2 mm	优	不推荐	不推荐
高碳钢	—	优	不推荐	好①
铸铁	—	优	不推荐	好①
耐热合金	—	优	不推荐	好①
难熔合金	—	优	不推荐	不推荐

表 3-1-4(续)

被焊金属		直流		交流
		正极性	反极性	
铝合金	≤0. 6 mm	不推荐②	好	优
	>0. 6 mm	不推荐②	不推荐	优
	铸件	不推荐②	不推荐	优
铍	—	优	不推荐	好①
铜及铜合金	黄铜	优	不推荐	好①
	脱氧铜	优	不推荐	不推荐
	硅青铜	优	不推荐	不推荐
镁合金	≤3. 2 mm	不推荐②	好	优
	24. 8 mm	不推荐②	不推荐	优
	铸件	不推荐②	不推荐	优
银	—	优	不推荐	好①
钛合金	—	优	不推荐	不推荐

注:①应比直流正接所用的电流高约 25%。

②除非待焊处经机械或化学清理。

焊接电流的大小主要根据工件的厚度、空间位置和钨极直径来选择。过大或过小的焊接电流都会使得焊缝成形不良或产生焊接缺陷。所以,必须在不同钨极直径允许的焊接电流范围内正确地选择焊接电流。焊接电流与钨极直径的对应关系见表 3-1-5。

表 3-1-5　不同直径钨极的许用电流范围

钨极直径/mm	直流正接/A	直流反接/A	交流/A
1. 0	15~80	—	20~60
1. 6	70~150	10~20	60~120
2. 4	140~235	15~30	100~180
3. 2	225~325	25~40	160~250
4. 0	300~400	40~55	200~320
5. 0	400~500	55~80	290~390

②焊接电压

焊接电压主要由弧长决定,弧长增加,电弧电压增大,焊缝宽度增加,熔深减小,但弧长太长,易引起未焊透及咬边且保护效果也不好;电弧太短,不易操作,既看不清熔池,又容易引起短路,加大钨极烧损,容易夹钨。通常在保证不短路的情况下,应尽量采用较短的电弧进行焊接。不加填充焊丝焊接时,弧长以控制在 1~3 mm 之间为宜,加填充焊丝焊接时,弧长 3~6 mm。

电极端头的几何形状也影响焊接电压的大小。在钨极尖端到工件距离相同的条件下，较尖的锥形电极的焊接电压要高些。可根据具体产品及电源类型任选电弧电压的控制方法，但应控制焊接电压保持相对的稳定。

③焊接速度

电弧穿透深度通常与焊接速度成反比。金属的导热性、构件的厚度和尺寸是控制焊接速度的主要考虑因素。改变焊接速度的目的是保持恒定电弧穿透力所要求的恒定热量。

焊接速度一般应遵循以下原则。

a. 焊接铝等高热导率金属时，为了减小变形，应采用较快的焊接速度。

b. 焊接有热裂倾向的合金时，不能采用高速焊接。

c. 焊缝熔池的尺寸直接受焊速影响，当在非平焊位置时，只能是较小的熔池以避免铁水下淌，应适当提高焊接速度。

d. 焊接电流脉冲控制技术的发展，在低热导率的金属（如钛）和固定管子及厚壁管子的焊接时，对接头熔池的控制十分有利。

焊接速度影响焊接线能量，因此影响熔深及熔宽。通常根据板厚来选择焊接速度，而且为了保证获得良好的焊缝成形，焊接速度应与焊接电流、预热温度及保护气流量适当匹配。焊接速度太快时，易出现未焊透、咬边等缺陷；而焊接速度太慢时会出现焊缝太宽、烧穿等缺陷。

④钨极直径及端部形状

钨极直径的选择原则是：在保证钨极许用电流大于所用焊接电流的前提下，尽量选用直径较小的钨极。当焊接电流较小、钨极直径较大时，由于电流密度较低，钨极端部温度不够，电弧会在钨极端部不规则漂移，电弧很不稳定，破坏了保护区，使熔池被氧化。焊接电流较大而钨极直径较小时，由于电流密度太高，钨极端部的温度较高，当温度达到或超过钨极的熔点时，端部就会出现熔化现象，熔化的钨极会在端部形成一个小尖状突起，逐渐变大形成熔滴，电弧随熔滴尖端漂移，很不稳定，破坏了氩气保护区，使熔池氧化，焊缝成形不好，还会产生夹钨等缺陷。选择合适的焊接电流和钨极直径才能保证电弧的稳定性。

实践表明，钨极端部的表面质量和形状尺寸对焊接许用电流的大小和焊缝成形有一定的影响。一般情况下，在焊接薄板和焊接电流较小时，可用小直径的钨极并将其磨成尖锥角（约 30°），这样，容易引弧且电弧稳定，如图 3-1-15（a）所示。但在电流较大时仍用尖锥角，会使末端过热熔化，增加烧损，使弧柱明显扩大、漂移不稳，影响焊缝成形。因此，在大电流焊接时，要求钨极端部磨成带有平顶的锥形，如图 3-1-15（b）所示。采用交流钨极氩弧焊时，一般钨极末端磨成半圆球状，如图 3-1-15（c）所示。

⑤喷嘴孔径及氩气流量

喷嘴孔径越大，保护区越大，但太大时，熔池及电弧的可观察性变差。对于一定的喷嘴孔径，保护气流量有一个合适的范围，流量太小时，气体挺度差，保护效果不好；流量太大时，气流层中出现紊流，空气易卷入，保护效果也不好。喷嘴孔径及氩气流量通常根据电流的种类和大小、极性来选择，见表 3-1-6。

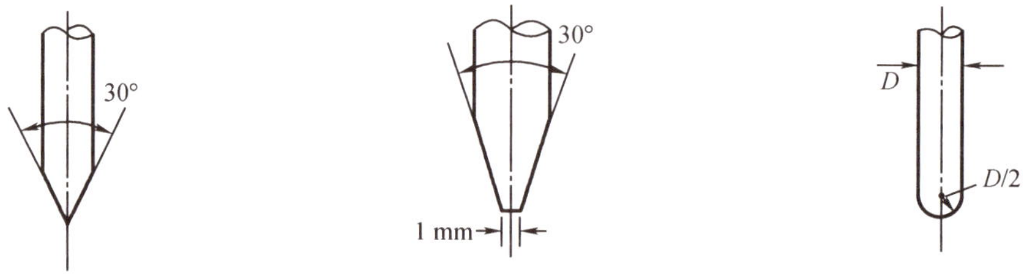

(a)尖锥角钨极端头　(b)平顶的锥形钨极端头　(c)半圆球状钨极端头

图 3-1-15　钨极端部形状

表 3-1-6　喷嘴孔径及氩气流量的选择

焊接电流/A	直流正接(DCSP)		直流反接(DCRP)	
	喷嘴孔径/mm	氩气流量/(L/min)	喷嘴孔径/mm	氩气流量/(L/min)
10~100	4~9.5	4~5	8~9.5	6~8
101~150	4~9.5	4~7	9.5~11	7~10
151~200	6~13	6~8	11~13	7~10
201~300	8~13	8~9	13~16	8~15
301~500	13~16	9~12	16~19	8~15

⑥钨极伸出长度

通常将露在喷嘴外面的钨极长度叫作钨极的伸出长度。伸出长度过大时,钨极易过热,且保护效果差;而伸出长度太小时,喷嘴易过热。因此钨极伸出长度必须保持一适当的值。对接焊时,钨极的伸出长度一般保持在 5~6 mm;焊接 T 形焊缝时,钨极的伸出长度最好为 7~8 mm。

⑦喷嘴离工件的距离

喷嘴离工件的距离要与钨极伸出长度相匹配。一般应控制在 8~14 mm 之间。距离过小时,影响工人的视线,且易导致钨极与熔池的接触短路,使焊缝夹钨并降低钨极寿命;距离过大时,气体保护效果差,电弧不稳定。

(2)钨极氩弧焊工艺参数的选择

碳钢手工钨极氩弧焊的工艺参数见表 3-1-7,铝及铝合金手工钨极氩弧焊的工艺参数见表 3-1-8,不锈钢手工钨极氩弧焊的工艺参数见表 3-1-9,8-18 不锈钢手工钨极氩弧焊的工艺参数见表 3-1-10,铜、镁、镍及其合金手工钨极氩弧焊的工艺参数见表 3-1-11,钛及钛合金手工钨极氩弧焊的工艺参数见表 3-1-12。

表 3-1-7　碳钢手工钨极氩弧焊的工艺参数

项目	内容		
材料厚度/mm	1.5~3.0	3.0~6.0	6.0~12
接头设计	直边对接	V 形坡口	X 形坡口

表 3-1-7(续)

项目	内容		
焊接电流/A	50~100	70~120	90~150
极性	直流正接	直流正接	直流正接
焊接电压/V	12	12	12
钨极种类	钍钨极	钍钨极	钍钨极
电极尺寸/mm	2.4	2.4	3.2
填充金属尺寸/mm	1.6~2.5	2.5~3.2	2.5~3.2
保护气体流量/(L/min)	Ar 8~12	Ar 8~12	Ar 10~14
背面保护气体流量/(L/min)	Ar 2~4	Ar 2~4	Ar 2~4
喷嘴尺寸/mm	8~10	8~10	10~12
喷嘴到工件距离/mm	≤12	≤12	≤12
最低预热温度/℃	15	15	15
最高层间温度/℃	250	250	250

表 3-1-8　铝及其合金手工钨极氩弧焊的工艺参数

板厚/mm	坡口形式	焊接层数(正/反面)	钨极直径/mm	焊丝直径/mm	预热温度/℃	焊接电流/A	氩气流量/(L/min)	喷嘴孔径/mm
1	卷边	正 1	2	1.6	—	45~60	7~9	8
1.5	卷边或 I 形	正 1	2	1.6~2.0	—	50~80	7~9	8
2	I 形	正 1	2~3	2~2.5	—	90~120	8~12	8~12
3	Y 形坡口	正 1	3	2~3	—	150~180	8~12	8~12
4		1~2/1	4	3	—	180~200	10~15	8~12
5		1~2/1	4	3~4	—	180~240	10~15	10~12
6		1~2/1	5	4	—	240~280	16~20	14~16
8		2/1	5	4~5	100	260~320	16~20	14~16
10		3~4/1~2	5	4~5	100~150	280~340	16~20	14~16
12		3~4/1~2	5~6	4~5	150~200	300~360	18~22	16~20
14		3~4/1~2	5~6	5~6	180~200	340~380	20~24	16~20
16		4~5/1~2	6	5~6	200~220	340~380	20~24	16~20
18		4~5/1~2	6	5~6	200~240	360~400	25~30	16~20
20		4~5/1~2	6	5~6	200~260	360~400	25~30	20~22
16~20	X 形坡口	2~3/2~3	6	5~6	200~260	300~380	25~30	16~20
22~25		3~4/3~4	6~7	5~6	200~260	360~400	30~35	20~22

表 3-1-9　不锈钢手工钨极氩弧焊的工艺参数

板厚/mm	坡口形式	焊接层数(正/反面)	钨极直径/mm	焊丝直径/mm	预热温度/℃	焊接电流/A	氩气流量/(L/min)	喷嘴孔径/mm
1.0	对接	1	2	1.6	—	7~28	3~4	12~17
1.2	对接	1	2	1.6	—	15	3~4	25
1.5	对接	1	2	1.6	—	5~19	3~4	18~32

表 3-1-10　8-18 不锈钢钨极氩弧焊的工艺参数

材料厚度/mm	1.5~3.0	3.0~6.0	6.0~12
接头设计	直边对接	V 形坡口	X 形坡口
焊接电流/A	50~90	70~120	100~150
极性	直流正接	直流正接	直流正接
焊接电压/V	12	12	12
钨极种类	钍钨极	钍钨极	钍钨极
电极直径/mm	2.5	2.5	2.5
填充金属类型及填丝直径/mm	8-18 型,ϕ1.6~2.5	8-18 型,ϕ2.5~3.2	8-18 型,ϕ2.5~3.2
材料厚度/mm	1.6~3.0	3.0~6.0	6.0~12
保护气体流量/(L/min)	Ar 8~12	Ar 10~14	Ar 10~14
背面保护气体流量/(L/min)	Ar 2~4	Ar 2~4	Ar 2~4
喷嘴尺寸/mm	8~10	10~12	10~12
喷嘴到工件距离/mm	≤12	≤12	≤12
最低预热温度/℃	15	15	15
最高层间温度/℃	250	250	250

表 3-1-11　铜、镁、镍及其合金手工钨极氩弧焊的工艺参数

合金类型	板厚/mm	焊道数	钨极直径/mm	喷嘴孔径/mm	焊丝直径/mm	焊接电流/A	焊接速度/(cm/min)	气体流量/(L/min)
铜及其合金	1.6	1	1.6	6.4	1.6	90~155	25.2	8.5
	3.2	1	2.4	7.9	2.4	150~245	20.4	8.5
	4.8	1	3.2	9.5	3.2	175~255	20.4	17.0
	6.4	1	3.2	9.5	3.2	200~285	18	17.0
	9.5	2	4.8	12.7	4.8	220~350	15	17.0
	12.7	3	4.8	15.9	6.4	300~500	15	21.2
	直流正接,板厚小于 4.8 mm 用氩气保护,其余用氦气,钍钨极							

表 3-1-11(续)

合金类型	板厚/mm	焊道数	钨极直径/mm	喷嘴孔径/mm	焊丝直径/mm	焊接电流/A	焊接速度/(cm/min)	气体流量/(L/min)
硅青铜	1.6	1	1.6	6.4	1.6	75~120	25.2	7.1
	3.2	1	1.6	6.4	2.4	95~150	25.2	7.1
	4.8	1	2.4	7.9	2.4	125~220	25.2	9.4
	6.4	2	2.4	7.9	3.2	140~275	20.2	11.8
	9.5	3	3.2	9.5	3.2	200~285	20.2	11.8
	12.7	7	4.0	9.5	3.2	240~300	20.2	11.8
	19.7	14	4.0	9.5	4.8	275~350	20.2	11.8
	25.4	20	4.8	11.1	6.4	300~365	20.2	11.8
	直流正接,氩气保护,钍钨极							
镁合金	0.9	1	1.6	9.5	2.4	25~45	51	7.1
	1.5	1	1.6	9.5	2.4	35~60	51	7.1
	1.9	1	2.4	9.5	3.2	50~80	43.2	7.1
	2.7	1	2.4	12.7	3.2	75~100	43.2	9.4
	3.0	1	2.4	12.7	3.2	95~120	43.2	9.4
	交流,氩气保护,纯钨极及其合金							
镍及其合金	0.6	1	1.6	9.5		8~10	20.2	7.5
	1.5	1	2.4	12.7	1.6	25~45	20.2	8.1
	3.2	1	3.2	12.7	2.4	90~175	28.2	11.8
	6.4	2	3.2	12.7	3.2	100~175	20.4	14.2
	直流正接,氩气保护,钍钨极							

表 3-1-12 钛及钛合金手工钨极氩弧焊的工艺参数

板厚/mm	坡口形式	焊接层数	钨极直径/mm	焊丝直径/mm	焊接电流/A	氩气流量/(L/min)			喷嘴孔径/mm	备注
						主喷嘴	拖罩	背面		
0.5	I形坡口	1	1.5	1.0	30~50	8~10	14~16	6~8	10	对接接头的间隙0.5 mm,也可不加钛丝,间隙1.0 mm
1.0		1	2.0	1.0~2.0	40~60	8~10	14~16	6~8	10	
1.5		1	2.0	1.0~2.0	60~80	10~12	14~16	8~10	10~12	
2.0		1	2.0~3.0	1.0~2.0	80~110	12~14	16~20	10~12	12~14	
2.5		1	2.0~3.0	2.0	110~120	12~14	16~20	10~12	12~14	
3.0	Y形坡口	1~2	3.0	2.0~3.0	120~140	12~14	16~20	10~12	14~18	坡口间隙2~3 mm;钝边0.5 mm;焊缝反面衬有钢垫板;坡口角度60°~150°
3.5		1~2	3.0~4.0	2.0~3.0	120~140	12~14	16~20	10~12	14~18	
4.0		2	3.0~4.0	2.0~3.0	130~150	14~16	20~25	12~14	18~20	
4.5		2	3.0~4.0	2.0~3.0	200	14~16	20~25	12~14	18~20	
5.0		2~3	4.0	3.0	130~150	14~16	20~25	12~14	18~20	
6.0		2~3	4.0	3.0~4.0	140~180	14~16	25~28	12~14	18~20	
7.0		2~3	4.0	3.0~4.0	140~180	14~16	25~28	12~14	20~22	
8.0		3~4	4.0	3.0~4.0	140~180	14~16	25~28	12~14	20~22	
10.0	双Y形坡口	4~6	4.0	3.0~4.0	160~200	14~16	25~28	12~14	20~22	坡口角度60°;钝边1 mm
13.0		6~8	4.0	3.0~4.0	220~240	14~16	25~28	12~14	20~22	
20.0		12	4.0	4.0	200~240	12~14	20	10~12	18	坡口角度55°;钝边1.5~2.0 mm
22.0		6	4.0	4.0~5.0	230~250	15~18	18~20	18~20	20	
25.0		15~16	4.0	3.0~4.0	200~220	16~18	26~30	20~26	22	坡口角度55°;钝边1.5~2.0 mm;间隙1.5 mm
30.0		17~18	4.0	3.0~4.0	200~220	16~18	26~30	20~26	22	

任务考核

1. 以下哪种符号表示钨极熔化极氩弧焊(　　)

A. TIG　　B. MIG　　C. GTAW　　D. MAG

2. 铜及铜合金采用钨极氩弧焊时的电源种类和极性是(　　)

A. 直流正接　　B. 直流反接　　C. 交流正接　　D. 交流反接

3. TIG 焊一般只用于焊接厚度在(　　)以下的焊件。

A. 4 mm　　B. 6 mm　　C. 8 mm　　D. 10 mm

4. 钨极氩弧焊机的调试不包括(　　)。

A. 焊枪的发热情况　　B. 控制系统性能

C. 焊剂的辅撤和回收　　D. 电源参数

5. 钨极氩弧焊机的电源调试不包括(　　)。

A. 电源的恒流特性　　B. 引弧的准确性和可靠性

C. 电流、电压的调节范围　　D. 焊枪有无漏气、漏水情况

6. 钨极氩弧焊机的控制系统调试包括(　　)。

A. 小车性能检测　　B. 引弧性能

C. 交流电源阴极雾化作用　　D. 输入电压变化时,输出电流的变化

7. 纯钨的熔点高达(　　),沸点约为(　　)。

A. 2 800 ℃,5 500 ℃　　B. 3 200 ℃,5 700 ℃

C. 3 400 ℃,5 900 ℃　　D. 3 600 ℃,6 100 ℃

8. 为了增加钨极发射电子的能力,可在纯钨中加入1%~2%的(　　)。

A. CuO　　B. ZnO　　C. Al_2O_3　　D. TuO_2

9. 以下不属于钨极氩弧焊的电极端部形状的是(　　)。

A. 圆柱形　　B. 平底锥形　　C. 尖锥形　　D. 圆球形

10. (多选)钨极氩弧焊可分为(　　)。

A. 手工钨极氩弧焊　　B. 半自动钨极氩弧焊

C. 自动钨极氩弧焊　　D. 钨极脉冲氩弧焊

Module Ⅲ
Handmade TIG Welding and Its Application

Project Ⅰ Fundamental Knowledge of TIG Welding

【Learning Objectives】

1. Understand the principle and characteristics of inert gas shielded welding;

2. Understand the working principle classification and characteristics of tungsten inert gas welding;

3. Master the equipment of tungsten inert gas welding;

4. Master the selection principles of welding materials and process parameters for tungsten inert gas welding.

The tungsten inert gas shielded welding method is an arc welding method that uses inert gas protection and tungsten rods as electrodes. Due to the common use of argon gas in China, it is often directly referred to as tungsten inert gas welding, abbreviated as TIG welding. Helium gas is also commonly used in other countries. Taking tungsten inert gas welding as an example, the principles and operating methods of other inert gases are similar. During tungsten inert gas welding, due to the fact that the tungsten electrode itself does not melt and only emits electrons to generate an arc, it is also known as non melting electrode argon arc welding. During welding, the argon gas sprayed from the nozzle forms a thick and dense gas protective layer to isolate the air. Surrounded by the laminar flow of argon gas, the arc burns between the tungsten electrode and the workpiece, using the heat generated by the arc to melt the welded area and fill the welding wire, connecting the two separated metals together to obtain a firm welding joint. At present, it is mainly used for welding thin parts or for backing welding of important products.

Task 1:Understand the Principle and Characteristics of Inert Gas Shielded Welding

1. Principle of Inert Gas Shielded Welding

The welding process of inert gas arc welding is shown in Fig. 3-1-1. The inert gas flow ejected from the welding gun's nozzle forms a thick and dense gas shielding layer in the welding area, isolating the air. Simultaneously, the arc heat generated by the combustion between the electrode and the weldment melts the welded part and joins the metals together, either by filling or not filling the welding wire, resulting in a strong welded joint.

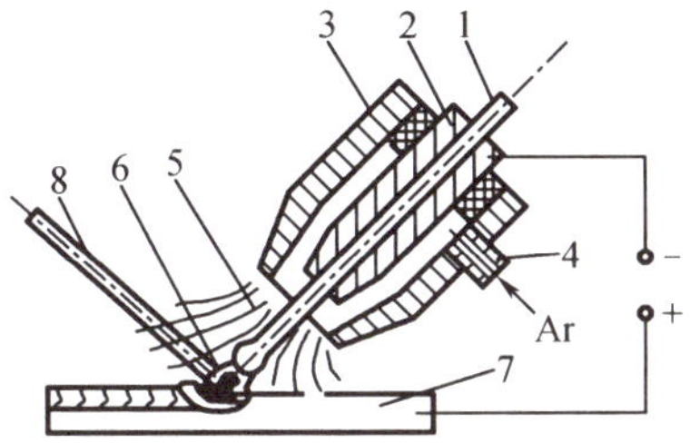

(a) non-melting inert gas shielding welding

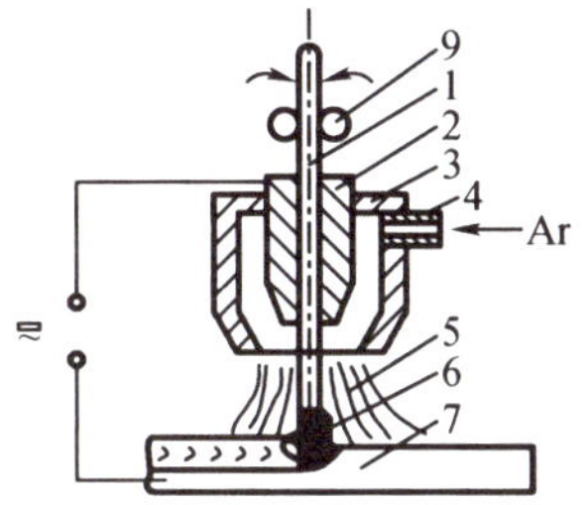

(b) melting inert gas shielding welding

1—Welding wire or electrode; 2—Current contact nozzle; 3—Nozzle; 4—Gas inlet pipe; 5—Inert gas flow; 6—Electric arc; 7—Workpiece; 8—Filler wire; 9—Wire feeding roller.

Fig. 3-1-1 Schematic Diagram of Inert Gas Shielded Welding

2. Characteristics of Inert Gas Shielded Welding

(1) High quality weld

The inert gas can form a stable barrier between the air and the weldment, ensuring that the alloy elements in the welded metal will not oxidize and burn at high temperatures. Additionally, the inert gas does not dissolve in liquid metal, thus effectively protecting the molten pool metal and achieving higher welding quality.

(2) Minimal welding deformation and stress

Due to the concentrated heat of inert gas shielded welding, the arc is cooled and compressed by the flow of inert gas, resulting in a narrow heat affected zone and minimal welding deformation and stress, making it particularly suitable for welding thin plates.

(3) Wide range of weldability

Almost all metal materials can be welded under inert gas. Generally, it is mainly used for welding non-ferrous metals such as stainless steel, aluminum, and copper, as well as their alloys. Occasionally, it is also employed for backing welding of welded components.

(4) Easy to master the operation technique

Inert gas is used to shield with no slag, and open arc welding is adopted. The electric arc and molten pool have excellent visibility, making it suitable for welding in various positions, and easy to achieve mechanization and automation.

Task 2: Understand the Working Principle Classification and Characteristics of Tungsten Inert Gas Welding

1. Classification and application scopeof inert gas shielded welding

According to the commonly used electrode materials, inert gas shielded welding can be divided into two types. One type is called tungsten electrode (non-consumable electrode) inert gas shielded welding, which uses a tungsten electrode that only emits electrons and generates an arc but does not melt itself. The other type is called consumable inert gas shielded welding, which uses a welding wire that emits electrons and generates an arc for filling weld joints, as shown in Fig. 3-1-1. It can be further classified into manual welding, semi-automatic welding, and automatic welding based on its operation mode. If a pulse device is added to the inert gas welding power supply, it can be divided into tungsten arc pulse welding and metal-impulse welding.

Due to its common usage as an inert gas, the process of inert gas shielded welding is often referred to as argon arc welding. The non-consumable electrode argon arc welding, which uses tungsten as the electrode, is known as tungsten inert gas (TIG) welding. On the other hand, the consumable electrode argon arc welding, which uses welding wire as the electrode, is known as metal inert gas (MIG) welding. Please refer to Table 3-1-1 for the applicable scope of argon arc welding.

Table 3-1-1 Scope of Application for Argon Arc Welding

Material to be welded	Weldment Thickness /mm	Welding method	Type and polarity of power supply
Titanium and titanium alloys.	0.5-3.0 >2.0	Tungsten inert gas welding Metal argon arc welding	DC straight polarity DC reverse polarity
Magnesium and magnesium alloys	0.5-5.0 >2.0	Tungsten inert gas welding Metal argon arc welding	AC or DC reverse connection DC reverse polarity
Aluminum and aluminum alloy	0.5-4.0 >3.0	Tungsten inert gas welding Metal argon arc welding	AC or DC reverse connection DC reverse polarity
Copper and copper alloys	>0.5 >3.0	Tungsten inert gas welding Metal argon arc welding	Direct current straight polarity DC reverse polarity
Stainless steel, heat-resistant steel	0.5-3.0 >2.0	Tungsten inert gas welding Metal argon arc welding	AC or DC reverse connection DC reverse polarity

Inert gas welding can be used for almost all types of steel, non-ferrous metals, and their alloys. However, due to its high cost, it is primarily utilized for welding high-alloy steel materials, nonferrous metals, their alloys, and refractory active metals such as molybdenum and niobium. Additionally, it is employed for repair welding and backing welding without a gasket on the reverse side. For instance, in shipbuilding production, manual argon tungsten arc welding is commonly employed for backing welds (one-side welding and double-side forming) during the welding of important piping systems made of carbon steel. This ensures the attainment of high-quality welds with uniform shape and no defects such as slag and inclusions in the pipes.

Since argon tungsten arc welding belongs to the category of gas metal arc welding in Module II, and the welding operation techniques are similar, only the commonly used tungsten arc welding method in non-gas metal arc welding is described here.

2. Working principleof argon tungsten arc welding

TIG welding utilizes the heat generated by the arc between a tungsten electrode and the workpiece to melt additional filler wire or automatically fed welding wire (or without filler wire) and the base metal, forming a molten pool and creating a weld. During the welding process, argon gas is continuously expelled from the nozzle of the welding torch, creating a tightly sealed protective gas layer in the arc zone. This layer isolates the electrode and the molten metal pool from the surrounding air, resulting in high-quality welded joints. The working principle of argon tungsten arc welding is illustrated in Fig. 3-1-2 below.

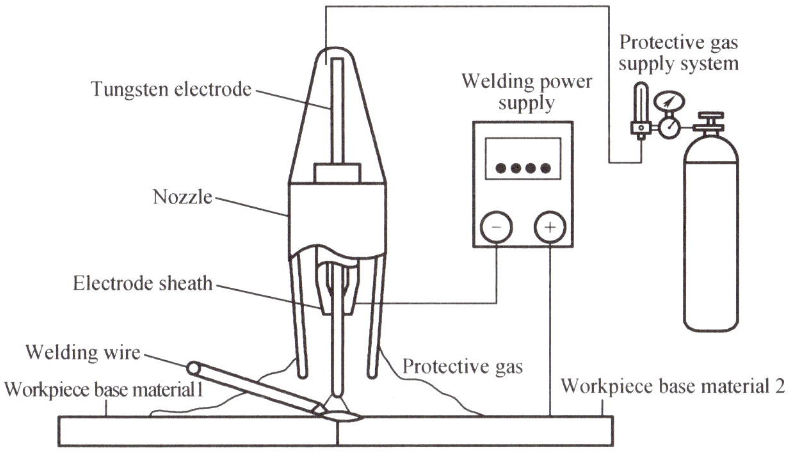

Figure 3-1-2 Schematic diagram of argon tungsten arc welding

3. Classification of argon tungsten arc welding

According to the type of current used, TIG welding can be divided into DC TIG welding, AC TIG welding, and pulsed TIG welding.

TIG welding can be divided into manual tungsten arc welding and automatic tungsten arc welding according to its operation mode.

During manual tungsten inert gas (TIG) welding, the welder holds the welding torch with one hand and the welding wire with the other hand. The welding wire is gradually fed into the molten pool as the welding torch swings and moves forward, as shown in Fig. 3-1-3. Sometimes, no filler wire is added, and only the interface edge is melted to form a weld. Manual TIG welding is widely used in actual production.

Automatic argon tungsten arc welding is a welding method where the welding gun is driven by a transmission mechanism, and the wire feeder follows the welding gun to provide continuous wire feeding, as shown in Fig. 3-1-4.

4. Characteristics of tungsten inert gas (TIG) welding

The welding process of this type of welding method exhibits excellent stability and facilitates the attainment of high-quality welds.

Fig. 3-1-3 Manual TIG Welding

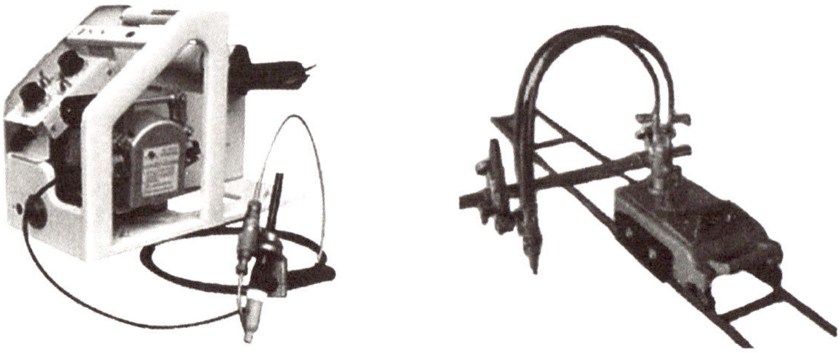

Fig. 3-1-4 Schematic Diagram of Semi-automatic TIG Welding and Automatic TIG Welding

(1) Advantages of TIG welding

Compared to other welding methods, argon tungsten arc welding has the following advantages.

①Stable welding process. The argon arc combustion is highly stable, with the tungsten rod remaining intact during welding. There are minimal factors causing interference in the arc length change, resulting in a highly stable welding process.

②Good welding quality. Argon, being an inert gas, does not dissolve in the liquid metal nor undergo any chemical reactions with the metal. Furthermore, argon readily forms an effective airflow isolation layer, preventing the entry of oxygen and nitrogen into the weld metal.

③Wide application. It is capable of welding nearly all metals and alloys, making it suitable for welding in various positions.

④Suitable for thin plate welding and all-position welding. Even with a small current of several amperes, the tungsten argon arc remains stable and provides concentrated heat, allowing for the welding of 0.3 mm thin plates. By utilizing a pulsed tungsten argon arc welding power supply, it can also facilitate all-position welding and one-side welding without the need for a liner or double-side forming welding.

⑤The welding process is easy to automate: Argon tungsten arc welding produces an open arc, with stable welding process parameters that are easily detectable and controllable. It is an ideal method for automated or even robotic welding.

⑥No slag in the welding area: Welders have a clear view of the molten pool and the formation process of the weld joint.

(2) Disadvantages of TIG welding

①Poor wind resistance: Argon tungsten arc welding utilizes gas protection, resulting in low lateral wind resistance. When the wind is weak, the protection effect can be maintained by reducing the distance between the nozzle and the workpiece and increasing the flow rate of the protective gas. However, when the wind is strong, windproof measures must be taken.

②High workpiece cleaning requirements: Due to the use of inert gas for protection, there is no metallurgical deoxidation or dehydrogenation. To prevent defects such as pores and cracks, it is essential to thoroughly remove oil stains and rust from the workpiece prior to welding.

③Low productivity: TIG welding has limited penetration capacity and slow welding speed due to the restricted current-carrying capacity of the tungsten electrode, especially during AC welding.

Task 3:Master the Equipment of Tungsten Inert Gas Welding

The manually operated argon tungsten arc welding equipment consists of a welder, a welding gun, a gas supply system, a cooling system, and a control system, as shown in Fig. 3-1-5. In addition to the aforementioned components, the automatic TIG welding equipment also includes a wire feeder and a welding trolley traveling mechanism.

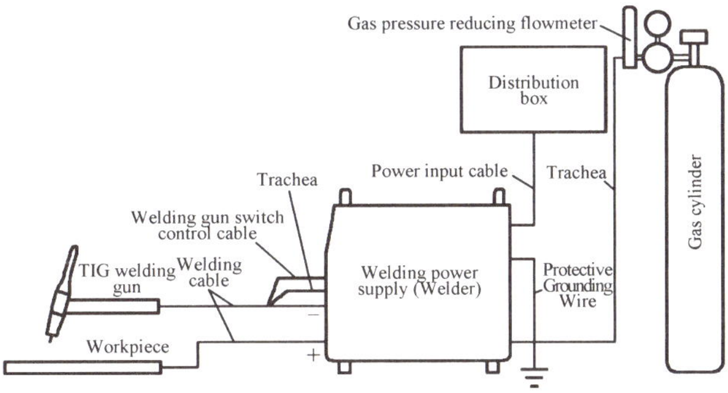

Fig. 3-1-5 Composition of Manual Tungsten Argon Arc Welding Equipment

1. Tungsten inert gas welding machine

The welding machine includes a welding power supply, high-frequency oscillator, pulse arc stabilizer, and DC component elimination device. If using the power supply for shielded metal arc welding, a separate control box should be provided. The welding machine for DC argon tungsten arc welding is relatively simple, and the high-frequency oscillator can be added to the DC welding power supply.

(1) Welding power supply

The power supply with steep drop external characteristics should be selected for argon tungsten arc welding. Generally, the power supply for shielded metal arc welding (such as arc welding transformer and rectifier) can be used as a manual TIG welding power supply, as shown in Fig. 3-1-6.

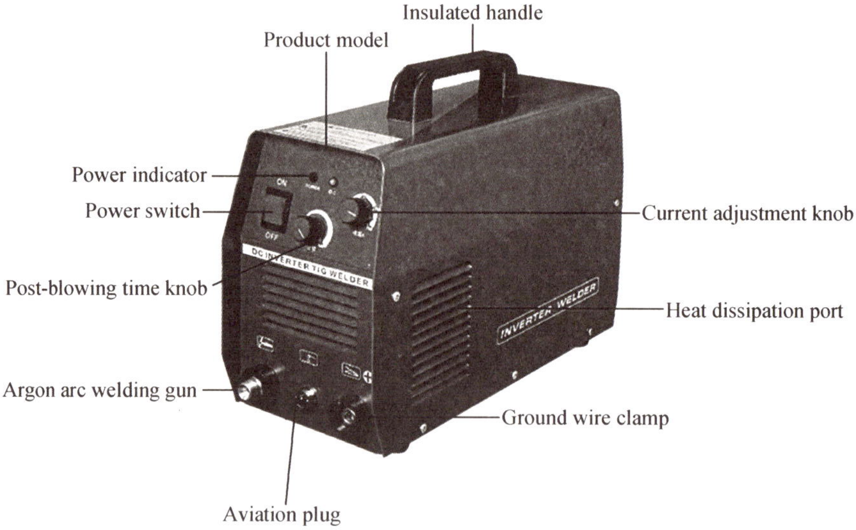

Fig. 3-1-6 TIG Welding Power Supply

Based on the power supply nature, TIG welding machines can be classified into DC TIG welding machines, AC TIG welding machines, AC/DC TIG welding machines, and pulsed TIG welding machines. The models of DC argon tungsten arc welding machines include WS-250 and WS-400, the models of AC argon tungsten arc welding machines include WSJ-300 and WSJ-500, the models of AC/DC argon tungsten arc welding machines include WSE-150 and WSE-400, and the models of pulsed argon tungsten arc welding machines include WSM - 200 and WSM-400.

(2) Arc ignition and arc stabilization device.

Due to the high ionization energy of argon, it is difficult to ionize and ignite the arc. However, it is not suitable to increase the no-load voltage. Therefore, TIG welding with tungsten electrode requires the use of a high-frequency oscillator to ignite the arc, as shown in Fig. 3-1-7. For AC power supply, since the current passes through zero point 100 times per second and the arc is unstable, it is also necessary to use a pulsed arc stabilizer to ensure repeated arc ignition and stabilization.

The high-frequency oscillator is a specialized arc ignition device in TIG welding equipment. It applies a high-frequency voltage of approximately 3,000 V between the tungsten electrode and the workpiece, while the no-load voltage of the welding power supply only needs to be around 65 V to achieve non-contact ignition arc between the tungsten electrode and the weldment. The high-frequency oscillator is mainly used for arc ignition and is immediately shut off after ignition, without being used for arc stabilization.

Pulse arc stabilizer applies a high - voltage pulse to initiate and sustain the continuous burning of the arc, thereby stabilizing its performance.

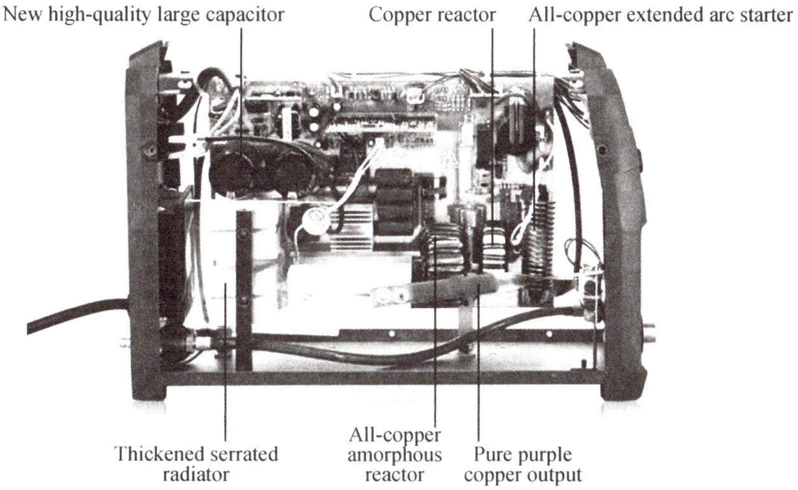

Fig. 3-1-7 Internal Structure of TIG Welding Power Supply

(3) DC component and its elimination

During AC welding, the current becomes asymmetric in the positive and negative half cycles due to the constant change in polarity, especially noticeable when welding aluminum and its alloys. This asymmetry in the positive and negative half cycles of current can be seen as comprising two components: one being the actual AC and the other being a DC component superimposed on the AC. This DC component is referred to as the DC component.

The presence of a DC component weakens the "cathode crushing" effect on one hand and can cause heat buildup and even damage to the welding transformer on the other hand. Therefore, it is necessary to eliminate the DC component during AC TIG welding. A common method of eliminating the DC component is by connecting capacitors in series in the welding circuit.

(4) Control system

The control system of argon tungsten arc welding achieves control over the action procedures in various stages such as power supply, gas supply, arc striking, and arc stabilization through control circuits. Fig. 3-1-8 illustrates the control procedure of AC manual TIG welding.

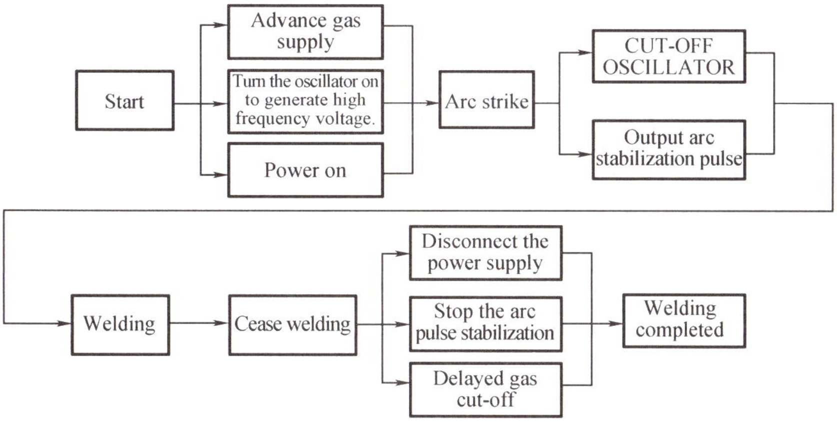

Fig. 3-1-8 Control Procedure Flow Chart of AC Manual TIG Welding

2. Argon tungsten arc welding torch

The function of the tungsten inert gas (TIG) welding gun is to clamp the electrode, conduct electricity, and transport argon gas flow. The TIG welding gun typically consists of a gun body, nozzle, electrode clamping mechanism, cable, argon input pipe, water pipe, switch, and button. The tungsten inert gas welding gun is divided into air-cooled welding gun (QQ series) and water-cooled welding gun (QS series). The air-cooled welding gun is convenient to use, but it is limited to low current (150 A) welding; the water-cooled welding gun is suitable for high current and automatic welding. The QQ series air-cooled tungsten inert gas welding gun is shown in Fig. 3-1-9(a), and the QS series water-cooled welding gun is shown in Fig. 3-1-9(b).

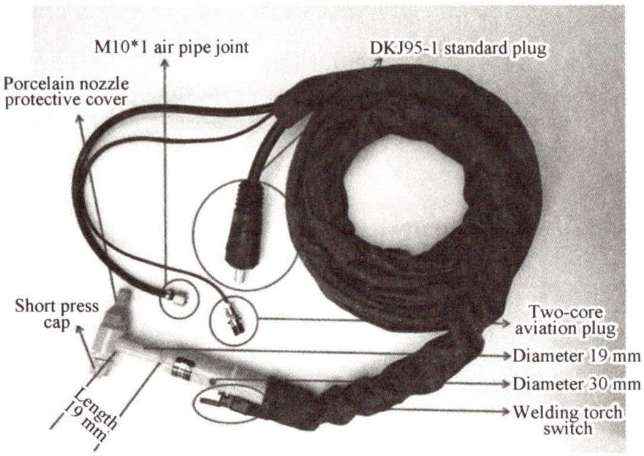

(a) Air-cooled

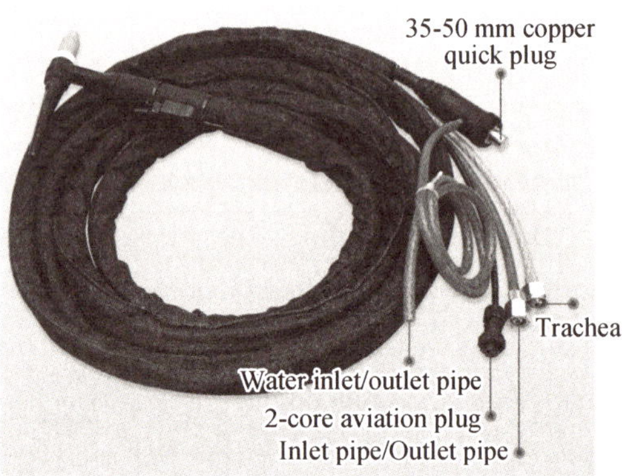

(b) Water-cooled

Fig. 3-1-9 Tungsten Argon Arc Welding Gun

The structure of the water-cooled TIG welding gun body is shown in the left fig. of Fig. 3-1-10, and the structure of the air-cooled TIG welding gun body is shown in the right fig. of Fig. 3-1-10.

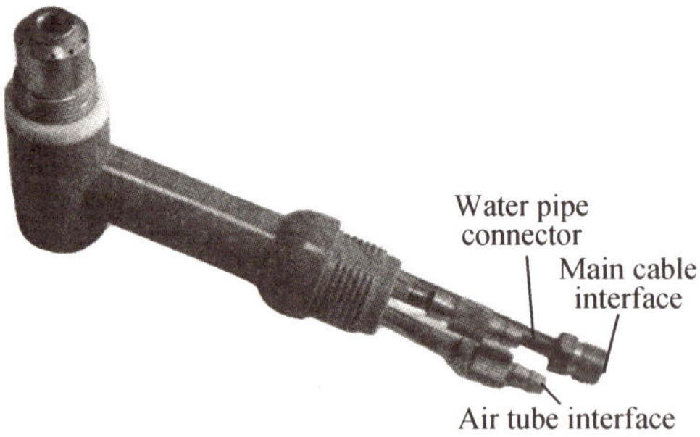

(a) Liquid-cooled

(b) Fan-cooled

Fig. 3-1-10 Structure of TIG Welding Torch Holder

The assembled structure of the TIG welding torch head is displayed in Fig. 3-1-11.

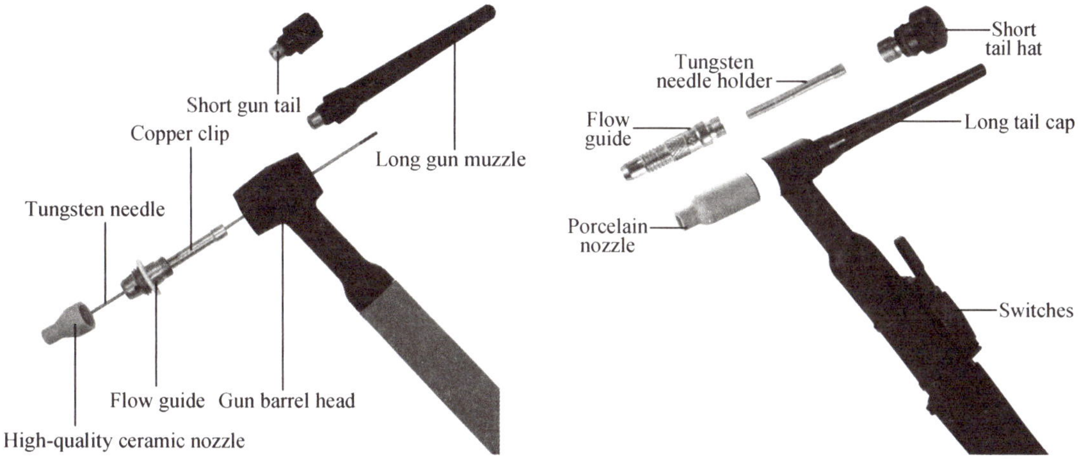

Fig. 3-1-11 Composite Structure of TIG Welding Torch Head

3. Air supply system

The gas supply system for TIG welding consists of an argon cylinder, pressure reducer, flowmeter, and solenoid valve. The outer surface of the argon cylinder is painted gray and marked with green "Argon" or "Argon", as shown in Fig. 3-1-12. The pressure reducer is used for decompression and pressure regulation, while the flowmeter is used to adjust and measure the argon flow. Nowadays, the pressure reducer and flowmeter are often integrated into one unit, which is called the argon flow regulator, as shown in Fig. 3-1-13. The solenoid valve is a device that controls the gas on-off.

Fig. 3-1-12 Argon Gas Cylinder

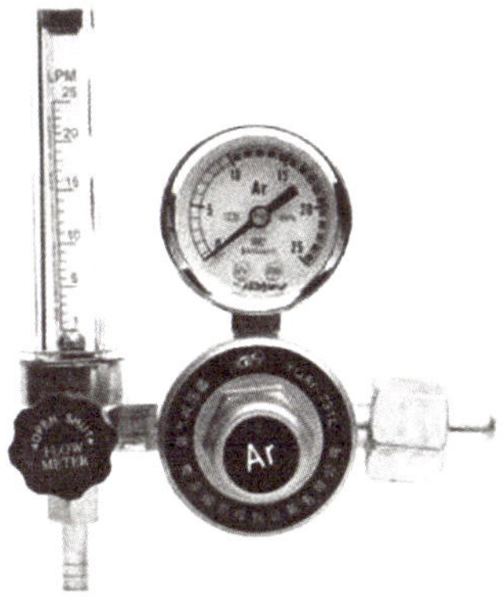

Fig. 3-1-13 Argon Flow Regulator

4. Cooling system

When the maximum welding current selected is above 150 A, water must be supplied to cool the welding gun and electrode. The welding equipment can only be started after the cooling water is connected and has a certain pressure. Usually, the water flow rate in TIG welding equipment is controlled by a hydraulic switch or manually.

Task 4:Master the Selection Principles of Welding Materials and Process Parameters for Tungsten Inert Gas Welding

1. Welding Materialsfor Argon Tungsten Arc Welding

The welding materials for TIG welding include tungsten needle (tungsten electrode), welding wire, and shielding gas.

(1) Tungsten needle (tungsten electrode)

The tungsten electrode is the electrode material for tungsten inert gas (TIG) welding, which greatly affects arc stability and weld quality. Generally, the tungsten electrode is required to have advantages such as high current capacity, low welding loss, and good arc starting and stabilizing performance, which mainly depend on its electron emission ability.

①Type of tungsten electrode

There are five types of tungsten electrodes: pure tungsten electrode, thoriated tungsten electrode, ceriated tungsten electrode, zirconiated tungsten electrode, and lanthanated tungsten electrode. Currently, the first three are commonly used.

a. Pure tungsten electrode. Pure tungsten electrode contains more than 99. 85% (mass fraction), has a very high melting point (about 3 390–3 479 ℃), and a very high boiling point (about 5 900 ℃). It is difficult to melt and evaporate, making it the earliest electrode material used. However, the pure tungsten electrode emits electrons at a higher voltage, requiring the welder to have a high no-load voltage. Additionally, pure tungsten is prone to burnouts. The higher the current, the more severe the burning loss. Therefore, it is seldom used at present.

b. Thoriated tungsten electrode. The addition of 1% to 2% (by mass fraction) of thorium oxide to the pure tungsten electrode results in a thoria-tungsten electrode. The presence of thorium element in the tungsten electrode rod enhances its ability to emit electrons, providing advantages such as good current carrying capacity, prolonged service life, excellent anti-pollution performance, easy arc striking, low required arc striking voltage, and stable arc. However, the drawback is the high cost, and the dust generated from thoriated tungsten electrodes contains traces of radioactivity. Protective measures should be taken while grinding the electrodes.

c. Cerium tungsten electrode. The tungsten electrode, with 2% (mass fraction) of cerium oxide added to pure tungsten electrode, is called a cerium tungsten electrode. It has greater advantages over thorium-tungsten electrode. The arc is slender, the heat is concentrated, and the current density can be increased by 5% to 8%. It has a low burning loss rate, long service life, easy arc striking, stable arc, and almost no radioactivity. It is an ideal electrode material and currently widely used in China. The superiority of cerium tungsten electrode is also evident in its lower loss when welding or plasma arc cutting with high current compared to low current.

②Grade and specification of tungsten electrode

a. Grade The grades of pure tungsten electrodes are W1 and W2 with a purity level exceeding 99.85% (by mass fraction). The grades of thorium-tungsten electrodes are WTh-7, WTh-10, and WTh-15. The grades of cerium-tungsten electrodes are WCe-5, WCe-13, and WCe-20.

b. Specification The manufacturer is required to supply tungsten electrodes ranging from 76mm to 610 mm in length. Common tungsten electrode diameters include 0. 5 mm, 1. 0 mm, 1. 6 mm, 2. 0 mm, 3. 2 mm, and 4. 0 mm.

For convenience of use, one end of the tungsten electrode is colored for easy identification, as shown in Fig. 3-1-14. For example, the thorium-tungsten electrode is painted red (representing 2% thorium dioxide), the cerium-tungsten electrode is painted gray (representing 2% cerium dioxide), and the pure tungsten electrode is painted green. Sky blue represents 2% lanthanum, blue represents 2% yttrium, and brown represents 4% zirconium.

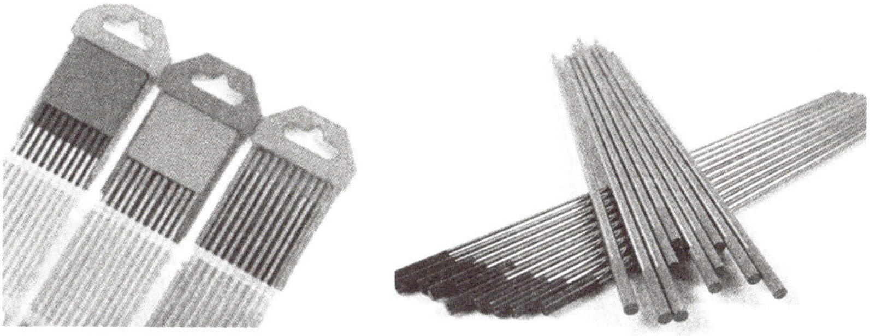

Fig. 3-1-14 Illustration of Tungsten Needle

Examples of cerium tungsten electrode grades are as follows:

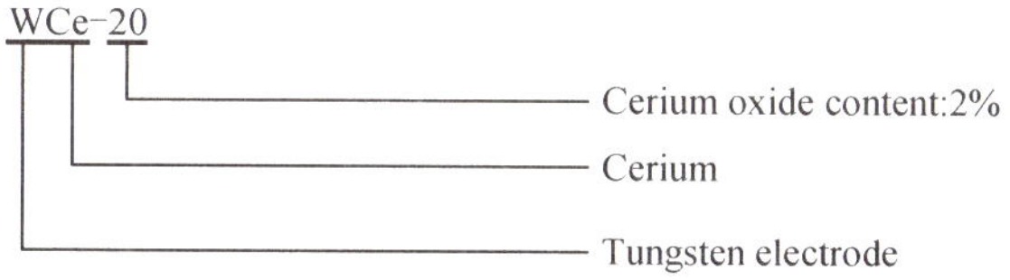

As far as possible, ceriated tungsten electrodes should be selected. When storing tungsten electrodes, it is preferable to store them in a lead box if the quantity is large.

(2) Welding wire

The principle for selecting electrodes and rods is to ensure that the chemical composition or mechanical properties of the deposited metal are equivalent to those of the materials being welded. Argon arc welding wires are mainly classified into two categories: steel welding wires and non-ferrous metal welding wires. The selection of welding wires can be based on corresponding international or national standards, such as China's national standard GB/T 8110 for Welding Electrodes and Rods for Gas Shielding Arc Welding of Carbon and Low Alloy Steel, and GB/T 20878 for Stainless Steel Welding Electrodes and Rods. The commonly used international standard is AWS.

Welding wires equivalent to the base metal are generally used for welding non-ferrous metals, such as copper and copper alloys. According to China's national standard GB/T 9460 "Welding Electrodes and Rods for Copper and Copper Alloys," please refer to Table 3-1-2 for the types, compositions, and uses of commonly used copper and copper alloy welding wires.

Table 3-1-2 Commonly Used Models, Composition, and Applications of Copper and Copper Alloy Welding Wires

Type of welding wire	Welding wire designation	Title	Main Chemical Components (Mass Fraction, %)	Melting point /℃	Usage
SCu1898 (CuSnl)	HS201	Pure copper welding wire	Cu(≥98.0), Sn(≤1.0), Si(≤0.5), Mn(≤0.5)	1083	Gas welding, oxygen arc welding, and plasma arc welding of pure copper.
SCu6560 (CuSi3Mn)	HS211	Bronze Welding Wire	Si (2.8~4.0), Mn (≤1.5), Zn (≤1.0), Sn (≤1.0), Fe (≤0.5), Pb (≤0.02), Al (≤0.01), others (≤0.5), the rest is Cu.	958	Bronze gas welding, argon arc welding, and plasma arc welding
SCu4700 (CuZn40Sn)	HS221	Brass welding wire	Cu (57~61), Sn (0.25~1.0), Pb (≤0.05), Al (≤0.01), others (≤0.5), and the rest is Zn.	886	
SCu6800 (CuZn40Ni)	HS222	Brass welding wire	Cu (56~60), Sn (0.8~1.1), Mn (0.01~0.50), Si (0.04~0.15), Fe (0.25~1.20), Ni+Co (0.2~0.8), Al (≤0.01), Pb (≤0.05), others (≤0.5), the rest is Zn	860	Gas welding, argon arc welding, and plasma arc welding for brass.
SCu6810A (CuZn40SnSi)	HS223	Brass welding wire	Cu (58~62), Si (0.1~0.5), Sn (≤1.0), Mn (≤0.03), Fe (≤0.02), Al (≤0.01), Pb (≤0.03), others (≤0.5), the rest is Zn.	905	

(3) Protective gas

①Properties of argon

Argon is a colorless and odorless monatomic inert gas with a density 1.4 times that of air. Because argon is heavier than air, it is not easily dispersed and floats during use. Therefore, it can form a better coverage layer above the molten pool, which is beneficial for protecting the weld metal. Additionally, when using argon gas shielded welding, less smoke is generated, making it convenient for observing and controlling the weld pool and arc.

Argon does not chemically react with any metal nor dissolve in the metal. This property allows it to prevent the burning loss of alloying elements in weld metal and avoid other welding defects caused by this. As a result, welding metallurgical reactions become simple and easy to control.

Another application characteristic of argon is its low thermal conductivity and monatomic nature, which means it does not decompose or absorb heat at high temperatures, resulting in lower heat loss during combustion in argon. Once the arc is ignited in argon, combustion remains stable. Among various shielding gases, argon arc provides the best stability, even at low voltages. Argon has minimal thermal contraction effects on the arc, so even slight changes in arc length do not significantly impact the arc voltage. Therefore, the arc remains stable and is highly suitable for manual welding.

②Requirements for argon purity.

Argon is a by-product of oxygen production and is produced through the fractional distillation of liquefied air. The boiling point of argon is between that of oxygen and nitrogen. Therefore, a certain amount of other impurities will remain during its preparation. If the impurity content is too high, it not only affects the protection of molten metal during welding but also easily leads to defects such as pores and slag inclusion in the welds, increasing the burning loss of the tungsten electrode. According to the current relevant standards, the purity of argon should reach 99.99% to fully meet the requirements of welding active metals such as aluminum and titanium. Currently, argon used for welding often comes in two purities: 99.99% and 99.999%, both of which can satisfy the welding requirements of various materials. The composition requirements are shown in Table 3-1-3.

Table 3-1-3 Composition Requirements of Argon for Welding (%)

Argon purity	N_2	O_2	H_2	C_nH_m	H_2O
≥99.99	<0.01	<0.015	<0.000 5	<0.001	30 mg/m^3
≥99.999	$\leqslant 10^{-4}$	$\leqslant 10^{-5}$	$\leqslant 5-10^{-6}$	10^{-5}	$\leqslant 2-10^{-5}$

③Storage and transportation of argon.

Argon can be stored and transported in liquid form at temperatures below −184 ℃, but during welding, it is mostly contained in steel cylinders for use by welders. The argon cylinder is a high-pressure steel container with a round shape. Currently, commonly used argon cylinders in China have volumes of 33 L, 40 L, and 44 L, and when the cylinder is full, the pressure is 15 MPa. The exterior of the cylinder is painted gray and marked with the word "Argon" in green. Argon cylinders should be placed upright during use. Knocking or colliding with them is strictly prohibited, and they should not be handled by electromagnetic cranes or exposed to sunlight. During shipment, the cylinder cap should be worn to avoid damage to the interface thread.

2. Process Parameters and Selection of Tungsten Inert Gas (TIG) Welding

(1) Process parameters of TIG welding

The process parameters of TIG welding primarily include the type and polarity of current, welding current, diameter and end shape of tungsten electrode, flow rate of shielding gas, etc. For automatic argon tungsten arc welding, it also includes the welding speed and wire feed speed. Once the materials to be welded are determined, the process parameters should be determined through process testing and procedure qualification.

①Types and polarities of welding current

Different types and polarities of the current have distinct process characteristics that are suitable for welding different materials. Therefore, the type and the polarity of the current should be selected based on the material of the workpiece. TIG welding has three types of welding currents, each with its own applicable range.

a. AC. With a moderate depth and width of fusion, AC welding is primarily used for welding aluminum, magnesium, and their alloys, as well as copper with an oxide film.

b. DC. DC welding is classified into straight connection and reverse connection. When in direct connection, the heat generated by the workpiece accounts for about 70%, while that of the tungsten electrode accounts for about 30%. Straight polarity can be used to weld almost all steel materials, whereas reverse polarity is rarely employed.

c. Pulse current. Pulse current can control and improve penetration and weld formation, making it suitable for welding in special positions.

Refer to Table 3-1-4 for the selection of TIG welding current types and polarities for different metal materials.

Table 3-1-4 The Selection of TIG Welding Current Types and Polarities for Different Metal Materials

Metal to be welded		DC		AC
		Straight polarity	Reverse polarity	
Low carbon steel	0.4-0.8 mm	Excellent	Not recommended	Good①
	0.8-3.2 mm	Excellent	Not recommended	Not recommended
High carbon steel	—	Excellent	Not recommended	Good①
Cast Iron	—	Excellent	Not recommended	Good①
Heat-resistant alloy	—	Excellent	Not recommended	Good①
Difficult-to-melt alloys	—	Excellent	Not recommended	Not recommended
Aluminum alloy	≤0.6 mm	Not recommended②	Good	Excellent
	>0.6 mm	Not recommended②	Not recommended	Excellent
	Castings	Not recommended②	Not recommended	Excellent

Table 3-1-4 (Continued)

Metal to be welded		DC		AC
		Straight polarity	Reverse polarity	
Beryllium	—	Excellent	Not recommended	Good①
Copper and copper alloys	Brass	Excellent	Not recommended	Good①
	Deoxidized copper	Excellent	Not recommended	Not recommended
	Silicon Bronze	Excellent	Not recommended	Not recommended
Magnesium alloys	≤3.2 mm	Not recommended②	Good	Excellent
	24.8 mm	Not recommended②	Not recommended	Excellent
	Castings	Not recommended②	Not recommended	Excellent
Silver	—	Excellent	Not recommended	Good①
Titanium alloy	—	Excellent	Not recommended	Not recommended

Note: ①It should be approximately 25% higher than the current used for direct current positive polarity.

②Unless the area to be welded undergoes mechanical or chemical cleaning.

The size of the welding current is primarily determined by the thickness, spatial position, and tungsten electrode diameter of the workpiece. Excessive or insufficient welding current can lead to poor weld formation or welding defects. Therefore, it is essential to select the welding current correctly within the allowable range for different tungsten electrode diameters. Refer to Table 3-1-5 for the corresponding relationship between welding current and tungsten electrode diameter.

Table 3-1-5 Allowable Current Range of Tungsten Electrodes with Different Diameters

Tungsten electrode diameter/mm	DC straight polarity/A	DC reverse polarity/A	AC/A
1.0	15-80	—	20-60
1.6	70-150	10-20	60-120
2.4	140-235	15-30	100-180
3.2	225-325	25-40	160-250
4.0	300-400	40-55	200-320
5.0	400-500	55-80	290-390

②Welding voltage

The welding voltage is primarily determined by the arc length. As the arc length increases, the arc voltage increases, and the weld width increases while the penetration decreases. However, if the arc length is too long, it can easily result in incomplete penetration, undercutting, and insufficient protection. Conversely, if the arc is too short, it becomes difficult to operate as it hinders clear visibility of the molten pool and can lead to short circuits, increased burning loss of the tungsten electrode, and tungsten inclusions. Generally, under the condition of ensuring no short circuit, it is advisable to use a shorter arc for welding whenever possible. The arc length should be controlled between 1 mm to 3 mm when welding without filler wire, and between 3 mm to 6 mm when welding with filler wire.

The geometry of the electrode tip also impacts the magnitude of the welding voltage. When the distance from the tungsten electrode tip to the workpiece is the same, the welding voltage of a sharper conical electrode is higher. The method for controlling arc voltage can be selected based on the specific product and power supply type, but the welding voltage should be controlled to maintain relative stability.

③Welding speed

The arc penetration depth is typically inversely proportional to the welding speed. Controlling factors for welding speed include the thermal conductivity of the metal, thickness and size of the component. The purpose of adjusting the welding speed is to maintain a consistent heat level required for a constant arc penetration force.

The welding speed should generally adhere to the following principles.

a. When welding metals with high thermal conductivity such as aluminum, a fast welding speed should be adopted to reduce deformation.

b. High-speed welding should not be adopted when welding alloys with a tendency to hot crack.

c. The size of the weld pool is directly affected by the welding speed. When not in a flat position, only a small pool should be used to prevent molten iron from flowing down, and the welding speed should be appropriately increased.

d. The development of welding current pulse control technology is very beneficial for controlling the molten pool in joints when welding metals with low thermal conductivity (such as titanium) and fixed and thick-walled pipes.

The welding speed affects the energy of the weld line, thereby influencing the depth and width of fusion. The welding speed is usually determined based on the thickness of the plate and should be appropriately matched with the welding current, preheating temperature, and shielding gas flow to ensure proper weld formation. When the welding speed is too fast, defects such as incomplete penetration and undercut are prone to occur. Conversely, when the welding speed is too slow, defects such as excessive weld width and burn-through will occur.

④Tungsten electrode diameter and end shape

The selection principle for tungsten electrode diameter is as follows: While ensuring that the allowable current of the tungsten electrode is greater than the welding current used, try to choose a smaller diameter tungsten electrode. When the welding current is small and the tungsten electrode diameter is large, the low current density and insufficient temperature at the end of the tungsten electrode cause the arc to drift irregularly. This makes the arc highly unstable, resulting in the destruction of the protective area and oxidation of the molten pool. On the other hand, when the welding current is large and the tungsten electrode diameter is small, the high current density leads to a relatively higher temperature at the end of the tungsten electrode. If the temperature reaches or exceeds the melting point of the tungsten electrode, the end will melt. This molten tungsten electrode will form a small sharp protrusion at the end, gradually growing into droplets. The arc drifts along with the tip of the droplet, leading to an extremely unstable arc. This disrupts the argon protection zone, oxidizes the molten pool, and results in poor weld joint formation, causing defects such as tungsten inclusion. Choosing the appropriate welding current and tungsten electrode diameter ensures arc stability.

Practical experience has shown that the surface quality and shape and size of the tungsten electrode end have a certain influence on the allowable welding current and weld formation. Generally, when welding thin plates and using a small welding current, a tungsten electrode with a small diameter can be used and ground to a sharp cone angle (around 30°), so that it is easy to strike an arc and the arc is stable, as shown in Fig. 3-1-15(a). However, using a sharp cone angle when the current is high will cause overheating and melting of the end, increase burning loss, significantly expand the arc column, cause unstable drift, and affect the weld formation. Therefore, during high-current welding, the tungsten electrode end should be ground into a cone with a flat top, as shown in Fig. 3-1-15(b). When using AC tungsten inert gas(TIG) welding, the tungsten electrode end is generally ground into a hemispherical shape, as shown in Fig. 3-1-15(c).

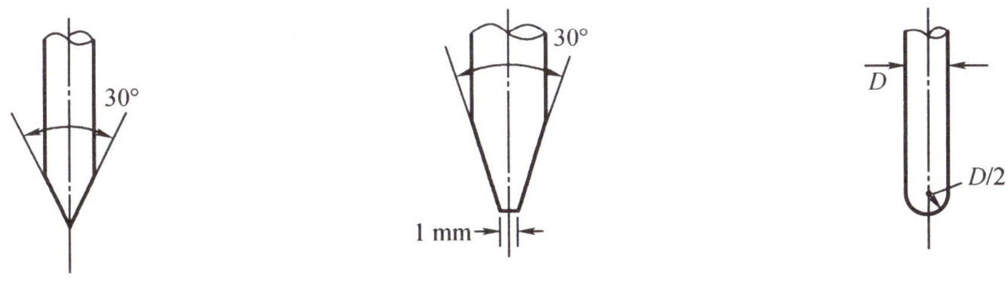

(a) Sharp-cone angled tungsten electrode tip

(b) Tapered tungsten electrode tip with a flat top

(c) Hemispherical-shaped tungsten electrode tip

Fig. 3-1-15 Shape of Tungsten Electrode End

⑤Nozzle aperture and argon flow

The larger the nozzle aperture is, the larger the protected area will be. However, when it is too large, the observability of molten pool and arc will be reduced. For a certain nozzle aperture, the protective gas flow rate has an appropriate range. If the flow rate is too small, the gas stiffness will be poor and the protection effect will not be good; if the flow rate is too large, turbulent flow will occur in the airflow layer, making it easy for air to be involved and the protection effect will not be good. The nozzle aperture and argon flow rate are usually selected according to the type, magnitude, and polarity of the current, as shown in Table 3-1-6.

Table 3-1-6 Selection of Nozzle Aperture and Argon Flow Rate

Welding current/A	DC straight polarity(DCSP)		DC reverse polarity (DCRP)	
	Nozzle diameter/mm	Argon flow rate /(L/min)	Nozzle diameter/mm	Argon flow rate /(L/min)
10-100	4-9.5	4-5	8-9.5	6-8
101-150	4-9.5	4-7	9.5-11	7-10
151-200	6-13	6-8	11-13	7-10
201-300	8-13	8-9	13-16	8-15
301-500	13-16	9-12	16-19	8-15

⑥Extension length of tungsten electrode

Generally, the length of the tungsten electrode exposed outside the nozzle is referred to as the extension length of the tungsten electrode. When the extension length is too large, the tungsten electrode is prone to overheating and provides poor protection. Conversely, when the extension length is too small, the nozzle is likely to overheat. Therefore, it is crucial to maintain an appropriate value for the extension length of the tungsten electrode. During butt welding, the extension length of the tungsten electrode is typically kept at 5-6 mm. For welding T-shaped joints, it is preferable to have an extension length of the tungsten electrode of 7-8 mm.

⑦Nozzle-to-workpiece distance.

The distance between the nozzle and the workpiece should match the extension length of the tungsten electrode. Generally, it should be controlled between 8 mm and 14 mm. If the distance is too small, it will impair workers' vision and easily cause a short circuit between the tungsten electrode and the molten pool, resulting in tungsten inclusion in the weld and reducing the tungsten electrode's lifespan. If the distance is too large, the gas protection effect will be poor and the arc will be unstable.

(2) Selection of TIG welding process parameters

Refer to Table 3-1-7 for process parameters of manual TIG welding of carbon steel, Table 3-1-8 for process parameters of manual TIG welding of aluminum and its alloys, Table 3-1-9 for process parameters of manual TIG welding of stainless steel, Table 3-1-10 for process parameters of manual TIG welding of 8-18 stainless steel, Table 3-1-11 for process parameters of manual TIG welding of copper, magnesium, nickel and their alloys, and Table 3-1-12 for process parameters of manual TIG welding of titanium and its alloys.

Table 3-1-7 Process Parameters of Manual TIG Welding of Carbon Steel

Item	Content		
Material thickness/mm	1.5-3.0	3.0-6.0	6.0-12.0
Joint design	Straight edge butt joint	V-groove	X-shaped groove
Welding current/A	50-100	70-120	90-150
Polarity	DC straight polarity	DC straight polarity	DC straight polarity
Welding voltage/V	12	12	12
Type of tungsten electrode	Thoriated tungsten electrode	Thoriated tungsten electrode	Thoriated tungsten electrode
Electrode dimension/mm	2.4	2.4	3.2
Size of filler metal/mm	1.6-2.5	2.5-3.2	2.5-3.2
Shielding gas flow rate/(L/min)	Ar 8-12	Ar 8-12	Ar 10-14
Back shielding gas flow rate /(L/min)	Ar 2-4	Ar 2-4	Ar 2-4
Nozzle size/mm	8-10	8-10	10-12
Distance from the nozzle to the workpiece/mm	≤12	≤12	≤12
Minimum preheating temperature/℃	15	15	15
Maximum interpass temperature/℃	250	250	250

Table 3-1-8 Process Parameters of Manual TIG Welding of Aluminum and Its Alloys

Plate thickness /mm	Groove form	Number of welding layers (Front /Back)	Tungsten electrode diameter /mm	Wire diameter /mm	Preheat temperature: /℃	Welding current /A	Argon gas flow /(L/min)	Nozzle orifice diameter /mm
1.0	Rolled edges	Go straight 1	2	1.6	—	45-60	7-9	8
1.5	Rolled edge or I-shaped	Go straight 1	2	1.6-2.0	—	50-80	7-9	8
2	I-shaped	Go straight 1	2-3	2-2.5	—	90-120	8-12	8-12

Table 3-1-8(Continued)

Plate thickness /mm	Groove form	Number of welding layers (Front /Back)	Tungsten electrode diameter /mm	Wire diameter /mm	Preheat temperature: /℃	Welding current /A	Argon gas flow /(L/min)	Nozzle orifice diameter /mm
3	Y-shaped groove	Go straight 1	3	2-3	—	150-180	8-12	8-12
4		1-2/1	4	3	—	180-200	10-15	8-12
5		1-2/1	4	3-4	—	180-240	10-15	10-12
6		1-2/1	5	4	—	240-280	16-20	14-16
8		2/1	5	4-5	100	260-320	16-20	14-16
10		3-4/1-2	5	4-5	100-150	280-340	16-20	14-16
12		3-4/1-2	5-6	4-5	150-200	300-360	18-22	16-20
14		3-4/1-2	5-6	5-6	180-200	340-380	20-24	16-20
16		4-5/1-2	6	5-6	200-220	340-380	20-24	16-20
18		4-5/1-2	6	5-6	200-240	360-400	25-30	16-20
20		4-5/1-2	6	5-6	200-260	360-400	25-30	20-22
16-20	X-shaped groove	2-3/2-3	6	5-6	200-260	300-380	25-30	16-20
22-25		3-4/3-4	6-7	5-6	200-260	360-400	30-35	20-22

Table 3-1-9 Process Parameters of Manual TIG Welding of Stainless Steel

Plate thickness /mm	Groove form	Number of welding layers (Front /Back)	Tungsten electrode diameter /mm	Wire diameter for welding /mm	Preheating temperature /℃	Welding current /A	Argon gas flow /(L/min)	Nozzle aperture diameter /mm
1.0	Butt joint	1	2	1.6	—	7-28	3-4	12-17
1.2	Butt joint	1	2	1.6	—	15	3-4	25
1.5	Butt joint	1	2	1.6	—	5-19	3-4	18-32

Table 3-1-10 Process Parameters of Manual TIG Welding of 8-18 Stainless Steel

Material thickness/mm	1.5-3.0	3.0-6.0	6.0-12.0
Joint design	Straight edge joint	V-groove	X-shaped groove
Welding current/A	50-90	70-120	100-150
Polarity	DC straight polarity	DC straight polarity	DC straight polarity
Welding voltage/V	12	12	12

Table 3-1-10(Continued)

Tungsten electrode types	Thoriated tungsten electrode	Thoriated tungsten electrode	Thoriated tungsten electrode
Electrode diameter/mm	2.5	2.5	2.5
Filler metal type and filler wire diameter/mm	Type 8-18, ϕ1.6-2.5	Type 8-18, ϕ2.5-3.2	Type 8-18, ϕ2.5-3.2
Material thickness/mm	1.6-3.0	3.0-6.0	6.0-12
Shielding gas flow rate/(L/min)	Ar 8-12	Ar 10-14	Ar 10-14
Back shielding gas flow/(L/min)	Ar 2-4	Ar 2-4	Ar 2-4
Nozzle size/mm	8-10	10-12	10-12
Nozzle-to-workpiece distance/mm	≤12	≤12	≤12
Minimum preheating temperature/℃	15	15	15
Maximum interpass temperature/℃	250	250	250

Table 3-1-11 Process Parameters of Manual TIG Welding of Copper, Magnesium, Nickel, and their Alloys

Alloy Type	Plate Thickness /mm	Number of weld passes	Tungsten electrode diameter /mm	Nozzle orifice diameter /mm	Welding wire diameter /mm	Welding current /A	Welding speed /(cm/min)	Gas flow /(L/min)
Copper and its alloys	1.6	1	1.6	6.4	1.6	90-155	25.2	8.5
	3.2	1	2.4	7.9	2.4	150-245	20.4	8.5
	4.8	1	3.2	9.5	3.2	175-255	20.4	17.0
	6.4	1	3.2	9.5	3.2	200-285	18	17.0
	9.5	2	4.8	12.7	4.8	220-350	15	17.0
	12.7	3	4.8	15.9	6.4	300-500	15	21.2
	DC positive polarity, argon shielding for plate thickness less than 4.8 mm, helium for the rest, thoriated tungsten electrode							
Silicon Bronze	1.6	1	1.6	6.4	1.6	75-120	25.2	7.1
	3.2	1	1.6	6.4	2.4	95-150	25.2	7.1
	4.8	1	2.4	7.9	2.4	125-220	25.2	9.4
	6.4	2	2.4	7.9	3.2	140-275	20.2	11.8
	9.5	3	3.2	9.5	3.2	200-285	20.2	11.8
	12.7	7	4.0	9.5	3.2	240-300	20.2	11.8
	19.7	14	4.0	9.5	4.8	275-350	20.2	11.8
	25.4	20	4.8	11.1	6.4	300-365	20.2	11.8
	DC positive polarity, argon shielded, thoriated tungsten electrode							

Table 3-1-11(Continued)

Alloy Type	Plate Thickness /mm	Number of weld passes	Tungsten electrode diameter /mm	Nozzle orifice diameter /mm	Welding wire diameter /mm	Welding current /A	Welding speed /(cm/min)	Gas flow /(L/min)
Magnesium Alloys	0.9	1	1.6	9.5	2.4	25~45	51	7.1
	1.5	1	1.6	9.5	2.4	35~60	51	7.1
	1.9	1	2.4	9.5	3.2	50~80	43.2	7.1
	2.7	1	2.4	12.7	3.2	75~100	43.2	9.4
	3.0	1	2.4	12.7	3.2	95~120	43.2	9.4
	AC, argon shielded, pure tungsten electrode and its alloy							
Nickel and its alloys	0.6	1	1.6	9.5		8~10	20.2	7.5
	1.5	1	2.4	12.7	1.6	25~45	20.2	8.1
	3.2	1	3.2	12.7	2.4	90~175	28.2	11.8
	6.4	2	3.2	12.7	3.2	100~175	20.4	14.2
	DC straight polarity, argon shielded, thoriated tungsten electrode							

Table 3-1-12 Process Parameters of Manual TIG Welding of Titanium and Its Alloys

Plate Thickness /mm	Groove form	Welding floor count	Tungsten electrode diameter/mm	Welding wire diameter/mm	Welding current /A	Argon flow rate/(L/min)			Nozzle orifice diameter/mm	Remarks
						Main nozzle	Drag cover	Back		
0.5	I-shaped groove	1	1.5	1.0	30-50	8-10	14-16	6-8	10	The butt joint clearance is 0.5 mm, or 1.0 mm without titanium wire
1.0		1	2.0	1.0-2.0	40-60	8-10	14-16	6-8	10	
1.5		1	2.0	1.0-2.0	60-80	10-12	14-16	8-10	10-12	
2.0		1	2.0-3.0	1.0-2.0	80-110	12-14	16-20	10-12	12-14	
2.5		1	2.0-3.0	2.0	110-120	12-14	16-20	10-12	12-14	
3.0	Y-shaped groove	1-2	3.0	2.0-3.0	120-140	12-14	16-20	10-12	14-18	Groove clearance: 2-3 mm; root face: 0.5 mm; steel backing plate is lined on the backside of the weld; groove angle: 60°-150°
3.5		1-2	3.0-4.0	2.0-3.0	120-140	12-14	16-20	10-12	14-18	
4.0		2	3.0-4.0	2.0-3.0	130-150	14-16	20-25	12-14	18-20	
4.5		2	3.0-4.0	2.0-3.0	200	14-16	20-25	12-14	18-20	
5.0		2-3	4.0	3.0	130-150	14-16	20-25	12-14	18-20	
6.0		2-3	4.0	3.0-4.0	140-180	14-16	25-28	12-14	18-20	
7.0		2-3	4.0	3.0-4.0	140-180	14-16	25-28	12-14	20-22	
8.0		3-4	4.0	3.0-4.0	140-180	14-16	25-28	12-14	20-22	
10.0	Double Y-shaped groove	4-6	4.0	3.0-4.0	160-200	14-16	25-28	12-14	20-22	Groove angle: 60°; root face: 1 mm
13.0		6-8	4.0	3.0-4.0	220-240	14-16	25-28	12-14	20-22	
20.0		12	4.0	4.0	200-240	12-14	20	10-12	18	Groove angle: 55°; root face: 1.5-2.0 mm
22.0		6	4.0	4.0-5.0	230-250	15-18	18-20	18-20	20	
25.0		15-16	4.0	3.0-4.0	200-220	16-18	26-30	20-26	22	Groove angle: 55°; root face: 1.5-2.0 mm; clearance: 1.5 mm
30.0		17-18	4.0	3.0-4.0	200-220	16-18	26-30	20-26	22	

Task Assessment

1. Which symbol represents argon tungsten – arc welding ( ) among the following options.

A. TIG　　B. MIG　　C. GTAW　　D. MAG

2. The type and polarity of power supply for argon tungsten – arc welding of copper and copper alloy are ( ).

A. DC positive connection　　B. DC reverse connection

C. AC positive connection　　D. AC reverse connection

3. TIG welding is generally only used for weldments with a thickness below ( ).

A. 4 mm　　B. 6 mm　　C. 8 mm　　D. 10 mm

4. The commissioning of the argon tungsten–arc welding machine does not include ( ).

A. Heating condition of welding gun

B. Performance of control system

C. Auxiliary removal and recovery of flux

D. Power supply parameters

5. The power supply commissioning of the argon tungsten – arc welding machine does not include ( ).

A. Constant current characteristics of power supply

B. Accuracy and reliability of arc striking

C. Adjustment range of current and voltage

D. Whether the welding gun leaks air or water

6. The control system commissioning of the TIG welding machine includes ( ).

A. Trolley performance test

B. Arc striking performance

C. Cathodic atomization of AC power

D. Changes in output current when the input voltage changes

7. The melting point of pure tungsten is as high as ( ), and the boiling point is approximately ( ).

A. 2 800 ℃, 5 500 ℃　　B. 3 200 ℃, 5 700 ℃

C. 3 400 ℃, 5 900 ℃　　D. 3 600 ℃, 6 100 ℃

8. To enhance the electron emission capability of tungsten electrodes, a 1%–2% ( ) addition can be made to pure tungsten.

A. CuO　　B. ZnO　　C. Al_2O_3　　D. TuO_2

9. The following does not belong to the electrode end shape of argon tungsten–arc welding ( ).

A. Cylinder shape　　B. Flat–bottomed cone

C. Pointed cone D. Sphere

10. (Multiple choices) Argon tungsten-arc welding can be divided into ( ).

A. Manual TIG welding B. Semi-automatic TIG welding

C. Automatic TIG welding D. Pulsed TIG welding

项目二　手工钨极氩弧焊基础操作技术

【学习目标】

1. 掌握手工钨极氩弧焊焊前准备程序及方法；
2. 掌握手工钨极氩弧焊基本操作技术。

任务1：掌握手工钨极氩弧焊焊前准备程序及方法

1. 钨极氩弧焊焊接过程的一般程序

为了获得优质焊缝，无论是手工钨极氩弧焊还是自动钨极氩弧焊，焊接过程的一般程序如下：

①起弧前必须提前 1.5~4 s 用焊枪向始焊点输送保护气，以驱赶管内和焊接区的空气。

②灭弧后应滞后一定时间(5~15 s)停气，以保护尚未冷却的钨极与熔池。焊枪须待停气后才离开终焊处，从而保证焊缝始末端的质量。

③在接通焊接电源的同时启动引弧装置。引燃电弧后即进入焊接，焊枪的移动和焊丝的送进也同时协调地进行。

④自动接通、切断引弧和稳弧电路，控制电源的通断。

⑤焊接即将结束时，焊接电流应能自动地衰减，直至电弧熄灭，以消除和防止弧坑裂纹。这对于环缝焊接及热裂纹敏感材料尤其重要。

⑥用水冷式焊枪时，送水与送气应同步进行。

图 3-2-1 所示为手工钨极氩弧焊和自动钨极氩弧焊焊接的一般控制程序，焊接由操作者和焊机的控制系统配合完成。

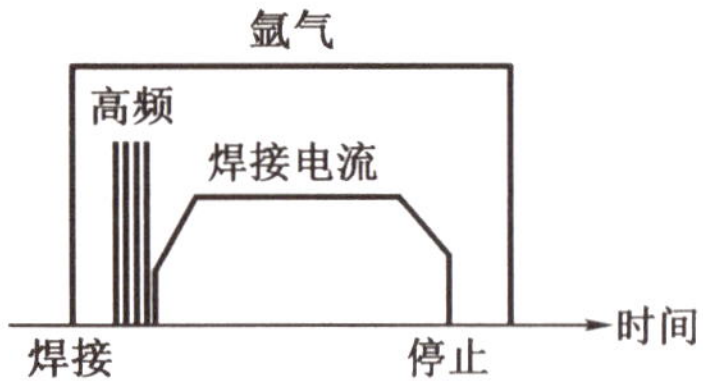

(a) 手工钨极氩弧焊

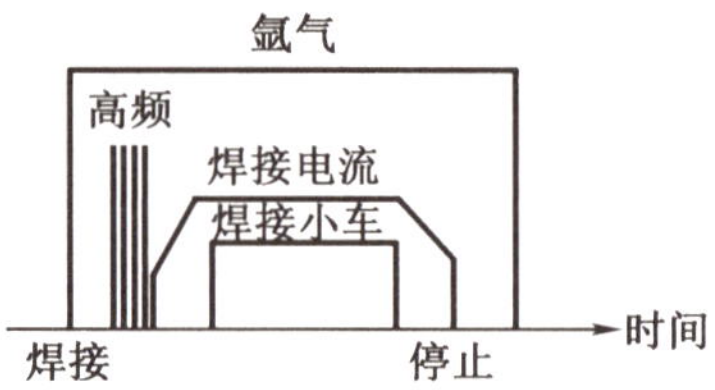

(b) 自动钨极氩弧焊

图 3-2-1　钨极氩弧焊的一般控制程序

2. 接头及坡口形式

钨极氩弧焊常用的接头形式有对接、搭接、角接、T 形接头、端接接头等，如图 3-2-2 所示。

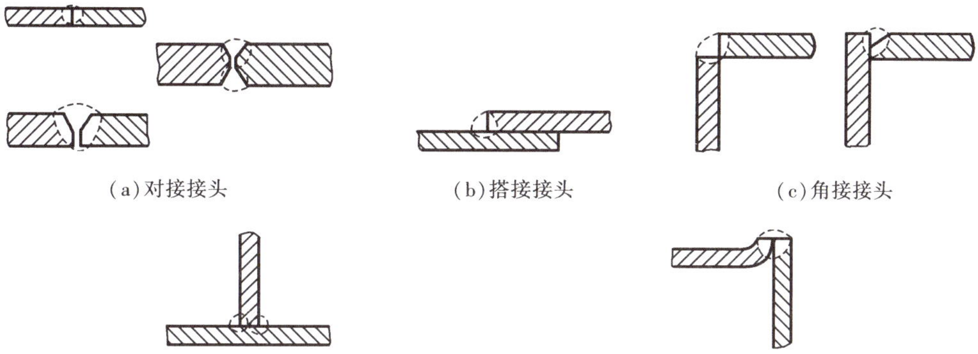

（a）对接接头　（b）搭接接头　（c）角接接头　（d）T 形接头　（e）端接接头

图 3-2-2　常见的五种基本接头形式

坡口形式及尺寸根据材料类型、板厚等来选择。一般情况下，板厚小于 3 mm 时，可开 I 形坡口；板厚为 3～12 mm 时，可开 V 形或 Y 形坡口。表 3-2-1 列出了铝及铝合金焊接接头的坡口形状及尺寸。关于各种钢的具体坡口形状及详细尺寸，可参照国家标准或行业标准选取。

表 3-2-1　铝及铝合金焊接接头的坡口形状及尺寸

接头及坡口形式		图示	板厚 δ /mm	坡口尺寸		
				间隙 b/mm	钝边 p/mm	坡口角度 α/(°)
对接接头	卷边	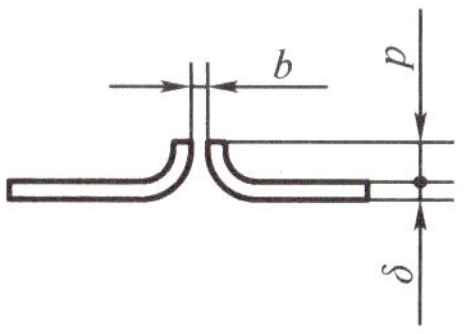	≤2	<0.5	<2	—
对接接头	I 形坡口	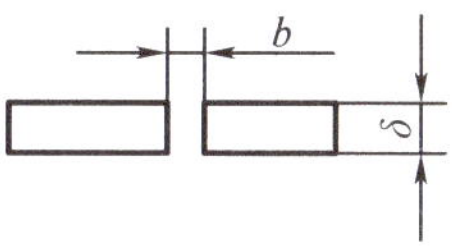	1～5	0.5～2	—	—
对接接头	V 形坡口	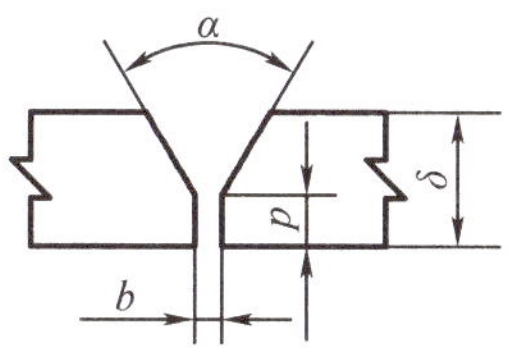	3～5	1.5～2.5	1.5～2	60°～70°
对接接头	V 形坡口		5～12	2～3	2～3	60°～70°
对接接头	X 形坡口	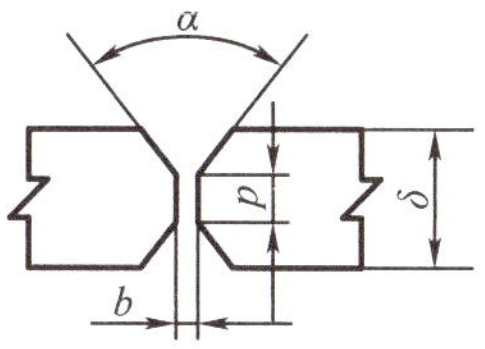	>10	1.5～3	2～4	60°～70°

表 3-2-1(续)

接头及坡口形式		示图	板厚 δ /mm	坡口尺寸		
				间隙 b/mm	钝边 p/mm	坡口角度 α/(°)
搭接接头		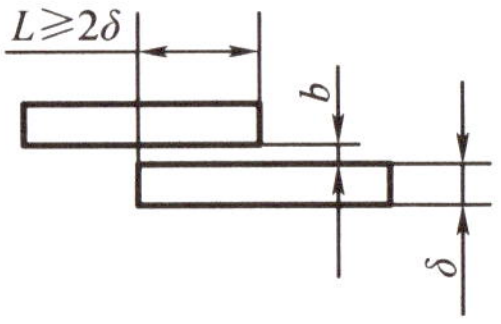	<1.5	0~0.5	$L\geqslant 2\delta$	—
			1.5~3	0.5~1	$L\geqslant 2\delta$	—
角接接头	I 形坡口	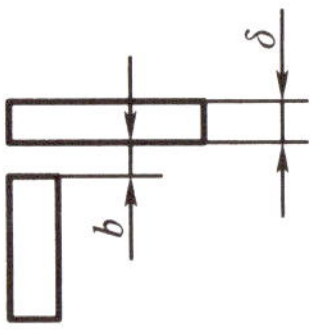	<12	<1	—	—
	V 形坡口	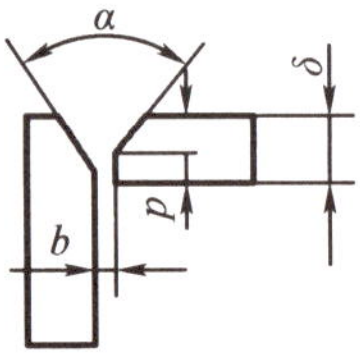	3~5	0.8~1.5	1~1.5	60°~70°
			>5	1~2	1~2	60°~70°
T 形接头	I 形坡口	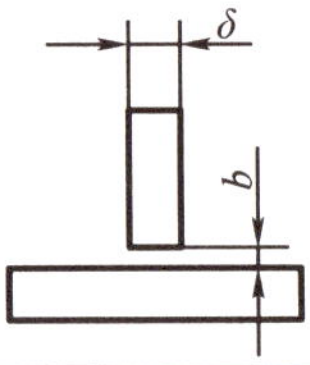	3~5	<1	—	—
			6~10	<1.5	—	—
	K 形坡口	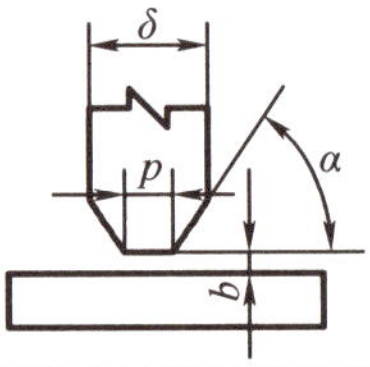	10~16	<1.5	1~2	60°

3. 焊前清理

氩气、氦气均是惰性气体,在焊接过程中不与液态金属发生任何化学反应,因此钨极氩弧焊无去氢、脱氧作用。钨极氩弧焊对材料表面质量要求很高,为了保证焊接质量,焊前必须清理工件坡口及坡口两侧表面至少 20 mm 范围内的氧化膜、油脂及水分。否则在焊接过程中将影响电弧稳定性,恶化焊缝成形,并可能导致气孔、夹杂、未熔合等缺陷。清理方法主要有机械清理、化学清理,有时也采用两种方法交替进行。

(1)机械清理

该方法只适用于工件,对焊丝不适用。通常是采用钢丝刷、刮刀、砂布、喷砂或喷丸等机械方法去除工件表面的氧化膜、油污等。铝及其合金材质较软,通常采用刮刀或钢丝刷进行清理。对于大型钢质工件,可采用喷砂或喷丸的方法进行清理。而较小的不锈钢工件通常采用砂布打磨。机械清理效率低,去除氧化膜不彻底,一般只用于尺寸大、生产周期长或化学清洗后又局部沾污的工件。

(2)化学清理

该方法依靠化学反应去除工件及焊丝表面的氧化膜及油污,特别适合于铝合金、钛合金、镁合金母材及焊丝的焊前处理。化学清理溶液和方法因材料而异,通常先清洗油脂,可按表 3-2-2 的溶液配方和工艺进行,然后再清除氧化膜。表 3-2-3 列出了铝及铝合金氧化膜的化学清理配方及工艺条件。

表 3-2-2　工件表面去脂溶液的配方及清洗工艺

溶液配方/(g/L)	溶液温度/℃	脱脂时间/min	冲洗时间/min		清理方法
			热水(50~60 ℃)	流动冷水	
Na_3PO_4(40~50)、Na_2CO_3(40~50)、Na_2SiO_3(20~30)、H_2O(其余)	60~70	5~8	2	2	在 60 ℃溶液中浸泡 5~8 min,然后依次在热水中冲洗、在冷水中冲洗,最后用干净布擦干

表 3-2-3　铝及铝合金氧化膜的化学清理配方及工艺条件

材料	碱液			冲洗	中和光化			冲洗	干燥
	溶液	温度/℃	时间/min		溶液	温度/℃	时间/min		
纯铝	NaOH(6%~10%)	40~50	≤20	清水	HNO_3(30%)	室温	1~3	清水	先于100~110 ℃下烘干,再置于低温干燥箱中
铝镁合金、铝锰合金	NaOH(6%~10%)	40~50	≤7	清水	HNO_3(30%)	室温	1~3	清水	

注:①清理后至焊接前的储存时间一般不得超过 24 h。

②表中溶液的百分数指质量分数。

4. 装配

采用钨极氩弧焊制造的产品多为薄壁结构,控制焊接变形和保证熔透而不烧穿是制造中的关键技术。以薄板对接为例,对装配工作的基本要求是严格控制装配间隙和错边量,并尽可能使接头能在刚性固定的情况下施焊。焊接件越薄,制造难度越大。自动钨极氩弧焊对装配质量的要求比手工钨极氩弧焊更严格。

薄板(≤1 mm)对接不加填充金属钨极氩弧焊,一般是单面焊双面成形,不留装配间隙(或<0.15 mm),不能出现错边,通常是借助装配夹具来实现。手工钨极氩弧焊装配后允许用定位焊临时固定,板越薄焊点需越密,像琴键一样。自动钨极氩弧焊时,不能用定位焊,需要采用如图 3-2-3 所示装置,接头背面使用铜衬垫在夹紧状态下进行焊接。铜压块位于焊缝两侧,且沿焊缝均匀分布,板越薄压块越多、越密。

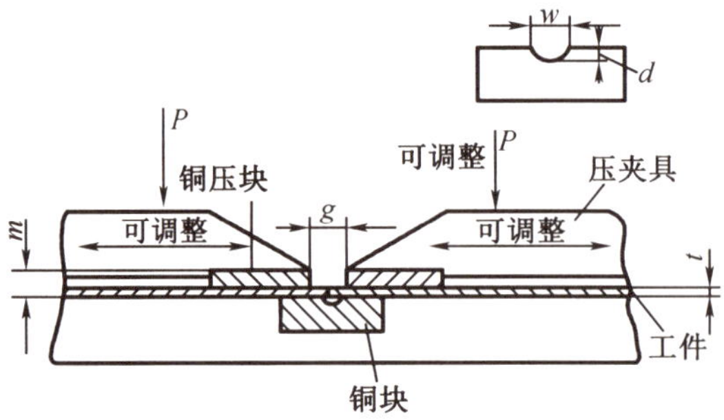

t/mm	g/mm
0.08~0.5 0.5~2.0 <2.0	0.08~0.5 2~4 (1.5~2)t
t/mm	P/(N/mm)
<0.1 10<t<3.0 >3.0	10 20 更大的力

$w=2t$
$d=0.25$或t(最小者)
$m=(1.5\sim2.0)t$

图 3-2-3　琴键式薄板对接焊的夹紧装置

焊接用的垫板一般不直接与对接接头对缝处紧贴，以免使焊缝背面成形不好或产生缺陷，可稍留槽隙，如图 3-2-4(a)、(b)所示。U 形对接接头的背面不与垫板直接接触，可以采用平垫板，如图 3-2-4(c)所示。

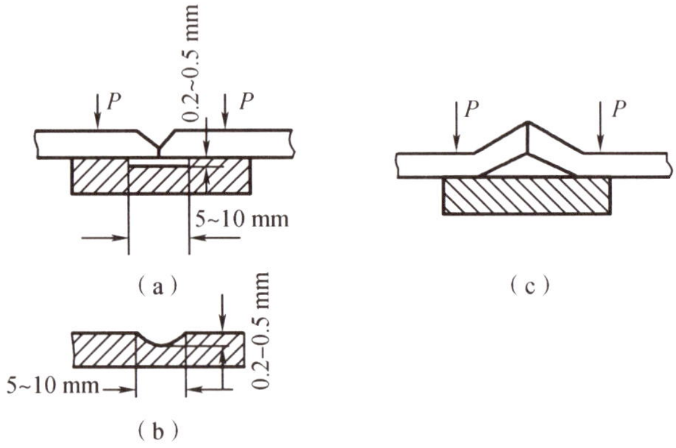

图 3-2-4　焊接垫板的准备情况

铜衬垫表面位于焊缝处常开槽，这是为了控制焊缝背面成形。为了保证背面焊缝不被空气污染，焊接时一般向槽内通入保护气体。焊接管子时，焊缝背面往往不能采用垫板，如有必要，可采用气垫的形式，也可采用玻璃质软带或其他带条贴在焊缝背面。

薄板通常在剪板机上剪切下料后即可装配焊接，不需再进行端面加工。如果遇到切边上有斜切口，装配时应注意正反向，如图 3-2-5 所示。

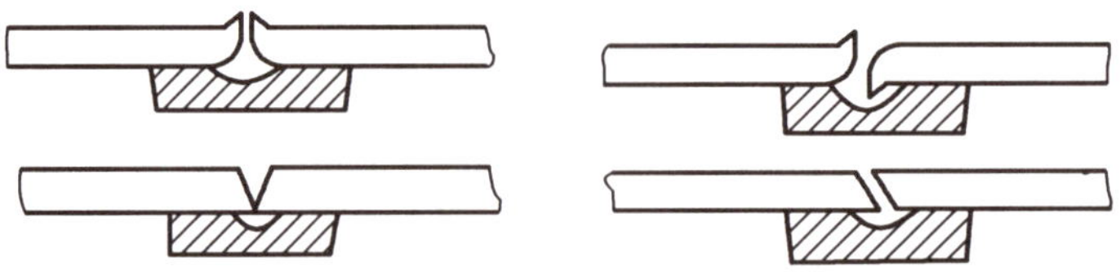

(a) 正确　　(b) 不正确

图 3-2-5　薄板对接剪切边的装配

为了保证手工钨极氩弧焊的质量，在焊接过程中要始终注意以下几个问题：

①保持正确的持枪姿势，随时调整焊枪角度及喷嘴高度，既有可靠的保护效果，又便于

观察熔池。

②注意焊后钨极形状和颜色的变化。在焊接过程中如果钨极没有变形，焊后钨极端部为银白色，则说明保护效果好；如果焊后钨极发蓝，说明保护效果差；如果钨极端部发黑或有瘤状物，则说明钨极已被污染，大多是在焊接过程中发生了短路，或沾了很多飞溅物，使钨极端头变成了合金，必须将这段钨极磨掉，否则容易产生夹钨。

③送丝要均匀，焊丝不能在保护区搅动，防止卷入空气。

④引弧。为了提高焊接质量，手工钨极氩弧焊多采用引弧器引弧，如高频振荡器或高压脉冲发生器，使氩气电离而引燃电弧。其优点是：钨极与焊件不接触就能在施焊点直接引燃电弧，钨极端部损耗小；引弧处焊接质量高，不会产生夹钨等缺陷。

⑤定位焊。为了防止焊接时焊件变形，必须保证定位焊缝的距离，可按表 3-2-4 选择。

表 3-2-4　定位焊缝的距离

项目	数值		
板厚/mm	0.5~0.8	1~2	>2
定位焊缝的间距/mm	约 20	50~100	约 200

由于定位焊缝是将来焊缝的一部分，故必须焊牢，不允许有缺陷。如果该焊缝要求单面焊双面成形，则定位焊缝必须焊透。

必须按正式的焊接工艺要求焊定位焊缝。如正式焊缝要求预热、缓冷，则定位焊焊前也要预热，焊后也要缓冷。

定位焊缝不能太高，以免焊接到定位焊缝处时接头困难。如果遇到这种情况，最好将定位焊缝磨低些，两端磨成斜坡，以便于焊接时接头。

如果定位焊缝上发现有裂纹、气孔等缺陷，应将这段定位焊缝打磨掉进行重焊，不允许用重熔的方法进行修补。

任务2：掌握手工钨极氩弧焊基本操作技术

1. 焊接

(1)打底焊

打底焊最好不在中途停止，如中途有停止时，则接头必须严格按要求进行打磨。而且，打底焊缝应有一定厚度：对于壁厚不大于 10 mm 的管子，其厚度不得小于 2 mm；壁厚大于 10 mm 的管子，其厚度不得小于 4 mm。打底焊缝需经自检合格后，才能进行填充焊接。

(2)焊接

焊接时要保证焊枪的角度及送丝位置，力求做到送丝均匀，以保证焊缝成形。

为了获得比较宽的焊道，保证坡口两侧的熔合质量，焊枪也可做横向摆动，但摆动频率不能太高，幅度不能太大，以不破坏熔池的保护效果为原则，由操作者灵活掌握。

打底层焊完后，在进行第二层焊接时，应注意不得将打底焊道烧穿，防止焊道下凹或背面剧烈氧化。

(3)焊接接头质量的控制

无论打底层焊接还是填充层焊接，控制焊接接头的质量是很重要的。因为接头是两段焊缝交接的地方，由于温度的差别和填充金属量的变化，接头处易出现超高、缺肉、未焊透、夹渣或夹杂、气孔等缺陷，所以焊接时应尽量避免停弧，减少接头次数。但在实际操作时，由于需要更换焊丝、更换钨极以及焊接位置的变化，或要求对称分段焊接等必须停弧，所以接头是不可避免的，因此就应尽可能地设法控制接头的质量。控制焊接接头的质量有以下方法：

①接头处要有斜坡，不能有死角。

②重新引弧的位置在原弧坑后面，使焊缝重叠 20~30 mm，重叠处一般不加或只加少量焊丝。

③熔池要贯穿到接头的根部，以确保接头处熔透。

2. 填丝

(1)填丝的基本操作技术

①连续填丝。这种填丝操作技术较好，对保护层的扰动小，但比较难掌握。在连续填丝时，要求焊丝平直，用左手拇指、食指、中指配合动作送丝，无名指和小指夹住焊丝控制方向，如图 3-2-6 所示。

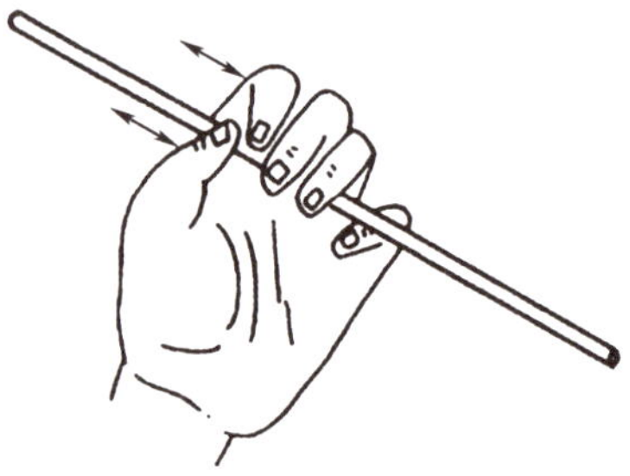

图 3-2-6　连续填丝操作技术

连续填丝时手臂动作不大，待焊丝快用完时才前移。当填丝量较大，采用较大的焊接参数时，多采用此法。

②断续送丝。以左手拇指、食指、中指捏紧焊丝，焊丝末端应始终处于氩气保护区内。填丝动作要轻，不得扰动氩气层，以防止空气侵入。更不能像气焊那样在熔池中搅拌，而是靠手臂和手腕的上、下反复动作，将焊丝端部的熔滴送入熔池。全位置焊时多采用此法。

③焊丝贴紧坡口或钝边一起熔入。将焊丝弯成弧形，紧贴在坡口间隙处，焊接电弧在熔化坡口钝边的同时也熔化了焊丝。由于坡口间隙应小于焊丝直径，此法可避免焊丝遮住操作者视线，适用于困难位置的焊接。

(2)填丝注意事项

①必须等坡口两侧熔化后才填丝，以免造成熔合不良。

②在填丝时，焊丝应与焊件表面夹角成 15°，快速地从熔池前沿点进，随后撤回，如此反复动作。

③填丝要均匀，快慢要适当。过快焊缝余高大；过慢则产生焊缝下凹和咬边。焊丝端头应始终处于氩气保护区内。

④当坡口间隙大于焊丝直径时，焊丝应跟随电弧做同步横向摆动。无论采用哪种填丝动作，送丝速度均应与焊接速度相匹配。

⑤在填充焊丝时，不应把焊丝直接放在电弧下面，但把焊丝抬得过高也是不适宜的，不

可让熔滴向熔池“滴渡”。填丝位置的正确与否的示意图,如图 3-2-7 所示。

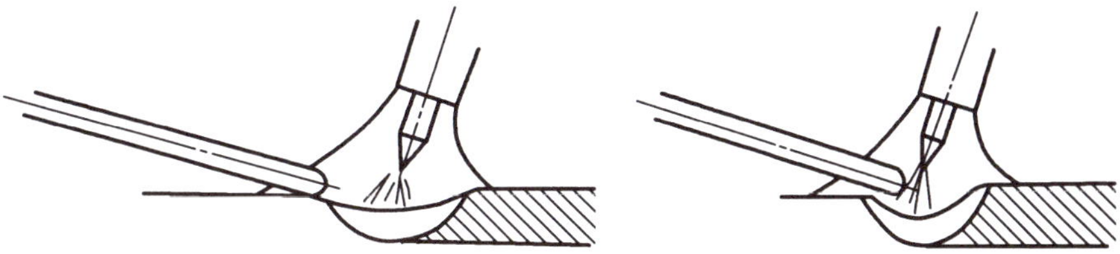

(a)正确　　(b)不正确

图 3-2-7　填丝的位置

⑥在操作过程中,如不慎使钨极与焊丝相碰,发生瞬时短路,将产生很大的飞溅和烟雾,会造成焊缝污染和夹钨。这时应立即停止焊接,用砂轮磨掉被污染处,直到磨出金属光泽。被污染的钨极,应在别处重新引弧熔化掉被污染的端部,或重新磨尖后方可继续焊接。

⑦当撤回焊丝时,切记不要让焊丝端头撤出氩气保护区,以免焊丝端头被氧化,在下次点进时送入熔池,造成氧化物夹渣或产生气孔。

3. 收弧

收弧不当,会影响焊缝质量,使弧坑过深或产生弧坑裂纹,甚至造成返修。一般氩弧焊设备都配有电流自动衰减装置,若无电流衰减装置时,多采用改变操作方法来收弧。其基本要点是逐渐减少热量输入,如改变焊枪角度、拉长电弧、加大焊速等。对于管子封闭焊缝,最后的收弧一般多采用稍拉长电弧,重叠焊缝 20~40 mm,在重叠部分不加或少加焊丝。停弧后,氩气开关应延时 10 s 左右再关闭(一般设备上都有提前送气、滞后关气的装置),防止金属在高温下继续氧化。

4. 左向焊与右向焊

左向焊与右向焊如图 3-2-8 所示。

在焊接过程中,焊丝与焊枪由右端向左端移动,焊接电弧指向未焊部分,焊丝位于电弧运动的前方,称为左焊法。如在焊接过程中,焊丝与焊枪由左端向右端施焊,焊接电弧指向已焊部分,填充焊丝位于电弧运动的后方,则称为右焊法。

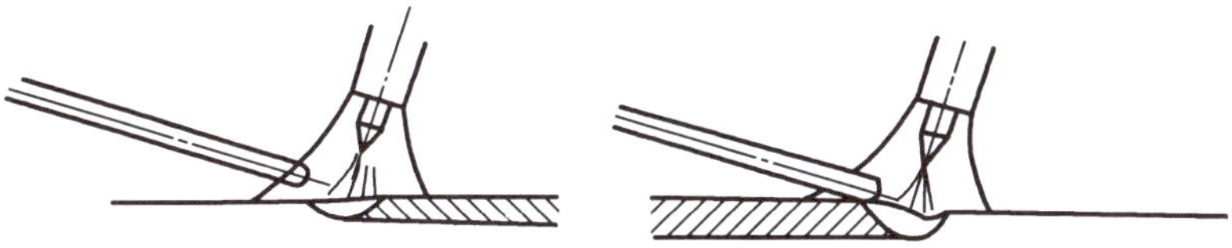

(a)左向焊　　(b)右向焊

图 3-2-8　左向焊与右向焊

(1)左焊法的优缺点

①优点

a. 操作者的视野不受阻碍,便于观察和控制熔池情况。

b. 焊接电弧指向未焊部分,既可对未焊部分起预热作用,又能减小熔深,有利于焊接薄件,特别是管子对接时的根部打底焊和焊易熔金属。

c. 操作简单方便,初学者容易掌握。

②缺点

主要是在焊大焊件，特别是进行多层焊时，热量利用率低，因而阻碍了熔敷效率的提高。

(2)右焊法的优缺点

①优点

a. 当焊接电弧指向右侧已凝固的焊缝金属时，熔池冷却缓慢，这有利于改善焊缝金属组织结构，减小气孔、夹渣产生的可能性。

b. 由于电弧指向焊缝金属，因而提高了热利用率，在输入的线能量相同时，右焊法比左焊法熔深大，故特别适合于焊接厚度较大、熔点较高的焊件。

②缺点

a. 由于焊丝在熔池运动的后方，影响操作者的视线，不利于观察和控制熔池。

b. 无法在管道(特别是小直径管)上焊接。

任务考核

1. 钨极氩弧焊所焊板材厚度范围，从生产率考虑以(　　)mm 以下为宜。

A. 3　　B. 4　　C. 5　　D. 6

2. 以下不属于钨极氩弧焊的引弧方式的是(　　)。

A. 敲击引弧　　B. 接触短路引弧

C. 高频高压引弧　　D. 高压脉冲引弧

3. 钨极氩弧焊时，焊枪的横向摆动方式有(　　)种。

A. 2　　B. 3　　C. 4　　D. 5

4 钨极氩弧焊时，送丝方式有(　　)种。

A. 2　　B. 3　　C. 4　　D. 5

5. 钨极氩弧焊时，手动送丝方式有(　　)种。

A. 2　　B. 3　　C. 4　　D. 5

6. 钨极氩弧焊的焊前清理的方法有：________、________、________等方法。

7. 手工钨极氩弧焊一般采用________焊法，右手________，左手________。

8. 钨极氩弧焊电焊的灭弧方法主要有________法，________法，________法和________法四种。

9. 坡口准备主要是指____________以及________两部分。

10. 钨极氩弧焊常用的接头形式有________、________、________、________、________等。

任务操作

根据基本操作指南，对基本焊接要领的操作技术、焊前准备进行针对性实操训练。

Project Ⅱ Fundamentals of Manual TIG Welding Operations

【Learning Objectives】

1. Master the preparation procedures and methods for manual TIG welding;
2. Master the basic operation techniques of manual TIG welding.

Task 1:Master the Preparation Procedures and Methods for Manual TIG Welding

1. General procedure of the TIG welding process

To attain high-quality welds, regardless of whether it is manual TIG welding or automatic TIG welding, the typical procedure of the welding process is as follows:

①Prior to starting the arc, it is necessary to deliver shielding gas from the welding gun to the welding starting point 1.5~4 seconds in advance in order to remove air from inside the pipe and the welding area.

②After extinguishing the arc, the gas supply should be stopped after a certain period of time (5~15 seconds) to protect the uncooled tungsten electrode and molten pool. The welding gun should not leave the final welding position until the gas supply is stopped, ensuring the quality of the start and end points of the weld.

③When the welding power supply is turned on, activate the arc striking device. Once the arc is ignited, welding begins, and the movement of the welding gun and the feeding of the welding wire are coordinated.

④Automatically connect and disconnect the arc striking and stabilizing circuits, and control the power supply's on and off state.

⑤As welding nears completion, the welding current should automatically decrease until the arc is extinguished to eliminate and prevent crater cracks. This is particularly important for circumferential welding and materials prone to hot cracking.

⑥When using a water-cooled welding gun, the water supply and gas supply should be carried out simultaneously.

Fig. 3-2-1 illustrates the general control procedure for manual argon tungsten arc welding and automatic argon tungsten arc welding, which is performed by the operator in collaboration with the welder's control system.

2. Joint and groove type

The common types of joints used in argon tungsten arc welding include butt joint, lap joint, corner joint, T-joint, and end joint, as depicted in Fig. 3-2-2.

(a) Manual TIG welding (b) Automatic TIG welding

Fig. 3-2-1 General Control Procedure of TIG Welding

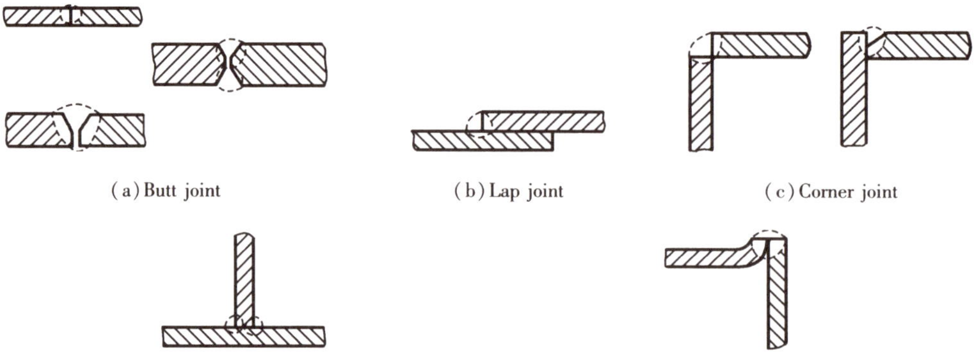

(a) Butt joint (b) Lap joint (c) Corner joint

(d) T-joint (e) End joint

Fig. 3-2-2 Five Common Basic Joint Forms

The selection of groove type and size shall be based on the type of material, plate thickness, etc. Generally, for plate thickness less than 3 mm, an I-shaped groove can be made. For plate thickness between 3-12 mm, a V-shaped or Y-shaped groove can be made. Table 3-2-1 provides the groove shape and size for welded joints of aluminum and aluminum alloy. The specific groove shape and detailed dimensions for various steels can be selected according to national or industry standards.

Table 3-2-1 Groove Shape and Size of Aluminum and Aluminum Alloy Welded Joints

Joint and groove form		Diagram	Plate thickness δ/mm	Groove dimension		
				Clearances b/mm	Blunt edge p/mm	Chamfer angle α/(°)
Butt joint	Edge rolling	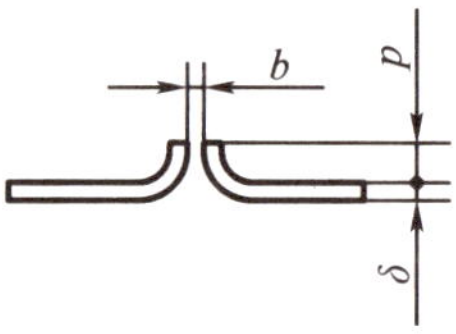	≤2	<0.5	<2	—
	I-shaped groove	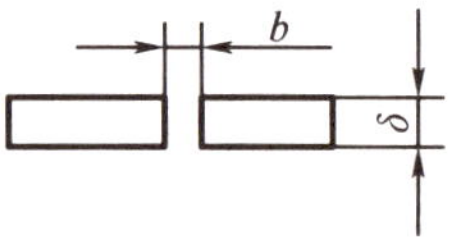	1-5	0.5-2	—	—

Table 3-2-1 (Continued)

Joint and groove form		Diagram	Plate thickness δ/mm	Groove dimension: Clearances b/mm	Groove dimension: Blunt edge p/mm	Groove dimension: Chamfer angle α/(°)
Butt joint	V-shaped groove	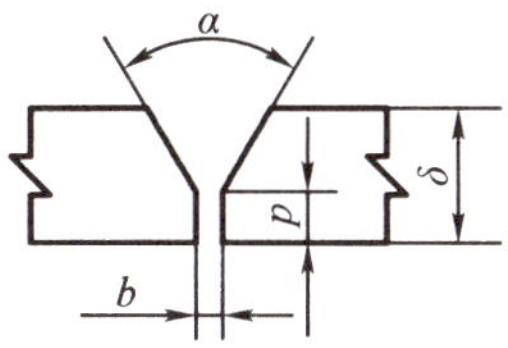	3-5	1.5-2.5	1.5-2	60°-70°
			5-12	2-3	2-3	60°-70°
	X-shaped groove	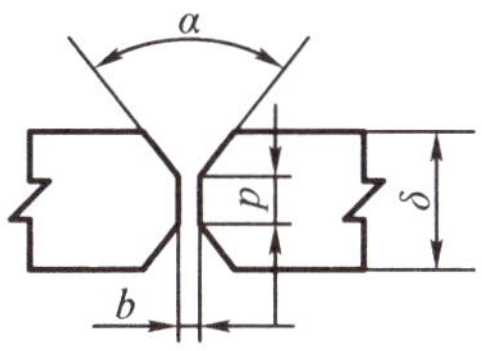	>10	1.5-3	2-4	60°-70°
Lap joint		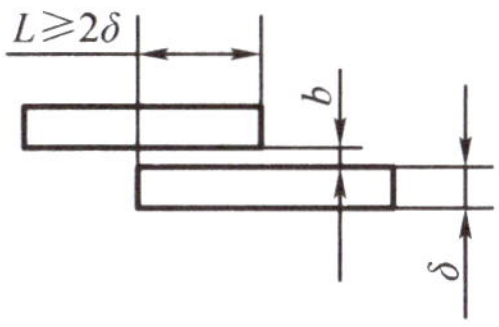	<1.5	0-0.5	L≥2δ	—
			1.5-3	0.5-1	L≥2δ	—
Corner joint	I-shaped groove	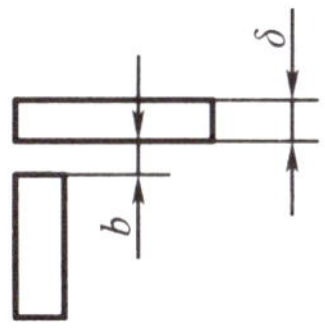	<12	<1	—	—
	V-shaped groove	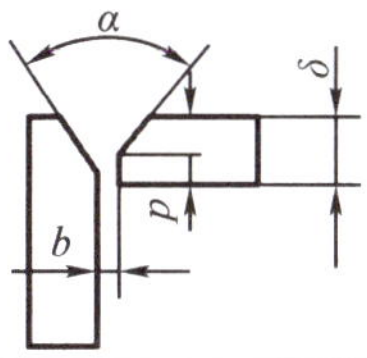	3-5	0.8-1.5	1-1.5	60°-70°
			>5	1-2	1-2	60°-70°
T-joint	I-shaped groove	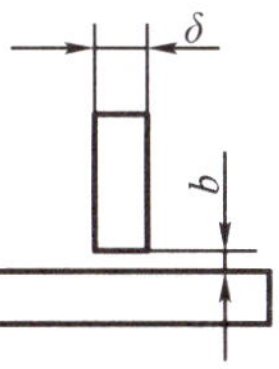	3-5	<1	—	—
			6-10	<1.5	—	—
	K-shaped groove	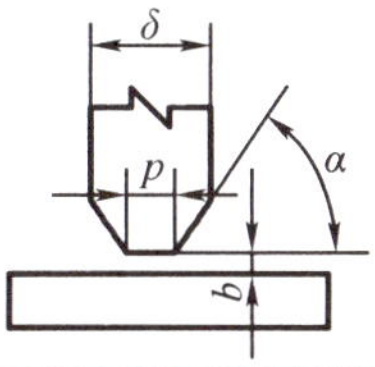	10-16	<1.5	1-2	60°

3. Cleaning before welding

Argon and helium are inert gases and do not undergo any chemical reaction with liquid metal during welding. Therefore, TIG welding does not have any dehydrogenation or deoxidation effect. Argon tungsten arc welding has high requirements for material surface quality. To ensure the welding quality, the oxide film, grease, and moisture within at least 20 mm of the workpiece groove and both sides of the groove must be cleaned before welding. Otherwise, it will affect the arc stability during welding, deteriorate the weld formation, and may lead to defects such as pores, inclusions, and incomplete fusion. The cleaning methods mainly include mechanical cleaning and chemical cleaning, and sometimes both methods are used alternately.

(1) Mechanical cleaning.

The method is suitable only for workpieces and not for welding wires. Mechanical methods such as wire brush, scraper, abrasive cloth, sand blasting, or shot blasting are commonly used to remove oxide film and oil stains from the surface of workpieces. Aluminum and its alloys are soft and are usually cleaned using scrapers or wire brushes. For large steel workpieces, sand blasting or shot blasting can be used for cleaning. Smaller stainless steel parts are usually polished with abrasive cloth. Mechanical cleaning has low efficiency and does not completely remove the oxide film. It is generally only used for workpieces that are large in size, have a long production cycle, or have localized contamination after chemical cleaning.

(2) Chemical cleaning

The method relies on chemical reactions to remove oxide films and oil stains from the surface of the workpiece and welding wire. It is particularly suitable for pre-welding treatment of aluminum alloy, titanium alloy, magnesium alloy base metals, and welding wires. Chemical cleaning solutions and methods vary depending on the materials. Generally, grease should be cleaned first according to the solution formulation and process provided in Table 3-2-2, followed by the removal of oxide films. Table 3-2-3 provides the chemical cleaning formulas and process conditions for aluminum and aluminum alloy oxide films.

Table 3-2-2 Formulatio and Cleaning Procedure for Degreasing Solution on Workpiece Surface

Solution formulation /(g/L)	Solution temperature /℃	Degreasing time /min	Rinsing time/min		Cleaning method
			Hot water (50-60 ℃)	Flowing chilled water	
Na_3PO_4(40-50), Na_2CO_3(40-50), Na_2SiO_3(20-30), H_2O(remainder)	60-70	5-8	2	2	Soak in a 60 ℃ solution for 5 to 8 minutes, then wash in hot and cold water, and wipe dry with a clean cloth

Table 3-2-3 Chemical Cleaning Formulations and Process Conditions for Aluminum and Aluminum Alloy Oxide Film

Materials	Alkali solution			Rinsing	Neutralization and photochemical reaction			Rinsing	Drying
	Solution	Temperature /℃	Time /min		Solution	Temperature /℃	Time /min		
Pure aluminum	NaOH 6%-10%	40-50	≤20	Clear water	HNO_3 (30%)	Room temperature	1-3	Clear water	Dry at 100-110 ℃ and then place in a low-temperature drying oven
Aluminum-magnesium alloy, aluminum-manganese alloy	NaOH 6%-10%	40-50	≤7	Clear water	HNO_3 (30%)	Room temperature	1-3	Clear water	

Note: ①The storage time between cleaning and welding should generally not exceed 24 hours.

②The percentage of solution in the table refers to mass fraction.

4. Assembly

Most of the products manufactured using argon tungsten arc welding are thin-walled structures. Controlling welding deformation and ensuring proper fusion without burning through are crucial techniques in the manufacturing process. Taking thin plate butt joints as an example, the assembly work requires strict control of assembly clearance and misalignment, and welding the joints under rigid fixation as much as possible. The thinner the welded part, the more challenging it is to manufacture. Automatic TIG welding has stricter requirements for assembly quality compared to manual TIG welding.

Argon tungsten arc welding without filler metal is typically used for butt joints of thin plates (≤1 mm). It involves single-sided welding and double-sided forming, with no assembly clearance (or <0.15 mm) and no misalignment allowed. Assembly fixtures are commonly employed to achieve this. After manual argon tungsten arc welding assembly, temporary fixation with tack welding is permitted. The welding spots are more condensed, resembling piano keys, as the plate becomes thinner. However, for automatic argon tungsten arc welding, tack welding cannot be used. The device depicted in Fig. 3-2-3 should be adopted, and the back of the joint should be welded with a copper gasket in a clamped state. Copper pressing blocks are positioned on both sides of the weld and evenly distributed along it. The number and density of pressing blocks increase as the plate gets thinner.

The backing plate for welding is generally not directly attached to the butt joint of the joint in order to prevent poor formation or defects on the back of the weld. A small slot gap can be left, as shown in Fig. 3-2-4(a) and (b). The back of the U-shaped butt joint is not in direct contact with the base plate, and a flat base plate can be used, as shown in Fig. 3-2-4(c).

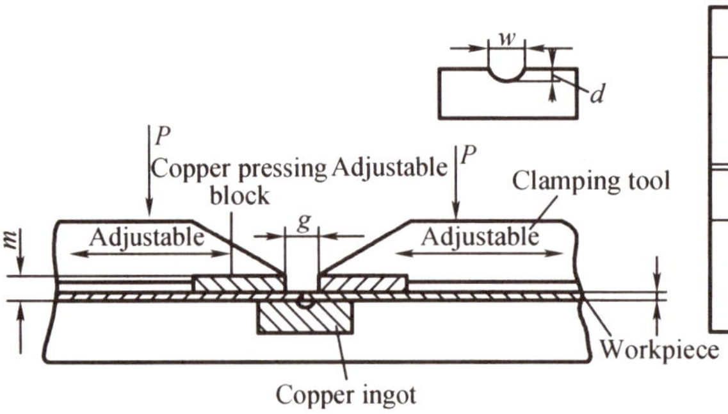

t/mm	g/mm
0.08~0.5 0.5~2.0 <2.0	0.08~0.5 2~4 (1.5~2)t
t/mm	P/(N/mm)
<0.1 10<t<3.0 >3.0	10 20 Higher power

w=2t
d=0.25 or the smaller of t
m=(1.5~2.0)t

Fig. 3-2-3 Piano-style Clamping Device for Thin Plate Butt Welding

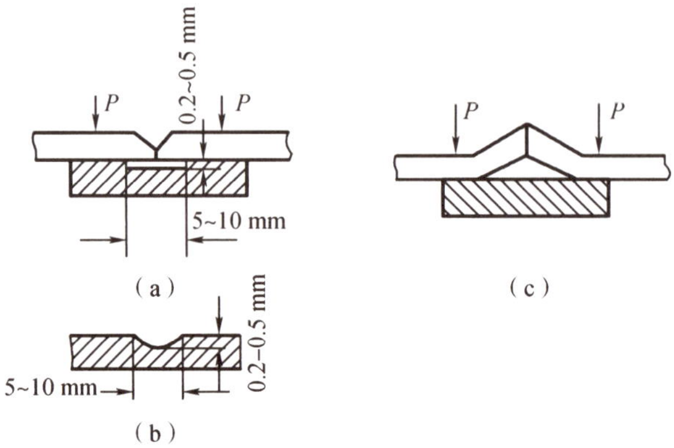

Fig. 3-2-4 Preparation of Welding Backing Plate

The copper backing surface is usually grooved at the weld to control the formation of the weld's backside. In order to prevent the back weld from being contaminated by air, protective gas is typically introduced into the groove during welding. When welding pipes, it is often not possible to use a backing plate on the back of the weld. If necessary, an air cushion can be used, or soft glass tape or other strips can be attached to the back of the weld.

Usually, thin plates can be assembled and welded after being cut on a plate shearing machine without the need for end face processing. If there is a bevel cut on the cutting edge, pay attention to the forward and backward directions during assembly, as shown in Fig. 3-2-5.

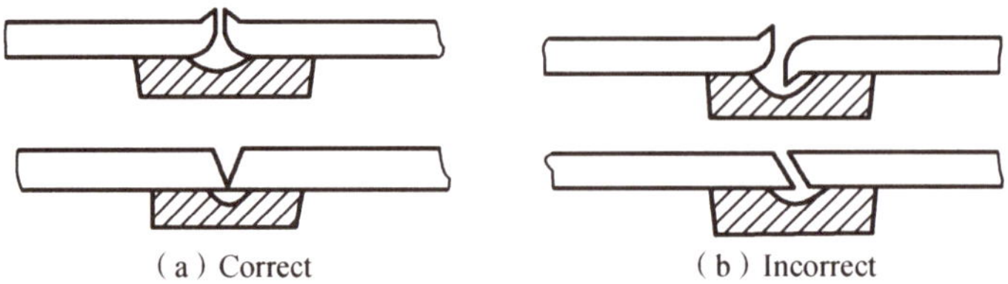

Fig. 3-2-5 Assembly of Butt Sheared Edge of Thin Plate

To ensure the quality of manual argon tungsten arc welding, it is necessary to always pay attention to the following issues during the welding process:

①Maintain a correct gun grip posture, and adjust the angle of the welding gun and the height of the nozzle at any time. This not only provides reliable protection, but also facilitates observation of the molten pool.

②Pay attention to changes in the shape and color of the tungsten electrode after welding. If the tungsten electrode remains undistorted and the end turns silvery white after welding, it indicates good protection; if the tungsten electrode turns blue, it indicates poor protection; if the tungsten electrode end appears black or has nodules, it indicates contamination of the tungsten electrode. Most of the contamination is caused by short circuits or excessive spatter during welding, which leads to alloy formation at the tungsten electrode end. This portion of the tungsten electrode must be ground off, otherwise tungsten inclusions may occur.

③The wire feeding should be uniform, and the welding wire should not be stirred within the protection area to avoid air contamination.

④Arc striking. In order to improve welding quality, manual argon tungsten arc welding often uses an arc-striking device, such as a high-frequency oscillator or high-voltage pulse generator, to ionize argon and ignite the arc. The advantages are: the arc can be ignited directly at the welding point without contact between the tungsten electrode and the workpiece, resulting in minimal loss at the tungsten electrode end; high welding quality and no defects like tungsten inclusions occur at the arc striking position.

⑤Tack welding. To prevent workpiece deformation during welding, the distance between tack welds must be maintained and can be selected according to Table 3-2-4.

Table 3-2-4 Distance between Locating Welds

Item	Value		
Plate thickness/mm	0. 5-0. 8	1-2	>2
Spacing between tack welds/mm	about 20	50-100	about 200

As the tack weld is a part of future welds, it must be firmly welded without any defects. If one-side welding and double-side shaping are required for this weld, the tack weld must be fully penetrated.

The tack weld must be welded in accordance with the formal welding process requirements. If preheating and slow cooling are necessary for formal welds, they must also be preheated before tack welding and slowly cooled after welding.

Tack welds should not be too high to make joint welding difficult. In such cases, it is preferable to grind the tack weld lower, with both ends sloped, to facilitate a good joint during welding.

If defects such as cracks and pores are found on the tack weld, this section of tack weld should be polished off and re-welded. Repair by remelting is not permitted.

Task 2:Master the Basic Operation Techniques of Manual TIG Welding

1. Welding

(1) Backing welding

It is recommended to avoid stopping the backing welding halfway. If there is a stop in the middle, the joint must be polished strictly as required. Additionally, the backing weld should have a certain thickness: for pipes with a wall thickness not exceeding 10 mm, its thickness should not be less than 2 mm; for pipes with a wall thickness greater than 10 mm, its thickness should not be less than 4 mm. The backing weld must pass the self-inspection before proceeding with the filling welding.

(2) Welding

Ensure the angle and wire feeding position of the welding gun during welding to achieve consistent wire feeding and ensure proper weld formation.

To achieve a wider weld bead and ensure the fusion quality on both sides of the groove, the welding gun can also be swung laterally. However, the swing frequency should not be too high and the amplitude should not be too large. The operator should control it flexibly based on the principle of not compromising the protective effect of the molten pool.

After completing the welding of the backing layer, caution must be exercised during the welding of the second layer to prevent burning through the backing weld pass and avoid the weld pass sinking or severe oxidation of the back surface.

(3) Control of quality of welded joints

It is important to control the quality of welded joints for both base layer welding and filler layer welding. Because the joint is the point where two sections of welds meet, defects such as excessive height, insufficient fusion, incomplete penetration, slag inclusion or impurity, and porosity are prone to occur at the joint due to temperature differences and changes in filler metal quantity. Therefore, arc stopping should be avoided as much as possible during welding to minimize the number of joints. However, in actual operation, it is necessary to replace the welding wire and tungsten electrode, change the welding position, or require arc stopping for symmetrical sectional welding, etc., which makes the occurrence of joints inevitable. Thus, the quality of the joint should be controlled as much as possible. The following methods can be employed to control the quality of welded joints:

①There should be a slope at the joint, with no blind spots allowed.

②The re-striking point of the arc is positioned behind the original crater, allowing a weld overlap of 20-30 mm. Generally, no or only a small amount of welding wire is added at the overlapping area.

③The molten pool should penetrate to the root of the joint to ensure complete fusion at the joint.

2. Filler wire

(1) Basic operation techniques for wire filling

①Continuous wire feed. This type of wire filling operation technology is superior and causes minimal disturbance to the protective layer, but it is more challenging to learn. When performing continuous wire filling, the welding wire must be straight. The left thumb, index finger, and middle finger are used to feed the wire, while the ring finger and little finger hold the welding wire to control its direction, as shown in Fig. 3-2-6.

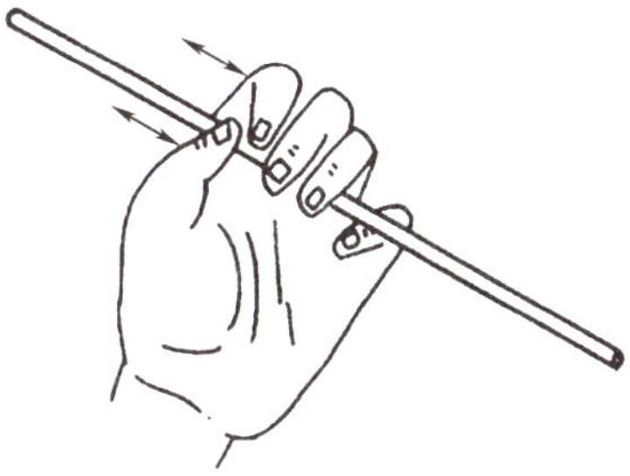

Fig. 3-2-6 Continuous Silk Filling Operation Technology

The arm should not move too much during continuous wire filling and should only move forward when the welding wire is nearly depleted. This method is often employed when there is a significant amount of filler wire and larger welding parameters are utilized.

②Intermittent wire feeding. Grasp the welding wire tightly with the left thumb, index finger, and middle finger. The end of the welding wire should always remain within the argon protection zone. The feeding action should be gentle to avoid disturbing the argon layer and prevent air from entering. It is also forbidden to stir in the molten pool like gas welding. Instead, the droplets at the end of the welding wire should be introduced into the molten pool through repeated up and down movements of the arms and wrists. This method is mostly used for welding in all positions.

③The welding wire is melted tightly into the groove or root face. The welding wire is bent into an arc and tightly adhered to the groove gap. The welding arc melts both the root face of the groove and the welding wire. Since the groove gap should be smaller than the diameter of the welding wire, this method can prevent the welding wire from obstructing the operator's line of sight and is suitable for welding in challenging positions.

(2) Wire filling precautions

①The wire must be filled only after both sides of the groove are melted in order to avoid poor fusion.

②During wire filling, the welding wire should form an angle of 15° with the surface of the weldment. The welding wire should be tapped quickly from the front edge of the molten pool and then withdrawn. Repeat this operation.

③Fill the thread evenly and at an appropriate speed. If it is too fast, the weld reinforcement will be large; if it is too slow, the weld joint will be concave and undercut. The welding wire end should always be in the argon protection area.

④When the groove gap is greater than the diameter of the welding wire, the welding wire should swing synchronously and transversely with the arc. Regardless of the filler wire action, the wire feed speed should match the welding speed.

⑤When filling the welding wire, it should not be placed directly under the arc, but lifting the welding wire too high is also inappropriate. The molten droplets should not "drip" into the molten pool. Refer to Fig. 3-2-7 for the correct position of the filler wire.

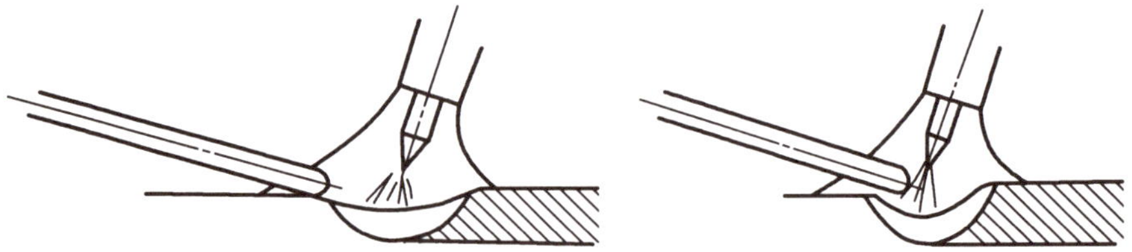

(a) Correct　　(b) Incorrect

Fig. 3-2-7　Position of Filler Wire

⑥During operation, if the tungsten electrode accidentally collides with the welding wire and an instantaneous short circuit occurs, a significant amount of splatter and smoke will be generated, which will contaminate the weld and cause tungsten inclusion. In such cases, welding should be immediately stopped and the contaminated area should be ground with a grinding wheel until a metallic shine is achieved. The contaminated tungsten electrode should be repositioned and melted at another location to remove the contaminated end, or it can be reshaped and sharpened before continuing the welding process.

⑦When retracting the welding wire, it is important to remember not to withdraw the end of the welding wire from the argon protection area. This is to prevent oxidation of the wire end and avoid introducing oxidized particles into the molten pool during the next welding process, which could result in the inclusion of slag or the formation of pores.

3. Arc termination

Improper arc termination will adversely affect the weld quality, leading to excessively deep craters or crater cracks, and even requiring repairs. Generally, argon arc welding equipment is equipped with an automatic current attenuation device. In the absence of such a device, the operation method is usually altered to terminate the arc. The key point is to gradually decrease the heat input, such as altering the angle of the welding gun, elongating the arc, and increasing the welding speed. For closed welds on pipes, a slightly elongated arc is commonly used for the final arc termination. The overlapping welds should be 20-40 mm, and no additional or minimal welding wire should be added to the overlapping sections. After the arc is terminated, the argon valve should be closed after a delay of approximately 10 seconds (typically, devices for advance gas supply and delayed gas closing are present on the equipment) to prevent further oxidation of the metal at high temperatures.

4. Leftward and rightward welding

Leftward welding and rightward welding as shown in Fig. 3-2-8.

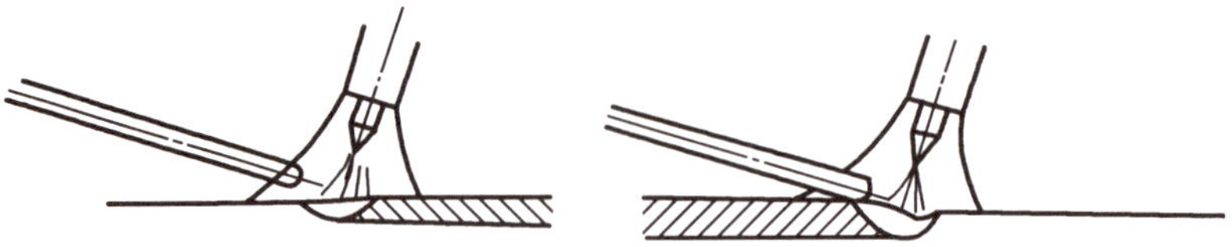

(a) Leftward welding　　(b) Rightward welding

Fig. 3-2-8　Leftward Welding and Rightward Welding

During the welding process, welding wire and welding gun move from the right end to the left end, with the welding arc pointing towards the unwelded part, and welding wire is positioned in front of the arc's movement, which is known as forehand welding. If, during the welding process, welding wire and welding gun are welded from the left end to the right end, with the welding arc pointing towards the welded part, and the filler wire positioned behind the arc's movement, it is called backhand welding.

(1) Advantages and disadvantages of forehand welding

①Advantages

a. The operator's field of vision is unobstructed, making it convenient for observing and controlling the molten pool.

b. The welding arc points towards the unwelded part, which can preheat the unwelded part and reduce fusion depth. This is beneficial for welding thin parts, especially root backing welding and fusible metal welding during pipe butt joint.

c. Simple and convenient operation, easy for beginners to master.

②Disadvantages

The low heat utilization rate particularly hampers the improvement of deposition efficiency when welding large weldments, especially during multi-layer welding.

(2) Advantages and disadvantages of backhand welding

①Advantages

a. As the welding arc points towards the solidified weld metal on the right side, the molten pool will cool slowly, resulting in an improved weld metal structure and reduced possibility of porosity and slag inclusion.

b. Since the arc is directed towards the weld metal, the heat utilization rate is increased. With the same line energy input, backhand welding offers greater penetration compared to forehand welding, making it particularly suitable for welding thick and high-melting point joints.

②Disadvantages

a. The movement of the molten pool obstructs the operator's vision as the welding wire is situated behind it, making it difficult to observe and control the pool.

b. Welding on pipes, especially small-diameter ones, is impractical.

Task Assessment

1. It is advisable to have a plate thickness range for TIG welded plates that is less than ( ) mm, considering productivity.

A. 3 B. 4 C. 5 D. 6

2. Which of the following is not an arc starting mode for TIG welding? ( )

A. Arc striking by tapping

B. Arc striking by short circuiting contact

C. High-frequency high-voltage arc striking

D. High-voltage pulse arc striking

3. During TIG welding, there are ( ) different transverse swing modes of the

welding gun.

A. 2 B. 3 C. 4 D. 5

4. During TIG welding, there are ( ) wire feeding modes.

A. 2 B. 3 C. 4 D. 5

5. During TIG welding, there are ( ) manual wire feeding modes.

A. 2 B. 3 C. 4 D. 5

6. Pre-weld cleaning methods for TIG welding include: ________, ________, and ________.

7. Manual TIG welding generally adopts the ________ welding method, with the right hand ________ and left hand ________.

8. There are four main arc extinguishing methods for TIG welding: ________, ________, ________, and ________.

9. Groove preparation mainly refers to ________ and ________.

10. The commonly used joint types for TIG welding include ________, ________, ________, ________, and ________.

Task Assessment

Carry out targeted practical training on the operation techniques of basic welding essentials, as well as pre-welding preparation, according to the guidelines for basic operations.

项目三　板对接平焊钨极氩弧焊

【学习目标】

1. 分析板对接平焊钨极氩弧焊的技术要求；
2. 掌握板对接平焊钨极氩弧焊的焊前准备；
3. 掌握板对接平焊钨极氩弧焊的焊接操作；
4. 掌握板对接平焊钨极氩弧焊的焊后处理与检查。

任务1：分析板对接平焊钨极氩弧焊的技术要求

图 3-3-1 为常见板对接平焊试件装配图及技术要求。

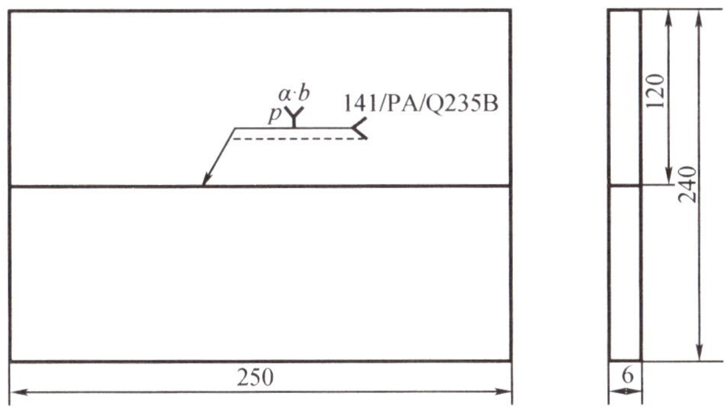

技术要求

1. 单面焊双面成形。
2. 坡口的坡口角为 60°，V 形带钝边。
3. 根部间隙和钝边尺寸自定。
4. 错边≤0.5 mm。
5. 角变形<3°。
6. 不允许有咬边。
7. 不允许有未焊透。
8. 不允许有裂纹、气孔、夹渣。
9. 焊缝余高≤1+0.15b。

图 3-3-1　常见板对接平焊试件装配图及技术要求（单位：mm）

钨极惰性气体保护焊方法是利用惰性气体保护，用钨棒做电极的一种电弧焊焊接方法，由于我国常用氩气，所以常直接称其为钨极氩弧焊，简称 TIG 焊，其他国家也常用氦气等，这里以钨极氩弧焊为例介绍，利用其他惰性气体的原理和操作方法相类似。钨极氩弧焊在焊接时由于钨极本身不熔化，只起发射电子产生电弧的作用，故也称非熔化极氩弧焊。焊接时，从喷嘴喷出的氩气形成一个厚而密的气体保护层，隔绝空气。在氩气层流的包围之中，电弧在钨极和焊件之间燃烧。利用电弧产生的热量熔化待焊处和填充焊丝，把两块分离的金属连接在一起，从而可获得牢固的焊接接头。目前主要用于焊接薄件或用于重要产品的打底焊。

本项目以实际工程中常用的低碳钢材质为例介绍板对接平焊钨极氩弧焊方法的焊前准备、焊接操作和焊后处理与检查等任务实施流程。

任务2：掌握板对接平焊钨极氩弧焊的焊前准备

1. 焊件准备及坡口清理

根据任务单要求，准备 6 mm×120 mm×250 mm 尺寸的 Q235B 材质焊件两块，单边开 30°的 V 形坡口。

焊前打磨清理坡口面及坡口边缘上下两侧 15~20 mm 范围，露出金属光泽，并打磨出 0~0.5 mm 的钝边。

2. 焊接工艺参数确定

结合本任务母材 Q235B 的焊接特性和板厚来看，选择直径 2.5 mm 的 ER50-6 焊丝（注意保持焊丝的干净，使用前可用砂布及棉纱擦净焊丝上的油、锈等污物，必要时还可用丙酮清洗），保护气体为氩气，纯度高于 99.99%，电极采用铈钨极，采用三层三道来焊接，具体焊接工艺参数如表 3-3-1 所示。

表 3-3-1　焊接工艺参数表

焊接层次	焊丝型号	焊丝直径/mm	焊接电流/A	焊接电压/V
打底层	ER50-6	2.5	80~100	12~16
填充层			100~120	12~16
盖面层			90~110	12~16
焊接层次	保护气体流量/(L/min)	钨极直径/mm	钨极伸出长度/mm	电源极性
打底层	7~9	2.5	3~6	直流正接
填充层	7~9	2.5	3~6	
盖面层	7~9	2.5	3~6	

3. 装配定位

将两块钢板水平放工装台上，两端对齐装配成对接接头，装配时焊件始焊端根部间隙设置为 2.0 mm，结束端为 3.0 mm，采取和打底相同的工艺参数在两端进行点固焊，焊点长度为 10~15 mm，必须焊透，不允许有缺陷，错边量不大于 0.5 mm，反变形预留量为 3°~5°，焊后应把焊点打磨成斜坡，以便接头，装配及焊点形式如图 3-3-2 所示。

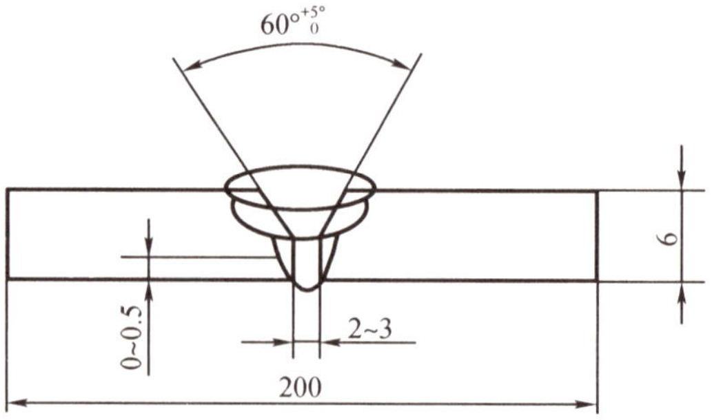

图 3-3-2　装配定位及焊点示意图（单位：mm）

如定位焊缝有缺陷,必须将有缺陷的定位焊缝磨掉后重焊,不允许用重熔的办法来处理定位焊缝上的缺陷。

任务3：掌握板对接平焊钨极氩弧焊的焊接操作

钨极氩弧焊焊炬的握法用右手握焊炬,食指和拇指夹住焊炬前身部位,其余三指作为焊件支点,也可用食指或中指做支点,呼吸要均匀,要稍微用力握住焊炬,保持焊炬的稳定,使焊接电弧稳定。关键在于焊接过程中钨极焊件或焊丝不能形成短路。

将焊件固定在操作台上,焊缝水平装夹,坡口面朝上,焊件高度应便于操作者操作,间隙小的一端放在右端,采取左焊法进行焊接,6 mm 厚板件常采用三层三道进行焊接。

1. 打底焊

①焊接时填丝方法可采用连续填丝法或断续填丝法,操作时左手拿焊丝的方法如图 3-3-3(a)所示,右手持枪方法如图 3-3-3(b)所示。

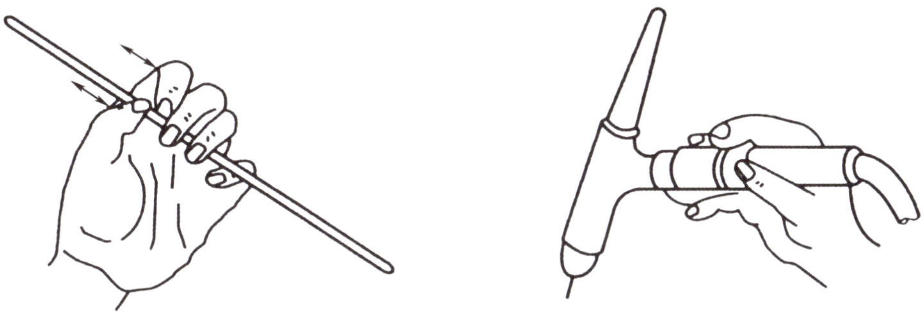

(a) (b)

图 3-3-3 钨极氩弧焊操作时手拿焊丝和焊枪的方法

②平焊操作时焊枪与焊丝的角度如图 3-3-4 所示。

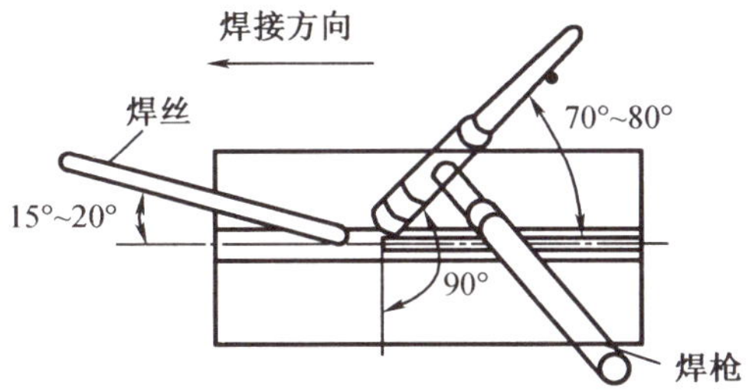

图 3-3-4 平焊时焊枪和焊丝的角度示意图

③在试件右端定位焊缝上引弧,并稍停顿进行预热,当定位焊缝左端形成熔池并出现熔孔后开始填丝,进行正常焊接,自右向左焊接打底层焊道,沿斜坡向坡口根部移动焊枪,至坡口根部后做锯齿形小幅度摆动,并在坡口两侧稍做停顿,焊枪沿坡口两侧做小幅度横向摆动,如图 3-3-5(a)所示,并控制电弧在离底边 2~3 mm 处燃烧,保持打底焊缝厚度不超过 4 mm,如图 3-3-5(b)所示。

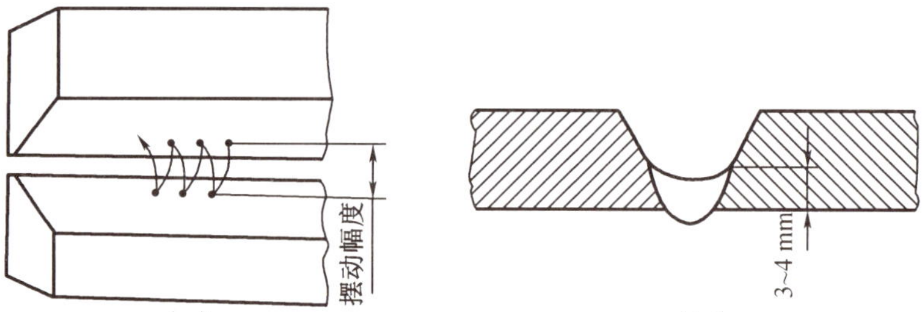

（a）　（b）

图 3-3-5　根部焊道轨迹及焊道大小示意图

④当坡口底部熔孔直径达 3~4 mm 时，转入正常焊接。尽可能维持熔孔直径不变，以获得宽窄和高低均匀的反面焊缝。焊接时要注意观察熔孔尺寸，熔孔直径应比坡口间隙大 0.5~1.0 mm。根据坡口间隙和熔孔直径的变化来调整焊枪横向摆动幅度和焊接速度。在打底焊时，应减小焊枪倾角，使电弧热量集中在焊丝上。采用较小的焊接电流，加快焊接速度和送丝速度，熔滴要小，以避免焊缝下凹和烧穿。

⑤打底焊时，采用较小的焊枪倾角和较小的焊接电流，而焊接速度和送丝速度应较快，以免使焊缝下凹和烧穿。焊丝填入动作要均匀、有规律，焊枪移动要平稳，速度要一致。焊接中应密切注意焊接熔池的变化，随时调节有关工艺参数，保证背面焊缝良好成形。当熔池增大、焊缝变宽并出现下凹时，说明熔池温度过高，此时应减小焊枪与焊件夹角，加快焊接速度。当熔池减小时，说明熔池温度低，应增加焊枪倾角，减慢焊接速度。

⑥接头。当焊丝用完需更换时，或因其他原因需要暂时中止焊接时，会有接头存在。接头前应先检查接头熄弧处弧坑质量，当保护较好，无氧化物等缺陷时，则可直接接头；当有缺陷时，则需将缺陷修磨掉，并使其前端成斜面。在焊缝中间停止焊接时，可松开焊枪上的开关，停止送丝。如果焊机有电流自动衰减装置，则应保持喷嘴高度不变，待电弧熄灭、熔池完全冷却后，再移开焊枪。如果焊机没有电流自动衰减装置，则在松开开关后稍抬高焊枪，待电弧熄灭、熔池冷却凝固到颜色变黑后再移开焊枪。接头时打开焊枪，在弧坑右侧 15~20 mm 处引弧，并慢慢向左移动，待弧坑处开始熔化并形成熔池和熔孔后，继续填丝焊接。

⑦收弧。如果焊机有电流自动衰减装置，则焊至焊件末端时，应减小焊枪与焊件间的夹角，让热量集中在焊丝上，加大焊丝熔化量，以填满弧坑，然后切断控制开关。这时焊接电流逐渐减小，熔池也不断缩小，焊丝回抽，但不要脱离氩气保护区。停弧后，氩气需延时 10 s 左右再关闭，以防熔池金属在高温下氧化。如果焊机没有电流自动衰减装置，则在收弧处要慢慢抬起焊枪，并减小焊枪倾角，加大焊丝的熔化量，待弧坑填满后再切断电流。

2. 填充焊

①焊接前，清理前道焊缝的焊渣和飞溅物。焊接填充层时的注意事项和步骤同打底焊。

②焊接时焊枪应横向摆动，一般做锯齿形摆动。焊枪的摆动幅度比打底焊时稍大，在坡口两侧稍停留，以保证坡口两侧熔合良好、焊道均匀。

③填充焊道应比焊件表面低 1~1.5 mm，不要熔化坡口的棱边。焊道如图 3-3-6 所示。

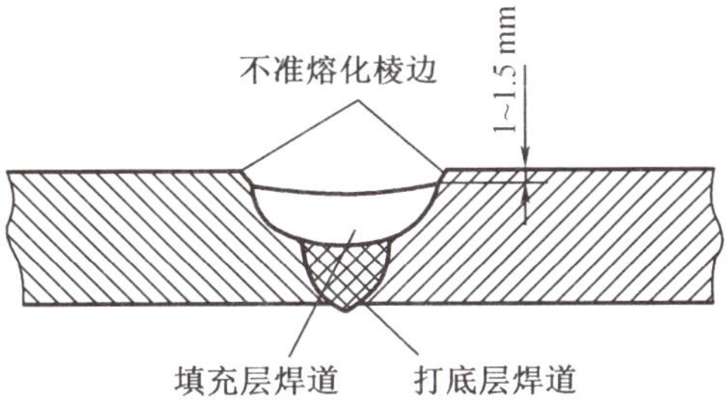

图 3-3-6　填充层焊道示意图

3. 盖面焊

①焊接前，清理前道焊缝的焊渣和喷嘴上的飞溅物。

②调节盖面层焊接工艺参数，从右端开始焊接。

③盖面焊时的焊枪角度、摆动方法与填充焊时相同，焊枪横向摆动幅度比填充焊时稍大，但要注意焊枪横向摆动幅度不宜过大，保证熔池两侧超过坡口棱边 0.5~1.5 mm 即可，否则易出现焊波粗大和咬边现象。尽量保持焊接速度均匀，避免盖面层焊道中间凹陷。焊枪在坡口两侧摆动应均匀、缓慢，以防止咬边。填丝速度与焊接速度决定了焊缝余高。

任务4：掌握板对接平焊钨极氩弧焊的焊后处理与检查

1. 焊缝清理

将焊好的焊件用钢丝刷反复刷擦，除去焊缝氧化层。焊缝应光滑、平整，应保证焊件的边齐、面平，包括焊件上开口边缘的垂直平行度，但不能破坏焊缝原始表面。

2. 焊缝质量检测

(1)焊缝外观检测

焊后对焊缝表面质量进行检测，肉眼观察或用低倍放大镜检查焊缝表面是否有气孔、裂纹、咬边等缺陷，用钢直尺、钢角尺、焊缝检验尺对焊缝进行外观质量和外观成形尺寸。常规具体检测项目及质量要求如表 3-3-2 所示。

表 3-3-2　焊缝目视检测的项目参考表

检测项目	检测部位	质量要求	备注
清理质量	所有焊缝及其两侧 25 mm 范围内	无阻碍检测的焊渣、飞溅及附着物	
几何形状	焊缝与母材的接头	焊缝接头完整且不得有漏焊，连接处应圆滑过渡	
	焊缝形状和尺寸急剧变化的部位	焊缝高低、宽窄及结晶焊缝波纹应均匀	可用焊接检测尺等测量
伤痕补焊	母材机械划伤部位	划伤部位不应有明显棱角和沟槽，伤痕深度不超过有关标准规定	

(2)焊缝检测常用评分标准

对焊件按规范进行焊后处理与检测评分，6 mm 厚板对接焊缝外观常用评分标准如表3-3-3所示，分值总分以60分计算，可以根据实际情况修改。内部质量检查参考模块二项目五。

表 3-3-3　板对接焊缝外观评分表

检查项目	评判标准及得分	评判等级				自测数据	自评分数	教师测量数据	教师评分	备注
		Ⅰ	Ⅱ	Ⅲ	Ⅳ					
焊缝余高	尺寸标准/mm	0~1	>1,≤2	>2,≤3	<0 或>3					
	得分	4	3	2	0					
焊缝高度差	尺寸标准/mm	0~1	>1,≤2	>2,≤3	>3					
	得分	8	4	2	0					
焊缝宽度	尺寸标准/mm	8~9	≥7,≤10	≥6,≤11	<6 或>11					
	得分	4	2	1	0					
焊缝宽度差	尺寸标准/mm	0~1	>1,≤2	>2,≤3	>3					
	得分	8	4	2	0					
咬边	尺寸标准/mm	无咬边	深度≤0.5		深度>0.5					
	得分	12	长度每 5 mm 扣 2 分		0					
正面成形	标准	优	良	中	差					
	得分	8	4	2	0					
背面成形	标准	优	良	中	差					
	得分	6	4	2	0					
背面凹度	尺寸标准/mm	0~0.5	>0.5,≤1	>1,≤2	长度>30					
	得分	2	1	0	0					
背面凸度	尺寸标准/mm	0~1	>1,≤2	>2						
	得分	2	1	0						
角变形	尺寸标准/mm	0~0.5	>0.5,≤1	>1						
	得分	4	2	0						
错边量	尺寸标准/mm	0~0.5	>0.5,≤1	>1						
	得分	2	1	0						
外观缺陷(裂纹、气孔、咬边、弧坑凹坑、夹渣、未熔合等)记录										

3. 工位工具清理点检与评分

参考模块二项目五。

完工后对工位按“6S”标准进行清理清扫整顿，并做好记录，按表 2-5-5 进行评分。

任务考核

1. 一般情况下，6 mm 厚工件板对接平焊钨极氩弧焊时应单边开（　　）V 形坡口。

A. 30°　　B. 45°　　C. 50°　　D. 60°

2. 板对接工件焊缝坡口处应进行打磨清理，清理范围一般为坡口面及坡口边缘上下两侧（　　）mm 范围。

A. 5～10　　B. 10～15　　C. 15～20　　D. 20～25

3. 6 mm 厚工件板对接平焊钨极氩弧焊时，坡口应打磨或加工（　　）mm 的钝边。

A. 0～0.5　　B. 0.5～1.0　　C. 1.0～1.5　　D. 1.5～2.0

4. 6 mm 厚工件板对接平焊钨极氩弧焊装配时，焊件始焊端和结束端的根部间隙常设置为（　　）mm。

A. 3.2、4.0　　B. 0、2.0　　C. 1.0、2.5　　D. 2.0、3.0

5. 钨极氩弧焊板对接平焊时，常采用（　　）焊法。

A. 左　　B. 右　　C. 前　　D. 后

6. 钨极氩弧焊板对接平焊打底层施焊时，焊枪与板件焊缝方向之间夹角可采用（　　）来摆动焊丝。

A. 45°～60°　　B. 50°～70°　　C. 70°～80°　　D. 80°～90°

7. 钨极氩弧焊板对接平焊打底层施焊时，焊丝与板件焊缝方向之间夹角可采用（　　）角度摆动焊丝。

A. 20°～30°　　B. 50°～70°　　C. 70°～80°　　D. 80°～90°

8. 利用钨极氩弧焊对低碳钢进行平焊，在填充层施焊时，保持焊道表面低于母材表面（　　）mm 左右，不能熔化坡口的棱边。

A. 1～1.5　　B. 1.5～2　　C. 2～2.5　　D. 2.5～3

9. 利用钨极氩弧焊对低碳钢进行平焊，在盖面层施焊时，焊丝摆动到坡口两侧时，焊丝对准坡口棱边，不要超过棱边，形成熔池后熔化棱边（　　）mm。

A. 0.5～1.5　　B. 0　　C. 1～2　　D. 0～1

10. 接头时打开焊枪在弧坑右侧（　　）mm 处引弧，并慢慢向左移动，待弧坑处开始熔化并形成熔池和熔孔后，继续填丝焊接。

A. 10～15　　B. 20～30　　C. 0　　D. 0～10

任务操作

按任务要求和流程顺序进行任务实施训练。焊后能够根据焊缝检查要求进行自检和进行工位工具整理。训练后进行考核，并按检测要求进行评分。

Project Ⅲ Flat TIG Welding for Board Butt Welding

【Learning Objectives】

1. Analyze the technical requirements of flat TIG welding for board butt welding;
2. Master the pre-welding preparation of flat TIG welding for board butt welding;
3. Master the welding operation of flat TIG welding for board butt welding;
4. Master the post-weld treatment and inspection of flat TIG welding for board butt welding.

Task 1: Analyze the Technical Requirements of Flat TIG Welding for Board Butt Welding

Fig. 3-3-1 shows the assembly drawing and technical requirements of common plate butt joint flat welding test pieces.

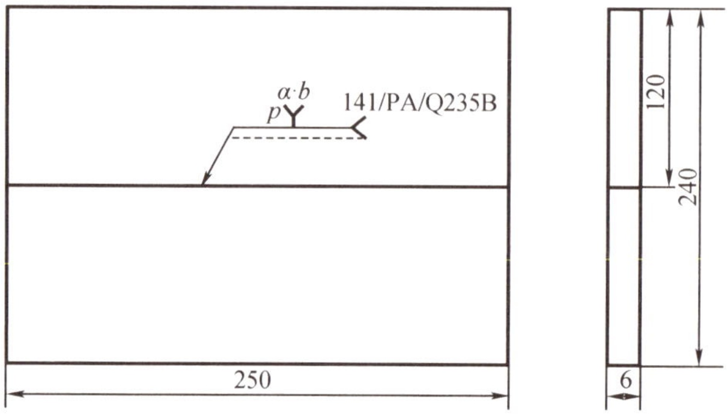

Technical requirements

1. Single-side welding double-side forming.
2. Groove: V-shape groove with a groove angle of 60° and a root face.
3. Self-determined root gap and root face size.
4. Misalignment ≤0.5 mm.
5. Angular deformation <3°.
6. Undercut is not allowed.
7. Incomplete penetration is not allowed.
8. Cracks, pores, and slag inclusion are not allowed.
9. Weld reinforcement ≤1+0.15*b*.

Figure 3-3-1 The Assembly Draming and Technical Requirements of Common Plate Butt Joint Flat Welding Test Pieces (Unit: mm)

The TIG method is an arc welding method that utilizes inert gas protection and a tungsten electrode as the electrode. Since argon is commonly used in China, it is often referred to as Tungsten Inert GasWelding (TIG for short). Helium is also commonly used in other countries. Here, TIG is used as an example for introduction. The principles and operation methods of other inert gases are similar. TIG is also known as non-consumable argon arc welding because the tungsten electrode itself does not melt and only emits electrons to generate an arc. During welding, the argon emitted from the nozzle forms a thick and dense gas protective layer to isolate the air. Surrounded by a laminar flow of argon, the arc burns between the tungsten electrode and the welding material. The heat generated by the arc melts the weld area and filling welding wire, connecting two separate metals to obtain a strong welded joint. Currently, it is mainly used for welding thin parts or as a backing welding technique for important products.

This project uses low carbon steel commonly used in practical engineering as an example to demonstrate the task implementation process of plate butt joint flat welding TIG method, including preparation before welding, welding operation, and post-weld treatment and inspection.

Task 2:Master the Pre-Welding Preparation of Flat TIG Welding for Board Butt Welding

1. Weldment preparation and groove cleaning

According to the task list requirements, two Q235B weldments with dimensions of 6 mm×120 mm×250 mm are prepared, with a 30° V-shaped groove opened on one side.

Before welding, the groove surface and the range of 15-20 mm on the upper and lower sides of the groove edge shall be polished and cleaned to expose metallic luster and polish a truncated edge of 0-0. 5 mm.

2. Determination of welding process parameters

Considering the welding characteristics and plate thickness of the base metal Q235B for this task, ER50-6 welding wire with a diameter of 2. 5 mm is selected (ensure the welding wire is clean. Before use, wipe off any oil, rust, or dirt on the welding wire using emery cloth and cotton yarn, and clean it with acetone if necessary). The protective gas used is argon with a purity higher than 99. 99%. Cerium tungsten electrode is used, and three layers and three beads are employed for welding. The specific welding process parameters are shown in Table 3-3-1.

Table 3-3-1 Welding process parameters

Welding layer	Welding wire type	Welding wire diameter/mm	Welding current/A	Welding voltage/V
Backing layer	ER50-6	2. 5	80-100	12-16
Filling layer			100-120	12-16
Covering layer			90-110	12-16

Welding layer	Shield gas flow rate /(L/min)	Tungsten electrode diameter (mm)	Extension length of tungsten electrode/mm	Power supply polarity
Backing layer	7-9	2. 5	3-6	DC straight polarity
Filling layer	7-9	2. 5	3-6	
Covering layer	7-9	2. 5	3-6	

3. Assembling and positioning

Place two steel plates horizontally on the tooling table, aligning both ends to form butt joints. Set the root gap at 2. 0 mm for the initial welding end and 3. 0 mm for the final end. Use the same process parameters for tack welding at both ends. The welding spot should be 10 – 15 mm in length and fully welded without defects. The misalignment should not exceed 0. 5 mm, with an anti–deformation allowance of 3° – 5°. After welding, grind the welding spot into a slope to achieve the joint, assembly, and welding spot as shown in Fig. 3–3–2.

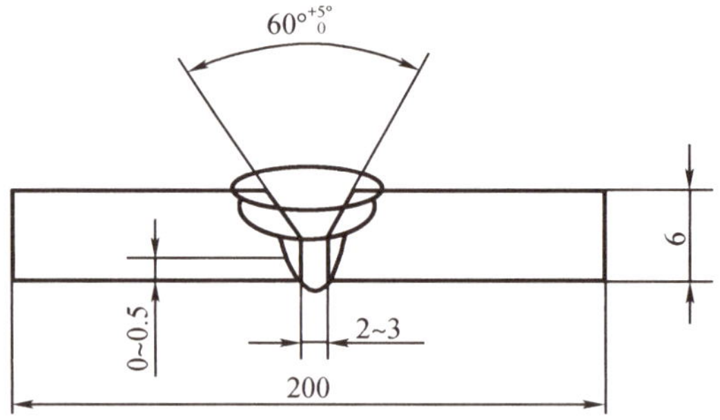

Fig. 3–3–2 Schematicdiagram of Assembly Positioning and Welding Spot(Unit:mm)

If the tack weld is defective, it must be ground off before re – welding. The re – melting method is not allowed to be used to deal with defects on the tack weld.

Task 3:Master the Welding Operation of Flat TIG Welding for Board Butt Welding

The holding method of the TIG torch is to grip the torch with the right hand, clamp the front part of the torch with the index finger and thumb, and the other three fingers can be used as the fulcrum of the workpiece . The index finger or middle finger can also be used as the fulcrum. Breathing should be even, and the torch should be held slightly firmly to maintain its stability and stabilize the welding arc. It is crucial that there is no short circuit formed by the tungsten electrode weldment or welding wire during welding.

Secure the weldment onto the operating table, clamp the weld horizontally with the groove surface facing upwards. The height of the weldment should be easy for the operator to operate. Place the end with a small gap on the right side and utilize the forehand welding. For 6 mm thick plates, it is commonly welded in three layers and three beads.

1. Backing welding

①The continuous wire filling method or intermittent wire filling method can be used during welding. During operation, hold the welding wire with your left hand as shown in Fig. 3–3–3(a), and hold the gun with your right hand as shown in Fig. 3–3–3(b).

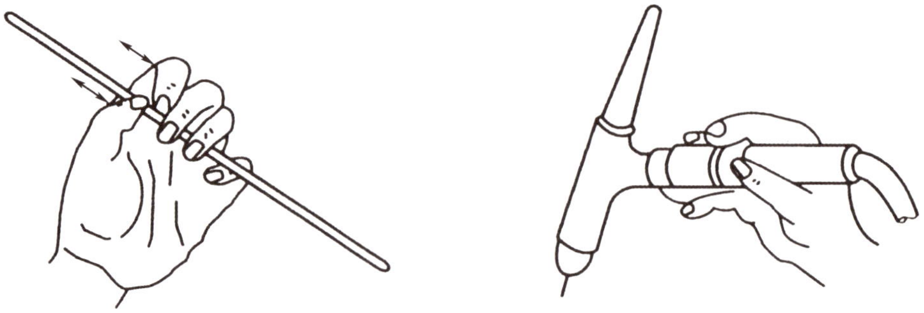

(a) (b)

Fig. 3–3–3 Method of Holding Welding Wire and Welding Gun by Hand during TIG

②The angle between the welding gun and the welding wire during flat welding is shown in Fig. 3-3-4.

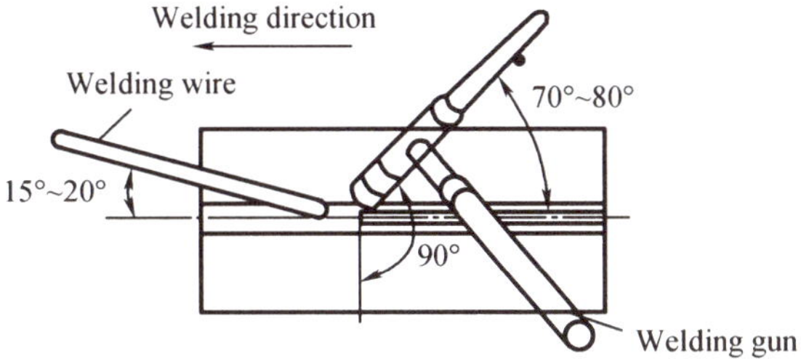

Fig. 3-3-4 Schematicdiagram of Arc Welding Gun and Welding Wire Angle during Flat Welding

③Strike the arc on the tack weld at the right end of the test piece and pause for preheating. When a molten pool is formed at the left end of the tack weld and a melting hole appears, start filling wire and carry out normal welding. Weld the backing layer bead from right to left, move the welding gun along the slope to the groove root, swing in a zigzag small range after reaching the groove root, and pause slightly on both sides of the groove. The welding gun makes small transverse swings along both sides of the groove, as shown in Fig. 3-3-5(a). The arc should be controlled to burn at a distance of 2-3 mm from the bottom edge, so that the thickness of the backing weld is kept not more than 4mm, as shown in Fig. 3-3-5(b).

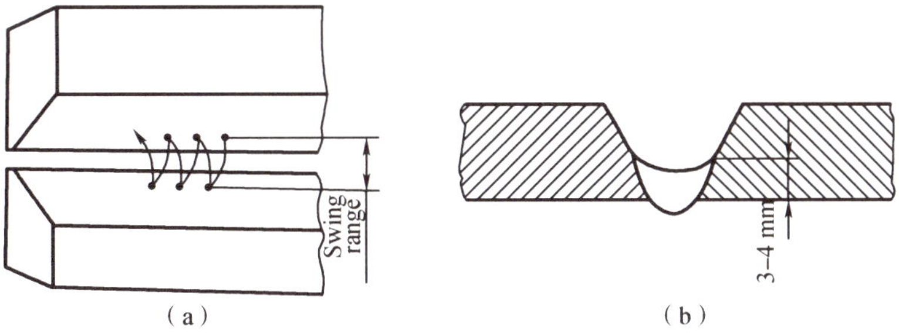

Figure 3-3-5 Schematicdiagram of Root Bead Track and Size

④When the diameter of the weld hole at the bottom of the groove reaches 3-4 mm, normal welding shall be carried out. The diameter of the melt hole should remain as constant as possible to achieve a reverse weld with uniform width and height. During welding, pay attention to observing the size of the melt hole, which should be 0.5-1.0 mm larger than the groove gap. Adjust the transverse swing amplitude and welding speed of the arc welding gun according to the changes in groove gap and melt hole diameter. During backing welding, reduce the inclination angle of the arc welding gun to concentrate the arc heat on the welding wire. Use a lower welding current to accelerate the welding speed and wire feeding speed. The molten droplets should be small to avoid concave and burn-through welds.

⑤During backing welding, use a smaller inclination angle and lower welding current for the welding gun, while increasing welding speed and wire feeding speed to avoid concave and burn-through welds. Ensure that the filling of welding wire is uniform and regular, and that the welding gun moves smoothly at a consistent speed. Pay close attention to the changes in the molten pool during welding, and adjust the relevant process parameters as necessary to ensure a good formation of the back weld. If the molten pool becomes larger, and the weld widens and sinks, it indicates that the temperature of the molten pool is too high. In this case, reduce the included angle between the welding gun and the weldment to speed up welding. If the molten pool decreases, it indicates that the temperature of the molten pool is low, and the inclination angle of the welding gun should be increased to slow down welding.

⑥Joint. When the welding wire is used up and needs to be replaced, or when it is necessary to temporarily suspend welding for other reasons, there will be a joint. Before joining, the quality of the arc extinguishing crater at the joint should be checked first. If the protection is good and there are no defects such as oxides, the joint can be made directly. If there are defects, they need to be grinded off and their front ends should be inclined. When welding is stopped in the middle of the weld, release the switch on the welding gun to stop wire feeding. If the welding machine has an automatic current attenuation device, keep the nozzle height unchanged. After the arc is extinguished and the molten pool is completely cooled, remove the welding gun. If the welding machine does not have an automatic current attenuation device, release the switch to slightly raise the welding gun, and then remove it after the arc is extinguished and the molten pool is cooled and solidified to a black color. During joining, open the welding gun to strike the arc at 15–20 mm on the right side of the arc crater and slowly move to the left. After the arc crater begins to melt and forms a molten pool and hole, continue filling wire welding.

⑦Arcending. If the welding machine is equipped with an automatic current attenuation device, when welding reaches the end of the weldment, the angle between the welding gun and the weldment should be reduced. This will concentrate the heat on the welding wire, increase the amount of welding wire melted to fill the arc crater, and then cut off the control switch. At this point, the welding current gradually decreases and the molten pool continuously shrinks. The welding wire is pulled back but remains within the argon protection area. After arc termination, the argon gas should be delayed for approximately 10 s before being turned off to prevent oxidation of the metal in the molten pool at high temperatures. If the welding machine does not have an automatic current attenuation device, slowly raise the welding gun at the arc ending point, reduce the inclination angle of the welding gun, increase the amount of welding wire melted, and cut off the current after the arc crater is filled.

2. Filling welding

①Before welding, clean the welding slag and spatter from the previous weld. The precautions and steps for welding the filling layer are the same as those for backing welding.

②During welding, the welding gun should swing horizontally, usually in a zigzag motion. The swing amplitude of the welding gun is slightly larger than that during backing welding, and stay on both sides of the groove for a while to ensure good fusion and a uniform bead on both sides of the groove.

③The filling layer bead should be 1–1.5 mm lower than the surface of the welded part, do not melt the edge of the groove. The bead is shown in Fig. 3-3-6.

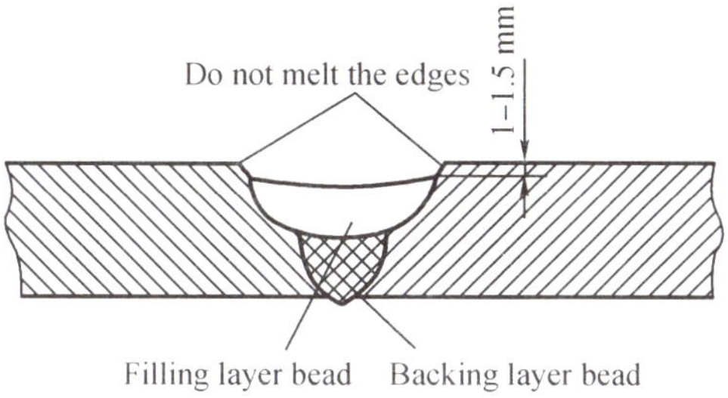

Fig. 3-3-6 Schematicdiagram of Filling Layer Bead

3. Covering welding

①Before welding, clean the welding slag and splashes on the previous weld and nozzle.

②Adjust the welding process parameters for the covering layer and start welding from the right end.

③The angle and swing method of the arc welding gun forcovering welding are the same as those for fill welding. The transverse swing amplitude of the arc welding gun should be slightly larger than that for fill welding, but it should not be too large. This ensures that both sides of the molten pool exceed the groove edge by 0.5–1.5 mm. Otherwise, rough weld waves and undercuts may occur easily. Maintain a uniform welding speed to avoid sagging in the middle of the covering layer bead. The arc welding gun should swing evenly and slowly on both sides of the groove to prevent undercutting. The wire filling speed and welding speed will determine the reinforcement of the weld.

Task 4:Master the Post-Weld Treatment and Inspection of Flat TIG Welding for Board Butt Welding

1. Weld cleaning

Repetitively brush the welded weldment using a wire brush, to remove the oxide layer from the weld. The weld should be smooth and even, ensuring the weldment has a flush edge and plane, including maintaining the vertical parallelism of the upper opening edge, without damaging the original surface of the weld.

2. Weld quality inspection

(1) Weld appearance inspection

After the welding process, the surface quality of the welds should be inspected. The weld surface should be visually examined or checked with low-power magnifying glasses to identify any defects such as pores, cracks, and undercut. The appearance quality and dimensional conformity of the welds should be checked using steel rulers, steel squares, and weld inspection rules. Refer to Table 3-3-2 for specific routine test items and quality requirements.

Table 3-3-2 Reference Table for Visual Inspection Items of Welds

Test item	Tested site	Quality requirement	Remarks
Cleaning quality	All welds and areas within 25 mm on both sides	No welding slag, splashes, and attachments that hinder inspection	
Geometry	Joint between weld and base metal	The weld joint shall be complete without any missed soldering, and the connection shall be smooth	
	Parts with sharp changes in weld shape and size	The weld height, width, and ripple of the crystalline weld should be uniform	A welding inspection ruler can be used for measurement
Scar repair welding	The scratched area of the base metal due to mechanical causes	The damaged part should not have obvious edges and grooves, and the depth of the scar should not exceed the relevant standards	

(2) Common scoring criteria for weld inspection

Post-weld treatment and testing scoring shall be carried out for weldments according to the specifications. The common scoring criteria for the appearance of butt welds of 6mm thick plates are shown in Table 3-3-3, and the total score is calculated as 60 points, which can be modified according to actual conditions. Refer to Project 5 of Module 2 for internal quality inspection.

3. Workstation tool cleaning inspection and scoring

Refer to Project Ⅴ of Module Ⅱ.

After completion, clean and tidy up the workstations according to the "6S" standard, make records, and score according to Table 2-5-5.

Table 3-3-3 Scoring for Appearance of Plate Butt Weldmm

Inspection items	Evaluation Standards and score	Evaluation grade				Self-test data	Self-assessment score	Teacher's measurement data	Teacher's evaluation score	Remarks
		Ⅰ	Ⅱ	Ⅲ	Ⅳ					
Weld height excess	Size standard/mm	0~1	>1, ≤2	>2, ≤3	<0 or >3					
	Score	4	3	2	0					
Difference in weld height	Size standard/mm	0~1	>1, ≤2	>2, ≤3	>3					
	Score	8	4	2	0					
Weld width	Size standard/mm	8~9	≥7, ≤10	≥6, ≤11	<6 or >11					
	Score	4	2	1	0					
Difference in weld width	Size standard/mm	0~1	>1, ≤2	>2, ≤3	>3					
	Score	8	4	2	0					
Undercut	Size standard/mm	No undercut	Depth≤0.5	Depth>0.5						
	Score	12	Deduct 2 points for every 5 mm in length		0					
Front forming	Standards	Excellent	Good	Average	Bad					
	Score	8	4	2	0					
Back forming	Standards	Excellent	Good	Average	Bad					
	Score	6	4	2	0					
Back concavity	Size standard/mm	0-0.5	>0.5, ≤1	>1, ≤2	Depth>30					
	Score	2	1	0	0					
Back convexity	Size standard/mm	0-1	>1, ≤2	>2						
	Score	2	1	0						

Table 3-3-3(Continued)

Inspection items	Evaluation Standards and score	Evaluation grade				Self-test data	Self-assessment score	Teacher's measurement data	Teacher's evaluation score	Remarks
		I	II	III	IV					
Angular distortion	Size standard/mm	0-0.5	>0.5, ≤1	>1						
	Score	4	2	0						
Incorrect edge measurement	Size standard/mm	0-0.5	>0.5, ≤1	>1						
	Score	2	1	0						
Appearance defects (such as cracks, porosity, edge biting, arc pits, slag inclusions, incomplete fusion, and other defects) defect records.										

Task Assessment

1. Generally, a ( ) V-shaped groove should be opened on one side during flat TIG welding for board butt welding of a 6 mm thick workpiece.

A. 30° B. 45° C. 50° D. 60°

2. The weld groove of the plate butt joint workpiece should be polished and cleaned, with a cleaning range generally of ( ) mm on both sides of the groove surface and edge.

A. 5-10 B. 10-15 C. 15-20 D. 20-25

3. For flat TIG welding for board butt welding of a 6 mm thick workpiece, the groove should be polished or processed with a ( ) mm root face.

A. 0-0.5 B. 0.5-1.0 C. 1.0-1.5 D. 1.5-2.0

4. When assembling a 6 mm thick workpiece using flat TIG welding for board butt wedling, the root gap between the starting and ending ends of the weldment is often set to ( ) mm.

A. 3.2,4.0 B. 0,2.0 C. 1.0,2.5 D. 2.0,3.0

5. The ( ) welding method is often used during flat TIG welding for board butt wedling.

A. forehand B. backhand C. front D. rear

6. When conducting backing welding usingplate butt joint flat welding TIG, the included angle between the welding gun and the direction of the plate weld can adopt ( ) to swing the welding wire.

A. 45°-60° B. 50°-70° C. 70°-80° D. 80°-90°

7. When conducting backing welding using flat TIG welding for board butt wedling, the included angle between the welding wire and the direction of the plate weld can adopt ( ) to swing the welding wire.

A. 20°-30° B. 50°-70° C. 70°-80° D. 80°-90°

8. TIG is used for flat welding of low carbon steel. When welding the filling layer, keep the bead surface approximately ( ) mm lower than the base metal surface, and do not melt the edge of the groove.

A. 1-1.5 B. 1.5-2 C. 2-2.5 D. 2.5-3

9. TIG is used for flat welding of low carbon steel. When welding on the covering layer, ensure that the welding wire aligns with the edge of the groove without exceeding it, when swinging to both sides of the groove. After forming a molten pool, melt the edge by ( ) mm.

A. 0.5-1.5 B. 0 C. 1-2 D. 0-1

10. During jointing, open the welding gun and strike the arc at ( ) mm to the right of the arc crater, slowly moving to the left. After the arc crater starts to melt and form a molten pool and hole, continue filling wire welding.

A. 10-15 B. 20-30 C. 0 D. 0-10

Task Operation

Carry out task implementation training according to task requirements and process sequence. After welding, carry out self-inspection and sort out station tools according to weld inspection requirements. After training, conduct assessment and score according to testing requirements.

项目四　板对接立焊钨极氩弧焊

【学习目标】

1. 分析板对接立焊钨极氩弧焊的技术要求；
2. 掌握板对接立焊钨极氩弧焊的焊前准备；
3. 掌握板对接立焊钨极氩弧焊的焊接操作；
4. 掌握板对接立焊钨极氩弧焊的焊后处理与检查。

任务1：分析板对接立焊钨极氩弧焊的技术要求

图 3-4-1 为常见板对接立焊试件装配图及技术要求。

钨极氩弧焊多用在薄板焊接或者厚板打底焊中，板对接立焊是焊接结构成形过程中经常遇到的焊接位置，操作比平焊难得多，主要特点是熔池金属容易向下坠，焊缝成形不平整，焊枪角度不稳定引起电弧方向变化造成咬边。除了具有平焊的操作技能外，还应选用较细的焊丝、较小的焊接电流，随时调整焊枪角度来控制熔池的凝固。立焊分从下向上和从上向下两种方法，从下向上焊容易保证焊透，氩弧焊很少采用从上向下立焊方法。

本项目以实际工程中常用的 06Cr19Ni10 不锈钢材质为例介绍板对接立焊钨极氩弧焊的焊前准备、焊接操作和焊后处理与检查等任务实施流程。

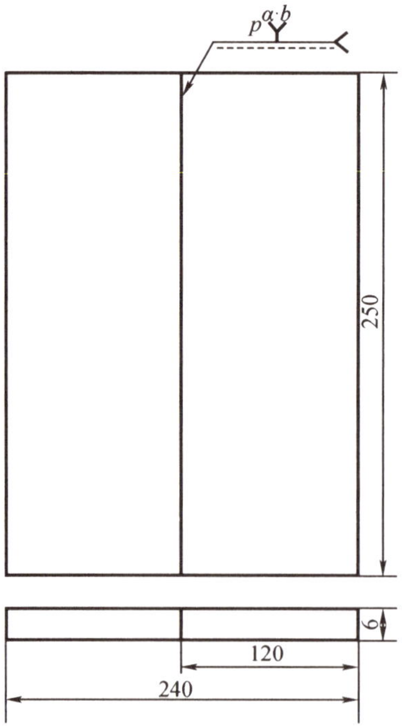

技术要求

1. 单面焊双面成形。
2. 坡口为 60°。
3. 根部间隙和钝边尺寸自定。
4. 错边≤0.5 mm。
5. 角变形<3°。
6. 不允许有咬边。
7. 不允许有未焊透。
8. 不允许有裂纹、气孔、夹渣。
9. 焊缝余高≤1+0.15b。

图 3-4-1　常见板对接立焊试件装配图及技术要求（单位：mm）

任务2：掌握板对接立焊钨极氩弧焊的焊前准备

1. 焊件准备及坡口清理

按任务单要求，准备 6 mm×120 mm×300 mm 尺寸的 06Cr19Ni10 不锈钢板材质焊件两块，单边开 30°的 V 形坡口。

焊前打磨清理坡口面及坡口边缘上下两侧 15~20 mm 范围，露出金属光泽，再用丙酮清洗。由于在手工钨极氩弧焊焊接过程中惰性气体仅起保护作用，无冶金反应，因此坡口的清洗质量直接影响焊缝的质量，并打磨出 0~0.5 mm 的钝边。

2. 焊接工艺参数确定

结合本任务母材 06Cr19Ni10 的焊接特性和板厚来看，选择直径 2.5 mm 的 ER308 焊丝（注意保持焊丝的干净，使用前可用砂布及棉纱擦净焊丝上的油、锈等污物，必要时还可用丙酮清洗），保护气体为氩气，纯度高于 99.99%，电极采用铈钨极，采用三层三道来焊接，具体焊接工艺参数如表 3-4-1 所示。

表 3-4-1　焊接工艺参数表

焊接层次	焊丝型号	焊丝直径/mm	焊接电流/A	焊接电压/V	保护气体流量/(L/min)	钨极直径/mm	钨极伸出长度/mm	电源极性
打底层	ER308	2.5	80~90	12~16	7~9	2.5	3~6	直流正接
填充层			90~100	12~16	7~9	2.5	3~6	
盖面层			90~100	12~16	7~9	2.5	3~6	

3. 装配定位

将两块钢板水平放工装台上，两端对齐装配成对接接头，装配时焊件始焊端根部间隙设置为 2.0 mm，结束端为 3.0 mm，采取和打底相同的工艺参数在两端进行点固焊，焊点长度为 10~15 mm，必须焊透，不允许有缺陷，错边量不大于 0.5 mm，反变形预留量为 3°~5°，焊后应把焊点打磨成斜坡，以便接头。装配示意图如图 3-4-2 所示。

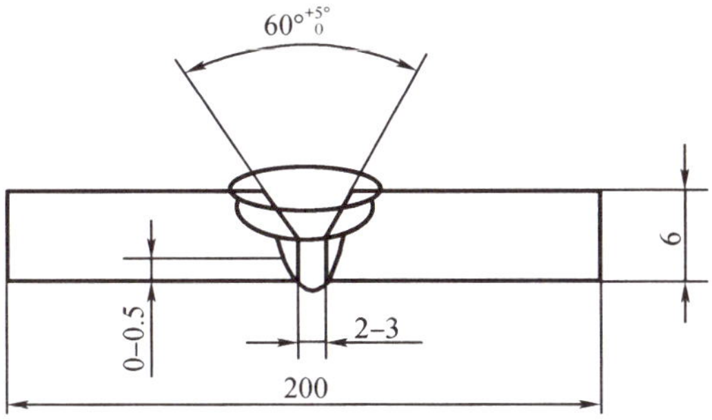

图 3-4-2　板对接装配定位示意图（单位：mm）

如定位焊缝有缺陷，必须将有缺陷的定位焊缝磨掉后重焊，不允许用重熔的办法来处理定位焊缝上的缺陷。

任务3：掌握板对接立焊钨极氩弧焊的焊接操作

钨极氩弧焊操作特点是：无论什么位置焊接时，焊枪角度、电弧长度、焊接速度、送入焊丝的位置和角度都是操作技术的基本要领。焊枪角度是控制熔池形状、熔深和熔宽的关键。电弧太短影响熔深和表面成形，电弧太长会造成焊道中间高和两侧咬边（平焊除外）。送入焊丝的位置及角度正确与否直接影响焊道表面成形和焊接能否顺利进行。

将焊件固定在操作台上，焊缝垂直装夹，坡口面朝向操作者，焊件高度适合操作者操作舒服的位置，间隙小的一端放在下端，采取立向上焊法进行焊接，6 mm 厚板件的焊接层次常采用三层三道。

1. 打底焊

立焊打底层焊接比平焊电流要小一点，以减小熔池，有利于焊缝成形。

①焊枪、焊丝位置及运动如图 3-4-3 所示，焊枪向下倾斜 10°～20°，以借助电弧向上的吹力来阻挡熔池金属下淌。焊丝与坡口中心线夹角为 20°～30°（即与板件焊缝方向 70°～80°），填丝位置在熔池的上边缘，并做锯齿形或反月牙形摆动，熔化的铁水缓慢向下流淌，有助于焊缝成形。若在熔池下部填丝，则熔池金属容易流到焊缝之外形成焊瘤。

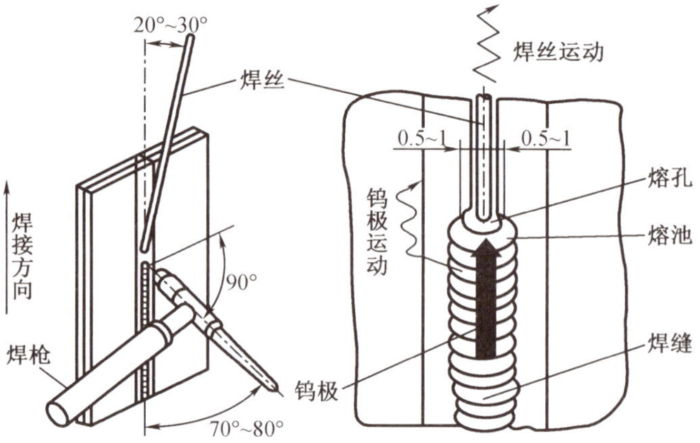

图 3-4-3　焊枪、焊丝位置、角度及运动示意图

向上立焊采用左焊法。操作时以肘关节为支点，以大臂带小臂，腕关节作小幅度左右摆动，弧长为 2～3 mm。

②引弧。为了确保熔池保护作用良好，引弧前应提前送气 5～10 s，然后将焊枪以 45°斜靠在坡口内，使钨极端部离母材表面 2～3 mm 进行引弧。引弧后先对焊缝位置进行预热，带板件达到熔融状态时就可以开始正式打底焊接。

③焊接。引弧后焊枪稍作摆动并向后倾斜 10°～20°，待熔池形成后逐渐前移至预先打磨好的斜坡处，待熔池形成并出现熔孔，两侧钝边各熔入 0.5～1 mm 时开始填丝向上焊接。焊枪做上反月牙形摆动，在坡口两侧稍做停顿，两侧停顿时间与摆动时间大致各占 1/3，以保证两侧熔化良好。

④焊接时注意，焊枪向上移动的速度要合适，控制好熔池的形状，熔池的下沿近似为椭圆形，不能向下凸出，否则成形不良。尽可能让已冷凝的焊道托住熔池，使熔池表面近似一个水平面匀速上升，以使焊缝外观平整。

⑤焊接中随时注意观察熔孔的形状和大小，发现熔孔不明显，应停止填丝，否则容易产生未焊透；若熔孔过大，熔池会向下坠，使焊缝背面形成焊瘤。为了保证焊缝背面成形饱满又不超高，焊丝贴着坡口根部均匀而有节奏地送进，当焊丝端部进入熔池熔化时轻轻挑向坡口根部。抽回焊丝准备下次送进，直至焊完打底层。焊丝与焊枪的动作要配合协调，同步移动，当间隙小时可同步直线上移；当间隙大时可做同步小幅度摆动匀速上移。

⑥接头。当焊丝用完需更换时，或因其他原因需要暂时中止焊接时，会有接头存在。接头前应先检查接头熄弧处弧坑质量，当保护较好，无氧化物等缺陷时，则可直接接头；当有缺陷时，则需将缺陷修磨掉，并使其前端成斜面，在弧坑前 5 ~ 10 mm 处引燃电弧引弧操作。

⑦收弧时要防止弧坑产生裂纹和缩孔，可利用电流衰减功能，逐渐降低熔池温度，同时延长氩气对弧坑的保护作用，直至熔池冷却。

2. 填充焊

①焊接前，清理前道焊缝的焊渣和飞溅物，焊接填充层时的注意事项和步骤同打底焊。

②与打底层相比电流稍大，焊枪、焊丝与焊件间夹角和打底层相同。

③焊接时，焊丝端头轻擦打底层焊缝表面，均匀规律地向熔池送进。由于填充层焊缝变宽，焊枪做锯齿形摆动，在两侧稍做停顿，以便熔化良好，且保持焊道表面低于母材表面 0.5 ~ 1 mm，不能熔化坡口的棱边，否则在盖面层焊接时将失去基准线，焊不出平直的面层焊道。

④接头应与底层接头错开 50 mm 以上，接头时在弧坑前 5 ~ 10 mm 处引燃电弧，焊枪做窄幅横向摆动，移至弧坑处时稍加焊丝使接头平整，转入正常焊接。

3. 盖面焊

①盖面层焊接焊枪摆幅稍大，其余与填充层相同。

②焊枪摆幅增大，在坡口棱边处稍做停顿，待棱边处熔化 0.5 ~ 1 mm，短弧施焊以免咬边，根据焊缝余高确定焊丝送进速度，保证两侧熔合良好圆滑过渡。其余与填充层相同。

任务4：掌握板对接立焊钨极氩弧焊的焊后处理与检查

同项目三。

任务考核

1. 一般情况下，6 mm 厚工件板对接立焊钨极氩弧焊时应单边开（　　）V 形坡口。

A. 30°　　B. 45°　　C. 50°　　D. 60°

2. 钨极氩弧焊板对接立焊时，常采用（　　）焊法。

A. 左　　B. 右　　C. 向上　　D. 向下

3. 钨极氩弧焊板对接立焊装配时焊件始焊端根部间隙设置为 2.0 mm，结束端为 3.0 mm，组合板件上架固定时，坡口面应朝向施焊者，间隙小的一端放（　　）面。

A. 左　　B. 右　　C. 上　　D. 下

4. 钨极氩弧焊板对接立焊打底层施焊时，焊枪应向下倾斜（　　），以借助电弧向上的吹力来阻挡熔池金属下淌。

A. 10° ~ 20°　　B. 30° ~ 40°　　C. 70° ~ 80°　　D. 80° ~ 90°

5. 钨极氩弧焊板对接立焊打底层施焊时，焊丝与板件焊缝方向之间夹角可采用（　　）

角度摆动焊丝，填丝位置在熔池的上边缘，熔化的铁水缓慢向下流淌，有助于焊缝成形。

A. 20°～30°　　B. 50°～70°　　C. 70°～80°　　D. 80°～90°

6. 钨极氩弧焊板对接立焊打底层施焊时，引弧前应提前送气(　　)s，然后将焊枪以45°位置斜靠在坡口内，使钨极端部离母材表面 2～3 mm 进行引弧。

A. 1～2　　B. 5～10　　C. 10～20　　D. 30～40

7. 钨极氩弧焊板对接立焊打底层施焊时，焊枪作(　　)形摆动，在坡口两侧稍作停顿，两侧停顿时间与摆动时间大致各占 1/3，以保证两侧熔化良好。

A. 上正月牙　　B. 上反月牙　　C. 下反月牙　　D. 下正月牙

8. 钨极氩弧焊板对接立焊在填充焊时，保持焊道表面低于母材表面(　　)mm 左右，不能熔化坡口的棱边。

A. 1～1.5　　B. 1.5～2　　C. 2～2.5　　D. 0.5～1

9. 钨极氩弧焊板对接立焊盖面焊时，焊丝摆动到坡口两侧时，焊丝对准坡口棱边，不要超过棱边，形成熔池后熔化棱边(　　)mm。

A. 1～1.5　　B. 0　　C. 1～2　　D. 0.5～1

10. 钨极氩弧焊板对接立焊过程中接头应与前一层的接头错开 50 mm 以上，接头时在弧坑前(　　)mm 处引燃电弧，焊枪作窄幅横向摆动，移至弧坑处时稍加焊丝使接头平整，转入正常焊接。

A. 10～15　　B. 20～30　　C. 0　　D. 5～10

任务操作

按任务要求和流程顺序进行任务实施训练，焊后能够根据焊缝检查要求进行自检和进行工位工具整理，训练后进行考核，并按检测要求进行评分。

Project Ⅳ Vertical TIG Welding for Board Butt Welding

【Learning Objectives】

1. Analyze the technical requirements of vertical TIG welding for board butt welding;
2. Master the pre-welding preparation of board butt welding with vertical TIG welding;
3. Master the welding operation of board butt welding with vertical TIG welding;
4. Master the post-weld treatment and inspection of board butt welding with vertical TIG welding.

Task 1:Analyze the Technical Requirements of Vertical TIG Welding for Board Butt Welding

Fig. 3-4-1 depicts the assembly diagram and technical requirements of common plate buttjoint vertical welding test pieces.

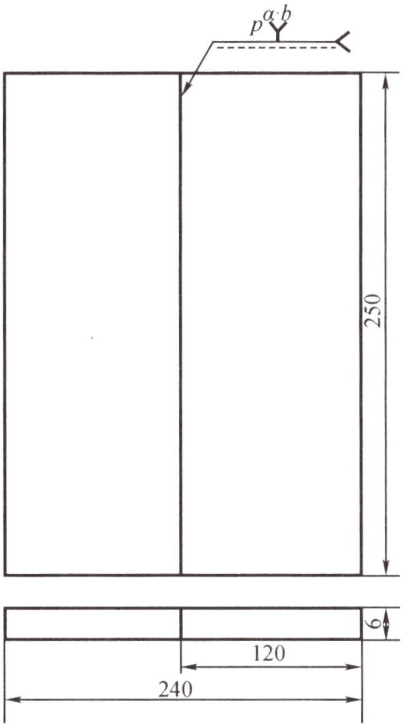

Technical requirements

1. Single - side welding double - side forming.
2. Groove with a groove angle of 60°.
3. Self-determined root gap and root face size.
4. Misalignment ≤0.5 mm.
5. Angular deformation <3°.
6. Undercut is not allowed.
7. Incomplete penetration is not allowed.
8. Cracks, pores, and slag inclusion are not allowed.
9. Weld reinforcement $\leq 1+0.15b$.

Fig. 3-4-1 The Assembly Diagram and Technical Requirements of Common Plate Butt Joint Vertical Welding Test Piecws(Unit:mm)

TIG is mainly used for thin plate welding or thick plate backing welding. Plate butt joint vertical welding is a common welding position in the forming process of a welded structure, and it is much more difficult to operate than flat welding. Its main characteristics include the tendency of the molten pool metal to fall down, uneven weld formation, and undercut caused by the unstable angle of the welding gun leading to changes in the arc direction. In addition to the skills required for flat welding, thinner welding wires and smaller welding currents should be selected. The angle of the welding gun should be adjusted at any time to control the solidification of the molten pool. Vertical welding can be performed using two methods: bottom-up and top-down. Bottom-up welding is easier to ensure penetration, while top-down vertical welding is rarely used in argon arc welding.

In this project, we take 06Cr19Ni10 stainless steel commonly used in practical projects as an example to introduce the task implementation process of plate butt joint vertical welding TIG, including preparation before welding, welding operation, and post-weld treatment and inspection procedures.

Task 2:Master the Pre-Welding Preparation of Board Butt Welding with Vertical TIG Welding

1. Weldment preparation and groove cleaning

Prepare two weldments made of 06Cr19Ni10 stainless steel plate with dimensions of 6 mm× 120 mm×300 mm, according to the requirements of the task list, and open a 30° V-shaped groove on one side.

Before welding, polish and clean the groove surface and the range of 15-20 mm on the upper and lower sides of the groove edge to expose metallic luster, and then clean with acetone. Since the inert gas only serves a protective role and has no metallurgical reaction during manualTIG, the cleanliness of the groove directly affects the welding quality, and a root face of 0-0.5 mm should be ground.

2. Determination of welding process parameters

Combining the welding characteristics and plate thickness of the base metal 06Cr19Ni10 in this task, a 2.5 mm diameter ER308 welding wire is selected (ensure the welding wire remains clean; before use, wipe off any oil, rust, or other dirt on the welding wire with emery cloth and cotton yarn, and if necessary, clean with acetone). The protective gas used is argon with a purity higher than 99.99%. A cerium tungsten electrode is adopted, and three layers with threebeads are used for welding. The specific welding process parameters are shown in Table 3-4-1.

Table 3-4-1 Welding Process Parameters

Welding layer	Welding wire type	Wire diameter /mm	Welding current/A	Welding voltage/V
Backing layer	ER308	2.5	80-100	12-16
Filling layer			90-100	12-16
Covering layer			90-100	12-16

Table 3-4-1(Continued)

Welding layer	Shield gas flow rate/(L/min)	Tungsten electrode diameter/mm	Extension length of tungsten electrode/mm	Power supply polarity
Backing layer	7-9	2.5	3-6	
Filling layer	7-9	2.5	3-6	
Covering layer	7-9	2.5	3-6	

3. Assembly and positioning

Place two steel plates horizontally on the tooling table and align both ends to assemble them into butt joints. Set the root gap at the initial welding end of the weldment as 2.0 mm and that at the final end as 3.0 mm. Use the same process parameters as backing for tack welding at both ends. The length of the welding spot should be 10-15 mm, fully welded without defects, with misalignment not exceeding 0.5 mm and an anti-deformation allowance of 3°-5°. After welding, polish the welding spot into a slope for easier connection. The assembly diagram is shown in Fig. 3-4-2.

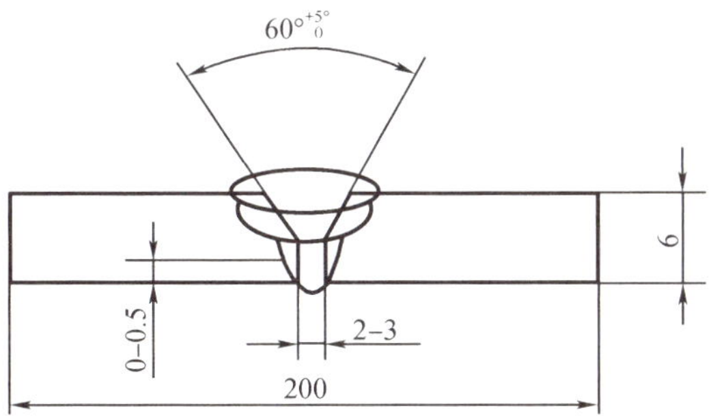

Fig. 3-4-2 Schematicdiagram of Plate Joint Assembly and Positioning(Unit: mm)

If the tack weld is defective, it must be ground off before re-welding. The remelting method is not allowed for dealing with defects on the tack weld.

Task 3: Master the Welding Operation of Board Butt Welding with Vertical TIG Welding

The operation characteristics ofTIG are as follows: Regardless of the welding position, the angle of the welding gun, the length of the electric arc, the welding speed, and the position and angle of wire feeding are all essential aspects of the operation technique. The angle of the welding gun is crucial in controlling the shape, penetration, and width of the molten pool. A too short arc will affect penetration and surface formation, while a too long arc will result in a high middle part of the bead and undercut on both sides (except for flat welding). The correct position and angle of wire feeding directly impact the formation of the bead surface and the smooth progression of the welding process.

Fix the weldment on the operating platform with the weld seam vertically clamped and the groove surface facing the operator. The height of the weldment should be suitable for the operator's comfortable operation position, and the end with a small gap should be placed at the lower end. Vertical upward welding method is adopted for welding. The welding layer of a 6 mm thick plate usually consists of three layers and three beads.

1. Backing welding

The current for backing welding in vertical welding is slightly smaller than that in flat welding to reduce the size of the molten pool and facilitate weld formation.

①The position and movement of the welding gun and welding wire are shown in Fig. 3-4-3. The welding gun is tilted downward by 10° to 20° to prevent the molten pool metal from flowing down with the upward blowing force of the arc. The angle between the welding wire and the center line of the groove is 20° to 30° (i. e. 70° to 80° in the direction of the plate weld). The filling wire is located at the upper edge of the molten pool and swings in a zigzag or reverse-crescent shape to facilitate the slow downward flow of molten iron, helping to form the weld. If the wire is filled in the lower part of the molten pool, the molten metal will easily flow outside the weld and form an overlap.

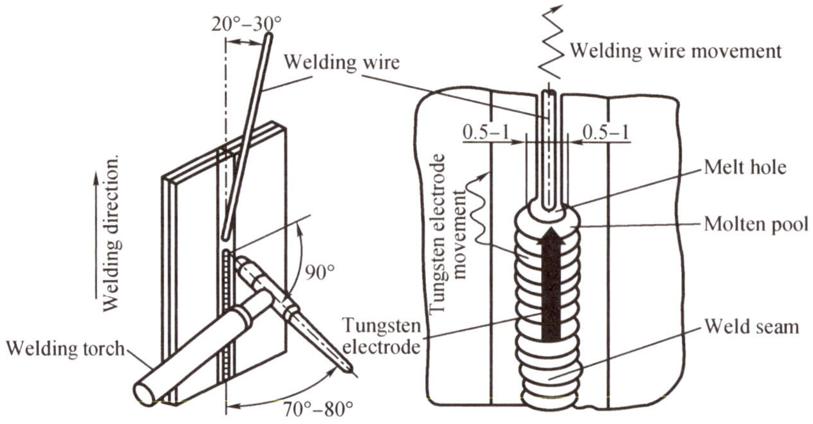

Fig. 3-4-3 Schematicdiagram of Position, Angle, and Movement of Welding Gun and Welding Wire (Unit: mm)

The left welding method should be used for vertical upward welding. During operation, the elbow joint acts as the fulcrum, the upper arm moves with the forearm, and the wrist joint swings left and right within a small range, with an arc length of 2-3 mm.

②Arc strike. To ensure good protection of the molten pool, gas should be supplied for 5-10 seconds before arc strike. Then, lean the welding gun against the groove at a 45° angle so that the tungsten electrode's tip is 2-3 mm away from the surface of the base metal for arc strike. After arc strike, preheat the weld position first, and start the formal backing welding when the strip plate reaches a molten state.

③Welding. Afterarc strike, the welding gun swings slightly and tilts backward by 10°-20°. Once the molten pool is formed, it gradually moves forward to the pre-polished slope. When the molten pool is formed and melt holes appear, fuse 0.5−1 mm of root faces on both sides and start filling wire upward welding. The welding gun swings in an upper reverse-crescent shape and pauses slightly on both sides of the groove. The pause time and swinging time on both sides account for roughly 1/3 respectively to ensure good melting on both sides.

④During welding, pay attention to the appropriate upward movement speed of the welding gun, and control the shape of the molten pool. The lower edge of the molten pool is approximately oval and should not protrude downwards; otherwise, the formation will be poor. The solidified bead should support the molten pool as much as possible, so that the surface of the molten pool rises uniformly at a horizontal plane, making the appearance of the weld smooth.

⑤Pay attention to the shape and size of the weld pool at all times during welding. If the weld pool is not clearly visible, stop feeding the wire, as incomplete penetration may occur. If the weld pool is too large, the molten pool will fall down, causing overlap on the back of the weld. In order to ensure a fully formed and appropriately sized back side of the weld, feed the welding wire evenly and rhythmically against the groove root. When the end of the welding wire enters the molten pool to melt, gently raise it towards the groove root. Withdraw the welding wire for the next feeding until the backing layer is welded. The movement of the welding wire and the welding gun should be coordinated and synchronized. For small gaps, move upward in a straight line synchronously; for larger gaps, move upward synchronously with a small range at a constant speed.

⑥Joint. When the welding wire is depleted and needs to be replaced, or when welding needs to be temporarily suspended for other reasons, there will be a joint. Prior to joining, the quality of the crater at the arc extinction point of the joint should be inspected first. If the protection is good and there are no defects such as oxides, the joint can be made directly; if there are defects, they need to be ground off and their front ends should be inclined, and the arc strike operation should be ignited 5−10 mm in front of the crater.

⑦Cracks and shrinkage cavities must be prevented from occurring in the arc crater during arcending. The current attenuation function can be utilized to gradually lower the temperature of the molten pool while prolonging the protective effect of argon on the arc crater until the molten pool is cooled.

2. Filling welding

① Before welding, clean the welding slag and spatter from the previous weld. The precautions and steps for welding the filling layer are the same as for backing welding.

②Compared with the backing layer, the current is slightly higher, and the angle between the welding gun, welding wire, and weldment is the same as that of the backing layer.

③During welding, gently wipe the end of the welding wire on the surface of the backing weld and feed it evenly and regularly into the molten pool. Due to the widening of the fill layer weld, the arc welding gun swings in a zigzag shape and pauses slightly on both sides for proper melting. The surface of thebead should be kept 0.5−1 mm lower than the surface of the base metal, and the edge of the groove should not be melted. Otherwise, the reference line will be lost during the covering layer welding, and the straight surface layer bead cannot be welded.

④The joint should be staggered with the bottom joint by more than 50 mm. During jointing, ignite the arc 5-10 mm in front of the arc crater. The welding gun should swing transversely within a narrow range. When reaching the arc crater, add a little welding wire to make the joint flat and continue with normal welding.

3. Covering welding

①The swing of the welding gun for the covering layer is slightly larger, while the rest is the same as that for the filling layer.

②The swing of the welding gun is increased, with a slight pause at the edge of the groove. When the edge melts by 0.5-1 mm, short arc welding should be carried out to avoid undercut. The feeding speed of the welding wire should be determined based on the reinforcement of the weld to ensure proper fusion and smooth transition on both sides. The rest is the same as that for the filling layer.

Task 4:Master the Post-Weld Treatment and Inspection of Board Butt Welding with Vertical TIG Welding

Same as Project Ⅲ.

Task Assessment

1. Generally, a (　　)V-shaped groove should be opened on one side during plate butt joint vertical welding TIG of a 6 mm thick workpiece.

A. 30°　　B. 45°　　C. 50°　　D. 60°

2. The (　　)welding method is commonly used forplate butt joint vertical welding TIG.

A. forehand　　B. backhand　　C. up　　D. down

3. During the assemblyusing plate butt joint vertical welding TIG, the root gap at the starting end of the weldment is set to 2.0 mm, while at the end it is set to 3.0 mm. When fixing the combined plate onto the jig, the groove surface should face the welder, and the end with the smaller gap should be placed on the (　　)surface.

A. left　　B. right　　C. up　　D. down

4. When conductingbacking welding using plate butt joint vertical welding TIG, the welding gun should be tilted downward (　　) to utilize the upward blowing force of the arc and prevent the molten metal from flowing downward.

A. 10°-20°　　B. 30°-40°　　C. 70°-80°　　D. 80°-90°

5. When conductingbacking welding using plate butt joint vertical welding TIG, the included angle between the welding wire and the direction of the plate weld can adopt (　　) to swing the welding wire. The filling wire is positioned at the upper edge of the molten pool, allowing the molten iron to flow slowly downwards and facilitating weld formation.

A. 20°-30°　　B. 50°-70°　　C. 70°-80°　　D. 80°-90°

6. When conductingbacking welding using plate butt joint vertical welding TIG, gas supply shall be initiated (　　) seconds in advance before arc strike. The welding gun should then be tilted at a 45°angle against the groove, ensuring that the tungsten electrode's tip is 2-3 mm away

from the surface of the base metal for arc strike.

A. 1-2 B. 5-10 C. 10-20 D. 30-40

7. Whenconducting backing welding using plate butt joint vertical welding TIG, the welding gun swings in a ( ) shape, pausing slightly on both sides of the groove. The pause time and swing time on both sides account for roughly 1/3 each, ensuring good melting on both sides.

A. upper positive crescent B. upper reverse crescent

C. lower reverse crescent D. lower positive crescent

8. When conducting filling welding using plate butt joint vertical welding TIG, keep the bead surface about ( ) mm lower than the base metal surface and do not melt the edges of the groove.

A. 1-1.5 B. 1.5-2 C. 2-2.5 D. 0.5-1

9. When covering welding using plate butt joint vertical welding TIG is adopted and the welding wire swings to both sides of the groove, it should align with the edge of the groove and not exceed it. The edge should be melted by ( ) mm after a molten pool is formed.

A. 1-1.5 B. 0 C. 1-2 D. 0.5-1

10. In the process of plate butt joint vertical welding TIG, the joint should be staggered from the joint of the previous layer by more than 50 mm. During jointing, the arc should be ignited at ( ) mm in front of the arc crater, and the welding gun should swing laterally within a narrow range. When moving to the arc crater, slightly add welding wire to make the joint flat, and then resume normal welding.

A. 10-15 B. 20-30 C. 0 D. 5-10

Task Operation

Carry out task implementation training according to task requirements and process sequence. After welding, carry out self-inspection and sort out station tools according to weld inspection requirements. After training, conduct assessment and score according to testing requirements.

项目五　板对接仰焊手工钨极氩弧焊

【学习目标】

1. 分析板对接仰焊钨极氩弧焊的技术要求；
2. 掌握板对接仰焊钨极氩弧焊的焊前准备；
3. 掌握板对接仰焊钨极氩弧焊的焊接操作；
4. 掌握板对接仰焊钨极氩弧焊的焊后处理与检查。

任务1：分析板对接仰焊钨极氩弧焊的技术要求

图 3-5-1 为常见板对接仰焊试件装配图及技术要求。

技术要求

1. 试件材质为 Q355R。
2. 接头形式为板-板对接接头，焊接位置为仰焊。
3. 焊接采取单面焊双面成形技术。
4. V 形坡口角度 $\alpha=60^\circ\pm5^\circ$，钝边 $p=0\sim0.5$ mm，根部间隙 $b=2.0\sim3.0$ mm。
5. 成形要求：焊缝表面无缺陷，焊缝波纹均匀，宽窄一致，高低平整，焊缝与母材圆滑过渡，焊后无变形，具体参照评分标准。

图 3-5-1　常见板对接仰焊试件装置图及技术要求(单位：mm)

平焊位绕焊缝轴线旋转 180°即为仰焊位置，这是容器制造和维修中常遇到的焊接位置之一。它是操作难度最大、对焊工操作技能要求最高的一种焊接位置。因其受重力的影响，熔滴难于向熔池过渡，焊缝背面容易产生凹陷而正面容易产生焊瘤，焊缝成形困难。熔池温度越高，表面张力越小，熔池越大，铁液下坠越严重。仰焊时劳动强度大，焊工需要仰头看电弧，两手高举焊枪和焊丝在头顶之上做运弧和填丝动作，所以很容易疲劳。另外，要预防熔滴下坠而灼伤身体，需要学习者特别注意。

本项目以实际工程中常用的低合金钢材质为例介绍板对接立焊钨极氩弧焊的焊前准备、焊接操作和焊后处理与检查等任务实施流程。

任务2：掌握板对接仰焊钨极氩弧焊的焊前准备

焊前准备任务常规实施路线：图样识读、焊件准备及坡口清理、焊接工艺参数确定、装配定位。

1. 焊件准备及坡口清理

任务单要求：准备 6 mm×120 mm×250 mm 尺寸的 Q355R 材质焊件两块，单边开 30° V 形坡口。

焊缝及坡口清理：焊前打磨清理坡口面及坡口边缘上下两侧 15~20 mm 范围，露出金属光泽，再用丙酮清洗。由于在手工钨极氩弧焊焊接过程中惰性气体仅起保护作用，无冶金反应，因此坡口的清洗质量直接影响焊缝的质量，并打磨出 0~0.5 mm 的钝边。

2. 焊接工艺参数确定

结合本任务母材 Q355R 的焊接特性和板厚来看，选择直径 2.5 mm 的 ER50-6 焊丝（注意保持焊丝的干净，使用前可用砂布及棉纱擦净焊丝上的油、锈等污物，必要时还可用丙酮清洗），保护气体为氩气，纯度高于 99.99%，电极采用铈钨极，采用三层三道来焊接，具体焊接工艺参数如表 3-5-1 所示。

表 3-5-1　焊接工艺参数表

焊接层次	焊丝型号	焊丝直径/mm	焊接电流/A	焊接电压/V	保护气体流量/(L/min)	钨极直径/mm	钨极伸出长度/mm	电源极性
打底层	ER50-6	2.5	80~90	12~16	7~9	2.5	3~6	直流正接
填充层			90~100	12~16	7~9	2.5	3~6	
盖面层			90~100	12~16	7~9	2.5	3~6	

3. 装配定位

将两块钢板水平放工装台上，两端对齐装配成对接接头，装配时焊件始焊端根部间隙设置为 2.0 mm，结束端为 3.0 mm，采取和打底相同的工艺参数在两端进行点固焊，焊点长度为 10~15 mm，必须焊透，不允许有缺陷，错边量不大于 0.5 mm，反变形预留量为 3°~5°，焊后应把焊点打磨成斜坡，以便接头。装配示意图如图 3-5-2 所示。

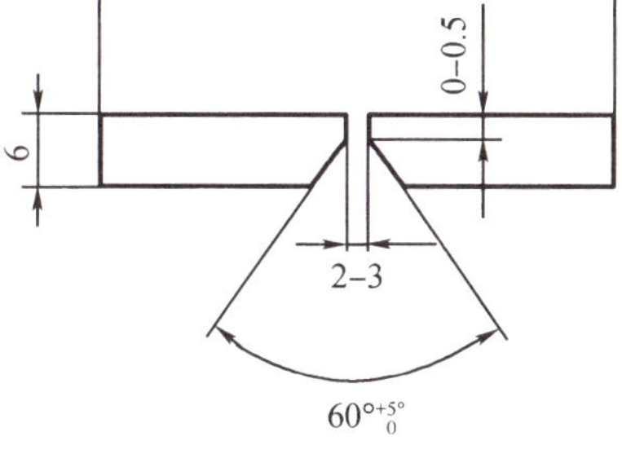

图 3-5-2　板对接装配定位示意图（单位：mm）

如定位焊缝有缺陷,必须将有缺陷的定位焊缝磨掉后重焊,不允许用重熔的办法来处理定位焊缝上的缺陷。

任务3:掌握板对接仰焊钨极氩弧焊的焊接操作

钨极氩弧焊仰焊必须严格控制焊接热输入和冷却速度,可以采用较小的焊接电流、较快的焊速,使熔池控制在较小的范围内,加快熔池的凝固速度,确保焊缝外形美观。由于氩气的密度比空气大,容易下沉,仰焊的保护效果较其他位置差,应加大氩气流量。

1. 打底焊

①将焊件固定在操作台上,焊缝水平装夹,坡口面朝下,焊件高度适合操作者操作舒服的位置,间隙小的一端放在右端,采取左焊法进行焊接,6 mm 厚板件的焊接层次常有三层三道。

②焊枪角度及位置如图 3-5-3 所示,焊枪与焊缝轴线右端夹角为 80°~90°,几乎垂直于焊件,焊丝与焊缝轴线左端的夹角为 30°~40°,大约为平焊的两倍。

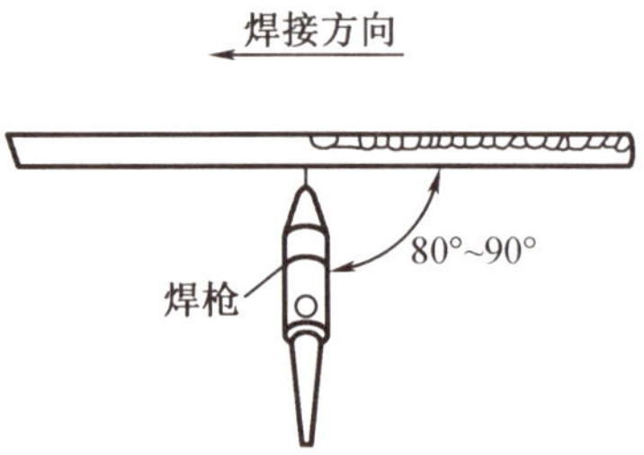

(a)焊枪倾斜角度

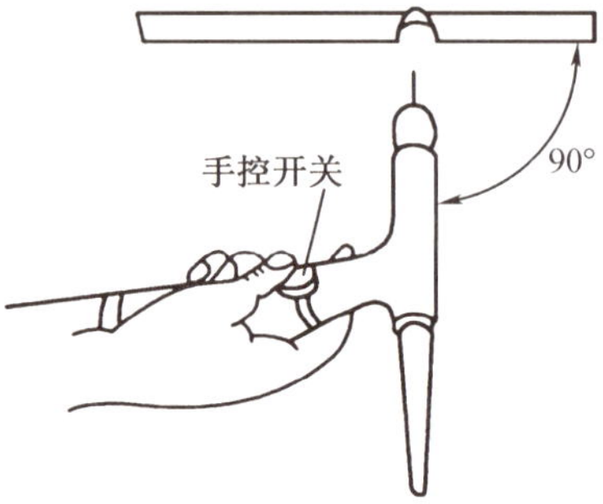

(b)电弧对中位置

图 3-5-3 焊枪角度及位置示意图

③引弧。引弧在焊件右端(间隙小的一端)定位焊缝上引燃电弧,为了确保熔池保护作用良好,引弧前应提前送气 5~10 s,然后将焊枪以 45°斜靠在坡口内,使钨极端部离母材表面 2~3 mm 进行引弧。引弧后先对焊缝位置进行预热,带板件达到熔融状态时就可以开始正式打底焊接。

④焊接。引弧后焊枪稍作摆动,待焊枪移至定位焊缝的斜坡处形成熔池和熔孔后,开始填丝并均匀向左焊接。施焊时以肘为支点,举起小臂,上身向左移动进行焊接。焊接中尽量压低电弧,焊枪做小幅度锯齿形摆动,在坡口两侧稍作停顿,注意观察熔池的形状和大小,防止熔池过大、温度过高,以钝边熔化 0.5~1 mm 为限,以免熔化金属下坠。

⑤填丝的方法是焊丝一定要沿坡口间隙送入熔池根部,此时电弧应移动到坡口的边缘,使电弧热量传递到焊件上,以降低熔池的温度,同时焊丝吸收熔池的热量而熔化;焊丝送入熔池后,应轻轻向上推,将熔化金属推向背面;在抽回焊丝时,焊丝应向上挑起,使熔化金属尽量向背面顶送,以控制焊缝背面成形;然后焊枪做横向摆动,将熔化金属敷平,防止焊道凸出,形成沟槽。

⑥施焊过程中尽量防止钨极与熔池接触而短路,一旦发生短路将产生夹钨,必须停弧处理掉夹钨并将钨极端部修磨成所需要的形状后,才能继续焊接。

⑦接头。首先检查原弧坑的焊缝质量,有缺陷应修磨掉,并将弧坑修磨成缓坡形。在

弧坑后 15~20 mm 处引弧，并慢慢向左移动至斜坡最高处加热，待原弧坑处形成熔池和熔孔后再填丝施焊，转入正常焊接。

⑧停弧和收弧。停弧时应松开焊枪上的按钮开关，停止送丝，利用焊机的电流衰减功能，保持焊枪高度不变，待电弧熄灭熔池冷却后，再移开焊枪；若焊机无电流衰减装置，则松开按钮开关后，稍抬高焊枪，待电弧熄灭熔池冷却至颜色变黑后，再移开焊枪。在焊缝末端收孤时，应减小焊枪与焊件间夹角，使热量集中在焊丝上，加大焊丝熔化量，填满弧坑，然后切断电源，待氩气延时 10 s 左右，直至熔池冷却后再移开焊枪和焊丝

2. 填充焊

①焊接前，清理前道焊缝的焊渣和飞溅物，焊接填充层时的注意事项和步骤同打底焊。

②与打底层相比电流稍大，焊枪、焊丝与焊件间夹角和打底层相同。

③填充层焊接时焊枪摆幅增大，两侧稍作停顿，保证坡口两侧熔化良好，避免咬边，焊道均匀平整，并比母材表面低 1mm 左右，不要熔化坡口棱边，以保持坡口边缘的原始状态，为盖面层焊接打好基础。

3. 盖面焊

①盖面层焊接焊枪摆幅比填充层稍大，其余与填充层相同。

②盖面层焊接焊枪与焊丝角度不变，只是焊枪的摆动幅度略大，并在两侧边缘稍 停，使两侧边缘各熔化 0.5~1 mm 为限，短弧施焊以免咬边，根据焊缝余高确定焊丝送进速度，保证两侧熔合良好圆滑过渡，送丝速度均匀适度，以确保焊缝尺寸符合要求。

任务4：掌握板对接仰焊钨极氩弧焊的焊后处理与检查

参见项目三。

任务考核

1. 钨极氩弧焊板对接仰焊时，焊枪与焊缝轴线右端夹角为(　　)。

A. 60°~70°　　B. 70°~80°　　C. 75°~85°　　D. 80°~90°

2. 钨极氩弧焊平对接仰焊时，焊丝与焊缝轴线左端的夹角为(　　)。

A. 20°~30°　　B. 30°~40°　　C. 40°~50°　　D. 50°~60°

3. (　　)是钨极氩弧焊内填丝。

A. 焊丝从焊件的正面送入，焊丝与焊枪在同一侧

B. 焊丝从焊件的反面送入，焊丝与焊枪在同一侧

C. 焊丝从焊件的正面送入，焊丝与焊枪不在同一侧

D. 焊丝从焊件的反面送入，焊丝与焊枪不在同一侧

4. (　　)是钨极氩弧焊工件装配的错误操作。

A. 板材对接时，没有错边　　B. 为了保证质量，强行对口

C. 预留好一定的反变形　　D. 预留合适的坡口间隙

5. 钨极氩弧焊仰焊时，焊接电流要(　　)，焊接速度要(　　)，坡口和根部间隙要适当(　　)。

A. 小，快，小　　B. 大，快，小　　C. 小，慢，小　　D. 大，慢，小

6. (判断题)钨极氩弧焊时喷嘴与工件的距离保持在 20~24 mm。(　　)

7. (判断题)钨极氩弧焊时，熄弧及接头的质量也非常重要。(　　)

8. (判断题)钨极氩弧焊的坡口形式有 I 形、V 形、X 形等。(　　)

9. (判断题)钨极氩弧焊时,钨极电流过大或与焊丝碰撞而使端头熔化落入熔池会造成夹钨。(　　)

10. (判断题)钨极氩弧焊时,如定位焊缝有缺陷,可以用重熔的办法来处理定位焊缝上的缺陷。(　　)

任务操作

按任务要求和流程顺序进行任务实施训练。焊后能够根据焊缝检查要求进行自检和进行工位工具整理。训练后进行考核,并按检测要求进行评分。

Project Ⅴ Manual TIG Welding of Low Alloy Plate–Butt Overhead Welding

【Learning Objectives】

1. Analyze the technical requirements of upward welding TIG welding for board butt welding;
2. Master the pre–welding preparation for board butt welding with TIG welding;
3. Master the welding operation of upward welding TIG welding for board butt welding;
4. Master the post–weld treatment and inspection of board butt welding with welding.

Task 1:Analyze the Technical Requirements of Upward Welding TIG Welding for Board Butt Welding

Fig. 3–5–1 displays the assembly diagram and technical requirements of commonly used butt joint overhead welding test pieces.

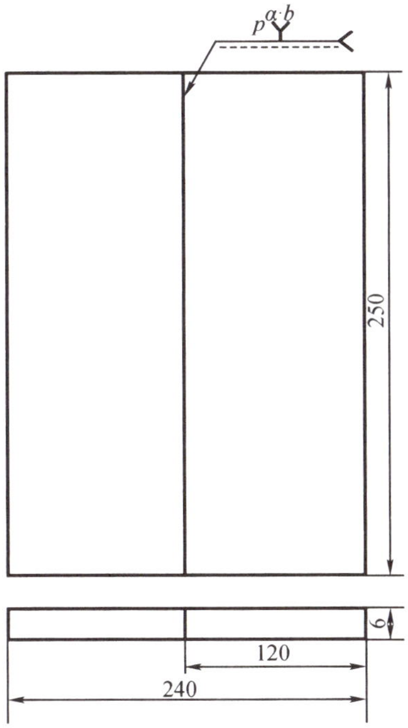

Technical requirements

1. The test piece material is Q355R.
2. The joint form is a plate–to–plate butt joint, and the welding position is overhead welding.
3. Single–side welding and double–side forming technology should be used for welding.
4. The V–shaped groove angle $\alpha = 60° \pm 5°$, root face $p = 0–0.5$ mm, root gap $b = 2.0–3.0$ mm.
5. Forming requirements: The weld surface should be free of defects, with uniform and consistent weld ripples in width and flatness, smooth transition between the weld and base metal, and no deformation after welding. Please refer to the scoring standard for details.

Fig. 3–5–1 The Assembly Eiagram and Technical Requirements of Commonly Used Butt Joint Overhead Welding Test Pieces(Unit:mm)

The flat welding position rotates 180° around the weld axis, which is one of the commonly encountered welding positions in vessel manufacturing and maintenance. It is a welding position with the highest operational difficulty and the highest requirements for the welder's operating skills. Due to the influence of gravity, the transfer of droplets to the molten pool is difficult, and the backside of the weld is prone to depression while the front side is prone to overlap, making it difficult to form the weld. The higher the temperature of the molten pool, the smaller the surface tension, the larger the molten pool, and the more serious the falling of liquid iron. During overhead welding, the labor intensity is high. The welder needs to look up at the arc, hold the welding gun and welding wire with both hands above their head to perform arc operations and wire filling actions, thus making it easy to fatigue. Additionally, learners need to pay special attention to prevent their body from being burned by falling droplets.

This project takes low-alloy steel materials commonly used in practical engineering as an example to introduce the implementation process of tasks such as pre weld preparation, welding operation, and post weld treatment and inspection for plate butt welding tungsten inert gas arc welding.

Task 2: Master the Pre-Welding Preparation for Board Butt Welding with TIG Welding

Conventional implementation route of pre-welding preparation tasks: Interpretation of drawings, preparation of weldments and groove cleaning, determination of welding process parameters, and assembly positioning.

1. Weldment preparation and groove cleaning

Task list requirements: Prepare two Q355R steel weldments with dimensions of 6 mm×120 mm×250 mm, and create a 30° V-shaped groove on one side.

Weld and groove cleaning: Before welding, polish and clean the groove surface, as well as the 15-20 mm range on the upper and lower sides of the groove edge, to reveal a metallic luster. Then, clean it with acetone. Since the inert gas only serves a protective function and does not have any metallurgical reaction during manual argon tungsten arc welding, the cleaning quality of the groove directly affects the weld quality. The root face should be ground to an accuracy of 0-0.5 mm.

2. Determination of welding process parameters

According to the welding characteristics and plate thickness of base metal Q355R in this task, a 2.5 mm diameter ER50-6 welding wire is selected (ensure the welding wire is clean by wiping off any oil, rust, or dirt with emery cloth and cotton yarn before use, and acetone can be used for cleaning if necessary). The protective gas used is argon with a purity higher than 99.99%. A cerium tungsten electrode is used, and three layers and three passes are applied for welding. The specific welding process parameters are provided in Table 3-5-1.

Table 3-5-1 Welding Process Parameters

Welding layer	Type of welding wire	Wire diameter /mm	Welding current /A	Welding voltage /V
Backing layer	ER50-6	2.5	80-90	12-16
Filling layer			90-100	12-16
Covering layer			90-100	12-16

Welding layer	Protective gas flow/(L/min)	Diameter of tungsten electrode /mm	Tungsten electrode extension length /mm	Power supply polarity
Backing layer	7-9	2.5	3-6	DC straight polarity
Filling layer	7-9	2.5	3-6	
Covering layer	7-9	2.5	3-6	

3. Assembling and positioning

Place two steel plates horizontally on the tooling table, aligning both ends to assemble them into butt joints. Set the root gap at the initial welding end of the weldment as 2.0 mm and 3.0 mm at the final end. Use the same process parameters as backing for tack welding at both ends. The length of the welding spot should be 10-15 mm and must be fully welded without defects. The misalignment should not exceed 0.5 mm, and the permissible deformation allowance should be 3°-5°. After welding, grind the welding spot into a slope for easier connection. The assembly diagram is depicted in Fig. 3-5-2.

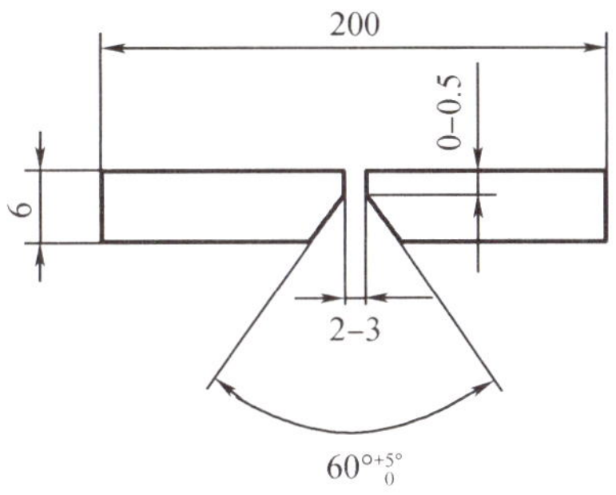

Fig. 3-5-2 Schematic Diagram of Plate Butt Joint Assembly and Alignment (Unit: mm)

If there is a defect on the tack weld, it must be ground off before re-welding. The use of remelting method to address defects on the tack weld is not allowed.

Task 3: Master the Welding Operation of Upward Welding TIG Welding for Board Butt Welding

The welding heat input and cooling speed must be strictly controlled for overhead TIG welding. Smaller welding current and faster welding speed can be adopted to control the molten pool within a smaller range, accelerate the solidification speed of the molten pool, and ensure the aesthetic appearance of the weld joint. As the density of argon is higher than that of air and it tends to sink, the protection effect of overhead welding is weaker than in other positions, so the oxygen flow should be increased.

1. Backing welding

①Secure the weldment onto the operating platform, horizontally clamp the groove surface facing downwards. The height of the weldment should be suitable for comfortable operator operation. Place the end with a small gap on the right end and use the left welding method. There are often three layers of welding and three passes for a 6 mm thick plate.

②The welding gun angle and position are shown in Fig. 3-5-3. The included angle between the welding gun and the right end of the weld axis is 80°-90°, nearly perpendicular to the weldment. The included angle between the welding wire and the left end of the weld axis is 30°-40°, approximately double that of flat welding.

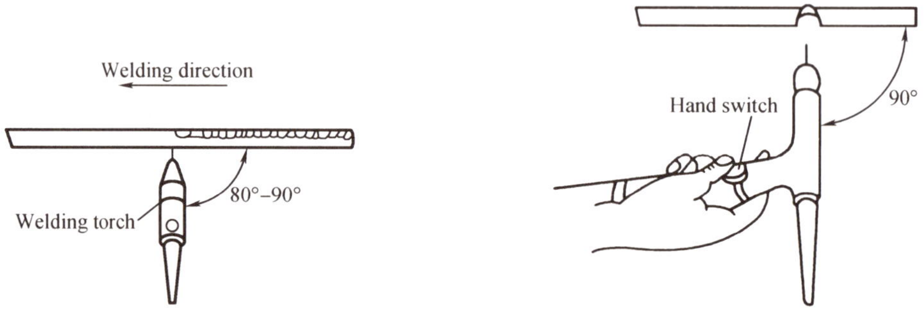

(a) Angle of inclination of welding gun (b) Position of arc centering

Fig. 3-5-3 Schematic Diagram of Welding Gun Angle and Position

③Arc striking. Ignite the arc on the tack weld at the right end of the weldment (end with a small gap). To ensure good protection of the molten pool, supply gas for 5-10 s before arc striking, then incline the welding gun against the groove at a 45° angle so that the tungsten electrode's end is 2-3 mm away from the base metal surface for arc striking. After arc striking, preheat the weld position first, and begin formal backing welding when the strip plate reaches a molten state.

④Welding. After striking an arc, the welding gun should swing slightly. When the welding gun moves to the slope of the tack weld to form a molten pool and a hole, start filling the wire and weld evenly to the left. During welding, use the elbow as a support, lift the forearm, and move the upper body to the left for welding. The arc should be lowered as much as possible during welding. The welding gun should swing in a small zigzag pattern and pause on both sides of the groove. Pay attention to observing the shape and size of the weld pool to prevent it from being too large and the temperature from being too high. The depth of the melted root face should be 0.5-1 mm to prevent the molten metal from falling.

⑤The method of wire filling is that the welding wire must be fed into the root of the molten pool along the groove gap. At this time, the arc should move to the edge of the groove to transfer the heat of the arc to the weldment in order to reduce the temperature of the molten pool.

Meanwhile, the welding wire absorbs the heat of the molten pool and melts. After the welding wire is fed into the molten pool, it should be gently pushed up to push the molten metal backwards. When withdrawing the welding wire, it should be lifted up so that the molten metal can be pushed to the back as much as possible to control the formation of the back of the weld. Then, the welding gun swings horizontally to level the molten metal, in order to prevent the weld bead from protruding and forming a groove.

⑥During welding, try to prevent the tungsten electrode from coming into contact with the molten pool and causing a short circuit. If a short circuit occurs, tungsten inclusion will happen. The arc must be stopped to remove the tungsten inclusion, and the end of the tungsten electrode must be ground into the required shape before continuing welding.

⑦Joint. First, check the weld quality of the original arc crater. If there are any defects, they should be repaired and ground into a gentle slope shape. Strike the arc 15-20 mm behind the arc crater, and slowly move to the left to the highest point of the slope for heating. After the original arc crater forms a molten pool and melting hole, fill wire for welding, and switch to normal welding.

⑧Arc stopping and extinguishing. When stopping the arc, release the button switch on the welding gun to stop wire feeding. Use the current attenuation function of the welder to maintain the height of the welding gun. Once the arc is extinguished and the molten pool is cooled, remove the welding gun. If the welder does not have a current attenuation device, after releasing the button switch, slightly lift the welding gun. Once the arc is extinguished and the molten pool cools to a black color, remove the welding gun. When closing the arc at the end of the weld, reduce the included angle between the welding gun and the weldment to concentrate the heat on the welding wire, increase the melting amount of the welding wire, fill the arc pit, then cut off the power supply. Wait for approximately 10 s for the argon gas until the molten pool is cooled before removing the welding gun and welding wire.

2. Filling welding

①Before welding, clean up the weld slag and spatter from the previous weld. The precautions and steps for welding the filler layer are the same as those for backing welding.

②Compared to the backing layer, the current is slightly higher, and the included angle between the welding gun, welding wire, and workpiece is the same as that of the backing layer.

③When welding the filler layer, increase the swing of the welding gun and briefly pause on both sides to ensure proper fusion on both sides of the groove and prevent undercut. The weld bead should be uniform and flat, about 1mm lower than the base metal surface. Do not melt the edge of the groove to maintain its original state, providing a good foundation for welding the cover layer.

3. Covering welding

①The swing range of the welding gun for the covering layer is slightly larger than that of the filling layer, and the rest is the same as the filling layer.

②The angle between the welding gun and the welding wire for covering layer welding remains unchanged, but the swing range of the welding gun is slightly larger, and it stops at the edges on both sides to melt the edges on both sides by 0.5–1 mm respectively. Short arc welding is carried out to avoid undercut. The feeding speed of the welding wire is determined according to the excess weld metal height to ensure good fusion and smooth transition on both sides. The wire feeding speed is uniform and appropriate to ensure that the weld size meets the requirements.

Task 4:Master the Post-Weld Treatment and Inspection of Board Butt Welding with Welding

Same as Project Ⅲ.

Task Assessment

1. During overhead butt welding with argon tungsten-arc welding plate, the angle between the welding gun and the right end of the weld axis is (　　).

A. 60°–70°　　B. 70°–80°　　C. 75°–85°　　D. 80°–90°

2. During flat butt overhead welding using argon tungsten-arc welding, the angle between the welding wire and the left end of the weld axis is (　　).

A. 20°–30°　　B. 30°–40°　　C. 40°–50°　　D. 50°–60°

3. (　　) is the filler wire used in argon tungsten arc welding.

A. The welding wire is fed into the weldment from the front, and the welding wire and the welding gun are on the same side

B. The welding wire is fed into the weldment from the reverse side, and the welding wire and the welding gun are on the same side

C. The welding wire is fed into the weldment from the front, and the welding wire and the welding gun are not on the same side

D. The welding wire is fed into the weldment from the reverse side, and the welding wire and the welding gun are not on the same side

4. (　　) is the incorrect operation of workpiece assembly for TIG welding.

A. There is no misalignment when the plates are butted

B. To ensure quality, they are forcibly aligned

C. Reserve a certain amount of anti-deformation

D. Reserve appropriate groove clearance

5. For argon tungsten-arc overhead welding, the welding current shall be (　　), the welding speed shall be (　　), and the gap between groove and root shall be appropriate (　　).

A. small, fast, small　　B. large, fast, small

C. small, slow, small　　D. large, slow, small

6. (True or false) The distance between the nozzle and the workpiece should be kept between 20 mm and 24 mm during TIG welding. (　　)

7. (True or false) Arc extinguishing and joint quality are also very important during TIG welding. (　　)

8. (True or false) The groove forms for TIG welding include I shape, V shape, and X

shape. (   )

9. (True or false) During TIG welding, excessive current of the tungsten electrode or collision with the welding wire will cause the end to melt and fall into the molten pool, resulting in tungsten inclusion. (   )

10. (True or false) During TIG welding, if the tack weld is defective, remelting can be used to treat the defects on the tack weld. (   )

Task Operation

Carry out task implementation training according to task requirements and process sequence. After welding, perform self-inspection and organize station tools according to weld inspection requirements. After training, conduct assessment and score based on testing requirements.

项目六　管对接水平固定手工钨极氩弧焊

【学习目标】

1. 分析管对接水平固定手工钨极氩弧焊的技术要求；
2. 掌握管对接水平固定手工钨极氩弧焊的焊前准备；
3. 掌握管对接水平固定手工钨极氩弧焊的焊接操作；
4. 掌握管对接水平固定手工钨极氩弧焊的焊后处理与检查。

任务1：分析管对接水平固定手工钨极氩弧焊的技术要求

图 3-6-1 为常见管对接水平固定焊试件装配图及技术要求。

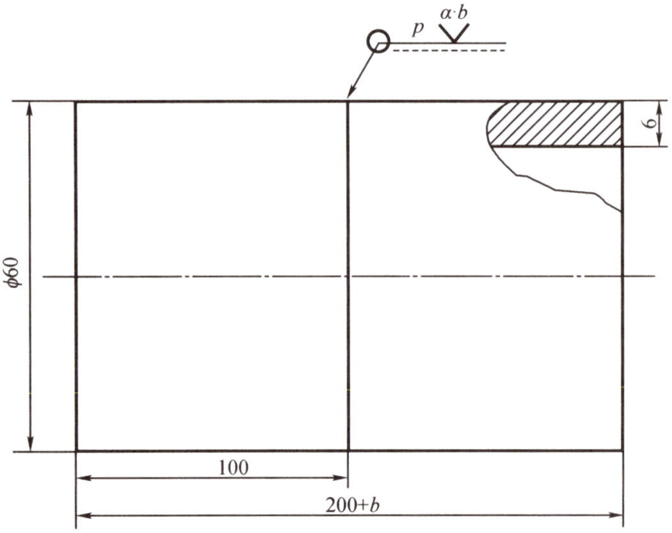

技术要求

1. 试件材质为 Q355R。
2. 接头形式为管-管对接接头，焊接位置为水平固定。
3. 焊接采取单面焊双面成形技术。
4. V 形坡口角度 $\alpha=60°\pm5°$，钝边 $p=0.5\sim1$ mm，根部间隙 $b=2.0\sim3.0$ mm。
5. 成形要求：焊缝表面无缺陷，焊缝波纹均匀，宽窄一致，高低平整，焊缝与母材圆滑过渡，焊后无变形，具体参照评分标准。

图 3-6-1　常见管对接水平固定焊试件装配图及技术要求（单位：mm）

在锅炉、化工、电力、原子能等工业部门的管线及换热器生产和安装中经常会需要管道的焊接，其中手工钨极氩弧焊占据着很大的比重，特别是在现场安装施工中，往往出现管道固定不动的焊接情况，这对它的焊接操作技术有一定的要求。

本单元以实际工程中常用的低碳钢材质为例介绍板对接平焊熔化极气体保护焊的焊前准备、焊接操作和焊后处理与检查等任务实施流程。

任务2：掌握管对接水平固定手工钨极氩弧焊的焊前准备

焊前准备任务常规实施路线：图样识读、焊件准备及坡口清理、焊接工艺参数确定、装配定位。

根据任务单可知，钢管材料为Q355R，规格为ϕ60 mm×6 mm×100 mm，两根管对接，坡口角度为60°±5°，V形坡口，间隙为2~3 mm，钝边为0.5~1 mm，进行管子水平固定全位置焊接。要求单面焊双面成形良好，焊件一经施焊，不得任意更换和改变焊接位置。

1. 焊件准备及坡口清理

规格为ϕ60 mm×6 mm×100 mm的管子，坡口面角度为30°±2.5°，每组两根，共一组。

将焊丝表面和焊件坡口内及其正反两侧20 mm范围内的油、锈、水分及其他污物清除干净，直至露出金属光泽。由于在手工钨极氩弧焊焊接过程中惰性气体仅起保护作用，无冶金反应，所以坡口的清洗质量直接影响焊缝的质量，应特别重视对坡口的清理工作。

2. 焊接工艺参数确定

Q355R属于低合金钢，焊接性良好，焊接时一般不需要采取特殊的工艺措施。

管对接水平固定焊，由于存在着平、立、仰等多种位置的操作，也称为全位置焊接。焊接时，由于随着焊接位置的改变，焊枪的角度和焊接操作时的手形、身形都将发生较大的改变，因此，要特别注意整个焊接过程中各方位焊接操作的变化与调整。焊接电流的大小要合适，严格采用短弧，控制熔池存在的时间。

根据管件材质和板厚，可选择ER50-6焊丝，直径为2.5 mm；电极选用铈钨极，直径为2.5 mm，钨极端头磨成30°圆锥形，锥端直径为0.5 mm；Ar气体纯度要求达到99.99%。采取两层两道焊。

可选择推荐工艺参数如表3-6-1所示。

表3-6-1　Q355R管对接水平固定焊的焊接参数

焊接层次	焊丝型号	焊丝直径/mm	焊接电流/A	焊接电压/V	保护气体流量/(L/min)	钨极直径/mm	钨极伸出长度/mm	电源极性
打底层	ER50-6	2.5	90~100	10~15	7~10	2.5	3~6	直流正接
盖面层			80~90	10~15	7~10	2.5	3~6	

3. 装配定位

(1)管道的装配对口及定位焊

管子焊接质量的优劣与装配组对和定位焊关系密切。管道组对要求坡口端面的平面度小于0.5 mm，焊口拼装错位不得大于1 mm，组对处的弯曲度不得大于1/400。有时转动起来比较费力，同时也为防止因转动时振动而使焊口根部出现裂纹，在组对前，应将管子放在平整的能有效固定定位的转动支架或滚杠上，如图3-6-2(a)所示，便于操作。同时，定位焊焊缝必须有足够的强度,如果采取支点式支架则靠近焊口的两个支点距离最好不大于管径的1.5~2倍,如图3-6-2(b)所示。焊接厚壁管子时,转动比较费劲,最好每一焊段焊接两层后再转动一次。

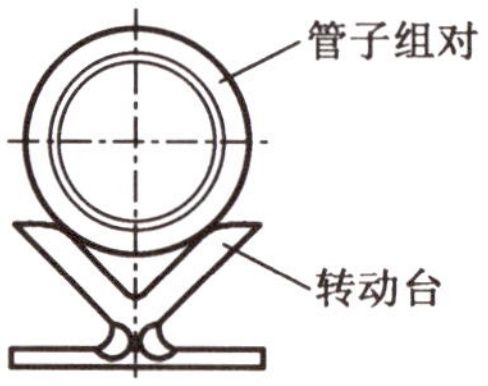

(a)管子定位转动台

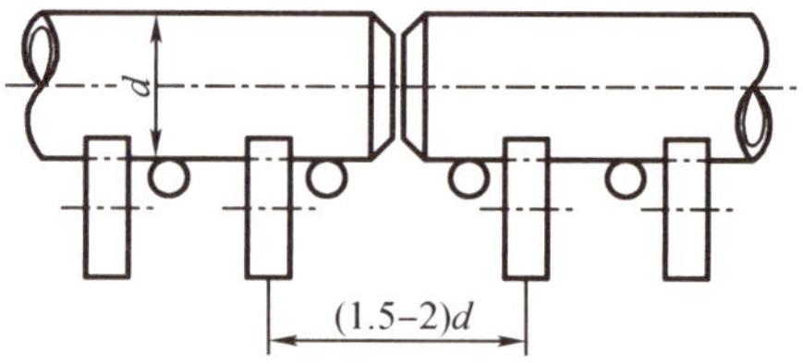

(b)管子滚动支点的布置

图3-6-2　管子装配定位支架示意图

定位焊时,对于直径小的管子,可以采取一点或两点定位,一点定位位置可以设置在时钟11点钟或者1点钟位置,两点定位位置对称设置在两侧,如图3-6-3(a)所示,或者在10点钟和2点钟方向定位。管径大的可定位焊3点或更多的焊点定位,焊点应均布,如图3-6-3(b)所示。定位焊焊点的尺寸应适宜,当管壁厚度小于或等于5 mm时,则焊点厚度为3~5 m,若管壁厚度大于5 mm时,则焊点厚度为5~8 mm,定位焊长度为20~30 mm。为便于接头熔透,焊点的两个端都必须修成缓坡形。

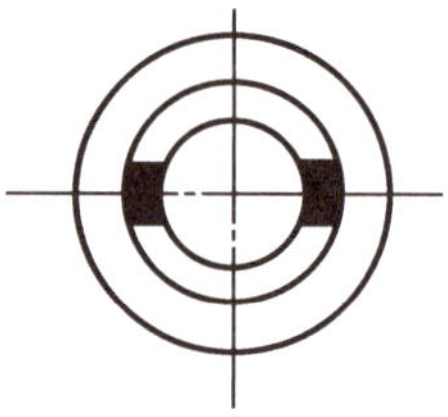

(a)2点点焊法

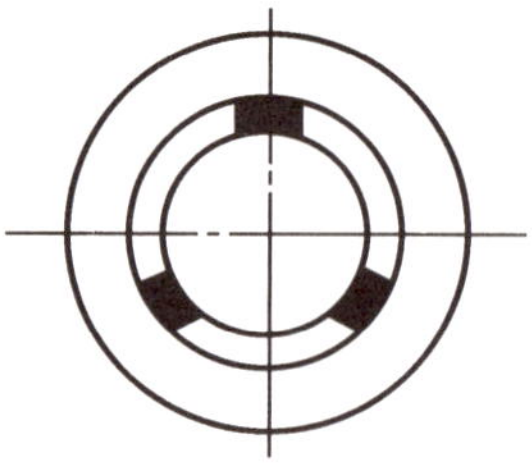

(b)3点点焊法

图3-6-3　定位焊点数量及位置示意图

具体装配焊点还与焊接位置和具体焊接情况有关,水平转动管定位焊一般不超过两点,即可以焊1点或2点,垂直固定、水平固定、斜45°管一般不超过3点,即可以焊1点、2点或3点。

(2)管对接装配定位要领

①将管件放在管件组对架上进行固定,确保管件同轴。

②在管件放置的12点钟位置进行1点定位,采用与正式焊接相同牌号的焊丝进行定位焊,定位焊焊点长度10~15 mm,厚度5~8 mm,确保背面焊透。考虑到单面焊双面成形操作,组对间隙预留略大,一般按上大下小设置,管顶部3 mm,底部2 mm,焊后管件错边量不大于0.5 mm,如图3-6-4所示。

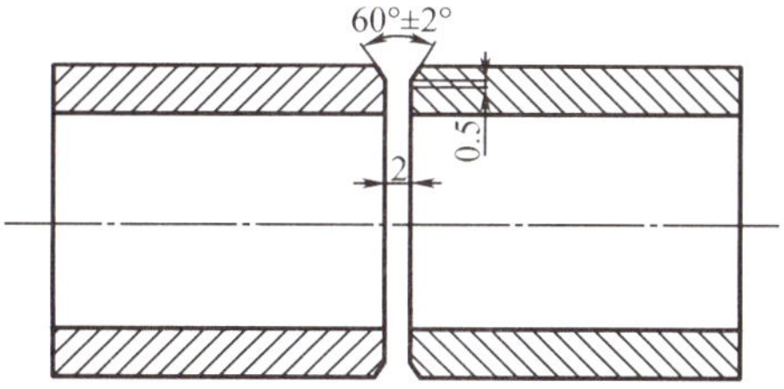

图 3-6-4　试件定位焊位置示意图(单位:mm)

(3)打磨

使用角磨机对固定焊点进行打磨,焊点打磨成双 U 形坡口即缓坡形,注意不要将固定点中心打磨过薄,以免在焊时造成管件变形,如图 3-6-5 所示。

图 3-6-5　组对点焊后焊点示意图

任务3:掌握管对接水平固定手工钨极氩弧焊的焊接操作

焊件为两层两道,焊接过程中,焊枪、焊丝随焊接位置而变化如图 3-6-6 所示。

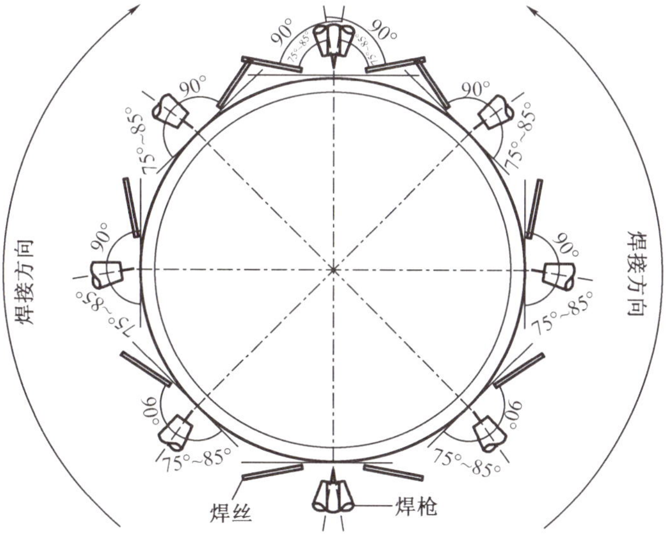

图 3-6-6　焊枪、焊丝随焊接位置而变化示意图

1. 打底焊

采用内填丝法和外填丝法，如图 3-6-7 所示，分前、后半部进行打底焊，自下而上单面焊双面成形。

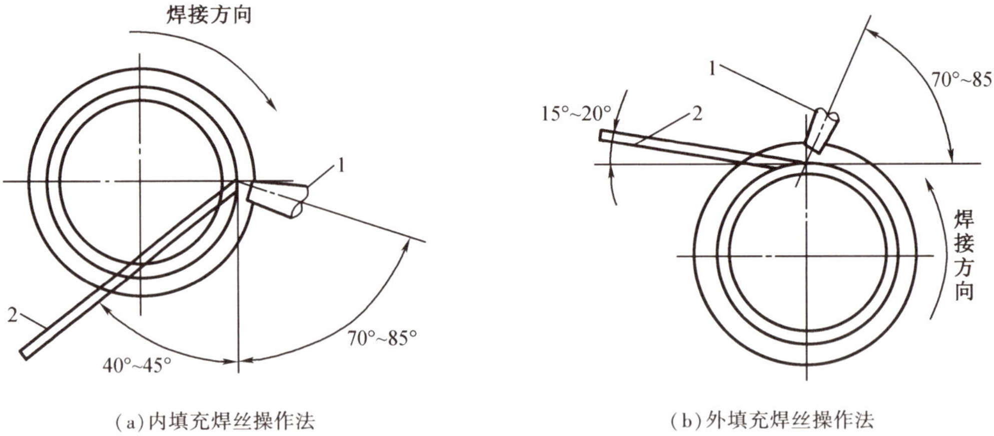

1—喷嘴；2—焊丝。

图 3-6-7 内填丝法与外填丝法

(1)打底焊从仰焊位置中心线后方 5~10 mm 处起焊，按逆时针方向先焊前半部，焊至平焊位置越过管中心线 5~10 mm 收弧，之后再按顺时针方向焊接后半部，如图 3-6-8 所示。

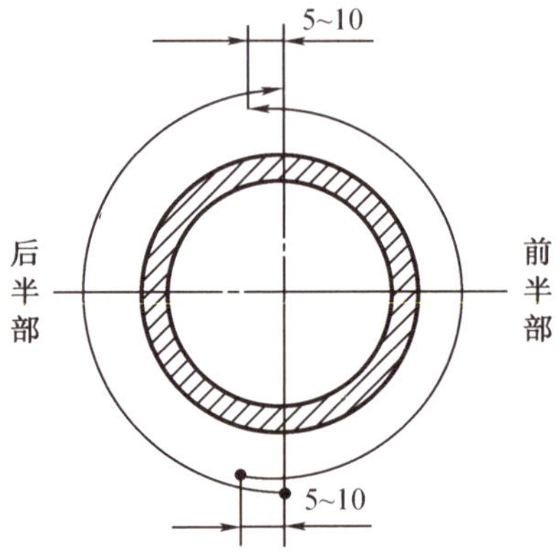

图 3-6-8 水平固定管起弧和收弧操作示意图(单位：mm)

(2)焊接过程中，焊枪角度和填丝角度要随焊接位置的变化而变化，如图 3-6-6 所示。

①电弧引燃后，在坡口根部间隙两侧用焊枪划圈预热，待钝边熔化形成熔孔后，将伸到管子内侧的焊丝紧贴熔孔，在钝边两侧各送一滴熔滴，通过焊枪的横向摆动，使之形成搭桥连接的第一个熔池。此时，焊丝再紧贴熔池前沿中部填充一滴熔滴，使熔滴与母材充分熔合，熔池前方出现熔孔后，再送入另一滴熔滴，依此循环。当焊至立焊位置时，由内填丝法改为外填丝法，直至焊完打底焊的前半部。

②后半部分为顺时针方向的焊接，操作方法与前半部分相同。当焊至距定位焊缝

3～5 mm 时，为保证接头焊透，焊枪应划圈，将定位焊缝熔化，然后填充 2～3 滴熔滴，将焊缝封闭后继续施焊（注意定位焊缝处不填焊丝）。当底层焊道的后半部分与前半部分在水平位上还差 3～4 mm 即将封口时，停止送丝，先在封口处周围划圈预热，使之呈红热状态，然后将电弧拉回原熔池填丝焊接。封口后停止送丝，继续向前施焊 5～10 mm 停弧，待熔池凝固后移开焊枪。打底层焊道一般以 2 mm 为宜。

（3）在焊接过程中，根据不同的焊接位置（仰焊、立焊、平焊），焊枪角度和填丝角度发生变化，具体操作如图 3-6-6 所示。

2. 盖面焊

（1）采用月牙形摆动进行盖面焊，盖面焊焊枪角度与打底焊时相同，填丝采用外填丝法。

（2）在打底焊上位于 6 点钟处引弧，焊枪做月牙形摆动，在坡口边缘及打底层焊道表面熔化并形成熔池后，开始填丝焊接。焊丝与焊枪角度同步摆动，在坡口两侧稍加停顿，各加一滴熔滴，并使其与母材良好熔化。如此摆动、填丝进行焊接。在仰焊部位填丝量应适当少一些，以防熔敷金属下坠；在立焊部位，焊枪的摆动频率要适当加快以防熔滴下淌；到平焊部位时，每次填充的焊丝要多些，以防焊缝不饱满。

（3）整个盖面层焊接运弧要平稳，钨极端部与熔池距离保持在 2～3mm。熔池的轮廓应对称焊缝的中心线，若发生偏斜，随时调整焊枪角度和电弧在坡口边缘的停留时间。

任务4：掌握管对接水平固定手工钨极氩弧焊的焊后处理与检查

1. 焊缝清理

将焊好的焊件用钢丝刷反复刷擦焊缝，除去焊缝氧化层。焊缝应光滑、平整，应保证焊件的“同轴、面平”，清理过程中不能破坏焊缝原始表面。

2. 焊缝质量检测

（1）焊缝外观检测

焊后对焊缝表面质量进行检测，肉眼观察或用低倍放大镜检查焊缝表面是否有气孔、裂纹、咬边等缺陷，用钢直尺、钢角尺、焊缝检验尺对焊缝进行外观质量和外观成形尺寸。常规具体检测条目及要求如表 3-6-2。

表 3-6-2　焊缝目视检测的项目参考表

检测项目	检测部位	质量要求	备注
清理质量	所有焊缝及其两侧 25 mm 范围内	无焊渣、飞溅及阻碍检测的附着物	
几何形状	焊缝与母材连接处	焊缝完整不得有漏焊，连接处应圆滑过渡	
	焊缝形状和尺寸急剧变化的部位	焊缝高低、宽窄及结晶焊缝波纹应均匀	可用焊接检测尺等测量
伤痕补焊	母材机械划伤部位	划伤部位不应有明显棱角和沟槽，伤痕深度不超过有关标准规定	

(2)焊缝检测常用评分标准

对焊件按规范进行焊后处理与检测评分,6 mm 厚板对接焊缝外观常用评分标准如表 3-6-3 所示,分值总分以 60 分计算,可以根据实际情况修改。

表 3-6-3　板对接焊缝外观评分表

检查项目	评判标准及得分	评判等级				自测数据	自评分数	教师测量数据	教师评分	备注
		Ⅰ	Ⅱ	Ⅲ	Ⅳ					
焊缝余高	尺寸标准/mm	0~1	>1,≤2	>2,≤3	<0 或>3					
	得分	4	3	2	0					
焊缝高度差	尺寸标准/mm	0~1	>1≤2	>2,≤3	>3					
	得分	8	4	2	0					
焊缝宽度	尺寸标准/mm	8~9	≥7,≤10	≥6,≤11	<6 或>11					
	得分	4	2	1	0					
焊缝宽度差	尺寸标准/mm	0~1	>1,≤2	>2,≤3	>3					
	得分	8	4	2	0					
咬边	尺寸标准/mm	无咬边	深度≤0.5		深度>0.5					
	得分	12	长度每 5 mm 扣 2 分		0					
正面成形	标准	优	良	中	差					
	得分	8	4	2	0					
背面成形	标准	优	良	中	差					
	得分	6	4	2	0					
背面凹度	尺寸标准/mm	0~0.5	>0.5,≤1	>1,≤2	长度>30					
	得分	2	1	0	0					
背面凸度	尺寸标准/mm	0~1	>1,≤2	>2						
	得分	2	1	0						
角变形	尺寸标准/mm	0~0.5	>0.5,≤1	>1						
	得分	4	2	0						
错边量	尺寸标准/mm	0~0.5	>0.5,≤1	>1						
	得分	2	1	0						
外观缺陷(裂纹、气孔、咬边、弧坑凹坑、夹渣、未熔合等)记录										

3. 工位工具清理点检与评分

与模块二项目五相同。

完工后对工位按“6S”标准进行清理清扫整顿,并做好记录,按表 2-5-5 进行评分。

任务考核

1. 对接管水平固定位置向上焊接时，焊条的角度应随着焊接位置的变化而变化，但焊接位置中没有(　　)。

A. 平焊　　B. 立焊　　C. 横焊　　D. 仰焊

2. 对接管水平固定位置向上焊接(　　)进行。

A. 按整圆　　B. 分两个半圆　　C. 分四个半圆　　D. 分六个半圆

3. 钨极氩弧焊水平管对接焊时，坡口面角度为(　　)。

A. 30°±2.5°　　B. 32°±2.5°　　C. 35°±2.5°　　D. 40°±2.5°

4. 钨极氩弧焊水平管对接，在填丝时，焊丝应与工件表面夹角成(　　)左右。

A. 10°　　B. 15°　　C. 20°　　D. 30°

5. 钨极氩弧焊水平管对接，如中途停顿，再度起焊，将端头打磨并使焊缝重叠(　　)mm。

A. 4~6　　B. 5~7　　C. 6~8　　D. 7~9

6. 钨极氩弧焊水平管对接，在进行打底焊时，选择(　　)焊丝更好。

A. H08A　　B. ER50-6　　C. H08Mn2A　　D. H08Mn2SiA

7. 钨极氩弧焊水平管对接，在打底焊时，焊至(　　)位置，用外填丝法。

A. 平焊　　B. 立焊　　C. 横焊　　D. 仰焊

8. 钨极氩弧焊水平管对接，打底焊从仰焊位置中心线后方(　　)mm 处起焊。

A. 4~8　　B. 5~10　　C. 6~12　　D. 7~9

9. 钨极氩弧焊水平管对接，水平转动管定位焊一般不超过(　　)点。

A. 2　　B. 3　　C. 4　　D. 5

10. 钨极氩弧焊水平管对接，使用角磨机对固定焊点进行打磨，焊点打磨成双(　　)形坡口。

A. V　　B. Y　　C. U　　D. X

任务操作

按任务要求和流程顺序进行任务实施训练。焊后能够根据焊缝检查要求进行自检和进行工位工具整理。训练后进行考核，并按检测要求进行评分。

Project Ⅵ Manual TIG Welding for Butt Horizontal Fixing of Low Alloy Steel Pipe

【Learning Objectives】

1. Analyze the technical requirements of manual TIG welding for horizontal fixation of pipe joints;

2. Master the pre-welding preparation for manual TIG welding with fixed pipe docking level;

3. Master the welding operation of manual TIG welding for horizontal fixation of pipe joints;

4. Master the post-weld treatment and inspection of manual TIG welding for horizontal fixation of pipe joints.

Task 1: Analyze the Technical Requirements of Manual TIG Welding for Butt Horizontal Fixation of Low Alloy Stell Pipe

Fig. 3-6-1 depicts the assembly diagram and technical requirements of common pipe butt horizontal fixed welding test piece.

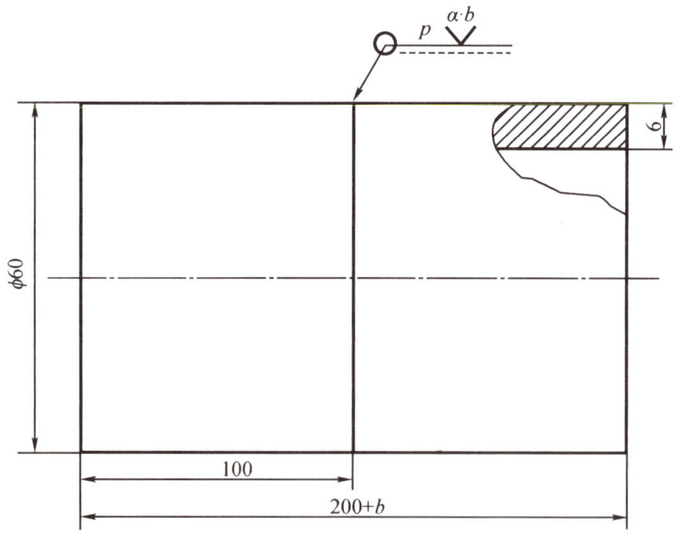

Technical requirements

1. The test piece material is Q355R.
2. The joint form is a pipe-to-pipe butt joint, and the welding position is horizontally fixed.
3. Single-side welding and double-side forming technology should be adopted for welding.
4. The V-shaped groove angle is $\alpha = 60° \pm 5°$, the root face is $p = 0.5$–1 mm, and the root gap is $b = 2.0$–3.0 mm.
5. Forming requirements: The weld surface should be defect-free, with uniform and consistent weld ripples in terms of width and flatness, smooth transition between the weld and base metal, and no deformation after welding. Please refer to the scoring standard for specific details.

Fig. 3-6-1 The Assembly Diagram and Technical Requirements of Common Pipe Butt Horizontal Fixed Welding Test Piecws (Unit: mm)

Pipeline welding is often required in the production and installation of pipelines and heat exchangers in industrial sectors such as boilers, chemical industry, electric power, atomic energy, etc. Manual argontungsten arc welding holds a significant proportion, particularly during on-site installation and construction, where stationary pipeline welding often occurs, imposing certain requirements on its welding operation technology.

Task 2:Master the Pre-welding Preparation for Manual TIG Welding with Fixed Pipe Docking Level

Conventional implementation route for pre-welding preparation tasks: reading of blueprints, weldment preparation and groove cleaning, determination of welding process parameters, and assembly positioning.

According to the task list, the steel pipe material is Q355R with the specification of ϕ60 mm×6 mm×100 mm. Two pipes are to be butt joined with a groove angle of 60°±5° using a V-shaped groove, with a clearance of 2-3 mm and a blunt edge of 0. 5-1 mm. The pipe should be horizontally fixed and welded in all positions. It is required that both sides of the one-side welding have a well-formed appearance. Once the weldment is welded, it is not permitted to replace or change the welding position arbitrarily.

1. Weld preparation and groove cleaning

For ϕ60 mm×6 mm×100 mm pipes, the groove angle is 30°±2. 5°, with two pipes in each group (one group in total).

The oil, rust, moisture, and other dirt on the surface of the welding wire, inside the groove of the weldment, and within a 20 mm range on both sides should be thoroughly removed until a metallic luster is exposed. Since the inert gas only serves a protective role without any metallurgical reaction during manual argontungsten arc welding, the quality of the groove cleaning directly affects the weld quality. Special attention should be given to cleaning the groove.

2. Determination of welding process parameters

Q355R is a type of low alloy steel with excellent weldability. Typically, there is no need for special process measures during welding.

Pipe butt horizontal fixing welding is also known as all-position welding due to operations in various positions such as flat, vertical, and overhead. During welding, significant changes occur in the angle of the welding gun, hand shape, and body shape, depending on the welding position. Therefore, special attention should be given to adjusting and adapting welding operations in all directions throughout the welding process. The welding current should be appropriate, and a short arc should be strictly maintained to control the duration of the molten pool.

According to the material and plate thickness of the pipe fittings, ER50-6 welding wire with a diameter of 2. 5 mm can be selected. A cerium tungsten electrode with a diameter of 2. 5 mm is chosen, and the tungsten end tip is ground into a 30° cone with a diameter of 0. 5 mm. The purity of Ar gas should reach 99. 99%. Two-layer and two-pass welding should be adopted.

Optional recommended process parameters are shown in Table 3-6-1.

Table 3-6-1 Welding Parameters for Horizontal Tack Weld of Q355R Pipe

Welding level	Welding wire model	Wire diameter /mm	Welding current/A	Welding voltage/V
Backing layer	ER50-6	2. 5	90-100	10-15
Covering layer			80-90	10-15
Welding layer	**Shielding gas flow/(L/min)**	**Tungsten electrode diameter/mm**	**Extension length of tungsten electrode/mm**	**Power supply polarity**
Backing layer	7-10	2. 5	3-6	DC straight polarity
Covering layer	7-10	2. 5	3-6	

3. Assembling and positioning

(1) Assembly, alignment, and tack welding of pipes

The quality of pipe welding is closely related to assembly and tack welding. For pipe fitting-up, it is required that the flatness of the groove end face should be less than 0. 5 mm, the displacement of the welded joint assembly should not exceed 1 mm, and the curvature at fitting-up should not exceed 1/400. Sometimes it is laborious to rotate, and in order to prevent cracks at the root of the welded joint due to vibration during rotation, the pipe should be placed on a flat rotating support frame or rolling bar before assembly to effectively fix the positioning, as shown in Fig. 3-6-2(a), for easy operation. At the same time, the tack welding seam must have sufficient strength. If a fulcrum support is used, the distance between two fulcrums near the weld junction should not be greater than 1. 5 to 2 times the pipe diameter, as shown in Fig. 3-6-2(b). When welding thick-walled pipes, rotating is relatively difficult. It is preferable to rotate once after welding two layers for each welding section.

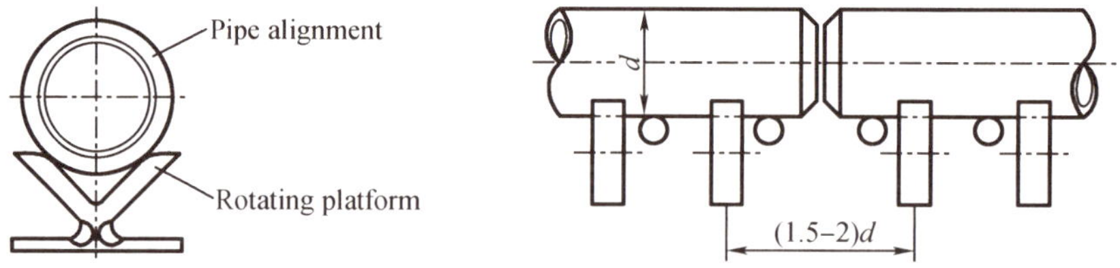

(a) Pipe positioning rotary table (b) Arrangement of pipe rolling fulcrum

Fig. 3-6-2 Schematic Diagram of Pipe Assembly Positioning Bracket

During tack welding, one-point or two-point positioning can be used for small diameter pipes. The one-point positioning can be set at the 11 o'clock or 1 o'clock position, while the two-point positioning is symmetrically set on both sides, as shown in Fig. 3-6-3(a), or located at the 10 o'clock and 2 o'clock directions. For larger pipe diameters, three or more welding spots can be positioned using tack welding, and the welding spots should be evenly distributed, as shown in Fig. 3-6-3(b). The size of the tack welding spot should be appropriate. When the pipe wall thickness is less than or equal to 5 mm, the thickness of the welding spot should be 3-5 mm. When the pipe wall thickness is greater than 5 mm, the thickness of the welding spot should be 5-8 mm, and the length of the tack welding should be 20-30 mm. To facilitate joint penetration, both ends of the welding spot must be trimmed into a gentle slope.

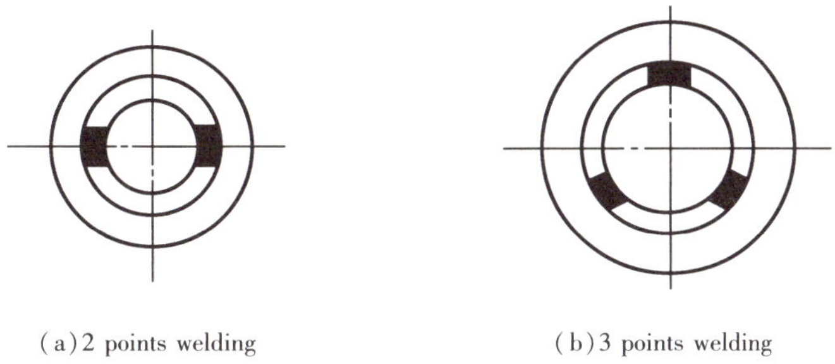

Fig. 3-6-3 Quantity and Position Illustration of Tack Welding Spots

The specific assembly welding spots are also dependent on the welding position and specific welding conditions. Generally, for horizontally rotating pipes, the tack welding should not exceed two points, meaning that either 1 or 2 points can be welded. For vertically fixed, horizontally fixed, and inclined 45° pipes, the tack welding should generally not exceed 3 points, meaning that either 1, 2, or 3 points can be welded.

(2) Key points for assembly and positioning of pipe butt joint

①Place the pipe fittings on the pipe fitting assembly and secure them to ensure coaxial alignment.

②Carry out pinpoint positioning at the twelve o'clock position where the pipe fittings are placed. Use welding wire of the same grade as that for formal welding for tack welding. The tack welding spot should have a length of 10-15 mm and a thickness of 5-8 mm to ensure complete penetration on the back side. Considering the single-side welding and double-side forming operation, the reserved assembly gap is slightly larger, generally arranged with a larger gap at the top and a smaller gap at the bottom, with 3mm at the top of the pipe and 2 mm at the bottom. The misalignment of pipe fittings after welding should not exceed 0.5 mm, as shown in Fig. 3-6-4.

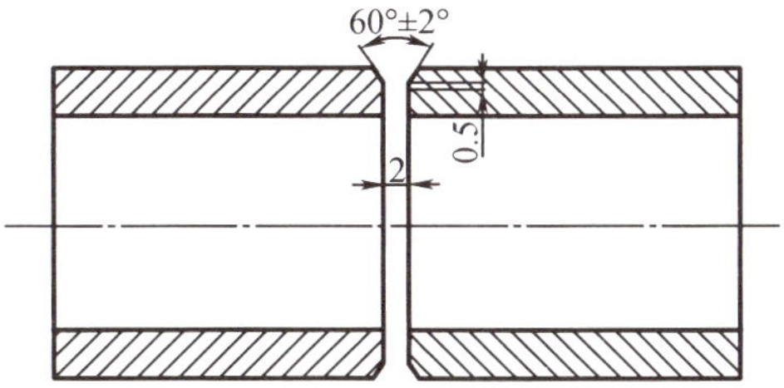

Fig. 3-6-4 Schematic Diagram Depicting Welding Positions for Fixturing the Test Piece (Unit: mm)

(3) Polished

Use an angle grinder to polish the fixed welding spot into a double U-shaped groove, known as a gentle slope type. Take care not to polish the center of the fixed point too thin, in order to prevent deformation of the pipe fittings during welding, as shown in Fig. 3-6-5.

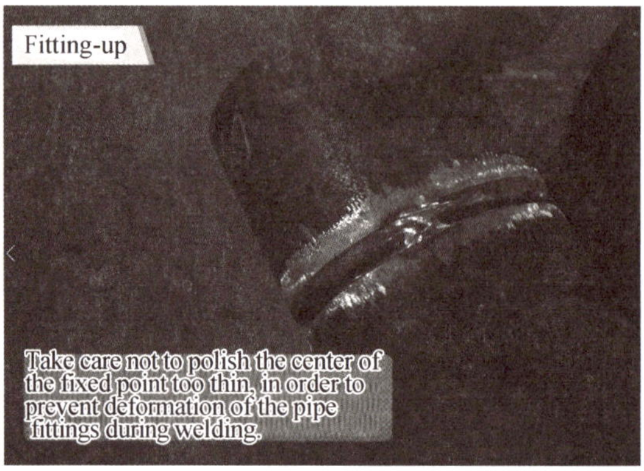

Fig. 3-6-5 Schematic Diagram of Weld Spots after Assembly and Spot Welding

Task 3:Master the Welding Operation of Manual TIG Welding for Horizontal Fixation of Pipe Joints

The weldment consists of two layers and two passes. Throughout the welding process, the welding gun and welding wire adapt to the welding position, as illustrated in Fig. 3-6-6.

Fig. 3-6-6 Schematic Diagram Illustrating the Variation of Welding Gun and Welding Wire with Welding Position

1. Backing welding

The internal filler wire method and external filler wire method are used for backing welding of the front and rear parts, as shown in Fig. 3-6-7. One-sided welding is performed from bottom to top, resulting in a double-sided formation.

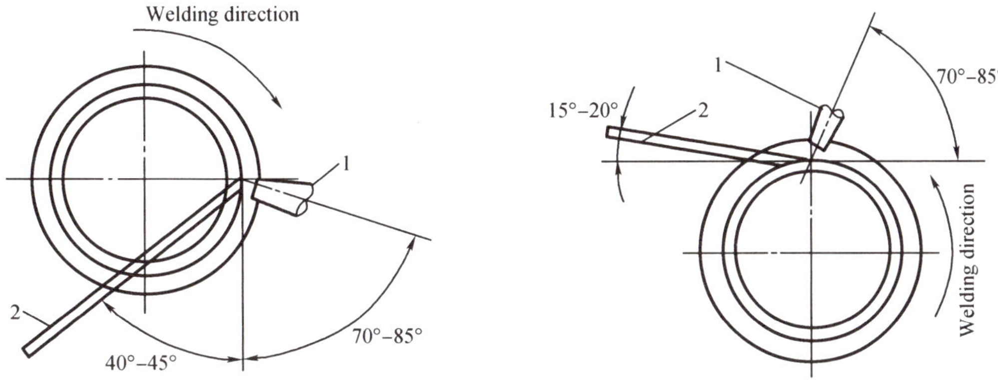

(a) Inner welding wire operation

(b) Outer welding wire operation

1—Spray nozzle; 2—Welding wire.

Fig. 3-6-7 Inner Strand Filling Technique and Outer Strand Filling Technique

(1) Backing welding starts from 5-10 mm behind the centerline of the overhead welding position. The front half is welded counterclockwise until it crosses the pipe centerline by 5-10 mm for arc stopping at the flat welding position, and then the rear half is welded clockwise, as shown in Fig. 3-6-8.

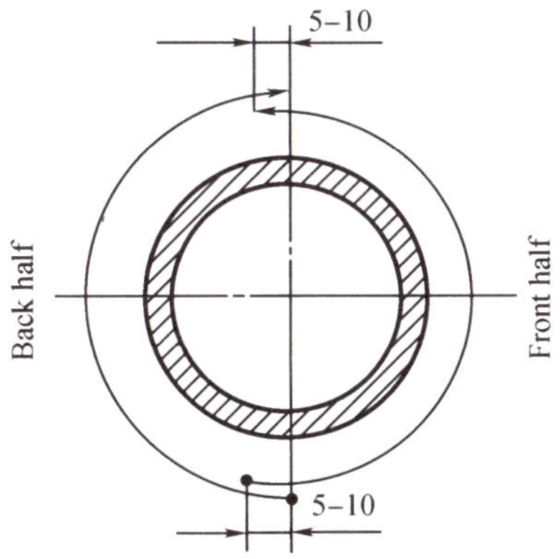

Fig. 3-6-8 Schematic Diagram of Arc Ignition and Termination Operations for Horizontally Fixed Tube (Unit: mm)

(2) During the welding process, the angles of the welding gun and filler wire should change according to the welding position, as demonstrated in Fig. 3-6-6.

①After the arc is ignited, the root gap at both sides of the groove shall be preheated by drawing circles with an arc welding gun. Once the blunt edge melts and forms a weld hole, the welding wire extended into the inner side of the pipe shall be tightly attached to the weld hole, and one drop of metal shall be deposited on each side of the blunt edge. By transversely swinging the arc welding gun, the first molten pool connected by the bridge shall be formed. At this point, the welding wire should be filled with a droplet close to the middle of the leading edge of the molten pool, ensuring complete fusion between the droplet and the base metal. After a melting hole appears in front of the molten pool, another droplet should be added, and so on. When welding in the vertical position, switch from the internal filler wire method to the external filler wire method until completing the first half of the backing weld.

②The rear half is welded in a clockwise direction, and the operating method is the same as that of the front half. When welding to a distance of 3-5 mm from the tack weld, in order to ensure that the joint is fully welded, the arc welding gun should draw a circle to melt the tack weld, and then fill 2-3 drops of molten droplets to seal the weld. The welding should be continued (note that no welding wire should be filled at the tack weld). When the second half and the first half of the bottom weld pass are about to be sealed with a horizontal position difference of 3-4 mm, wire feeding should be stopped. A circle should be drawn around the sealing part for preheating until it becomes red hot, and then the arc should be pulled back to the original molten pool for filling wire welding. After sealing, wire feeding should be stopped, and welding should be continued forward for 5-10 mm before stopping the arc. The welding gun should be removed after the molten pool solidifies. The backing layer weld bead is generally 2 mm.

(3) In the welding process, the angle of the welding gun and filling wire changes according to different welding positions (overhead position welding, vertical position welding, and flat position welding). The specific operation is shown in Fig. 3-6-6.

2. Covering welding

(1) The covering welding shall be performed using a crescent swing motion. The angle of the welding gun for covering welding is the same as that for backing welding, and the wire filling shall be done using the external wire filling method.

(2) Strike the arc at 6 o'clock on the backing welding, and swing the welding gun in a crescent shape. After the groove edge and the surface of the backing pass melt and form a molten pool, start wire welding. The welding wire and the angle of the welding gun swing synchronously. Pause slightly on both sides of the groove, add a droplet respectively, and ensure it melts well with the base metal. Weld by swinging and filling wire like this. Use less wire filling for overhead welding to prevent metal deposition from falling. Accelerate the swing frequency of the welding gun for vertical welding to prevent molten droplets from flowing down; when reaching the flat welding position, fill more welding wire each time to ensure the weld joint is fully formed.

(3) The welding arc of the entire cover layer must be smooth, and the distance between the tungsten tip and the molten pool should be maintained within 2-3 mm. The contour of the molten pool should be symmetrical to the centerline of the weld. If there is deflection, adjust the angle of the welding torch and the dwell time of the arc at the edge of the groove at any time.

Task 4:Master the Post-weld Treatment and Inspection of Manual TIG Welding for Horizontal Fixation of Pipe Joints

1. Weld cleaning

Repeatedly brush the welded joint with a wire brush to remove the oxide layer from the weld. The joint should be smooth and flat, ensuring that the weldment remains "coaxial and flat", without damaging the original surface of the weld during the cleaning process.

2. Weld quality inspection

(1) Weld appearance inspection

After welding, the surface quality of the welds must be inspected. Visual examination or the use of low-power magnifying glasses should be employed to check for defects such as pores, cracks, and undercuts on the weld surface. The appearance quality and dimensional characteristics of the welds should be evaluated using steel rulers, steel squares, and weld inspection tools. Refer to Table 3-6-2 for specific requirements and criteria for routine testing.

Table 3-6-2 Reference Table for Visual Inspection Items of Welds

Test item	Tested location	Quality requirements	Remarks
Cleaning quality	All welds and their surrounding 25 mm on both sides	No welding slag, splashing, or attachments that hinder inspection	
Geometry shape	Joint between weld and base metal	The weld joint shall be complete without any missing solder, and the connection shall be smooth in transition	
	weld areas with abrupt alterations in both form and dimensions	The weld height, width, and crystalline weld ripples should be uniform	A welding inspection ruler can be used for measuring
Scar repair welding	Mechanical scratches on the base metal surface	There should be no obvious edges and grooves in the damaged area, and the depth of the scar should not exceed the relevant standards	

(2) Common scoring criteria for weld inspection

Please carry out post-weld treatment and testing scoring for weldments according to the specifications. Refer to Table 3-6-3 for common scoring criteria for the appearance of butt welds of 6mm thick plates. The total score is calculated as 60 points, which can be adjusted based on actual conditions.

Table 3-6-3 Scoring Chart for External Appearance of Plate Butt Weldmm

Inspection items	Evaluation standards and score	Evaluation grade				Self-test data	Self-assessment Score	Teacher's measurement data	Teacher's evaluation score	Remarks
		Ⅰ	Ⅱ	Ⅲ	Ⅳ					
Weld height excess	Size standard/mm	0-1	>1, ≤2	>2, ≤3	<0 or >3					
	Score	4	3	2	0					
weld height	Size standard/mm	0-1	>1, ≤2	>2, ≤3	>3					
	Score	8	4	2	0					
Weld width	Size standard/mm	8-9	≥7, ≤10	≥6, ≤11	<6 or>11					
	Score	4	2	1	0					
Difference in weld width	Size standard/mm	0-1	>1, ≤2	>2, ≤3	>3					
	Score	8	4	2	0					
Undercut	Size standard/mm	No burr	Depth≤0. 5	Depth>0. 5						
	Score	12	Deduct 2 points for every 5 mm in length		0					
Front forming	Standards	Excellent	Good	Average	Bad					
	Score	8	4	2	0					
Back molding	Standards	Excellent	Good	Average	Bad					
	Score	6	4	2	0					
Back concavity	Size standard/mm	0-0. 5	>0. 5, ≤1	>1, ≤2	Depth>30					
	Score	2	1	0	0					
Back curvature	Size standard/mm	0-1	>1, ≤2	>2						
	Score	2	1	0						

Table 3-6-3 (Continued)

Inspection items	Evaluation standards and score	Evaluation grade				Self-test data	Self-assessment Score	Teacher's measurement data	Teacher's evaluation score	Remarks
		Ⅰ	Ⅱ	Ⅲ	Ⅳ					
Angular distortion	Size standard/mm	0-0.5	>0.5, ≤1	>1						
	Score	4	2	0						
Incorrect edge measurement	Size standard/mm	0-0.5	>0.5, ≤1	>1						
	Score	2	1	0						
Appearance defects (such as cracks, porosity, edge biting, arc pits, slag inclusions, incomplete fusion, and other defects) defect records.										

3. Station Tool Cleaning Spot Check and Scoring

It is the same as Project Ⅴ in Module Ⅱ.

After completion, clean and organize the workstations according to the "6S" standard, make records, and score according to Table 2-5-5.

Task Assessment

1. When the butt joint pipe is welded in an upward horizontal fixed position, the angle of the electrode should change according to the welding position, but there should be no ( ) within the welding position.

A. Flat welding B. Vertical welding

C. Horizontal welding D. Overhead welding

2. The butt joint pipe should be welded in an upward direction at the horizontally fixed position ( ).

A. According to the entire circle. B. Divide into two semicircles.

C. Divide into four semicircles. D. Divide into six semicircles.

3. For butt welding of horizontal pipes by argon tungsten-arc welding, the angle of the groove surface should be ( ).

A. 30°±2.5° B. 32°±2.5° C. 35°±2.5° D. 40°±2.5°

4. For butt joint of horizontal pipes by argon tungsten-arc welding, the included angle between the welding wire and workpiece surface should be approximately ( ) during wire filling.

A. 10° B. 15° C. 20° D. 30°

5. 5. Welding a horizontal pipe joint using argon tungsten arc welding. If it halts midway, resume the welding process, polish the end, and overlap the weld by ( ) mm.

A. 4-6 B. 5-7 C. 6-8 D. 7-9

6. For butt joint of horizontal pipe by argon tungsten-arc welding, it is better to use ( ) welding wire for the backing weld.

A. H08A B. ER50-6 C. H08Mn2A D. H08Mn2SiA

7. For the butt joint of horizontal pipes using argon tungsten-arc welding, weld up to the ( ) position during the backing welding process, employing the external wire filling method.

A. Flat welding B. Vertical welding

C. Horizontal welding D. Overhead welding

8. For the butt joint of horizontal pipes by argon tungsten-arc welding, backing welding shall start ( ) mm behind the centerline of the overhead welding position.

A. 4-8 B. 5-10 C. 6-12 D. 7-9

9. Argon tungsten-arc welding is used for butt joints of horizontal pipes, and the positioned welding of horizontally rotating pipes generally does not exceed ( ) points.

A. 2 B. 3 C. 4 D. 5

10. For the butt joint of horizontal pipes welded using argon tungsten-arc welding, the fixed welding spots should be ground with an angle grinder, forming double ( ) grooves.

A. V　　B. Y　　C. U　　D. X

Task Operation

Carry out task implementation training according to task requirements and process sequence. After welding, conduct self-inspection and sort out station tools according to weld inspection requirements. After training, carry out assessment and score according to testing requirements.

参 考 文 献

[1] 中国机械工程学会焊接学会. 焊接手册：第 1 卷 焊接方法及设备[M]. 北京：机械工业出版社，2016.

[2] 中国机械工程学会焊接学会. 焊接手册：第 2 卷 材料的焊接[M]. 北京：机械工业出版社，2016.

[3] 中船舰客教育科技（北京）有限公司. 特殊焊接技术（基础知识）[M] . 北京：高等教育出版社，2020.

[4] 中船舰客教育科技（北京）有限公司. 特殊焊接技术（初级）[M] . 北京：高等教育出版社，2020.

[5] 中船舰客教育科技（北京）有限公司. 特殊焊接技术（中级）[M] . 北京：高等教育出版社，2021.

[6] 中船舰客教育科技（北京）有限公司. 特殊焊接技术（高级）[M] . 北京：高等教育出版社，2022.

[7] 张应立，周玉华. 焊工手册[M]. 北京：化学工业出版社，2015.

[8] 施殿宝，从零开始学技术——电焊工[M]. 北京：中国铁道出版社，2012.

[9] 徐越兰，庞怀信. 电焊工简明实用手册[M]. 南京：江苏科学技术出版社，2010.

[10] 潘继民. 焊工操作质量保证指南[M]. 北京：机械工业出版社，2010.

[11] 杨海民. 焊工快速提高[M]. 北京：北京理工大学出版社，2010.

[12] 胡宝良. 焊工快速掌握精要问答[M]. 上海：上海科学技术出版社，2010.

[13] 陈裕川. 焊接工艺设计与实例分析[M]. 北京：机械工业出版社，2020.

[14] 史耀武. 焊接技术手册（上）[M]. 北京：化学工业出版社，2009.

[15] 苍井晃. 双色图解焊接知识与技能[M]. 王营瑞，译. 北京：机械工业出版社，2017.

[16] 刘云龙. 焊工（初级）[M]. 北京：机械工业出版社，2014.

[17] 周树春，何忠刚. 气体保护焊接技术[M]. 北京：北京理工大学出版社，2015.

[18] 于增瑞. 钨极氩弧焊[M]. 北京：化学工业出版社，2014.

[19] 邱言龙，聂正斌，雷振国. 手工钨极氩弧焊技术快速入门[M]. 上海：上海科学技术出版社，2016.

[20] 王兵. CO2 气体保护焊一学就会[M]. 北京：化学工业出版社，2014.